Schooling the New South

THE FRED W. MORRISON SERIES IN SOUTHERN STUDIES

Schooling

The
University
of North
Carolina
Press

Chapel Hill
& London

the New South

James L. Leloudis

Pedagogy, Self, and Society

in North Carolina, 1880–1920

© 1996 The University
of North Carolina Press

Manufactured in the
United States of America

The paper in this book
meets the guidelines for
permanence and durabil-
ity of the Committee on
Production Guidelines for
Book Longevity of the
Council on Library Re-
sources.

This book's major themes
were outlined in "School-
ing the New South: Peda-
gogy, Self, and Society in
North Carolina, 1880–
1920," *Historical Studies in
Education/Revue d'histoire
de l'éducation* 5 (Fall
1993): 203–29. Portions
of Chapter 5 appeared as
"School Reform in the
New South: The Woman's
Association for the
Betterment of Public
School Houses in North
Carolina, 1902–1919,"
*Journal of American
History* 69 (March 1983):
886–909. These sections
are reprinted with the
permission of the pub-
lishers.

Library of Congress Cataloging-in-Publication Data
Leloudis, James L.
Schooling the New South : pedagogy, self, and society
in North Carolina, 1880–1920 / James L. Leloudis.
    p.   cm. — (Fred W. Morrison series in Southern
studies)
Includes bibliographical references (p.   ) and index.
ISBN 0-8078-2265-5 (cloth: alk. paper)
ISBN 0-8078-4808-5 (pbk.: alk. paper)
    1. Public schools—North Carolina—History—19th
century.   2. Public schools—North Carolina—
History—20th century.   3. Education—Social
aspects—North Carolina—History—19th century.
4. Education—Social aspects—North Carolina—
History—20th century.   5. Ability grouping in
education—North Carolina—History—19th
century.   6. Ability grouping in education—North
Carolina—History—20th century.   I. Title.
II. Series.
LA340.L45   1996
370'.9756'09041—dc20   95-26137
                                                          CIP
02   01   00   99   98   6   5   4   3   2

For my daughters,

Kirsten Elizabeth and Rebecca Michelle

Contents

Illustrations

Preface

Educational work in [the South] is . . . something more than
the teaching of youth; it is the building of a new social order.
—Walter Hines Page, *The Rebuilding of Old Commonwealths*

This is a book that I felt compelled to write. Its origins lie in my own childhood and the social upheavals of the 1960s. In the fall of 1963, I entered the third grade at the all-white Fairview Elementary School in Rocky Mount, North Carolina, a small tobacco town located in the eastern part of the state. Like most of my classmates, I was only vaguely aware of the battle for civil rights that was raging in the world beyond. We had all seen the pictures on television and heard adults talking, but matters of race seldom intruded into our daily lessons and playground games. Or at least they didn't until that year. By springtime, another boy and I were being shunned because our parents had stood up in a PTA meeting to defend the simple justice of desegregation. Brent and I became best friends before the term was out. At the time, the experience registered as little more than the pain of exclusion. Later, I realized that my school had become a battleground in the struggle to re-make southern life, and that even eight-year-olds could be recruited for the cause.

When I entered graduate school in the late 1970s, those memories steered me toward the study of education. I wanted some historical context in which to understand my experiences. By that time, revisionist scholars had begun to challenge the prevailing view of public education as the capstone of democracy. Their accounts of schools deeply mired in class and racial conflicts helped make sense of both the segregated world in which I had grown up and the concerns of teachers who complained of blackboard jungles and dull, repressive classrooms. But the revisionists' emphasis on the school as an instrument of social reproduction was less than satisfying. The classroom remained a black box. We knew what went in and what came out, but we understood very little about what happened inside. How were classroom lessons related to the patterns of daily life? And more important, how, in times of turmoil, could seemingly ordinary childhood experiences be made into tools for social change?[1]

Those questions led me to explore another critical juncture in southern history: the period from 1880 through the mid-1920s, when reformers had labored once before to make a New South through the agency of public education. During those years, North Carolina led the way in building thousands of new schoolhouses, professionalizing teacher training, and developing an elaborate bureaucracy to administer the instruction of youth. New South advocates touted those reforms as the region's bridge from a plantation to a commercial economy. They looked to the classroom to induct future generations into the habits of wage labor and market production; they relied on schooling to discipline race relations in a world of hardening segregation and black disfranchisement; and through the reform enterprise itself, they shaped new notions of womanhood and manhood that reflected the primacy of the self in a society becoming increasingly less attentive to traditional relations of family and community. In short, reformers viewed the classroom as the progenitor of a new culture and a new way of life. Today, more than a century on, we still wrestle with the legacies of their labor.

Southern educational reform turned on the crucial but largely unexplored transition from common school to graded school pedagogy. The practices of graded education have become so embedded in our everyday lives that it is difficult to imagine that children ever learned in any other way. But until the 1880s, most students mastered their lessons in classrooms filled with youngsters of all ages and abilities. Few made extensive use of textbooks, and formal examinations and report cards were virtually unknown. Chapter 1 examines these early approaches to public instruction and the assault made upon them by proponents of a more rational pedagogy. The method I employ there might be best described as an experiment in historical ethnography. With the help of parents' letters, students' reminiscences, and a variety of schoolhouse writings—both fictional and prescriptive—I attempt to peer into the classrooms of the past in order to discover how age-graded schooling became a metaphor to live by.[2]

The graded school movement drew its most outspoken advocates from a generation of men and women buffeted by the backwash of the Civil War and Reconstruction. Chapter 2 looks specifically at the graduates of the University of North Carolina in the late 1870s and early 1880s. Too young to have taken up arms, they neither formed lasting attachments to the Old South nor felt the need to justify the Lost Cause. Instead, they became bitter critics of their fathers' world, assuming the task of rehabilitating their region through a wholesale reformation of state and society. Public school careers offered sons of the university the means of carving out new identities set apart from the rituals of partisan politics that had shaped men's lives in the past.

Chapter 3 turns to the white middle-class women who became the university graduates' loyal allies. When North Carolina opened its first normal college for white women in 1891, only four out of every ten teachers in the state were female; by 1920, the balance had shifted, with women claiming 86 percent of the state's classroom jobs.[3] Through the recruitment of vast numbers of women "helpers," graded school men secured their own positions as superintendents, principals, and normal school professors. But despite low pay and subordinate status, women answered the call to teach for reasons of their own. Educational work offered them a public voice, an opportunity to live independently outside of marriage, and their own institutions of higher learning. The story of white women's movement into the classroom reveals a turn-of-the-century female world that was more dynamic than stereotypes of southern ladies and rigid sex roles might suggest.

Not all North Carolinians embraced the new education so enthusiastically. Chapter 4 explores the battle over alternative paths of southern development that erupted during the late 1890s. That contest pitted reformers against opponents who feared the centralization of economic and pedagogical power. The most determined challenge came from Baptists within the Populist movement, whose church traditions were founded on the preservation of local autonomy, and African Americans, who had watched the white graded schools advance at the expense of their own children's education. These schoolhouse dissidents championed a brand of democratic localism that was in many respects an overly simple response to feelings of powerlessness and dislocation, yet their vision did hold out the possibility of more equitable schooling in a society headed rapidly toward one-party rule and unyielding racial segregation.

With the passage in 1900 of a state constitutional amendment that disfranchised blacks and many poor whites, New South boosters crushed their opponents and cleared the way for the new education to take possession of the countryside. Chapters 5 and 6 round out the story by looking at reformers' efforts to consolidate their classroom revolution. Fortified by the wealth of northern philanthropists, they set out to win the hearts and minds of rural children and to construct a new racial peace built on civility and willing subordination rather than the politics of repression that had characterized the late nineteenth century. Of special interest in Chapter 6 are the black women teachers who, in this world robbed of politics, used the classroom to affirm a sense of racial dignity and to renegotiate the black place in a white South. For those teachers, their students, and the parents who sustained them both, the classroom stood as a last refuge for claims to common citizenship and as the key to realizing a future founded on principles of simple justice and equality. Black educators pursued that agenda in the interstices of white reformers' designs, and in doing so they made the schools of the New South into contested terrain of the most significant kind.

This account of school reform is circumscribed in obvious ways by the peculiarities of place and time, but its significance is not merely provincial. In the broadest terms, it speaks as much to the origins and uses of modern education as to the unique history of a single state and region. The pedagogical ideas that helped to make the New South sprang initially from the European Enlightenment and by the mid-nineteenth century had transformed schooling throughout much of urban North America. During the 1880s and 1890s, they spread even farther afield, reshaping life—albeit to quite different ends—in two postemancipation societies, the American South and Czarist Russia. Then, in the decades that followed, lessons of what reformers liked to call the "southern laboratory" were themselves carried abroad, most notably to the African colonies of the British Empire. Viewed from that perspective, the story of southern school reform becomes a chapter in the much larger tale of the market and disciplinary revolutions that have ricocheted through the Western world during the last two hundred years. Where it seemed appropriate, I have tried to point to those connections, so that students of schooling and society in other places might consider the parallels between their stories and my own.[4]

In writing this book, I have also pursued two other purposes that readers should know about. The first is a desire to open historical dialogue to new voices. The story of school reform has often been told as if students, parents, and teachers were passive objects of change rather than active historical subjects. As a result, we know less than we should about how modern schools have been shaped by their clients as well as their creators. My second concern is to integrate educational history into the mainstream of American history writing. In my university, as in many others, courses in the field have traditionally been viewed as service offerings best left to schools of education. But that attitude ignores compelling reasons for historians and educators to begin talking more directly with one another. The benefits of such a conversation seem clear. By placing education in the context of larger patterns of historical change, we can deepen our understanding of schooling's critical role in our society, a role we routinely acknowledge but seldom scrutinize. And by including education in the "master narrative" of America's past, we may finally take appropriate notice of the institution that in modern times has assumed responsibility for much of the work once done by the family, church, and community in shaping our children's personalities and their capacity to imagine the future. My hope, in the end, is that *Schooling the New South* will help to lower the barriers that too often separate educators, historians, and the larger public they mean to engage.

The image of the lone scholar laboring in creative solitude is perhaps the most enduring myth of academic life. In truth, research and writing are collaborative endeavors shared with friends, family, and colleagues. Frank Ryan, John Kasson, and Willis Brooks kindled my determination to become a historian. Donald Mathews welcomed me into graduate school and, together with Peter Walker, convinced me to turn an early seminar paper on education and the New South into a full-length study. Wayne Durrill, Pamela Dean, and Helen Evans gave generously of insights from their own work; Michael Trotti helped with much of the research on which Chapter 6 is based; and even though we are now scattered far and wide, Lu Ann Jones and Anastatia Sims have continued to offer their support through countless letters and telephone calls. At a critical juncture, Clarence Mohr went out of his way to express excitement over my graduate school writings—and to this day he remains a valued friend and colleague. Closer to home, Leon Fink, David and Kim Hall, Roger and Becky Hall, Tom Hanchett, George and Dayna Leloudis, and Rosalie Radcliffe have been constant sources of encouragement and good cheer. Bob Korstad deserves special thanks. Over the years, he has listened enthusiastically as I rambled on about school reform and has given me the benefit of incisive and careful criticism. John Kasson, Bill Barney, Harry Watson, and Joel Williamson also helped me to recognize the study's weaknesses and to make the good passages better. As always, my parents never lost faith in my work. I owe them perhaps the greatest debt of all, for they taught me early on important lessons about the obligations of life in a democratic society.

The burden of research expenses was lightened by a George E. Mowry Dissertation Fellowship from the Department of History at the University of North Carolina at Chapel Hill, along with grants from the Rockefeller Archive Center and the Duke University and University of North Carolina Women's Studies Research Center. A Spencer Dissertation Fellowship from the Woodrow Wilson National Fellowship Foundation, a Spencer Postdoctoral Fellowship from the National Academy of Education, a Fellowship for Recent Recipients of the Ph.D. from the American Council of Learned Societies, and a Phillip and Ruth Hettleman Faculty Fellowship from the University of North Carolina's Institute for the Arts and Humanities all provided much-needed free time for travel and writing. A publication grant from the University Research Council of the University of North Carolina at Chapel Hill paid for the photographs.

My work was also made easier by the generous assistance of many librarians and archivists, especially Alice Cotten, Bob Anthony, Jerry Cotten, Jeff Hicks, and Harry McKown at the North Carolina Collection; Richard Shrader, John White, and Mike Martin of the Southern Historical Collection and University of North Carolina Archive; and Stephen Massengill of the North Carolina Division of Archives and History. Emilie Mills, Ella Ross, and Betty Carter at the University of North Carolina at Greensboro shared their knowledge of that institution's beginnings as the State Normal and Industrial School and guided me through the seemingly endless boxes of the Charles D. McIver Papers. At Fisk University, Beth House introduced me to the treasures contained in the records of the Rosenwald Fund. Melissa Smith of the Rockefeller Archive Center answered with good cheer a barrage of questions about photographs, and Tom Rosenbaum offered not only knowledgeable advice about the center's remarkable manuscript collections but also delightful dinner conversation that relieved the tedium of long research trips.

Jacquelyn Hall has been both friend and adviser. Since we first met in her oral history course in 1979, I have had deep respect for her intellectual integrity, good humor, and devotion to graduate education. Many in the academy are excellent teachers, but only a few can truly be called mentors. Jacquelyn is one of that rare number. She read this work through numerous drafts and always offered comments that at once buoyed my spirits and prodded me to think harder about the issues at hand. I hope that the pages that follow reflect in some small measure her insistence on graceful writing and imaginative scholarship.

At the University of North Carolina Press, I owe a special debt to Lewis Bateman, who has stood by this project since its inception. He is one of those rare editors from whom authors can still expect a critical and engaged reading of their work. I am also thankful to Christi Stanforth for her skill as a copyeditor and for her good cheer in shepherding this book into print.

My wife Dianne has lived with this project almost as long as she has lived with me, and her constant faith and encouragement have contributed to this study in ways that are beyond calculation. Words can scarcely express my love and gratitude. Our daughters Kirsten and Rebecca were born in the years while I was beginning a new teaching job and laboring to make a dissertation over into a book. They have brought me great joy and have given my work new meaning. This is for them, with hopes that knowing the past might brighten their future.

Schooling the New South

A Classroom Revolution

The present is a period of transition.

Old things are passing away and

all things are becoming new.

—Frank A. Daniels, "New South,"

University Monthly (April 1883)

The tiny market town of Wilson took on a carnival-like air in late June 1881. Up and down the main street, merchants and townspeople prepared for the opening of a new summer normal school for white teachers. The school lasted three weeks and attracted educators and visitors from surrounding towns and counties throughout eastern North Carolina. They came to see old friends, shop in Wilson's stores, and take in the lectures of a distinguished faculty that included a British "teacher of elocution and oratory" and a professor of vocal music from Paris. Evening sessions offered "literary and musical entertainments," most notably the exhibition of a "hand-painted Panorama of the Apocalyptic Vision of Saint John on the Isle of Patmos" and a series of stereopticon lectures on astronomy presented by Professor Sylvester Hassell, the principal of a local academy. The normal school quenched local residents' thirst for contact with a world beyond the solitude of scattered farms and commercial crossroads. By all accounts, it was the social event of the season.[1]

The normal school exercises might have proceeded uneventfully had it not been for a series of speeches delivered by Alexander Graham of Fayetteville. Graham, who had taught for several years in New York State, brought news of the graded schools that were gaining popularity in the cities of the Northeast and in North Carolina's larger towns. Unfortunately, there is no record of what he said, but his words must have been inspiring. White residents of Wilson gathered in a mass meeting on July 6 to make plans for joining the graded school movement. On a motion from the floor, B. S. Bronson, a local minister, was directed to compile a list of potential trustees and "to stir up a lively interest in the community on the subject."[2]

At a second meeting, one week later, Bronson presented his nominees, all of them leading citizens: the clerk of superior court, an attorney, four merchants, three influential landholders, and a miller. Wilson township was then divided into districts, and canvasers were appointed to solicit support for a graded school in the form of voluntary subscriptions. By early August, the campaign was going well, and the county commissioners had agreed to give the trustees Wilson's share of the public funds allotted for white education. The graded school opened on Monday, September 5, 1881, with five teachers and more than two hundred students organized into eight grades.[3]

Wilson's new school became a major public attraction. People traveled from all across the state to see for themselves "the practical workings" of graded education. By June 1882, the town's two thousand residents had hosted 8,291 curious guests. As many as one hundred visitors at a time crowded into the halls and classrooms on the busiest days. The Wilson graded school also attracted national attention when Amory Dwight Mayo, an educational evangelist from New England, came to inspect its operation. Mayo was so impressed that he prepared a special report for the *Boston Journal of Education*, encouraging his "Northern friends, travelling South . . . to stop and see the Wilson" experiment. "With no disposition to exaggerate," he wrote, "we can honestly say we never saw so much good work done. . . . The children were there in force . . . and the enthusiasm of the youngsters over their work was something beautiful to behold." But "the most interesting sight of all was the community in its relations to the new graded school. It had become the passion of the place; the sight to which the best people took their friends from abroad; the town-talk." Mayo concluded by advising progressive communities across the South to send delegations of their "best men and women to bring home a report" on Wilson's "model system of . . . instruction."[4]

Why did the Wilson graded school stir such curiosity and excitement? After all, North Carolina had supported a system of public instruction since the 1840s. What was it about the graded school that so fired the imagination? To answer those questions, we must begin with the antebellum past and with the common schools that graded education aimed to replace.

On the eve of the Civil War, North Carolina was an economic backwater, known even among its own inhabitants as the "Rip Van Winkle State," the "Ireland of America." Lacking a major seaport and a system of easily navigable rivers, it never sustained great plantations like those boasted by its neighbors, South Carolina and Virginia. But the state's fortunes were shaped nonetheless by the economics of slavery. Political power rested in the hands of eastern slave owners who held the great bulk of their wealth in the form of human rather than real property. Unlike land, that investment was movable, and its value bore little relation to local development. As a result, North Carolina's governing elite gave scant attention to improving the countryside through the construction of railroads, canals, villages, and factories. They sought instead to maximize the return on their investment in slaves. When the soil wore out, planters—particularly those of more modest means—picked up and moved to unexploited land elsewhere in the state or to the fertile fields of Alabama, Mississippi, and western Tennessee. Between 1790 and 1860 that footloose behavior helped to drop North Carolina's population from fourth to twelfth largest in the nation. Those planters who remained produced cotton, tobacco, and rice—crops that oriented them toward the coastal export trade rather than inland commerce. For that reason, they offered only limited support for efforts to pierce the state's interior with plank roads and rail lines. Local investors and the state legislature financed a fledgling rail system on the coastal plain during the 1830s and 1840s, primarily to service the cotton and tobacco economy, but until 1856 no track extended farther west than Raleigh, the state capital, which lay just one hundred and fifty miles from the shore.[5]

Underdevelopment left most North Carolinians in the upcountry Piedmont and mountain regions living in rural isolation. Poor transportation hobbled commercial agriculture and reinforced a system of general farming and direct exchange among local producers. White yeomen and a smaller group of tenants raised corn, wheat, and other grains to feed their families; in the woods and meadows that surrounded their fields, they herded cattle and hogs, hunted wild game for the table, and harvested timber for fuel and shelter. People found dignity in working with their hands,

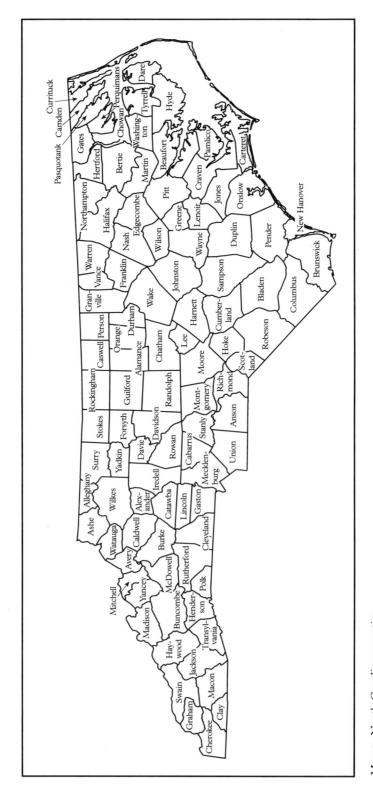

Map 1. North Carolina counties

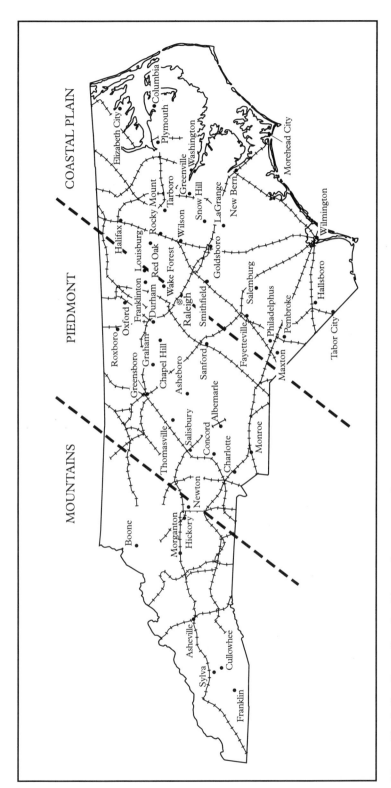

Map 2. North Carolina railroads, cities, and towns, ca. 1894

treasured control over their labor, and considered ownership of land—or at least access to the means of subsistence—a common right. Although they were not unaware of events in the outside world, they grounded their identities in a familiar circle of family, neighbors, and friends. Calvin Henderson Wiley, who took office as the first state superintendent of common schools in 1852, thought of North Carolina as less a state than "a confederation of independent communities." "Whoever travels over North Carolina," he observed, "will meet with great apparent diversity of character, manners, and interest; and if he be much attached to the ways . . . of his own community, will hardly ever feel himself at home from the time that he crosses the boundaries of his county." Nearly thirty years later, another traveler found most North Carolinians to be "independent and happy, but very far from the rest of the world."[6]

The state's common schools bore the stamp of that rural society. Before the mid-1880s education was primarily a local enterprise that served to integrate children into webs of personal relations defined by kinship, church, and race. North Carolina first provided for a system of public education in 1839, when lawmakers empowered individual counties to collect school taxes supplemented by payments from a state Literary Fund. This fund, established fourteen years earlier, drew its revenues from bank and navigation company stocks, taxes on auctioneers and distillers, and profits from the sale of state-owned swamplands and other public holdings. By the time of the Civil War, those resources supported the instruction of more than 100,000 children—roughly half the white school-aged population— enrolled in 3,488 districts scattered across the countryside.[7]

Under the Reconstruction Constitution of 1868, the benefits of schooling were extended to African American children, and a tax-supported, four-month term was made a legal requirement rather than a local option. Black Republicans fought for those provisions on behalf of constituents who viewed education as the key to realizing their dream of independence on the land. For the freedmen, illiteracy was both a badge of servitude and a serious liability in their dealings with white landlords and merchants. They embraced the common school as a means of putting "as great a distance between themselves and bondage as possible." But in other fundamental ways, the antebellum system of public instruction survived relatively unaltered. In the years immediately after the Civil War, schooling in black and white communities alike continued to stand on what one observer described as a foundation of "home rule and self-government."[8]

State law provided for an educational bureaucracy with only limited power. Throughout much of the mid-nineteenth century, politicians considered the state superintendency a "little office," and its occupants labored under the constraints of a vague legal mandate to "direct the operations of the system of public schools." Until 1885, the legislature refused even to supply a clerk to help the superintendent manage his correspondence. In the same year, lawmakers made provisions for the appointment of county boards of education and expanded the power of county superintendents to intervene in day-to-day schoolhouse affairs. But because board members served without pay and superintendents received only a modest per diem, few gave the work their full attention. In many counties, the superintendent never visited the schools in his charge. Meaningful authority remained largely in the hands of the three committeemen selected in each school district by the boards of education to oversee the hiring of teachers, the arrangement of the school calendar, and the disbursement of appropriated funds.[9]

The appointment of district committeemen reflected local hierarchies and served as an extension of the political process in which men vied for power, respect, and standing for themselves and their families. In Orange County, for example, Democrats used the school districts as basic units of political organization. During the spring, the party faithful in each district gathered to advise the county board of education on who should be named to the school committees and to select delegates to the party convention. Farther east, in counties with heavy black populations, the selection of district committees also reflected the politics of race. Under informal agreements with ruling Democrats, black community leaders often claimed at least one, and sometimes all three, of the committee posts attached to their neighborhood schools. White officeholders, mindful of the political clout of black voters, viewed such compromises as the price of power. While they retained ultimate authority over the allocation of school funds, they ceded to black parents a basic measure of day-to-day "control over their own schools."[10]

District committeemen kept themselves well apprised of their neighbors' opinions. Unless parents approved of a local committee's actions, they would neither enroll their children nor help secure the land and supplies necessary for building and maintaining schoolhouses. Most common schools stood on private property and were constructed without direct state assistance. When a district needed a new school, local committeemen mobilized their neighbors to undertake the construction. J. M. White of Concord remembered how his community went about replacing a dilapidated log schoolhouse in 1883. The district committee "decided not to have any school one winter" and diverted the money that otherwise would have been used to hire a teacher into a special building fund. A carpenter in the neighborhood drew up plans for a new frame structure, and a generous farmer offered all the necessary "field pine timber," provided that his neighbors agreed to "come with wagons and hands to chop and haul." The families then passed the hat to collect extra money for shingles, nails, and homemade desks. On the appointed day, men and boys gathered early in the morning to assist the carpenter, while the women prepared hot meals for all who joined in the task. In the evening, the neighbors celebrated their accomplishment and congratulated themselves on building "the best country schoolhouse in Cabarrus county."[11]

Perhaps justified in this case, such pride more often belied the conditions under which children learned their lessons. One student described her school as a "very common" structure "situated in the woods nearly half a mile from the public road. When it rains the yard is covered with water and is very muddy. The house is not plastered and there are some very large cracks all about." At another school, a young teacher found "nothing . . . to absolutely repel one, but . . . equally as little to attract." The walls, "which had once been white," were "ornamented by the hieroglyphics of incipient pensmen" and "smoked almost to blackness" by misuse of the fireplace. A "scratched and shabby-looking blackboard" stood at the front of the room, flanked by rows of "heavy, clumsy desks, so awkwardly constructed as more to resemble a contrivance for punishment than a comfortable seat for the 'human form divine.' " Still other teachers were terrified by the snakes that coiled around schoolhouse rafters or entertained by the lizards that crawled in and out of the walls, feasting on flies.[12]

Nevertheless, the neighborhood school both shaped and reflected a sense of community. If the families in a district got along, the school expressed their harmony. If they were at odds, it fell prey to partisan bickering. According to the state superintendent, people in some neighborhoods could "get up more enmity, hatred, and raise a bigger row in general, over the public schools . . . than could be stirred up upon any other subject in the world, except politics."[13]

In fact, conflicting political loyalties often provoked "public school wrangle[s]." W. D. Glenn, a dry goods merchant in a Gaston County settlement known as Crowder's Creek, charged that "under Radical rule" he and his Democratic neighbors in school district number 47 had been "robbed" by Republicans in district number 50, who had redrawn the boundary lines and claimed a mile of their territory. The expropriation caused little trouble until the mid-1880s, when the residents of the Republican district built a schoolhouse in the disputed area and, according to Glenn, "seduced our people to go to their school." Since most of the county educational fund was distributed on a per capita basis, Glenn and his neighbors received only $70, compared to their rivals' $100. Glenn's faction convinced the Democratic school board to restore the old boundary, but they had less success with the defectors, who continued to send their children to the Republican school. Apparently, they had not been seduced after all. "Some of these live ¼ mile some about ½ mile inside our district," Glenn complained to state superintendent Sidney Finger. "Can a man belong where he pleases and go where he pleases across the dist[rict] line. What is a line for if they can cross it any time they please."[14]

Superintendent Finger and local authorities were at a loss to resolve the dilemma. The state school law itself recognized the necessity of "consulting as far as practicable the convenience of the neighborhood" in drawing district boundaries. The boundary lines represented not so much permanent legal entities as changing social alliances shaped by politics, fluctuations in the school-aged population, quarrels over denominational influences in education, and petty squabbles kindled by "personal spite." County officials usually sought a compromise that would satisfy both of the warring parties; otherwise, they risked escalating the hostilities, perhaps even provoking the losers to such desperate measures as schoolhouse arson.[15]

Local disputes were largely responsible for the proliferation of school districts during the late nineteenth century. Between 1880 and 1902, the number of white and black districts grew from 6,392 to an all-time high of 8,094. Parents insisted on sending their children to schools that mirrored their own sympathies and allegiances, regardless of the consequences. To the dismay of reformers, such concerns always seemed to carry more weight "than longer terms, than better teachers, than a more perfect system."[16]

Similar considerations influenced the employment of teachers. State law required that every prospective teacher obtain a certificate of proficiency by passing a written examination administered by the county superintendents. Graded certificates were issued according to average test scores: 90 percent or higher for a first-grade certificate; 80 percent or more for a

second-grade certificate; and better than 70 percent for a third-grade certificate. The law required that the superintendents quiz teachers on spelling, reading, writing, arithmetic, grammar, geography, and history, but in
reality the tests seldom consisted of more than a few simple questions in
each category. Local school officials showed far greater interest in discerning their applicants' moral character. Their ideal pedagogue would teach
"thousands to read, but not one to sin."[17]

Well into the 1880s, county schoolmen echoed Calvin Wiley's belief that
"no amount of scholarly qualification will atone for the want of good moral
character; and that a teacher of bad habits, or opinions opposed to the
truth of God's revealed Word, is not a fit companion, much less instructor,
of the children." In 1887, residents of Steel Creek township in Mecklenburg County sought advice from the state superintendent on removing a
teacher who had seemed quite upstanding at first but through reports from
his former employers had now been exposed as "an *infidel.*" The man often
carried "Tom Paine's Age of Reason to school and [read] it to the scholars;
and by such conduct . . . had poisoned the minds of some of the most
promising young men in his neighborhood." In the assessment of moral
fitness officials found it "impossible to be too strict: there should be no
compromise here, no allowances." Since standards of character and morality could vary greatly from one community to the next, and because their
enforcement demanded constant vigilance, teaching certificates expired
after one year and were valid only in the county in which they were issued.[18]

Once they had passed muster before the county superintendent, teachers could begin their job search through an informal process of visiting,
going "first to one and then another of the committeemen" to negotiate a
salary and the length of the school term. Under such circumstances, the
influence of friends and kinfolk often proved decisive. Unemployed teachers frequently grumbled that committeemen ignored the issue of competence and hired "too many . . . 'pets,' favorites, or relatives." In 1887, for
example, a woman from Iredell County wrote to the state superintendent
complaining that in her district a "father and son and a *particular friend* of
theirs are school committeemen, and the result is that no one can secure the
position to teach in the public school . . . but a relative or *warm personal
friend*, regardless of their competency or fitness as a teacher."[19]

Nepotism was surely a problem, especially when committeemen made
appointments calculated to improve their own family finances, yet modern
eyes can easily misread the past. In an age unacquainted with public wel-

fare services, favoritism often shaded into civic responsibility. Myrther Wilson, a prospective teacher from Wayne County, was shocked to learn that a job she seemed certain to win had been given to another, but the reason was obvious. "As the public schools of North Carolina are *charitable* institutions," she explained, "the school was given to a woman of little education and very little culture, *because she needed it.*"[20]

Unlike Myrther Wilson and her rival, most common school teachers were not women. As late as 1890, two-thirds of them were men, averaging twenty-six years of age, who had "not chosen the work as a profession, but merely as a step to something else." Three-fourths taught for no more than four months a year, usually to earn tuition money for college or "pocket change" to supplement a farm income. Few had studied beyond the common school curriculum or undertaken any formal pedagogical training. "Indeed, it is the simple truth," reported the state superintendent in 1890, "that a large part of our public school money is expended on teachers whose geography does not extend much further than their localities and horizons; whose science is the multiplication table and simple arithmetic; and whose language, history and belles lettres are about comprised in Webster's Spelling-book." As a result, each teacher tended to view his school as the entire "educational world, of which he was the center and the sovereign." A majority of " 'neighborhood schools' . . . were conducted on no fixed plan whatever." Teachers derived their methods from their own common school experiences and the demands of their patrons rather than from abstract pedagogical principles.[21]

Neighborhood residents expected teachers to conform to their ways of doing things. With no bureaucracy to serve as a buffer between parents and the schoolroom, and with little sense of belonging to a profession, teachers found themselves at the mercy of the community. They often encountered the sort of "interference" suffered by Hope Caldwell, the protagonist in a late-nineteenth-century novel about common school teaching in North Carolina. On her first day in the classroom, Hope met "the widder Simmons" and her sons. "What I come to tell you is this," said Simmons. "My two boys is very different in their turns. . . . George—*he* has a turn for 'rithmetic and he's kinder mischievous, which I don't want you to pay no 'tention to, 'cause it's his disposition, and he don't mean no harm by it, but Tommie is as good a boy as the sun ever shined on, only he don't love books. . . . You see I'm their mother, and I understand them. . . . They both must be coaxed, they must be dealt kindly with, and I wants you to treat them jest as good as if they was the richest boys in the land." Mr. Liggins, one of widow Simmons's neighbors, had different ideas. "I likes your teachin'," he told Hope, "I likes it very well but for one thing. You ain't tight enough. Boys like mine need the hickory two or three times a week to season them." And still other parents offered advice on classroom thrift. "I wish, Miss Hope," said Aunt Rachel Tyler, "you would make the children bring their copies home every Friday. They get stolen sometimes here when left Saturday and Sunday. When I went to school paper was paper; children was keerful with everything, but now-a-days things is wasted. . . . Pencils, too! I can't keep [my children] in pencils to save my life. I do not mean to complain, but you know it is aggravatin'."[22]

Real-life teachers did well to take a lesson from Hope Caldwell by swallowing their pride and answering their petitioners in "a dignified manner." They seldom signed formal contracts with the committeemen who employed them; instead, they were retained and paid on the basis of their ability to satisfy the school's patrons. Like the widow Simmons, many parents sent their children to school on a trial basis. "I'll try them both awhile," Simmons warned, "and ef they don't get along I'll take them away." Parents who found fault with a teacher simply kept their youngsters at home, forcing the school to close and denying the teacher any further pay. Teachers who failed to take the hint and move on could face unwanted trouble. In 1887, a district committeeman from the Fork Church settlement in Davie County used his position on the grand jury to drive an unpopular teacher out of the community. The schoolmaster had quite innocently "carried a pistol one night with some young men to shoot a 'mad dog.' " Seizing the opportunity, the committeeman "had a bill found against [the] Pedagogue for carrying concealed weapons" and demanded revocation of his teaching certificate "on the grounds of 'open conviction in court.' "[23]

Teachers and committeemen were particularly mindful to arrange the school calendar according to the cycles of agricultural life. Although the law called for an annual session of four months, few schools met that requirement or remained open for a full term without interruption. In most communities, schooling was an on-again, off-again affair, with closings during the cold months of midwinter and at planting and harvest times. The school day usually ran from sunrise to sunset so that children could come and go according to the varying patterns of household routines. A mother might send her daughter to school early so that she could have her help in the afternoon to milk the cows, while an older son might arrive late because he was needed to light the morning fires and feed the livestock. When the burden of chores grew particularly heavy, children stayed away from school for days at a time. One seventeen-year-old boy presented a note to his teacher explaining a string of absences: "Dear Cir—Pleze to eggscuse Henry. . . . We made sour-krout, and he had to tromp it down. Also he had to Help butcher too pigs. Respeckful yuers, His Pap."[24]

Parents placed little value on regular attendance. Between the ages of six and twenty-one, children moved in and out of school according to family needs, often attending when they were very little, then remaining at home for several years, and finally returning when younger brothers and sisters were old enough to relieve them of field work and household duties. For that reason, nineteenth-century school census figures could be quite misleading. In 1887, the state superintendent reported that among blacks and whites alike only 58 percent of school-aged children were enrolled, but he warned against concluding that the others would never know the benefits of the classroom. They were likely to attend for at least a term or two sometime before their twenty-first birthdays.[25]

Casual attitudes toward attendance made sense in a society in which formal schooling constituted only a small part of children's education. Young people learned vocational skills on the farm or in the craftsman's shop; civic and moral instruction took place in church and on county court day, when neighbors met to gossip and talk politics. Schooling was but one of many paths to adulthood, meant to provide only the basic knowledge of reading, writing, and ciphering necessary for survival in a face-to-face world governed more by custom and personal reputation than by the written word.[26]

The common school curriculum consisted of whatever books parents could obtain or afford. On the first day of school, teachers regularly discovered that their pupils had "not a dozen text books alike." Among spellers, Webster's, or " 'the blue-backed spelling book,' as the children called it, took the lead. . . . The readers . . . were by every author who had written since the Revolution . . . grammar[s] by as many different authors, ditto arithmetic." Teachers who tried to impose some measure of uniformity confronted the intransigence of parents who clung to family heirlooms out of poverty or a belief in the power of books to "interlock one generation with the other." Under such circumstances, instruction followed no standard course of study or plan of advancement. Students moved ahead at their own pace and stayed in school until they had exhausted the neighborhood cache of readers and spellers or until their parents decided that they had acquired enough book-learning.[27]

Classroom lessons generally took the form of memory work—an approach one observer described as "a method of implicit belief . . . of learning, believing, and conforming." In arithmetic, that meant mastering a host of rules for practical problem-solving. The student's task was to match the problem to the correct formula and grind out the solution mechanically. Most youngsters plowed their way through rules for addition and subtraction, multiplication and division, and the addition of fractions and compound numbers without realizing that they were performing variations of the same operation. One educator offered this description of the process:

> The pupil learns a rule, which, to the man that made it, was a general principle; but with respect to *him*, and oftentimes to the instructor himself, it is so far from it, that it hardly deserves to be called even a mechanical principle. He performs the examples, and makes the answers agree with those in the book, and so presumes they are right. He is soon able to do this with considerable facility, and is then supposed to be master of the rule. He is next to apply this rule to practical examples, but if he did not find the examples under the rule, he would never so much as mistrust they belonged to it. But finding them there, he applies his rule to them, and obtains the answers, which are in the book, and this satisfies him that they are right. In this manner he proceeds from rule to rule through the book.

Such devotion to formal precepts and memory work reinforced "the idea that knowing facts constitutes education."[28]

The Rule of Three, a technique for solving problems of proportion that was first devised in the countinghouses of fifteenth-century Venetian merchants, marked the pinnacle of common school arithmetic. Mastery of its many permutations was often considered a sign of high scholarship. One prospective teacher recalled an encounter with a rival: "He put me through a kind of examination, giving me some of his hard questions, his hardest being a sum in the Double Rule of Three, which I readily worked, and so my reputation [in the neighborhood] was established."[29]

The Rule of Three inspired such awe partly because of its capacity to generate confusion. Consider an example: if 5 bushels of corn cost $1.75,

An unidentified rural school in the late nineteenth century. The children have brought their arithmetic slate outdoors to show the photographer. (Courtesy of the North Carolina Division of Archives and History, Raleigh)

how much would 8 bushels cost? Today's students would set up a simple algebraic equation to solve the puzzle, but nineteenth-century school-children had no recourse to algebra to help them approach the problem logically. The Rule of Three instructed them to write in their notebooks "5:1.75::8" and then to multiply the middle number by the last and divide the product by the first. Students often erred by putting the numbers down in the wrong order, but the real difficulty was that the first operation produced a meaningless result: $1.75 times 8 bushels equals 14 dollar-bushels. Only with the final division did the procedure make any sense.[30]

The rule's power to intimidate also revealed the limited role of numbers in the daily lives of most North Carolinians. Well into the late nineteenth century, farmers still planted their crops and craftsmen still made their wares from experience rather than from calculations of acreage and production or from precise mathematical plans. Intuition and common sense provided solutions for most ordinary challenges. Beyond simple addition and subtraction, arithmetic was virtually unnecessary in the management of day-to-day affairs.[31]

Memory drills dominated reading lessons just as they did ciphering lessons. Common school students learned to read by learning to spell. "Over and over again" was the rule of the day in most classrooms, as children labored to conquer lists of words without definitions. Textbook authors assumed that their young audiences would communicate through speech more than writing and that patterns of local usage would supply meaning. In most communities, reading was an oral, often collective activity, not the private and silent one it is today. Observers frequently described the common schools as "loud" or "howling schools" because teachers required students "to repeat their lessons . . . while memorizing them." When all of the pupils were hard at work, the classroom rang with "a constant hum & hubub" and the "babel-jargon of voices."[32]

Within this setting, the roles of students and teachers often overlapped, and for this reason, reform-minded critics complained that systematic instruction frequently gave way to mere "*school keeping.*" Older students helped "to hear some of the primary lessons," guiding the efforts of younger brothers and sisters, nephews, nieces, and cousins. For many adolescents, such exercises offered preparation for a year or two of teaching before marriage or the pursuit of a settled livelihood.[33]

That the common schools privileged sound over sight in reading instruction was no accident. The choice reflected the pattern of human relationships that shaped and conditioned literacy in nineteenth-century rural society. Modern observers might easily dismiss the clamor of the common school as a detriment to learning, but that judgment only suggests how alien common school pedagogy has become to our way of experiencing the world. Parents and educators valued reading less as an instrument of autonomy for the individual than as a means of reaffirming the moral bonds of everyday life. They wanted children to read so that they could understand "the Bible and the laws of the state"; they valued memory work because it tied the present to the past, making "what has already been done a pattern of good counsel to the future." At the end of the year, neighbors gathered for a "school breaking" to celebrate the youngsters' newfound skills. Before an assemblage of parents and friends, students demonstrated their facility with words through spelling bees and public declamations, oral exercises well-suited to a cultural world of speech and hearing.[34]

By the same token, schoolhouse discipline expressed the values of a society in which authority was personal and direct. Students who misbehaved found themselves seated on the "dunce block," or worse, subjected to the sting of the rod. Teachers regarded corporal punishment as indispensable, and they whipped "the backs of . . . offenders like threshing peas." Such punishments were meant to humiliate. Administered publicly, they chastened wrongdoers through shame rather than guilt, placing them momentarily beyond the fellowship of neighborhood and classroom life.[35]

But teachers did not always hold the upper hand. They often succumbed to a "turning out," particularly at Christmastime. On the appointed morning, all of the boys in the school would arrive early to fortify the classroom; then they would deny their instructor entry until they were granted a holiday. A mock battle often ensued, especially if the teacher was a man. After an exchange of sticks and insults, the teacher usually gave in, much to the delight of the parents who by this time had gathered to witness the confrontation. For one teacher in western North Carolina, the restoration of order cost a "half a gallon of brandy for an egg nog." When "the eggs could not be had," the "brandy and the milk were put into a kettle, and put on the fire, and a kind of a stew was made that couldn't exactly be named, and it was thus dealt out to the crowd." This upending of classroom authority made the neighborhood claim on the school visible, even palpable. Students and parents took possession of the schoolhouse, reminding teachers that they owed their positions to local favor and approval.[36]

All in all, the common schools were well-adapted to the lives of middling farmers, men and women who placed scant faith in acquisitiveness and social mobility but labored instead for a competence and a respectable start in life for their children. Parents and teachers recognized and rewarded students' individual achievements, but at every turn those accomplishments were tied to the rhythms of collective life. Youngsters went to school to learn their way around a densely personal world, not to make preparations for striking out on their own. The common school embodied what one historian has described as a "peasant pedagogy"—one more attuned to survival than to getting ahead.[37]

By the 1880s, economic forces unleashed by the Civil War and emancipation had begun to produce dramatic changes in the neighborhood-oriented world of the common school. Alexander Foushee of Person County remembered that "many of the people who had grown to maturity in the old days, thought . . . things would settle back to the old ways. The slaves were free, it was true, but surely" most North Carolinians would "toil and labour as before." At first those expectations seemed to mirror reality. The eternal rhythms of the sun and the seasons—of plowing, planting, and harvesting—continued to set the pace of everyday life. Farmers grew the same crops they had tended before the war—cotton, tobacco, and corn—and, as they had always done, they relied on the muscle of man and beast to break the land. But beneath the outward appearances of continuity, a new way of life was taking root.[38]

When the Thirteenth Amendment was ratified in 1865, slaveholders who had once been laborlords became landlords. Contemporary observers pointed out the profound implications of that shift in property rights. They argued that slavery had bound whites as well as blacks by choking off entrepreneurial energies, and they rejoiced that the Civil War liberated "not only the black slaves but a large class of white slaves" as well. "Our labor has become free, our doors have been thrown open to ideas of money," exclaimed Edwin Alderman, one of the architects of the graded school movement. "In short, we have passed from the patriarchal to the economic stage of society, where . . . the orators and dreamers of old must, at least, share the stage with the manufacturer, the producer, the industrial man." Alexander Foushee agreed. "The end of the war," he recalled, "brought new ideas; the individual demanded a place and a reward no matter what was his family backing. . . . Energy, business ability and general efficiency were the watchwords that opened the door to success now. We were living in a new world."[39]

Historians have often dismissed such exultations as mythmaking by publicists who overestimated the forces of upheaval in the postwar South. To be sure, change did not occur overnight. It proceeded in ever-building waves, only gradually eroding familiar habits of life. Nevertheless, New South promoters were, as they claimed, witnesses to the birth of a "new civilization."[40]

Emancipation forced white North Carolinians to rethink "fundamental points of view, social, political, and economic." As long as slavery survived, the state's elite took little interest in local development. But black freedom introduced new economic incentives. Masters without slaves had no choice but to redirect their investments and their politics toward raising land yields and land values. Across the South, coalitions of furnishing merchants and large landholders campaigned for fence laws and the enclosure of the common range; championed the construction of railroads and towns; lobbied for new taxes to finance public improvements; and built factories to turn the resources of the land into profitable goods. Denied property of their own or recognition of the common rights that had made a semisubsistence way of life possible, and burdened by higher taxes and the pressure to grow more cash crops instead of food, large numbers of freedmen and white yeomen began to work other men's land as sharecroppers or abandoned the plow to sell their labor for wages.[41]

Railroads blazed the way for an expanding commercial economy. Financed by local stockholders and outside investors, track mileage increased substantially. In 1880, 1,500 miles of rail snaked across North Carolina; by 1900, track mileage had grown by more than 250 percent. As railroads penetrated the backcountry, they introduced smallholders to the opportunities and dangers of the marketplace. A resident of western Carolina reported that the arrival of trains "wrought a great revolution" in his part of the state. "People who had no market at all, and who had no ambition to sell farm produce more than sufficient to pay their annual tax and keep a few dollars stowed away in the red chest as a keepsake," found themselves caught up in moneymaking, "selling their lumber, cattle, potatoes, and apples." At every turn, it seemed, the "cash basis of life" was gaining ground. "This is emphatically a money age," L. L. Wright of Thomasville told a gathering of teachers in 1884. "The great tread of popular anxiety is in the line of money. History presents no parallel. All classes and ages have caught the infection. The material is in the ascendant."[42]

Along the rail lines, old towns awoke and new towns sprang up to service the needs of farmers and to become centers of cotton and tobacco manufacturing. In 1870, only the port city of Wilmington could claim a population of more than 10,000; by the turn of the century it enjoyed the company of Asheville, Charlotte, Greensboro, Raleigh, and Winston. The number of towns with 5,000 to 10,000 people grew from two to six; one of them— Durham—did not even show up on the federal census in 1870 but reported 7,000 citizens by century's end. Even more striking was the rise of small settlements with populations of 1,000 to 5,000 : from fourteen in 1870 to fifty-two in 1900. As towns grew, so did the number of manufacturing establishments. Between 1880 and 1900, for example, investors built an average of six new cotton mills a year. Those mills, along with other industries, enticed thousands of struggling farm families off the land with the promise of regular cash wages.[43]

Burgeoning towns and cities became symbols of a "new North Carolina" that had gotten "the frenzy and fever of accumulation . . . into its blood." Taken with the sights of commerce, observers often resorted to hyperbole, describing the state's nascent urban centers as great, bustling metropolises. Visitors found Winston to be "literally a world of boxes, carts, drays, wagons, buggies, coaches, carriages and busses, all seemingly on a 'grand bust.' Women, children, men and boys, going, coming, laughing, talking, moving, running, rushing, flying. We could find no place for a pause on the street without being in somebody's way and having no time to dodge." In Durham, newcomers discovered "a delightful freedom, frankness, and independence in the very atmosphere." With its cotton mills and tobacco factories, Durham stood for "something brand new in North Carolina"—the "idea of a town that had an almost purely manufacturing basis. . . . It is along the right line. It is to-day not yesterday. It looks to the future, not backward at all. It is North Carolina under the new conditions."[44]

These commercial centers were home to the "*novus homo*"—the "progressive man of business" who was "cold, hard, and astute." For him, "sentiment" never "interfere[d] with the strict working of the principle of self-advantage." In an age increasingly attentive to the main chance, bonds of family, neighborhood, and friendship seemed diminished in value. The *Carolina Messenger* warned its readers to trust no one and to take nothing for granted. "No matter how intimate you may be with the friend with whom you may have business transactions put your agreement in writing. . . . Each word in our language has its peculiar meaning and memory may, by a change in a sentence convey an entirely different idea from that intended. When once reduced to writing ideas are fixed, and expensive lawsuits avoided."[45]

This "new order" of life called, in turn, for a "radical readjustment" in the way that children were educated. Wickliffe Rose, an outspoken proponent of school reform, explained that in a society of free labor and cash exchange, each individual had "to win for himself his place, and must show himself worthy of [that] place by winning it anew every day. In the new South not birth but worth determines place, and the criterion of worth is social efficiency." Here was a transformative ideology, what one schoolman termed a new "culture of the self" that defined exertion, striving, enterprise, and achievement as the keys to happiness and a rewarding life.[46]

Beginning in North Carolina's market towns, educators and civic leaders searched for an institutional form capable of translating that ideology into everyday practice. They found their answer in graded education. The first graded schools in the United States were organized in Boston in 1848, and from there the idea spread rapidly to other urban centers. Its appeal on both sides of the Mason-Dixon line signaled a critical shift of emphasis in the rhetoric and purpose of public education.[47]

Antebellum promoters of the common schools had most often explained their labor through a language of politics and morals. In a society confronted with a swelling tide of immigrants, deepening divisions between rich and poor, and perennial concerns over liberty's temptations to vice and personal excess, they turned to the classroom as a source of common citizenship. "The chief end" of education, declared the Illinois state superintendent in 1862, "is to make GOOD CITIZENS. Not to make precocious scholars . . . not to impart the secret of acquiring wealth . . . not to qualify directly for professional success . . . but simply to make good citizens."[48]

In North Carolina, Superintendent Wiley shared that view, albeit for reasons that his northern colleagues must have abhorred. The mission of the common school, he explained, was to produce a united citizenry "governed by common laws . . . advancing with a common step towards a common end." In a slave society, that purpose seemed especially important, for the most fundamental relations of property and authority depended on vigilant enforcement of the distinctions of race. More worrisome than the prospect of black insurrection, Wiley argued, was the danger posed by "vicious" whites who sank "into the bosom of the African community." Their "degeneracy" challenged the moral legitimacy of slaveholding itself by blurring the line between master and slave—the line that separated a ruling race elevated by "centuries of [Christian] progress" from a subject people "just emerging from a long and debasing thraldom to the lowest form of idolatry." Such intermingling also threatened to redefine the fundamental divisions of southern society in terms of class rather than color, thereby encouraging "fierce and bloody hostility . . . between the rich and poor." Thus, Wiley concluded, state lawmakers and county officials served their own interests by "strain[ing] every nerve to push forward the religious and mental development of the [white] masses." Only in that way could they hope to preserve a social order governed by a spirit of "respect, harmony, and subordination," and in which "all who are entitled to command [are] cheerfully submitted to in their proper place."[49]

Education for citizenship remained a driving concern for school reformers well into the twentieth century, but among graded school enthusiasts it found expression more often through a language of markets and competitive individualism than through one of civic virtue and self-sacrifice. For

Wilson graded school at the turn of the century. This brick building replaced the interim wooden structure that housed the school when it opened in 1881. (Courtesy of the North Carolina Division of Archives and History, Raleigh)

graded school promoters, the classroom was not so much a crucible of community as a staging ground for the great race of life. That difference in outlook could sometimes strain relations between first- and second-generation educators. Graded school leaders deified Calvin Wiley as the father of public education in North Carolina and often invoked his name to lend their work historical credibility. Nevertheless, they seldom invited the old man to assume an active role in promoting their cause. One reason, perhaps, lay buried in the annual reports that Wiley had once submitted to the state legislature. In 1860 he described in uncompromising language the kind of society he hoped the common schools would hold at bay: it was, he wrote, a world of "Ishmaelites, everywhere lying in wait for each other, and fighting over the natural fountains and fruits of the earth." As the former superintendent looked upon the changes wrought by war and emancipation, those words must have returned to his mind, ringing with the sound of prophecy.[50]

Graded school fever consumed townsfolk throughout the new North Carolina. Wilmington and Greensboro established the state's first graded schools in 1868 and 1870, respectively; Raleigh and Charlotte followed by 1876; and Fayetteville joined the movement in 1878. But it was the opening of schools in Wilson and nearby Goldsboro in 1881 that effectively spread enthusiasm across the state. Goldsboro was a major railroad center, and Wilson stood strategically placed twenty miles away on a through north-south line. Easy rail access to the towns brought thousands of visitors—parents and teachers who returned home with "a militant desire for public graded schools for their own children." By the late 1890s, more than two dozen communities had approved special taxes to support graded education, in most cases for black and white students alike.[51]

A new emphasis on professionalism and standardization marked the abandonment of common school instruction in those scattered outposts of the new North Carolina. In Goldsboro, for example, trustees of the black graded school established a private institute to train their own supply of "good, competent," forward-looking teachers. Without such classroom laborers, they argued, the graded school experiment would "fail of accomplishing" its transformative work, and the benefits of the new education would be lost to black children in "the great belt of the country in which the colored people are most thickly settled." Next door, in Wilson, white school officials pursued a similar purpose, although at first they moved with caution and circumspection. The trustees bowed to old ways by appointing a superintendent and teaching staff chosen to balance denominational interests. Julius Tomlinson, the superintendent, belonged to a prominent Quaker family from far-away Randolph County. Since Wilson had no Quaker community of its own, Tomlinson could easily stand apart from local religious rivalries. His two senior teachers, on the other hand, represented the leading churches: one was a Methodist, the other a Missionary Baptist. That capitulation to denominational politics, however, was the exception that proved the rule. Tomlinson, like the superintendents in other towns, labored to develop a teaching corps that sought direction from within its own ranks. Twice a month, he held training sessions for his staff, encouraging them to base their classroom work on a "scientific method of teaching which is abreast with the times." As a matter of expediency, Tomlinson and his colleagues might compromise with tradition, but their ultimate goal remained clearly in view: they labored to erect a profession guided by its own principles rather than the idiosyncratic concerns of parents and patrons.[52]

With that aim in mind, graded school teachers replaced the personalistic ways of the common school with a "single standard of honor." They measured children's success and made promotions from one grade level to the next on the basis of an ability to perform according to uniform criteria. Advancement was to be earned, not awarded on the basis of family, friendship, patronage, or some other particularistic relation. Such innovations obviously mimicked dramatic changes in public life, but the graded school did more than simply record the cultural consequences of a commercial revolution. As reformers themselves were quick to point out, a market economy could thrive only in a market society. Graded schools, explained a contributor to the *North Carolina Teacher*, operated both as a "reflex of things existing" and as a "motor imparting its force" to a new social machinery; they were at once a product of the New South and a condition of its possibility. That dual positioning accounted for graded education's capacity to inspire awe as well as civic pride. Its purpose was nothing less than the reformulation of individual identity. Within the graded school classroom, the ways of the marketplace were "moulded into pupils" so that they came to be lived as a sense of self.[53]

First encounters with the graded school must have been strange, perhaps even frightening, experiences for children accustomed to the rhythms and routines of common school instruction. When Wilson opened its school, the trustees set aside the first four days of the term for "examining and classifying the scholars." At nine o'clock each morning, parents delivered their children to the schoolhouse, where teachers administered a battery of tests and then assigned the students to the appropriate grade levels according to age and ability. As children took those tests, they left behind the anchors of an older way of life. Cut loose from the relations of family, neighborhood, and church, they entered classrooms where each would be furnished "an opportunity to work out his own salvation."[54]

The need to rank students and measure their individual performance demanded the rejection of casual attitudes toward attendance. Graded schools kept regular hours and remained open for an eight- or nine-month term that varied little from year to year. Once only a minor part of childhood, schooling became a defining element in young people's lives. Graded school administrators maintained detailed records of absences and tardiness and published the results each month in local newspapers. Superintendent Tomlinson took great pride in announcing that by the end of its second year the Wilson graded school had achieved an average attendance of 97 percent, with a tardiness rate of .004 percent. The children who proved most regular in attendance had their names placed on a "roll of honor" and displayed in the newspapers for all to see. Such reports became important tools for reminding parents that punctuality and regularity were essential to the success of the graded school enterprise. Unless children faced the challenges of the classroom together in an orderly and structured way, the hierarchical arrangement of graded education would collapse. A shared experience was essential if each pupil was "to measure his natural powers as compared with the powers of his fellows."[55]

The "inner workings" of the graded school encouraged emulation and competition at every turn. In their daily lessons, teachers appealed to what some might have considered the least admirable of human passions. "In common with all other animals," one school official observed, "man's first motive to activity is his desire . . . for superiority over others. . . . Selfish ambition, by which sin the poet tells us the angels fell, is also the beginning of progress and is the embryo from which results a standard of excellence." A certain anxiety was meant to haunt graded school children. Once having set upon the race for honor and distinction, they were ever-mindful of the price of failure. To lose the contest was to experience something more than defeat, for only success brought the notice and approbation of others.[56]

Both the organization of the classroom and teachers' methods of evaluation reflected that ideal. Graded school students sat aligned in neat rows of individual desks, all oriented toward a teacher who stood on a rostrum at the front of the room and parsed lessons from standardized texts. They learned at the pace of the group, not at a pace determined by their own or their parents' needs and desires, and rather than recite their lessons together, they worked their way through written examinations in quiet solitude. "Only individual exercises test the individual pupil," one teacher explained. In the common schools, spelling bees, recitations, and elocution exercises had sorted out "good" and "bad" scholars. But as elements of an ordinal system of evaluation, they furnished only relative measures of individual performance. By contrast, written tests and numerical scores imposed normalizing judgments. Those instruments applied a standard measure to the entire school population and attached a specific value to each student. Grades became, in effect, a figurative—and sometimes even literal—form of capital by which individual profit and loss could be calculated. One schoolteacher, for example, reported that she had established "a sort of currency called *merits*," with each daily exercise having a precise value. At the end of the term, her pupils could tally their accounts and learn where they stood in relation to their peers. The system, she advised fellow teachers, "was sufficient to induce every pupil to take good care of his exercises, and led to a more careful attention to the school record."[57]

In Wilson, a similar scheme was implemented not only in individual

A classroom scene from the Washington, North Carolina, graded school, ca. 1905 (Courtesy of the North Carolina Division of Archives and History, Raleigh)

classrooms but throughout the school. Each month the principal awarded a "very beautiful and costly gold medal" to the boy (girls seem not to have been eligible for this particular contest) who obtained the "highest general average in attendance, deportment, and scholarship." The winner bore the title of "chief officer" of the student body until the honor was "wrested from him by some more successful rival." During his reign, the medal holder commanded the services of a group of monitors made up of other outstanding boys and girls from each grade. Every day the monitors watched over their classmates, making sure that "the ranks [were] well kept in marching from the school room to the play grounds." Advanced students who in the common schools would have helped slower children through difficult lessons now supervised their peers' behavior. In the schoolyard as in the outside world, ambition and achievement were coupled with power and privilege.[58]

The graduation exercises that marked the end of the school year reinforced that association. On the surface, the ceremony resembled the old custom of "school breaking," but its purpose was less to affirm the bonds of neighborhood life than to sort out winners and losers. Most students enjoyed graduation day as a time of "happy self-congratulations." But for the few who were left behind, it could only have been a wrenching experience, especially in the graded schools' early years, when such sorting was still a novelty. A child might have been "very irregular in attendance" or unable to give "sufficient application" to classroom assignments because of sickness or home duties, but those excuses seldom figured into the "examinational data" compiled by teachers. In any case, the pain of one child's failure taught all of the students a lesson. School officials admonished each pupil to recognize that promotion depended "upon the strength of his own ability, and that he [had] every chance to prosper." Children learned that success in school—like success in life—was a matter of personal motivation and "self-denying drudgery" disconnected from the circumstances of birth, family, and community. In a world founded on the distinction between winners and losers, graded school lessons provided a theory of "morally acceptable inequality."[59]

The champions of graded education insisted that getting ahead in the New South required an ability to manipulate the world rather than simply abide it. In order to prepare youngsters for that challenge, they gave up a pedagogy based on memory work and authority in favor of an approach that encouraged experimentation and self-directed discovery. Like the market itself, new teaching methods shoved aside old barriers and opened new avenues of experience and understanding. Graded schools fostered intellectual curiosity and acquisitiveness by observing a fundamental rule: never tell a child "that which he can find out for himself."[60]

Graded school teachers translated that maxim into practice by employing "object methods" of instruction. Rather than "forcing upon [students] rules and statements of authority," they encouraged children to learn by interacting with the physical world. Proponents of object teaching argued that in the common schools children had acquired only "passive knowledge," or "simply the capacity to receive information, and to imitate what they see done by others." By contrast, the graded schools sought to cultivate "active" intelligence and the "ability to produce effects." Learning through the manipulation of objects rather than by precept had two results: "one . . . is the possession of new knowledge; the other is an increased facility in the exercise of the powers by whose activity knowledge is acquired." True education, the graded school advocates insisted, "does not consist in knowing isolated facts, but in knowing things in their relations to each other." Object methods put a premium on children's ability "to get [information] for themselves," to generalize from their discoveries, and to use their new knowledge in further exploration and reshaping of the world around them. "Our aim is very definite," one graded school administrator explained. "It is to develop in children the power of thought, the capacity for learning, and the impulse and the desire for knowledge. We want to make men, not fill them. We want to educate rather than inform."[61]

That enthusiasm for object teaching grew primarily from the work of Francis Wayland Parker, who was described by his admirers as "the most brilliant, out-and-out apostle of . . . the New Education." Born in New Hampshire in 1837, Parker might have become little more than a respected New England schoolmaster had an aunt not left him a modest inheritance. In 1872 he set off for Europe to study at the University of Berlin and to travel extensively through Holland, Switzerland, Italy, France, and Germany. During that tour, he visited a number of schools founded on the educational philosophies of Johann Heinrich Pestalozzi, Friedrich Froebel, and Johann Friedrich Herbart. Earlier in the century, those reformers had drawn on the Enlightenment writings of Locke and Rousseau to outline a distinctively modern pedagogy based on the assumption that children were by nature active and creative rather than merely receptive. Instruction, they insisted, should be a participatory exercise that encouraged students to learn through observation and to build new ideas, one upon another, at a pace attuned to the gradual unfolding of their innate capacities. Taken by those precepts, Parker returned home in 1873 determined to transplant European ideas to American soil.[62]

He found his first opportunity while working as superintendent of the graded schools in Quincy, Massachusetts, where his new techniques won national acclaim as the "Quincy System." In 1880, the *New York Tribune* heralded his innovations as the "starting point in the reorganization" of American schooling. Three years later, Parker accepted an appointment as principal of the Cook County Normal School in Chicago. He remained there until his death in 1902, laboring to train a teaching corps devoted to "child-centered" instruction. Along the way, he also served as mentor to both John Dewey and G. Stanley Hall. Little of what Parker advocated was entirely new to American educators. Henry Barnard, editor of the *Connecticut Common School Journal*, had labored as "an active Pestalozzian propagandist" during the late 1830s and 1840s; at roughly the same time, Froebel's views of childhood had crossed the Atlantic with the early infant school and kindergarten movements. But it was largely through Parker's work that the ideas of European reformers came to define the mainstream of American pedagogical practice. His two major treatises— *Talks on Teaching*, published in 1883, and *Talks on Pedagogics*, which appeared eleven years later—became handbooks for a new generation of "progressive" reformers and laid the foundation for efforts to define a science of teacher training.[63]

Parker visited North Carolina in 1885 to deliver a series of lectures before the annual meeting of the state's Teachers Assembly, a conclave for white educators and lay enthusiasts that had been founded two years earlier. Public reaction to the event was overwhelming: newspapers reported daily on his lessons, while an educational publishing house in Raleigh blanketed the state with a special commemorative issue of the assembly's complete proceedings. Much of that excitement flowed from the connection between Parker's pedagogics and the public schools of Prussia, which New South reformers took as a model for their own region. Prussia had suffered a crushing defeat during Europe's Napoleonic Wars, but in the decades that followed, the German state remade itself into a formidable economic and military power, in part by liberalizing its system of public education. Graded school enthusiasts saw in Parker's teachings a reflection of that triumph. He seemed to offer them the means of freeing students from the stale formalism of the common school and, at the same time, of yoking the experiences of childhood to the disciplinary logic of the marketplace. Such reforms, declared one graded school proponent, had launched Prussia toward "leadership of all the nations of Europe." Now, he advised fellow reformers, North Carolina should seize the same advantage "in the race with [her] sister states for material prosperity."[64]

Practitioners of Parker's object methods revolutionized arithmetic instruction. Graded school teachers introduced their students to elementary mathematics with the aid of straws, beads, marbles, and peas. The idea was to have children discover through tactile experience the meaning of addition, subtraction, multiplication, and division rather than simply to have them master "empty formulas." "Our plan of teaching arithmetic may be briefly stated," a graded school superintendent reported. " 'First, the thought; then the expression of the thought by the aid of figures.' " Under this plan, another explained, "all rules and definitions are discarded except those which the children are able to invent, and the science of numbers is taught only by reference to the numbers themselves." In graded school classrooms across the state, teachers joined in a crusade to sweep "the old routine, empirical work . . . practically . . . out of existence."[65]

The new arithmetic stood the old on its head by emphasizing inductive reasoning, moving from examples to fundamental principles rather than the other way around. Children devised their own strategies for solving simple problems and were then guided by the teacher in restating their methods as generalizable laws. Ideally, the process recapitulated the development of arithmetic as an integrated system of thought. Teachers still provided the rules, but children were more likely to understand those principles rather than simply commit them to memory. C. L. Dowell of Raleigh explained this approach in an essay on multiplication and division published in the *North Carolina Teacher*. Since he spoke to the philosophical heart of the new education, his remarks deserve consideration at some length:

> As soon as children become passably conversant with the elementary principles of addition and subtraction . . . they should begin the study of multiplication and division. These latter subjects are so intimately connected that the one merges into the other, and they should be learned simultaneously. The old method of teaching the former of these rules was to place the multiplication table in the hands of the child, and, without any explanation relative to the import of the subject, require him to commit to memory the entire table, and in the case of failure . . . the most pleasant and impressive elucidation resorted to was the 'birch.' Of the import of the table, from whence it came, and its connection with what had been learned previously, the child knew nothing. There is however, a more simple and natural mode of presenting the subject. . . .
>
> [M]ultiplication should not be treated as something entirely foreign, having no sympathy or connection with what has been previously learned. The teacher should endeavour [instead] to make every new subject appear as familiar and as simple as practicability will admit. Multiplication should be taught as a brief process of addition, and in this way the pupil will associate this subject with what he has studied before. . . . He should be taught that two 2's are 4, because $2+2=4$, and that three 3's are 9, because $3+3+3=9$, etc.
>
> Instead, therefore, of the pupil's entering upon multiplication as a new and independent process, he will form an idea of the nature of the subject, and the mode of reasoning by which the operation is adduced. He

will trace the origin of the multiplication table, understand its meaning and use, and can reproduce it for himself. He will also understand why he should commit it to memory—that he may not have to derive these consecutive products on every occasion when he is required to make use of them.

The aim of Dowell's pedagogy was to make arithmetic into a way of thinking about the world numerically rather than a body of formulas mechanically applied to specific categories of problems.[66]

Francis Parker's disciples worked a similar transformation in reading instruction by promoting what they described as a shift from "ear-mindedness to eye-mindedness." A visitor to the graded schools would have been struck at once by the silence of the classrooms. Graded school students learned to read through the "word method," which relied on vocabulary recognition rather than rote spelling drills. In fact, proponents of the word method held spelling skills in low esteem, teaching them only "for convenience and not for mental culture." If that implied "a condemnation of Webster's Spelling Book," they exclaimed, "so much the better. The use of this old book has dwarfed and damaged many a child."[67]

Graded school advocates insisted that the common school had made the teacher "a mere oracle and the pupil an humble follower; the teacher a fugleman and the pupils obedient repeaters." The word method stood to change all of that. As with numbers in the new arithmetic, students first mastered words "as wholes," associating them with objects in their surroundings. Then they broke those words into the "elementary sounds" that served as ground rules for reading and pronunciation. By combining those sounds, children could "learn new words without assistance from the teacher" and could acquire for themselves "the power to *use* words freely." The word method promised to liberate students from "oracular authority, blind obedience, [and] dead results[,] . . . enkindling in their minds the power of seeing truth for themselves." When educated properly, each child would become a "discoverer" who not only learned to read but also learned from reading.[68]

There is little evidence that children acquired basic literacy skills any faster under one method or the other, but for the graded school reformers the choice of technique was packed with social significance. The rejection of "ear-mindedness" signaled a desire to weaken the link between reading and the oral culture of local life, heightening literacy's capacity to cultivate independence of mind. Graded school enthusiasts found the most eloquent statement of their purpose in the words of the fourteenth-century Italian poet Petrarch, who wrote of books:

> I have friends whose society is extremely agreeable to me; they are of all ages and of every country. . . . It is easy to gain access to them, for they are always at my service, and I admit them to my company, and dismiss them from it whenever I please. They are never troublesome, but immediately answer every question I ask them. . . . Some teach how to live, others how to die; some by their vivacity drive away my cares and exhilarate my spirits; while others give fortitude to my mind, and teach me . . . how to . . . depend wholly upon myself. . . . In return for their services, they only ask me to accommodate them with a convenient chamber in some corner of my humble habitation, where they may repose in peace; for these friends are more delighted with the tranquility of retirement than with the tumults of society.

Here was a conception of literacy easily recognized by twentieth-century readers. In the graded schools, reading lost much of its association with family Bible lessons, storytelling, and the public rituals of church and courthouse. Conditioned less by the social world of speech and hearing, it became a private pursuit that took place within the silence of an individual mind.[69]

Of course, even in the graded schools these new ways did not win immediate and universal acceptance. The old "method of authority" faded slowly. In one instance, the father of a prospective graded school teacher complained of the "tyranny" of his daughter's arithmetic instructor. This woman required that her students figure all of their problems "as she wishes, step for step, word for word, under heavy penalties for violations." Where, he pleaded, "is the development of the individuality of the pupil? Where is the stimulation of independence in thought and action?" If his daughter and others repeated such mistakes in their own classrooms, the man warned, they would "bring tears, mortification, disappointment, failure, and unhappiness to many." Of that he was certain, having suffered in his own common school days "this same tyranny, this same mental slavery."[70]

Philander Priestley Claxton, superintendent of the Wilson and Asheville graded schools and later U.S. commissioner of education, also lamented the errors of backsliders. Like most graded school superintendents, Claxton routinely made surprise visits to his teachers' classrooms. On one occasion, he heard a geography lesson on Moscow that asked the students to imagine themselves "approaching the great city on a festival day. You see many domes covered with burnished gold and towering spires piercing the sky." The teacher went on to explain how the citizens of Moscow had burned the city in 1812 to drive Napoleon's invading army out into the harsh Russian winter. When the lesson was over, Claxton asked a few questions. "What is a dome?" There was no answer; to the students it was only d-o-m-e. Remembering that the city had been burned, one child guessed that "burnished gold" was burned gold used for covering domes. And a spire, another supposed, was "one of them men that goes about seeing things." Claxton was stunned, for earlier in the day the teacher had described this as her most "perfect lesson."[71]

But even teachers who found the old ways hard to shake recognized the "radical significance of the New Education." An arithmetic based on understanding rather than memory encouraged a habit of calculation—a proclivity for weighing risks and figuring advantages that was suitable to a society animated by a spirit of gain. By the same token, "intelligent eye-mindedness" armed youngsters with the ability to discern in "written or printed words all their delicate shades of . . . meaning." In a society governed less by the face-to-face encounters of the neighborhood and more by wages, contracts, and money, the new education provided vital means of fixing certainty in human relationships. What had once been left to faith and supposition was, in the New South, to be enumerated and codified.[72]

An increasingly impersonal world also demanded a new sort of discipline. As family and community began to lose their moral claim on the individual, public order relied ever more on obedience to conscience and civic duty. The graded schools drilled students daily in a catechism of citizenship: "A GOOD CITIZEN is one who is orderly . . . able to control himself, has a high sense of honor, knows how to use money, is thorough, truthful, respects authority, [and] does not shirk responsibility." Teachers sought to show each child "how to get along without being crushed by his fellows, or, on his part, [casting] stones of offense [at] others." Well-trained pupils learned to temper individual striving with "a sense of justice & right." Through the balanced cultivation of "hunger, ambition, [and] conscience," advocates of the new education explained, the graded schools aimed to produce a personality suited to survival and social order in the "fierce life of the present and the fiercer life of the future."[73]

Those civics lessons were reinforced by a pedagogy of guilt and love that rejected shame and "bodily pain" as instruments of classroom governance. Graded school administrators took pride in abandoning corporal punishment for all students except those who "had bad raising or bad inheritances." "We must love these little people, and we can teach them and teach them well," insisted Edward Pearson Moses, superintendent of the Raleigh graded schools. "Love is indeed an essential element in every true teacher, and no one who has not love for the little ones should be permitted to undertake the training of them." Accordingly, his staff labored to "command obedience by *respect . . .* rather than by *fear.*"[74]

The use of love as a form of discipline encouraged students to act according to their own sense of right and wrong. When children misbehaved, they felt the sting of conscience rather than the schoolmaster's hickory switch. In a *North Carolina Journal of Education* article describing a typical day in her school, one teacher exposed the relationship between love and guilt. She once kept five students after class for their unruliness. "One little girl, whose chief fault is disturbing us with too much talk, burst out crying before I said a word," pleading " 'Miss Brooks, please try me again.' " The teacher said she would, and she asked the girl to stay until the others had left. "I wanted her to help me a little. I had kept her in twice before, and we had a long talk about helping each other and helping ourselves to grow stronger. So all I did was to thank her for helping me water my flowers and say, just as she was leaving, 'I believe you are going to try harder than ever before. Let me know if I can help you.' " Such discipline required no public pronouncement of wrongdoing. Instead, teachers reached into students' souls in an attempt to temper their "inclinations" and make them into "their own guardians." Those lessons were particularly appropriate to a society inhabited by increasingly autonomous—and often anonymous— individuals, who were bound less tightly than their elders in a system of direct, personal authority. In an expanding world of strangers, children would take their moral bearings from an internal compass rather than the judgments of others.[75]

Altogether, the various elements of graded education worked to foster what we would recognize as a "modern" personality—optimistic, receptive of risk, outgoing, and open to the world beyond. Shortly after the turn of the century, a young graded school teacher offered himself as evidence of the new education's power to remake the individual. Born at the dawn of reform, he had suffered the misfortune of entering school under an "old teacher, who was evidently the last of his race." The " 'professor' " governed his classroom with "iron-bound rules" that left the children in perpetual terror. "Silence began to reign in our [school] when the distant knock of his wooden leg was sounded in the doorway. If I remember rightly, he lost his leg at the battle of Chickamauga, and how often we wished that his head had come in contact with the ball instead. . . . 'Get by heart, study your books,' were the constant cries of this pedagogue. It is true that our minds were active, but in the same sense that a mill is active when it grinds corn."

The young man complained that his early education dulled his intellect and stifled his lust for life. "Up to the age of fifteen years," he remembered, "my greatest ambition was to be able to make a plow and handle a young mule like my father, and I only regretted that I was not 'left-handed' like him. . . . I was in a little world of my own." He might never have escaped that world had his family not moved to town, where he could attend a graded school and then go on to college. Under the "wise instruction" of a new teacher, his eyes were opened. "I now had a glimpse of the riches . . . spread out before me. . . . To-day I am in a great living, moving, intellectual world. . . . I see and hear and feel things that used to be hidden from my vision. I see and understand things that I never knew were in existence ten years ago." The graded school had worked a profound transformation in the young man's life; and out of gratitude, he resolved to have a school of his own one day.[76]

Apostles of the New South

The things that are behind *must* be forgotten and *buried*.
"O Thou first and with the last, annul our ruined past."
—Journal of Cornelia Phillips Spencer, June 1901

The graded school movement drew its leaders from a generation of young men who had grown up amid the cataclysm of civil war. Contemporaries described them as "a new order of prophet" called forth by the perils of a "transitional age." Their destinies, like those of all prophets, were shaped in part by accidents of birth. Born in the early 1860s, the graded school men were too young to have taken up arms or developed loyalty to the Lost Cause. Edwin Anderson Alderman, one of the chief advocates of school reform, recalled that for men of his generation, the Civil War did not "unfold . . . any of its marching splendours and waving banners." They witnessed "only the filthy backwash of war, its ruin and bitterness." Such childhood experiences produced little nostalgia for the Old South. While their elders mourned the loss of a past world, the graded school men longed for the South's reunification with the North and its integration into the modern world of industry, commerce, and science. "Like Elijah and Isaiah of old," they were "reverent of the past"; yet, certain of their own historical uniqueness, they stood with "faces turned toward the future."[1]

With few exceptions, the graded school men developed their commitment to reform during their student years at the University of North Carolina. When Edwin Alderman arrived in Chapel Hill in 1878 he met another newcomer named James Yadkin Joyner and a seasoned sophomore named Charles Duncan McIver. Proud of his urban upbringing, Alderman at first dismissed McIver as little more than a "great big country boy." But the three men soon formed a lasting "companionship of dreaming and work, of hope and accomplishment." A decade later, that bond would ease their way to leadership of a regionwide school reform movement. By the 1890s they had emerged as the "tight . . . inner core" of a group of nearly thirty university graduates who found their life's calling in education.[2]

Alderman believed that there had been "no better place . . . for the making of leaders" than Chapel Hill in the last quarter of the nineteenth century. Those years were a time when "life seemed very grand and duty easy and opportunity precious." The campus pulsed with challenge and possibility. In 1875, the university had traded in its past for a curriculum and a professorate attuned to the New South quest. The remodeled college and its young graduates came of age together. Alderman and his classmates played a key role in the creation of a new academic culture, and that culture in turn provided the bearings by which they charted their public lives. The reformers' own identities were closely bound to the difference between what the university had been and what it was in the process of becoming.[3]

Leaders of the antebellum university had no doubts about their mission: it was to make young men into masters. Sons of the slaveholding elite ventured to Chapel Hill from every corner of the South. By the 1850s, 35 percent of the student body came from out of state, and with an enrollment approaching five hundred, the college ranked second only to Yale in size. The university stood at "the very head and heart of . . . Southern civilization," preserving and passing on to the next generation the culture of a slaveholders' world. As defenders of human inequality in an age of natural rights, its patrons felt uneasy with the ideas of progress and reform that prevailed throughout much of the rest of the Western world. Parents wanted their sons to get an education that affirmed the fixity of human relations and instilled a habit of command. Young men came to Chapel Hill to confirm their place in society rather than discover a prescription for remaking the world.[4]

Bourgeois notions of human perfectibility, competitive individualism, and free inquiry found little recognition in campus life. The university's curriculum, like that of the common schools, rested on authority and received wisdom. Students followed a prescribed course dominated by instruction in Greek, Latin, and mathematics. Although the curriculum also provided for the study of constitutional law, moral philosophy, and belles lettres, those subjects received only cursory attention, primarily as a capstone in the senior year. Science teaching was similarly abbreviated and was more often didactic than experimental. As one student explained, he and his classmates valued the study of natural philosophy less for its practical uses than as a means of discerning God's plan for humanity in the divine order of creation. "Science," he observed, "leads [the mind] to the great storehouses of Nature, discloses her arcana, and exhibits man as he is—a poor worm in the dust."[5]

The classics had defined the core of higher learning since the Renaissance and the West's rediscovery of ancient wisdom. But the university's antebellum curriculum traced its more immediate origins to the tide of reaction that swept across Europe and America in the wake of the French Revolution. When the college opened in 1795, its faculty offered a course of study inspired by the utilitarian philosophy of French and English radicals. History, science, and modern languages stood on equal footing with the classics, and students were free to pursue their choice of two diplomas. One was in Latin, for young men who wished to master an ancient tongue; the other was in English, for those who concentrated on science and literature and read the classics only in translation. Bemused by that curriculum, one observer quipped that in Chapel Hill, "the *age of reason* has surely come."[6]

The university's experiment in Enlightenment pedagogy survived less than a decade. It collapsed quickly after 1799, when students rose up in rebellion against the disciplinary authority of the faculty. A sparse archival record makes details hard to come by, but the trouble appears to have started with an especially popular young man's expulsion for misconduct. Other students rallied to his defense, and in the week of rioting that followed, they horsewhipped the president, "waylaid and stoned" one of the professors, and harassed the others with threats of similar harm. Most of the faculty resigned immediately; those who remained armed themselves in fear that the violence might spill over into the next term. For critics of the university, the disturbance proved the dangers lurking within the institution's "modern French Jacobine System of Education." Unless it was abandoned, they argued, the Enlightenment curriculum would soon perpetuate in America the same forces of infidelity, freethinking, and moral decay that had ignited France's Reign of Terror. Spurred by that warning and by their own concern for the preservation of proper deference, the university's trustees beat a hasty retreat to the classics. By 1804, they had abolished the English diploma and had restored Greek and Latin as the twin pillars of instruction.[7]

At first glance, Chapel Hill's return to the classical fold seems to have placed it well within the mainstream of American higher education. The student riot of 1799 was one of many such upheavals that rocked campuses across the nation as sons of the American Revolution tested the limits of a democratic society. From Harvard and Yale to tiny Transylvania University in the backwoods of Kentucky, college leaders responded with a common antidote. They administered heavy doses of classical learning and evangelical piety—one to discipline the mind, the other to tame the passions. James K. Polk, a student at Chapel Hill and later president of the United States, explained his teachers' suspicion of the unfettered intellect's capacity for speculation and abstraction. "Invention, that ennobling faculty of our nature," he observed, "has by progressive steps enabled man to soar from his earthly habitations and view the magnificence of creation, to explain phenomena that astonished nature's son, and deduce such natural laws as declare, 'The hand that made him was divine.'" But that same quality of mind could just as easily inspire "a Paine, a Hume and a Bolinbroke as the harbinger of infidelity." It was against such misuse of the mind's "inventive powers" that the classics were mobilized. The ancient languages were difficult to learn and therefore left students with little time for mental idleness and temptation. By the same token, the "writers of ancient Greece and Rome" supplied impressionable young men with "the purest precepts of . . . morality, delivered in the most concise and emphatic manner." Doubters might have questioned the wisdom of attempting to construct a Christian republic on a foundation of pagan texts, but proponents of the orthodox curriculum were armed with ready answers. "By the study of [the classics]," declared a North Carolina student, "we see the folly of [Greek and Roman] Gods and we are enabled to comprehend more clearly the superiority and omnipotence of our own." Just in case such lessons failed to register, he added, "every piece of immorality is carefully excluded from our text books."[8]

The architects of that retrenchment belonged to a transatlantic community of conservative thinkers who felt at odds with the age of revolution in which they lived. They distrusted popular democracy and defended the authority of the "best men" to govern. Over the next half century, their views shaped the political sensibilities of successive generations of college students. Robert H. Cowan, a member of the University of North Carolina's class of 1844, was one of them. His junior oration demonstrated how easily the ancient past could be turned to traditionalist purposes. Before an audience of classmates transfixed by his rhetorical skill, Cowan praised patrician Rome as a model of civil society. "As long as the relation between patron and client was recognized, as long as the plebeians acknowledged their dependence upon the higher order," he declared, "so long did peace and prosperity reign throughout the State. . . . But when the days of [Rome's] democracy drew nigh, 'Oh what a fall was there!' . . . A Barbarian chieftain [was] soon seated upon the throne of the Caesars. . . . Light, learning, civilization, and refinement fled the land, and eternal night shrouded the whole world as in one universal pale of deep, dark, and dismal ignorance." That reading of Roman history was—to say the least—creative, but such quibbling was beside the point. Rome's tragedy was undeniable, and to Cowan's way of seeing, it offered ample evidence that "the people, swayed as they are by prejudice and passion . . . must be governed by an aristocracy."[9]

Robert Cowan spoke to broad ideological principles that crossed regional lines and informed higher education throughout antebellum America. But such commonalities can hide as much as they reveal. They tend to obscure the fact that by the late 1830s many southern colleges had begun to steer their own course. The rise of abolitionism in the North gave a new twist to old arguments for the stabilizing influence of classical learning. In Chapel Hill, faculty and students charged antislavery activists with committing the same sin as the French philosophes: they had elevated human reason above divine revelation and, in their arrogance, had unleashed the demons of anarchy. Southern collegians viewed the abolitionist crusade as the leading edge of a false doctrine of perfectionism that denied the innate depravity of mankind and promised the world a redemption that only Christ could deliver. That misguided philanthropy spawned a host of other dangerous impulses—Mormonism, free love, feminism, spiritualism, and socialism—that threatened to burst the "ties of nature" and undermine all forms of establish authority. "Unless checked by some contrasting force," William Waightstill Avery warned in his senior oration, "this impetuous current" would soon "engulph in its whirlpool our government, our law, and even civilization itself." Avery and his teachers found their only promise of safety in "communion with departed ages"—in rejecting the contested truths of the present for the comforting certainties of the past. That

COURSE OF INSTRUCTION.

FRESHMAN CLASS.

FIRST TERM.
1. Livy—Six Books.
2. Anabasis of Xenophon.
3. Algebra.
4. *Geography.

SECOND TERM.
5. Cicero's Orations.
6. Virgil's Georgics.
7. Herodotus.
8. Algebra and Geometry.
9. Geography and History.

SOPHOMORE CLASS.

FIRST TERM.
10. Thucydides.
11. Homer's Iliad.
12. Horace—Odes and Satires.
13. Exercises in writing Latin.
14. Geometry completed.
15. Analytical Trigonometry.
16. Analytical Geometry.

SECOND TERM.
17. Horace completed (except the Art of Poetry.)
18. Juvenal—Six Satires.
19. Tacitus—Germania.
20. Homer's Iliad.
21. Demosthenes on the Crown.
22. French—Bolmar's Fables.
23. Navigation.
24. Surveying, Heights & Distances.
25. Analytical Trigonometry completed.
26. Analytical Geometry completed.
27. Mechanics.

JUNIOR CLASS.

FIRST TERM.
28. Tacitus—Agricola.
29. Natural Philosophy.
30. Differential and Integral Calculus.
31. Rhetoric.
32. French—Charles XII.

SECOND TERM.
33. Greek Tragedy.
34. Calculus completed.
35. Astronomy.
36. Rhetoric completed.
37. Logic.
38. Elements of History and Chronology.
39. French—Moliere.
40. Cicero—"Cato" and "Laelius."

SENIOR CLASS.

FIRST TERM.
41. Chemistry and Mineralogy.
42. Political Economy.
43. Moral Philosophy.
44. Greek Tragedy.
45. French—Moliere.
46. Mental Philosophy.

SECOND TERM.
47. National & Constitutional Law.
48. Chemistry and Geology.
49. Horace—"Art of Poetry."
50. Cicero—De Officiis.
51. French—Racine.

---

* Geography *should* form no part of the College course—being a study suited to the capacity of a child of from 7 to 10 years of age. But the lamentable ignorance of some who know more or less of Latin and Greek, renders it necessary to give it a hasty review. It is hoped that when Morse's excellent School Geography with Cerographic Maps shall come into general use, this will be unnecessary—so far at least as Modern Geography is concerned.

The university curriculum as outlined in the *Catalogue of the Trustees, Faculty, and Students of the University of North Carolina, 1848–49* (Courtesy of the North Carolina Collection, University of North Carolina at Chapel Hill) choice revealed just how far the university had strayed from its founders' vision. By the time of the Civil War, the college had become less a national institution than a provincial outpost, set apart by a festering ambivalence toward free thought.[10]

The fate of the university's astronomical observatory—one of the first to be built by an American college—revealed the depth of that discomfort. In 1824, university president Joseph Caldwell traveled to Europe at his own expense to purchase books and "a proper supply of apparatus" for the study of natural philosophy. He returned to Chapel Hill with more than a thousand volumes, two telescopes, and an astronomical clock. Six years later, Caldwell cleared a hilltop near the village graveyard and erected a small building to house the instruments. On cloudless evenings he invited colleagues to join in observations "on the longitude and latitude of various places, on Eclipses and on Comets and other celestial phenomena." But soon after Caldwell's death in 1835, the records of his work were lost, and the observatory "fell rapidly to decay." Reveling students set the structure ablaze in 1838. Under other circumstances the destruction of university property might have provoked legal action, but David Lowry Swain, Caldwell's successor, merely scolded the incendiaries and breathed a sigh of relief. Swain was a popular ex-governor who had been appointed to the presidency with a view toward increasing the university's endowment and enrollment rather than extending its reputation "in the literary and scientific world." He noted wryly in his report to the trustees that the observatory was an "ill-starred building" that had "from the period of its creation been a nuisance rather than a benefit to the institution."[11]

Swain and his faculty thought of knowledge as a set of fixed and final truths rather than as methods of investigation and discovery. Kemp Plummer Battle, a graduate of 1849 and later president of the university, remembered that in his day "much attention was paid to pure Mathematics, less to its application." His teachers defended that approach on grounds that it offered admission to the mind of God. Mathematics revealed "the laws by which the works of an all wise Creator are governed" and in so doing led students to a more perfect conception of "the vastness of [God's] plans, the inexhaustableness of His resources, the unlimitedness of His power, the infiniteness of His wisdom." A similar rule governed the classics. The faculty offered no instruction in Latin or Greek composition. Nor did they give much notice to the capacity of literature to illuminate the historical workings of society and mind. Instead, the professors demanded "a minute acquaintance with the meanings and derivations of words, the cases and gender of nouns, the tenses of verbs, and the rules of grammar and prosody." Kemp Battle and his classmates mastered the dead languages in order to translate the wisdom of the ancients, not in order to give voice to their own thoughts.[12]

Education in the antebellum university was a passive enterprise aimed at propagating, but not necessarily enlarging, the existing store of knowledge. The faculty's teaching methods offered one case in point, and the college library another. Although professors occasionally lectured to their students, they much preferred the recitation as a means of instruction. Members of each class—freshmen, sophomores, juniors, and seniors—gathered for their lessons three times a day. The students sat on straight-backed benches and rose in turn to participate in an oral quiz designed to gauge their command of the day's assignment. Lyman Bagg offered a description of such exercises at Yale that students in Chapel Hill would have easily recognized. Imagine the scene as one student was "asked to read or scan a short passage, another to translate it, a third to answer questions as to its construction": "The reciter is expected simply to answer the questions which are put to him, but not to ask any of his instructor. . . . Sometimes, when a wrong translation is made or a wrong answer given, the instructor corrects it forthwith, but more frequently he makes no sign, though if the failure be almost complete he may call upon another to go over the ground again." By the time of graduation, college men had committed to memory the poetry of Horace, the orations of Cicero and Demosthenes, and the epic tales of Homer and Virgil. They had also learned from the ritual of recitation to seek knowledge in authoritative texts before their own interrogation of the world.[13]

That approach to learning made little use of reading outside the classroom. As a result, the college library came to serve more of a decorative than an instructional purpose. By 1836, the university's holdings amounted to nearly two thousand volumes, but under the administration of President Swain, new purchases ceased, even though books had become cheaper and more plentiful. The Reverend Fordyce Hubbard, professor of Latin and one-time curator of the collection, recalled that during his tenure "the College Library was never open to students . . . and almost never . . . used by members of the Faculty." To talk of a college library was, in fact, misleading. Before the Civil War, the university never gathered all of its books in one location. Most of them remained scattered across the campus, "carefully guarded under lock and key" in the rooms of the various professors.[14]

Neither faculty nor students placed much stock in scholarship for its own sake. As at other antebellum colleges, most of the professors were clergymen who possessed no specialized training in the subjects they taught. The university's trustees evaluated instructors primarily on their moral character and recruited faculty through family and church connections. Although academic competence was by no means ignored, it did not rank as a first consideration. Together, those factors worked to direct faculty loyalties inward toward local concerns, attenuating any sense of membership in a broader scholarly community or any commitment to the intensive cultivation of a specific discipline. Indeed, for most professors, it would have seemed incomprehensible to suggest that the moral and intellectual purposes of their labor were somehow distinct and separable.[15]

The faculty judged their students by similar standards. Kemp Battle recalled the rigors of college life at a time when he and his classmates were required to "attend prayers long before sunrise" and assemble for Sunday worship "even in bitter cold without fires." While the president sat on the rostrum with the officiating minister, other members of the faculty located themselves "so as to enclose the 'student body' with a cordon of watchers." Outside the chapel, the faculty maintained their surveillance of undergraduate life. Tutors occupied a room in each of the dormitories so that they might enforce the nightly curfew and "repress all disorder." For added effect, senior professors patrolled the dormitories in weekly shifts. Any student found in violation of college rules was punished with demerit marks, and in the case of serious infractions, offenders were called before the faculty "for such censure as they felt inclined to give." Demerits weighed equally with classroom performance in the decision to advance a young man to the next class or to grant him a diploma.[16]

Like their mentors, students prized intelligence, but not as the sole measure of prestige. While they may have treasured the fruits of classical learning, they held the etiquette of the classroom itself in rather low regard. Many cheated with impunity, especially during commencement week, when final examinations often took written form. Student lore told of answers hidden in plugs of tobacco or delivered through classroom windows wrapped around heavy stones. But "working the telegraph" was perhaps the most ingenious scheme. During the dead of night students would "cut a hole in the floor of the recitation room . . . beneath the benches," then once the exam was underway they would "lower the questions by a string, and haul up the answers worked out by a number of good scholars beneath."[17]

Cheating flourished in part because the cramped routines of the recitation hall failed to provide college men with a satisfactory field for honor and distinction. Antebellum students read the classics less as literature than as handbooks of virtuous manhood. "Our object in coming to college," explained William Lafayette Scott, "is to . . . acquire pungency and sprightliness from reading the keen sarcasm of Juvenal and the courtly wit of Horace—to polish and enrich our styles by poring over the tragic beauty of Sophocles and the stately and splendid numbers of Homer . . . in short, to prepare our[selves] for the great and masterly struggles of mind with mind in the court, in the pulpit, and in the council chamber." But few students believed that the ability to "*speak* and *act* as a *man*" could be acquired through study alone. In fact, most were convinced that a single-minded obsession with textbooks would make them into nothing more than dictionary rats and would leave them impotent "on the great battlefield of life." For lessons in "manly dignity," they turned away from their professors to a "separate world" of their own making.[18]

The Dialectic and Philanthropic Societies, founded soon after the university's opening in 1795, dominated student life outside the classroom. Each society maintained lavish quarters filled with fine furniture, portraits of distinguished alumni, and extensive collections of newspapers, journals, and books addressing the leading issues of the day. Those chambers were one area where professors and tutors did not rule. The Di-Phi operated as self-governing bodies; they granted their own diplomas and enforced rigorous codes of conduct through secret trials. "Fear of incurring their censure," one alumnus recalled, "was far greater than that of offending the Faculty."[19]

College men gathered within the society halls to pursue an informal curriculum of composition, declamation, and debate. Students who rarely wrote for their professors prepared essays for correction by their peers, so that they might sharpen their talent for "perspicacious & elegant expression." By performing the speeches of history's great orators, they mastered the "graces that can thrill a crowd with a glance . . . a smile or a gesture." And in public disputation, they forged their learning into the "weapons of intellectual warfare." The stakes were high in each of those exercises. As young men vied for the respect and admiration of their classmates, they

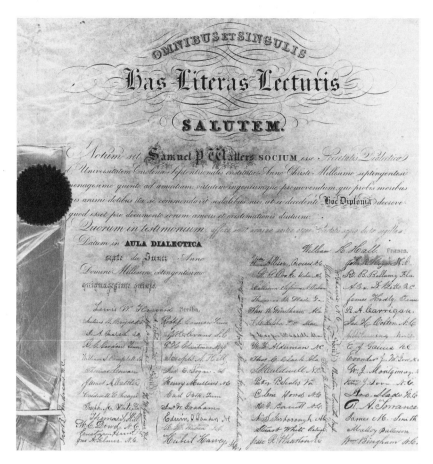

Students graduating from the university received diplomas from the debating societies as well as those given by the faculty. This diploma, bestowed on Samuel P. Watters in 1855, is signed by members of the Dialectic Society and decorated with that body's insignia, a wax seal and pale blue ribbon. (Courtesy of the University of North Carolina Archive, Chapel Hill)

were often tempted to hoot and jeer their rivals, or even to conspire against the success of an adversary. Presidents of the Di-Phi labored tirelessly to restrain that behavior by asserting the weight of a more noble fraternal ideal. Each society, they reminded their friends, was constituted as a "band of Brothers," dedicated to providing its members a refuge from the "prying gaze of . . . snarling critics." There, protected by "holy ties of intimacy," even the weakest debater could don the "toga virilis." "Without subjection to shame or dishonor," Angus McNeill explained, "you may fearlessly assail your antagonist, and though after repeated attacks, you may be at length overcome and forced to yield, you will have caused him to exert every energy of which he was master to sustain the [battle]." Whether one won or lost, such encounters were "emphatically a nursery of genius and eloquence."[20]

Students depended on the societies to cultivate that personal style and "polish of manners" which won little recognition in the classroom but which they considered essential to manly character. Chapel Hill was a tiny village where hogs wandered mud-choked streets and cows grazed on campus lawns; yet when the societies were in session, the place took on an air of self-conscious refinement. The principals in the weekly debates "studied their subjects well," often more thoroughly than they studied their lessons, while official critics filled the society minute books with sharp commentary that revealed how seriously students approached the contests. College men valued the lessons of the society halls because they soon would stake their fortunes on verbal persuasiveness and outward bearing. As lawyers, ministers, and politicians, their claims to authority would depend less on the possession of expert knowledge than on the ability to evoke the common truths of their society. Mastery of *the word*, as one student explained, was the "foundation for future eminence." On those grounds, college men often claimed for the Di-Phi a place of public honor no less than that of the faculty. "[E]very one must admit," insisted Alfred Foster, "that the two Societies in this Institution are her strongest props. Without them, she could not exist, or, if exist at all, it would be the existence of a weakly cripple deprived of a part of her limbs."[21]

All of student life, however, was not so high-minded as the society proceedings. Violence, too, figured prominently in this male world. College men armed themselves with pistols and knives and were quick to draw their weapons at the slightest affront to personal honor. The faculty and the courts regularly convicted them for "quarreling and fighting in their rooms." Students harassed country boys who wandered onto campus, and a group known as the "Ugly Club" routinely "gave gross insults to sundry citizens of the village, threatened violence to members of the Faculty and 'committed trespasses of peculiarly low and disgusting character on private property.'" But perhaps freshmen suffered most. Upperclassmen stole their belongings, kept them up all night before their recitations, and forced them to endure rituals of humiliation—not the least of which, in a slave-holding society, was the habit of blacking the "newies'" faces. But few freshmen complained. Having survived the ordeal, they considered themselves more manly than before.[22]

Students quickly learned that in college they could enjoy pleasures denied them at home. They stashed bottles of corn whiskey in their rooms and took delight in a "glorious drunk"; they gambled in defiance of college rules and went carousing in nearby towns long after curfew. Such rowdiness easily spilled into the recitation halls, where college men made a sport of tormenting the faculty. They piled blackboards into bonfires, pitched stones through the tutors' windows, doused professors with water "clean or foul," jammed the locks on classroom doors with pistol shot, and hoisted unsuspecting pigs into the recitation halls. Occasionally such "tricks" got out of hand and posed a threat to life and limb. In one instance, students placed a charge of gunpowder beneath their professor's desk. "When all were assembled the explosion came with unexpected violence," blasting the startled instructor "into the middle of the room."[23]

Disorder in the classroom arose partly from a "spirit of childish fun," but it also served a serious purpose. By "devilling" the faculty, college men cemented their loyalty to one another and sorted out who among them was suited to leadership. Students refused to judge one another's worth on the basis of academic standards alone. They placed a premium on courage and daring as well. By those measures, even the worst scholar could prove himself a man among men. Alfred Moore Waddell, a student in the 1850s, explained: "He may not have been an 'honor' man while here—he may not have tried to be—he may even have neglected his studies, and sometimes have engaged in the riots and rebellions which occurred; but he realized that . . . even these riots and rebellions, like the Athenian mobs, produced *men*, and leaders." To Waddell's way of thinking, this aspect of student life accounted for "the long list of statesmen" who reflected honor upon the university "by their lives and public services."[24]

College men insisted that the faculty take their appraisals of manhood seriously, particularly during the public celebrations that marked the end of the academic year. "The greatest man at Commencement, except the Governor of the State, the President of the University and the Orator before the two Societies," Kemp Battle recalled, "was the Marshal." Students filled that position with a member of the junior class "conspicuous for good manners, a handsome person, and *savoir faire*." Their choices often distressed the faculty. In 1852, the commencement marshal appointed as one of his assistants a young man notorious for absenting himself from recitations and prayers. When the professors forbade his elevation to such a position of honor, the marshal resigned and lodged a formal complaint with the trustees. No other student came forward to fill the vacancy, and the graduation ceremonies proceeded with "a distinct air of gloom."[25]

Commencement was less a time to celebrate academic achievement than to acknowledge students' passage into adulthood. Graduation week ended with a grand ball attended by "belles and rose-bud debutantes." The campus "rang with the sound of fast and furious fiddles," and the graduates turned out "clothed with such radiancy of glory" that "the President and Professors appeared absolutely inconsequential beside them." By the same token, a university diploma bore witness to manliness as much as scholarship. Bachelor of Arts degrees, though they offered uncertain proof of learning, were highly prized as "certificates of attendance on the University exercises." The degree signified that a young man "had learned much that gave him an advantage over his neighbors. . . . He had learned human nature and how to manage men. . . . He could think and speak on his feet. In county meetings he knew rules of order and how to conduct business. He had confidence in himself, and realized that he secures the fruit who has boldness to seize it and to hold it with tenacious grasp." Any alumnus who applied those lessons to a career in law, medicine, or the ministry could, after three years, acquire the Master of Arts degree by requesting it as recognition for success in public life. In either case, a university diploma marked its holder as a leader among men and confirmed his right to claim a place of authority, honor, and respect.[26]

University alumni fared well in the antebellum world. By the 1860s the school had produced a president and vice president of the United States, twenty governors, eight senators, forty-one members of the House of Representatives, and innumerable judges, state legislators, and justices of the peace. But that record offered diminishing comfort to a society threatened on all sides by the economic and ideological currents of an expansive bourgeois civilization. On the Chapel Hill campus, the 1850s brought forth new voices that demanded measures of individual worth less personal and more substantive than style.[27]

A handful of dissenters among the faculty and the board of trustees set out to compete with the North on its own terms. In 1852 they gained approval to establish a School for the Application of Science to the Arts. Conceived as part of a larger effort to modernize the South's slave economy, the program was meant "to prepare young men for professional life, as Engineers, Artisans, Chemists, Farmers, Miners, and Physicians." But the Bachelor of Science degree possessed none of the prestige of the B.A. and attracted few full-time students. Many college men simply substituted one of the school's courses for work in the ancient languages or constitutional law during the second term of their final year. Others expressed open opposition.[28]

Although critics of the scientific school gloried in the material progress of the nineteenth century, they distrusted the restless, speculative habit of mind on which those advances depended. In a series of remarkable indictments of the scientific spirit, James McNabb, Thomas Cowan, and David Worth warned their classmates that the "torch of civil war" was about to be lit by "the same genius that originated the railway and the steamship." The powers of inventiveness and imagination responsible for Samuel Morse's "Magnetic Telegraph" and John Ericsson's "Caloric engine," they declared, also stood accountable for the "wild dreams and dangerous speculations" of the "Hell hounds of abolitionism." The young men spoke those words with special urgency in the spring of 1857, in part because they had recently witnessed evidence of science's pernicious influence within their own institution. During the prior term, Benjamin Sherwood Hedrick, an honor graduate of the university in 1851 and Professor of Agricultural Chemistry, had been driven from campus after admitting his opposition to slavery and his support for John C. Frémont, the Republican candidate for president of the United States. The doubt and intolerance fed by Hedrick's apostasy—together with the indifference of President Swain, who "bought no books, and provided no apparatus for [laboratory] instruction"—left the scientific school in a precarious position. Without adequate funding or facilities, it limped along from one semester to the next, always on the margins of college life.[29]

Each student had his own reasons for turning away from a more open curriculum, but given the political climate of the 1850s, apprehension for the future clearly ranked chief among them. At a time when the forces of history seemed to be on the side of the South's enemies, ancient orthodoxies—not science—captured student loyalty. They affirmed the immutability of human inequality and offered assurance that the past was yet alive, that nothing need change. College men found among the Greeks and

Romans a society much like their own, a society in which slavery and political democracy coexisted in a purported balance of order and liberty. The senior faculty, too, sought refuge in tradition. By the time of the Civil War, President Swain and his elder colleagues had governed the university for a more than a quarter of a century. Their identities had been forged in service to the classical curriculum; they were too old to accept radical innovation. Their only option, as one historian has observed, was "to hold on, perhaps making minor concessions," hoping that they and their institution would survive the assault of a hostile world.[30]

They hoped in vain. Through heroic effort, Swain managed to keep the university open throughout the Civil War, despite a dwindling budget, student enlistments in the Confederate army, and Union occupation of Chapel Hill in April 1865. But the adversities of battle paled before the challenges of peacetime. The North's victory unleashed a barrage of criticism of the university from within and without. Confederate lieutenant general Daniel Harvey Hill led the attack in the first issue of his Charlotte-based magazine, *The Land We Love*. Hill blamed the South's defeat on a system of higher education that produced "orators and statesmen, but did nothing to enrich us, nothing to promote material greatness." Venom flowed from his pen: "The educated man of the South was like the hero of the fairy tale; in the legislative chamber he was a mail-clad warrior, armed at all points, ready to assail and invulnerable to attack; but as soon as he recrossed the portal of the enchanted hall, his armor fell off, his sword crumbled to dust, his tough and cord-like sinews became soft and flexible as those of a delicate woman. The invincible champion was changed into the feeble imbecile." Slavery had relieved the southern elite "of the necessity of scrambling for a livelihood" and had encouraged them to "turn their ambitious aims toward political power" instead. But emancipation changed all that by making the "struggle for property" and money the wellspring of human endeavor. Under such circumstances, preservation of the classical curriculum was "worse than folly"—it was "absolute madness."[31]

Anticipating Henry Grady and the New South advocates of the 1880s, Hill championed the benefits of industry and diversified agriculture and preached the necessity of educational reform as a means of achieving those goals. He argued that conditions required the South to "make a total radical change in our system of education" by abandoning "the aesthetic and the ornamental for the practical and the useful." Many university trustees and faculty members shared those sentiments. Andrew Dousa Hepburn, a young professor of logic and rhetoric, was the most outspoken. He wrote to President Swain in 1866 that "our only hope of prosperity is in being able to offer to the world a high & thorough scientific course. . . . A new life is commencing for Southern colleges; for those who can keep up with the times, there is a brilliant future; the others must sink. So I feel our first work is reform." William Horn Battle, a trustee and professor of law, concurred, adding that any adjustments should extend "to men as well as measures." If Hill, Hepburn, and Battle had their way, the old curriculum and its defenders would be buried "deep among the fossils of the past."[32]

President Swain found himself unable to resist the demands for change. He had few admirers among the reformers, and potential conservative allies were still bitter over his opposition to student conscription during the war, not to mention his daughter's marriage to a Union officer. Bowing to his critics, Swain tendered his resignation in July 1867. Kemp Battle, the son of William Horn Battle and himself a trustee, moved quickly to take advantage of the situation. He organized a special committee on curriculum reform and secured resignations from the remaining faculty in preparation for a "complete remodeling of the Institution."[33]

Battle's committee set to work in the midst of a general upheaval in higher education. During the 1860s, a number of forces came together to transform American colleges into modern research institutions. By law, the state land-grant colleges founded under the Morrill Act of 1862 supplemented classical studies with instruction in agriculture, "mechanic arts," pharmacy, medicine, and education. Americans studying abroad came home praising the German university, which emphasized research and academic specialization. And in the Northeast, Ezra Cornell and other philanthropists established new institutions to provide training in the emerging fields of engineering and commerce. In large measure, their efforts answered the demands of a nascent culture of professionalism, whose middle-class adherents valued the college diploma as a vocational credential rather than a certificate of "gentlemanly breeding." Guided by those developments, Battle and his colleagues devised a scheme that would have qualified their own university for federal land-grant funds. It called for abandoning the prescribed classical course in favor of a " 'University or elective system,' " dividing the institution into several degree-granting colleges, and allowing students the privilege of arranging their own academic programs.[34]

The politics of Reconstruction interrupted those plans. In April 1868, North Carolina adopted a new constitution, as mandated by Congress. A minor clause in that document placed the university under the control of a new board of trustees elected by the state board of education rather than the General Assembly. That provision was calculated to insulate the university from the influence of conservative Democrats in the legislature and to guarantee a Republican hold on its offices. Certain that they would soon lose their appointments, Battle and his colleagues abandoned their efforts at reform and reinstated Swain and his faculty. Their motives for doing so are unclear, although it seems probable that they sought to deflect any blame for uprooting the traditions of the old university onto their Republican adversaries.[35]

If that was Battle's plan, it worked admirably. When the new board of trustees met in the summer of 1868, it called on President Swain to deliver his annual report, then publicly humiliated him by declaring that his earlier resignation and those of his faculty were still in force. The university resumed operation in the spring of 1869 under the guidance of a new president and a faculty of five, all of whom were Republicans. The trustees chose Solomon Pool to head the institution. A native of Elizabeth City, an honor graduate of the university in 1853, and until 1866 an adjunct professor of mathematics, Pool might have been expected to curry favor among alumni. Instead, he denounced the antebellum college as " 'a nursery of treason' . . . governed by the aristocracy and family influence." Longtime friends of the institution shared the sentiments of Cornelia Phillips Spencer, daughter of a member of the antebellum faculty and one of the old university's most ardent defenders, who reported "a sensation of unmitigated disgust when I contemplate the whole affair."[36]

Under Pool's administration, the university's endowment dried up and its enrollment dwindled. In 1870, when the university had only thirty-six students, Pool proposed a plan of survival that would have turned the school over to various denominational colleges. But even his loyal trustees failed to see the wisdom of such drastic action; on February 1, 1871, they voted to close the university until circumstances improved. A simple inscription on a classroom wall recorded the event: "This old University has busted and gone to hell today."[37]

Over the next four years, the college's fortunes mirrored those of the Democratic Party. Through violence and fraud, party leaders managed to regain control of the legislature in 1870. Three years later, they won approval of a constitutional amendment reestablishing the General Assembly's authority to appoint university trustees, and in 1874 most members of the old board returned to power. Still wedded to the idea of curriculum reform, they again appointed a committee chaired by Kemp Battle to investigate the best course of action.[38]

The proposal the trustees finally adopted in 1875 closely resembled the "Battle plan" of 1867. It called for an institution made up of six colleges, each administered by an individual faculty member and subdivided into several schools, conferring the degrees of Bachelor of Arts, Bachelor of Science, Bachelor of Agriculture, and Master of Arts. Details of the plan deserve notice because they suggest how far the trustees distanced themselves conceptually from the antebellum curriculum. The remodeled university comprised six colleges: Agriculture, including the schools of scientific agriculture, practical agriculture, and horticulture; Engineering and Mechanic Arts, composed of the schools of mechanical engineering, civil engineering, and military science and tactics; Natural Science, embracing the schools of chemistry, zoology and botany, and geology and mineralogy; Literature, incorporating the schools of English language and literature, ancient languages, and modern languages; Mathematics, consisting of the schools of pure mathematics, physics, and commercial sciences; and Philosophy, containing the schools of metaphysics and logic, political economy and international and constitutional law, moral science, and history.[39]

The trustees selected this arrangement so that the university might "keep step with the century in its march of knowledge, invention and discovery." Their metaphors testified to a radically new vision of education and society. The university would serve no longer as a mere repository of knowledge; it would operate instead as "a great metropolis of thought whose ships bravely shall sail the ocean of life and even explore unknown seas." Just as the world's bustling seaports sustained the flow of commerce, the university's mission was to create a marketplace of ideas. By "gathering, creating and distributing knowledge," it would become "a potent force in the world's progress, a wide-felt influence throughout the State to make all men love and seek after learning." Satisfied with their handiwork, the trustees voted to open the school for the fall term in September 1875. During the following summer, they elected Battle to the presidency in recognition of his contributions as "the Father of the new University."[40]

The effects of curriculum reform rippled through every aspect of college life, altering the composition of the faculty, the methods of instruction, and

Faculty of the University of North Carolina, 1878. This picture was produced and widely distributed among friends and alumni of the university in celebration of its reopening at the end of Reconstruction. At the center is Kemp Plummer Battle, whom the trustees named president of the university in reward for his work as chief architect of the new curriculum. (Courtesy of the North Carolina Collection, University of North Carolina at Chapel Hill)

even "the habits and aspirations of students." In the selection of professors, the trustees labored to put aside "consideration of personal popularity, political necessity, family influence, sectarian interest, or local demand." Over the next two decades, clergymen and tutors disappeared from the faculty roster, replaced by men with graduate degrees. A significant minority held doctorates from leading European and American universities—still a rare credential in late-nineteenth-century America. The full force of the new professionals' ability to shape college life became apparent in 1900, when Francis Preston Venable, a chemist with a Ph.D. from the University of Göttingen, assumed the office of university president.[41]

As the teaching corps grew, so did undergraduates' freedom to chart their own plan of study. In 1875, a faculty of seven struggled with the new curriculum. George Tayloe Winston, a professor of Latin and German, recalled that he "represented in his single person five independent schools conferring certificates of proficiency and two complete colleges conferring certificates of graduation." But by 1894, two dozen instructors offered enough courses to extend the "elective system . . . to all studies of the Senior year, half of the Junior and two-fifths of the Sophomore." Within limits, each student could put together a degree program "to suit his tastes, talents or necessities."[42]

Although faculty and students still used the traditional class names, the class system itself had little meaning in the new university. In fact, only the power of "old customs" prevented abolition of the terms "freshman," "sophomore," "junior," and "senior." Under the new regime, students seldom followed the same daily schedule beyond their freshman year; each young man entered the classroom as an "isolated individual." There he competed for grades under a percentage system that replaced the antebellum marks of "very good," "respectable," "tolerable," and "bad." The classroom, once a place where students recited together and shared their answers, had become an arena in which "side by side they compete[d] for academic honors, and to each an equal opportunity [was] given to make the most of his powers and of his life." Nothing better illustrated the university's reincarnation as "both product and factor in the larger life about it."[43]

The professors, particularly those whose own training had included original research, brought new teaching methods to Chapel Hill. A revolution in science and technology gripped the late-nineteenth-century imagination. George Winston recalled that recent "triumphs of the intellect over the material world"—including the practical application of electricity, the germ theory of disease, "the Darwinian theory of life," and the invention of the telephone and the telegraph—"quickened the desire . . . for more experiments." Laboratory work and fieldwork became indispensable to undergraduate education in the sciences. Rather than watching as their professors demonstrated the principles of physics, chemistry, and biology, students probed the secrets of nature for themselves.[44]

The new professorate also transformed the teaching of Greek and Latin, the new university's inheritance from the old. Eben Alexander, appointed professor of Greek in 1886, and Karl Pomeroy Harrington, named professor of Latin in 1891, joined George Winston in bringing to Chapel Hill the methods of German philology. Under their tutelage, students began to examine the classics not as timeless texts but as historical products shaped by particular social, biographical, and cultural circumstances. "Greek and Roman literature as literature, poetry from the standpoint of poetical criticism, history with regard to its comparative accuracy and reliability," Harrington explained, "such are the topics in the classical instruction of today." Young men studied the ancient authors in order to acquire leverage over the moral, political, and aesthetic issues of their own time rather than a command of classical style and figures of speech. In the college catalog, that altered purpose translated into courses on comparative literature, literary history, and the history of grammar. Outside the classroom, it was sustained by the campus Philological Club, organized in 1893. Shortly after the turn of the century, the club began publication of its own journal, *Studies in Philology*, which featured both faculty and student writings.[45]

Lecturing, too, became commonplace in courses of all sorts. Students particularly admired Charles Phillips, a mathematician who had taught civil engineering in the antebellum university's scientific school and was the only member of the old faculty to retain his appointment after 1875. As a teacher he was "most thorough and learned, demanding not so much memorized reciting of the lessons assigned, but . . . inspiring, independent thought." Whether in the laboratory or the lecture hall, instructors encouraged students to gather information and devise their own conclusions. The goal of undergraduate education became the teaching of methods rather than the transmission of inherited wisdom. "Modern teaching is no longer a matter of dictionary and grammar grind," explained Edwin Alderman. "The key words of the new education are investigation[,] . . . research, discovery."[46]

For the first time, visits to the library occupied a significant part of student life outside the classroom. The new university was founded on the notion that "a student's life is nourished by books; that a real University is a great collection of books." But that ideal was haltingly achieved. The university and the Dialectic and Philanthropic Societies continued to maintain separate collections until their holdings were merged in 1886. Varying and irregular hours made access to books difficult; yet by the mid-1880s, the three libraries were circulating more than 3,500 volumes annually, compared to less than one hundred a year in the 1850s. "The student was now sent to the library," one professor explained, so that he might become a "reader, thinker and critic, as well as listener in the class room. His mental horizon was enlarged, his judgment strengthened, and a beginning was made of intellectual independence." Every subject offered topics of "special investigation" for which the libraries furnished material, and "every student became in some degree a specialist and an investigator."[47]

Changes in college discipline reflected this independence in intellectual matters. When considering their plan for the new university, many of the older trustees favored preserving the timeworn system of faculty "espionage" and punishment by demerits. But Kemp Battle preferred an approach based on "self-respect." After countless arguments, he finally won the day when "the good old Trustees . . . students of Caldwell and Swain, went up to the School of the Hereafter." Battle replaced the "college 'patroler' " with a simple honor code that forbade cheating and violation of acknowledged standards of gentlemanly behavior. Offenders were tried and punished by a jury of their peers rather than the president and were given the right of appeal to a special faculty committee. "Henceforth," Battle proclaimed, "a student may call on his friend in study hours [and] . . . no watchful eye will witness his sitting up beyond 10 o'clock. Henceforth he can go to the village in study hours, whether to buy fruit or call on . . . his ladylove." Under the honor system, there was "less compulsion by authority and more compulsion by public sentiment."[48]

Faculty and administrators boasted that the "inner life of the University, its very soul, heart and essence, rest[ed] upon the secure basis of self-development." Gone were the " 'good old times' . . . when student geniuses learned their lessons while walking from the Chapel to the recitation room" and proved themselves by deviling the faculty. Professors no longer labored to plane, saw, hammer, and chisel undergraduates into a "required conventional shape." Under the "new dispensation," academic accomplishment replaced style and bravado as the mark of manhood, the university diploma became "an evidence of merit," and the young man who sought that honor had to earn it by demonstrating "his power of original thought."[49]

The faculty could not have effected these changes in college life without student cooperation. In 1875, the university opened its doors to a student body that told "the whole story of the passing of an old order and the birth of a new." Statistics gathered in the 1890s revealed a fundamental shift in campus demographics. The university no longer served a regional elite; North Carolina provided more than 90 percent of the school's matriculates, a figure that represented the largest proportion of native students claimed by any state college in the country. Half of those undergraduates were the "sons of men who never knew the advantages of college training," and more than a quarter worked their way through school or financed their education with borrowed money. These young men came to Chapel Hill to find their place in a changing society rather than to acquire the mantle of gentility. An institution that had once educated the sons of slaveholders now ministered to the children of a budding middle class.[50]

Edwin Alderman, Charles McIver, and James Joyner were among the first of the new collegians. Alderman recalled that they often thought of themselves as "poor boys." In fact, poor boys found it all but impossible to muster the nearly $200 a year required to obtain a college diploma. But in another sense, Alderman was right. He and his classmates entered the university lacking not so much money as a secure future. They came from families that could not provide their sons an assured place of comfort in life. Their parents could only finance an education and then free their children to author their own fortunes. Alderman, McIver, and Joyner came of age under quite different circumstances, yet they followed a common path to New South adulthood.[51]

Passage into the New South came easily for Edwin Alderman. Born to James and Susan Jane Corbett Alderman on May 15, 1861, he grew up in Wilmington, antebellum North Carolina's primary seaport and only city of consequence. James Alderman earned his livelihood inspecting the lumber and naval stores that backcountry producers brought down the Cape Fear River on rafts. Forests of longleaf pine covered millions of acres along the sandy coastal plain and supplied the raw materials for a booming export

Edwin Anderson Alderman in the years soon after his graduation (Courtesy of the North Carolina Collection, University of North Carolina at Chapel Hill)

economy. The trees grew as tall as 120 feet; their straight, dense trunks made ideal masts and structural timbers for sailing ships. The longleaf also oozed a gummy sap that produced tar, pitch, and rosin for waterproofing and turpentine for use as a paint thinner and lamp fuel. By the 1850s, Wilmington produced two-thirds of America's naval stores and supplied international markets as well. That trade attracted hundreds of European immigrants and skilled artisans who found work as coopers, wheelwrights, carpenters, and brickmasons. Adventurous backcountry youths also came to labor on the docks as stevedores or to hire themselves out as sailors and see the world. On the eve of the Civil War, Wilmington was an outpost of the New South amid the old.[52]

Although a federal blockade paralyzed commercial activity throughout the war, Wilmington escaped occupation until January 1865. As Union forces made their assault on the fort that guarded the city's harbor, the Aldermans joined dozens of other merchant households fleeing inland to Fayetteville for safety. But within a year most had returned to pick up where they left off. James Alderman, like many others, took advantage of wartime confusion and the resurgence of trade to improve his situation. Sometime between 1865 and 1870 he set himself up as a naval stores broker as well as inspector. Eager to rejoin the Union and revive old business contacts, Wilmington's merchants presented themselves as a community that had forgotten the past. A writer for the 1867 city directory reported that when the war ended, a "great stone was rolled against those cavernous years. We are a new people; what we were before and during the war, we are not now. . . . Men have not time to think of the past; the present and the future claim each waking moment." Memories of the "olden days" came back only "at night, in dreams, when the soul is not our own."[53]

Such thinking left an indelible mark on young Alderman. He shared his townsmen's conviction that "the great war freed us all," that emancipation cleared the way for a new cast of players. With the death of plantation slavery, a once-feeble middle class came "to the front," ready to fashion a new civilization from the ashes of the old. In 1878, Edwin Alderman packed his bags for college, certain that the South's destiny depended on men of his kind. A university education would prepare him to answer the call.[54]

The war years were less kind to Charles McIver. He entered the world on September 27, 1860, the son of Matthew Henry and Sarah Harrington McIver. Both of his parents came from well-placed families and stood to inherit large holdings of land and slaves. But the promise of a comfortable future soon unraveled. One of Charles's most vivid memories was of the day his father left home "to 'go to war.'" He recalled the event in an autobiography written for his own children: "I remember how, when he was telling my mother goodbye, I begged him not to go. I didn't know what war was, but it was not hard for me to realize that there was something awful about the separation." Finally, Henry McIver spoke frankly, " 'I *must* go. If I don't, they will make me.'" Those words shattered the security of the boy's insular world, where his father had always been the "supreme power" who made other people do things. That childhood illusion suffered even further when Henry returned home in 1864, near death with typhoid fever.[55]

Henry recovered his health, but the war upended his financial prospects. His own father, Evander McIver, died a broken man in 1866. The war had taken the life of his eldest son and erased his considerable wealth in human chattel. A five-way division of Evander's estate left Henry with six hundred acres of land in Moore and Chatham Counties, but neither the labor nor the resources to bring in a crop. Henry quickly adapted to New South ways. He worked a small portion of the land with the help of his sons and leased the rest to tenants. He mined coal, cut timber, ran a gristmill, and went into business as a furnishing merchant in partnership with two kinsmen. Those enterprises provided Henry's family with an ample living, but nothing to match what he had once hoped for.[56]

Young Charles grew up in a household governed by shopkeepers' values and strict Presbyterian morality. In school, he penned essays on "Industry" and "Time," already worrying over what he would make of himself in adulthood. "Children should be industrious and improve their time," he scribbled in a notebook, "for old age will come upon them, and they will wish they had been more industrious in their early years, but it will be then too late. When Christ was on earth He said, 'I must work the work of Him that sent me, for the night cometh wherein no man can work.'" Barely thirteen years old, Charles was shadowed by the judgment of God and of a father who rarely praised his sons for fear of giving them "the big head."[57]

At times, the young man's seriousness could turn to self-doubt and brooding introspection. He wrote home during his second year in college, worried that his well-worn clothes would provoke ridicule from wealthier boys. His mother advised him to turn his attention to matters of the inner self rather than outward appearances: "Already I feel that many of my prayers have been answered in your behalf, why may I not hope that you may yet be a good and *noble* man serving the Lord wisely in whatever way His wisdom may direct." Those comforting words only added to Charles's burden. How could he live up to his mother's expectations? How could he ever match his father's determination and enterprise?[58]

James Joyner also knew the hardships of a wartime childhood. He was born a refugee on August 7, 1862, in Yadkin College, a small settlement located in the foothills of Davidson County. His father, John Joyner, had

Charles Duncan McIver during his student days (Courtesy of the North Carolina Collection, University of North Carolina at Chapel Hill)

64 · Apostles of the New South

James Yadkin Joyner and the class of 1881. Joyner is third from the left on the front row. (Courtesy of the North Carolina Collection, University of North Carolina at Chapel Hill)

been a prominent planter in the eastern county of Lenoir. In 1860, he owned more than 1,100 acres worked by thirty-nine slaves. James's mother, Sarah, was the daughter of Council Wooten, a prominent eastern politician. When Federal troops occupied the nearby port city of New Bern in the spring of 1862, both the Joyner and Wooten families abandoned their lands and fled west. The trip took a heavy toll. Sarah died six months after James's birth; eight months later, his father, already in ill health, followed her to the grave.

Once the war had ended, Council Wooten reclaimed part of his plantation in Lenoir County and headed back east to raise his grandson. But the old man died when James was ten, and the boy moved into the home of his maternal uncle, Shadrack Wooten. Only twenty-six years old and with a young wife and family of his own, Shadrack was in no position to give his orphaned nephew a start in life. James's inheritance provided funds for an education, but otherwise he had few prospects. In 1878, barely sixteen years old, he entered the university seeking the credentials that would establish him in one of the professions. His future was his alone to determine; what family he had left could offer little more than encouragement.[59]

These young men, and hundreds like them, embraced the university's new curriculum for the chance it offered to play out the drama of their individual lives. They thought of their years in Chapel Hill as a "period of preparation." Whatever pleasures the campus offered came second to the pursuit of academic achievement and worldly advancement. "Earthly *success* is the grand center around which the hopes and desires of most men collect," one student wrote in the *University Monthly*; "it is the goal that all would obtain." Serious students pushed ahead with a sense of urgency. "Fleeting time . . . is swiftly bearing us to our destiny," they warned one another. "We hold our fate in our hands. It does not depend upon circumstances.—We, and not eternal agencies, are to determine whether we shall enter Fame's temple, or live in obscurity. . . . We should determine that the sad and mournful strain, *it might have been*, shall never express the result of our lives."[60]

Such earnestness translated into hard work and stern self-discipline. The new collegians expressed open contempt for their less serious classmates. Three principles governed their own behavior: "systematic labor, perseverance, [and] a correct idea of saving time." Serious students wrote to campus publications, warning against the habit of "promiscuous and indiscriminate" visiting. They had come to college to improve their minds by "close application to text books," but all too often, rude and indolent intruders disregarded "the gentle hint of a locked door" and disturbed their studies. The young men feared for their own self-control: "It is impossible to fasten the attention under such temptations to idleness. All disposition to study, all ambition for success, that excites the boy when he first enters college, is swallowed up in the desperate indifference that takes possession of him."[61]

Ambitious students displayed the same intolerance for professors whose lectures were mere recitations of textbook lessons. They asked whether there was "any use in a professor's getting up and talking half an hour about something that any one can learn in five minutes from a good textbook," and the answer seemed obvious. While lectures were an invaluable means of imparting original thought, a student's time in college was "too short" to be wasted taking notes on assignments they had read the night before. It could be better "spent in studying, in learning something new." In a "'fast' age," the new collegians chided their instructors, "every man should be jealous of his time. We are in a mighty struggle for existence, and he who has used well his time has won half the battle."[62]

These students also took aim at the Dialectic and Philanthropic Societies. The debating clubs had long been a proving ground for young politicians, a place where college men formed the alliances that would later install them in seats of power. Critics complained that such electioneering furnished "no stimulus to a student to persevere in his studies, since he sees that the honors are not conferred as rewards for industry and true merit." Society politics tended "to put into office unworthy men—who are chosen rather on account of their loyalty to party than for their special fitness for the various positions." Since society membership remained mandatory until 1889, students had limited options for acting on those objections. Some, like Charles McIver, adopted a course of passive resistance, paying fines rather than participating in debates. Others sought reform from within. By the mid-1890s, the Di-Phi Societies had lost their place of distinction. Having become little more than intercollegiate debating clubs, they competed for members with a growing number of organizations catering to students' special interests in literature, history, philosophy, and science.[63]

As the new collegians reshaped campus life, they also redefined the standards of manhood. Unlike their antebellum counterparts, they judged one another more by the private mastery of classroom lessons than by public displays of physical daring and verbal power. "To be successful in our age," exclaimed William Pinckney Cline, "one must study, late and long, long and patiently." "*Mental efforts*," cried a classmate, "have gained high ascendancy over . . . pusillanimous physical exploits." That did not mean, however, that physicality no longer played a part in the masculine ideal. The rise of intercollegiate athletics—particularly football—during the last quarter of the nineteenth century offered ample evidence to the contrary. But on the university's playing fields, even physical prowess took on new meanings.[64]

Sports became a source of shared identity on a campus where students no longer studied a common curriculum or participated in campuswide debating unions. Young men might view themselves as historians, chemists, economists, or philosophers during most of the week, but on game day, they were all united as "Tar Heels." Athletic competition also recapitulated the lessons of the classroom. On the gridiron, as in academic pursuits, success required the mastery of a specialized knowledge of plays and strategy, and the difference between winning and losing was measured by a cold numerical score. The victorious athlete, like the triumphant scholar, had to apply himself constantly to self-improvement, for at any moment he might confront a rival who had been more resolute in his preparation. "Some may depend upon splendid talents," one of the new collegians warned, "but as a rule this will be a poor dependence. . . . [T]here will [be] other heroes in the field, who have talents and who have been trained to direct their minds in close and concentrated thought, before whom the talented but uneducated man will vanish as a 'morning mist before a noonday sun.' "[65]

Edwin Alderman offered a glimpse inside the new masculinity in his memories of a night spent with Charles McIver several years after their graduation. They were about to launch a statewide crusade for school reform. "We were to start out in a few days on a new and untried experiment. . . . I remember that we talked about our plans and purposes and difficulties until the cocks began to crow. I told [McIver] to let me say one more word and then let us both go to sleep. He replied . . . that he did not propose to be put to sleep and let me have the last word at the same time. We then decided to make a night of it, and talked on until the sun arose." Over the years, the two men "grew closer . . . in actual intimacy than ever before." Alderman recalled that they met often, "sleeping in the same rooms and talking in the night. . . . Each meeting . . . was a bath of youth and good feeling and courage, that left me cleaner and stronger and fresher for my own tasks." Alderman and McIver were bound together by a common quest for self-mastery and a shared determination to reconstruct their world.[66]

Of course, not all students subscribed to those sensibilities. Opposition came primarily from fraternity men, who tried to preserve traditional notions of style and manly bearing. Fraternities grew in popularity as the old ways passed from the center of student life. They first appeared in 1851 but established a permanent presence only in the early 1880s. By 1885, the faculty felt it had no choice but to lift the ban on Greek letter societies, provided that each organization supplied a list of its members and "pledged themselves not to use any intoxicating liquors." Nevertheless, fraternities became havens for young men who enjoyed strong drink, loose talk, gambling, and card playing. Their escapades "were more than enough to keep the friends of good government organized and vigilant."[67]

William Peele, a graduate of 1879, recalled the fraternity men's delight when more "orderly" students slipped from grace. Four-fifths of his classmates were "steady, hard-working and sober," but he found "no amusement" in recording such virtues. He much preferred the story of an otherwise upstanding young man who smuggled a jar of brandied peaches into his room, curious about how it felt to get drunk. "Not being sufficiently intimate with the multitude which 'run to the devil' to trust any of them with his secret," the student decided that it would be safest to conduct the experiment alone "or at least with no companion except the devil, who is understood to be present at every 'drunk and down.'" After carefully drinking all the brandy off the peaches, the lad was struck first by "how little of the peach flavor it had acquired," and then by a spinning in his head. "He observed, or rather experienced, a motion of the earth which was not only new to him but was not set down in any of the books on astronomy. The foot of his bed began slowly to rise . . . to an inclined plane of at least forty-five degrees. He continued in that position until he *felt* 'an aching void the world could never fill,' and then, he and his bed . . . returned to their *status quo*."[68]

The new collegians took such mockery seriously. They fired back, insisting that pretensions aside, fraternity men were "of no special importance, socially or otherwise," and would "soon be lost in the rubbish of the past." The fraternities took pride in "some old family tradition of wealth or distinction," never noticing that they lived "in an age in which there is no aristocracy but that of the intellect, and that he [who] has any true merit, is too distinguished to put on airs." Serious students admitted that they were often "*less* conspicuous" than fraternity men on campus but claimed that "the *people* [would] make them *more* conspicuous in after life." They viewed college "not as an *end*, but as a *means*," one observer explained. "They recognize that they have a mission to perform in this world, that there is a position of honor and trust awaiting them, if they will only make themselves worthy to fill it."[69]

Unlike their predecessors, the new collegians modeled themselves after the faculty and actively sought professorial approval. The faculty returned the favor, assuring them—in the words of one commencement speaker— that they were "destined to write [their] creed on other men's souls." To be a university student in the late nineteenth century was to be society's hope for the future and to be reminded of that responsibility at every turn. From the classroom lectern and the graduation stage, professors and alumni advised students that they had "grave responsibilities awaiting them when they . . . closed their text-books and assumed the duties of citizenship." Theirs was a "Lilliputian era in politics," governed by old men who found it easier to dream of "a time gone by" than to develop North Carolina's resources and educate her people for lives of productive labor. Only the young, who had "grown up under [the] new order of things," could grapple effectively with the social and economic revolution unleashed by the Civil War. "What an opportunity for usefulness," exclaimed Joseph Engelhard before the class of 1878, "what a field for glory."[70]

Such accolades encouraged the acting out of a peculiarly adolescent blend of self-sacrifice and egocentrism. The new collegians respected their elders, but they were also eager to remake the world in their own image. "The future is ours," they proclaimed in campus publications. "The past has perished as utterly as if the earthquake had opened its mouth and gulped it down." University students assigned themselves an essential role in creating the New South and organized their lives accordingly. In the privacy of his notebooks, Charles McIver compared himself to Julius Caesar, Napoleon Bonaparte, Patrick Henry, George Washington, and even Christ—all of whom, he wrote, "were young men when they first became great." He and his peers never questioned their fate; they had been chosen to serve as "missionaries . . . of the gospel of progress."[71]

But how could such zeal be turned to action? A quarter of a century earlier, similarly ambitious students would have gone on to read law in preparation for a career in politics. For many of the new collegians, however, that path bore the taint of the Old South. Echoing the words of Daniel Harvey Hill, they renounced the object of their forefathers' greatest pride. Freed from "common-place work" by other men's toil, slavemasters had assumed the role of statesmen and "made themselves easy" in "the study of politics." They commanded the halls of government, yet lived "essentially enervating" lives, producing in the place of wealth and letters "an indolent, haughty, and arrogant" culture that ultimately plunged the nation into civil war. That view of history conferred no honor on political life. The "mere orator, or politician," could never answer the challenges of the students' own "progressive and preeminently practical age."[72]

Many young men discovered an alternative to politics at the university's Summer Normal School. The state constitution of 1868 had required the establishment of such a program, but the legislature took no action until 1876, when a group of teachers from Guilford County joined with President Battle to press the issue and win an annual appropriation of $2,000. For six weeks each summer, hundreds of teachers, university students, and interested townspeople assembled in Chapel Hill to learn about the latest advances in the "science and art of teaching." During the day, they took part in demonstration classes led by noted graded school instructors from New York and Baltimore, as well as North Carolina's own fledgling city schools. At night, the students joined in " 'experience meetings' " to discuss common problems, or simply relaxed in their dormitories " 'talking shop.' " University officials described the normal as "a *great educational camp meeting*" where "the souls of the teachers were made stronger" and new converts were won to the graded school gospel. Like many undergraduates, Alderman, Joyner, and McIver spent at least one summer vacation attending the school and participating in its debating society. Years later, their friend and fellow reformer Marcus Noble singled out that experience as "the starting point of their life of devotion and labor in behalf of public education."[73]

After graduation, all three took teaching jobs. Alderman went to Goldsboro; McIver joined the faculty of Durham's graded school; and Joyner returned to the LaGrange Academy in Lenoir County, where he had prepared for college. In 1884, Joyner moved to the Winston graded school, following McIver, who had just been named its superintendent. The three men joined a growing number of their generation who were "turning away from the old groves of politics" to pursue educational careers. In 1854, 38 percent of the university's graduates made law their profession, while only 11 percent took up teaching as a regular occupation. By 1896, those figures had reversed: 19 percent of the graduates went on to read law, while 37 percent became full-time teachers.[74]

Education proved attractive for at least two reasons. It was an immature and expansive field in which a young man could easily make his mark. It also offered the new collegians an opportunity to translate their experiences into social action. Their years at the university had taught them to view schooling as the "great agency for moulding social and economic forces." Education had made the New South dream tangible in their own lives; surely it could do the same for the multitude still mired in poverty and illiteracy.[75]

But a teacher's life was fraught with doubts. Given the financial instability of the early graded schools, there was no promise of steady work or a dependable income. Years also passed before a young man witnessed the results of his labor. "Lawyers, physicians, preachers & business men have the advantage of dealing with the present generation," McIver complained, but the "dividends of gratitude and homage" from working with children often could not "be declared until the teacher is dead." Despite their distaste for political life, Alderman and McIver both read law in a "desultory fashion" and contemplated giving up their school work for a more lucrative and settled occupation. A friend advised McIver that there was "nothing in cranky dried up Professorships, and you will tire of teaching in a few years." Joyner seemed to agree. In 1886, he left the classroom and opened a law office in Goldsboro, partly to resolve his ongoing financial troubles and partly to be closer to his future wife. But his absence from teaching was only temporary. He found time to serve on the local county board of education, and when Alderman left his post in Goldsboro in 1889 for another appointment, Joyner filled the vacancy.[76]

For all three men, early misgivings quickly faded into self-confidence. They drew encouragement from others who shared their vision. Joseph DuPuy Eggleston, superintendent of the Asheville graded school, remembered how he and his colleagues met in Raleigh on holidays. "McIver, Alderman . . . [and] J. Y. Joyner . . . were always there. . . . We would have earnest discussions for two or three days and nights, and we always left these meetings with our ideals strengthened and hearts aflame with the desire to accomplish results." Eggleston's friends also enjoyed growing prestige. In 1886, McIver's co-workers elected him vice president of the North Carolina Teachers Assembly; a year later, Alderman occupied the presidency. By the 1890s, no member of the trio doubted his calling. Alderman and his classmates had found in graded school work "a cause to which a man might nobly attach himself . . . a social faith to hold, a philosophy of life to live and die by." For them, the creation of a new pedagogy became a means of self-creation as well.[77]

Servants of the State

You are not mere teachers of children as the widow and
the old scholar and the old preacher . . . were. You are . . .
the builders of a new social order.

—Walter Hines Page, *The Rebuilding of Old Commonwealths*

The graded school superintendents' zeal for reform belied the fact that they commanded only isolated out-
posts of the new education. Teachers, parents, and county officials across
the state resisted innovation and often expressed outright hostility toward
anyone who presumed to tell them how best to train their children. The
success of North Carolina's classroom revolution depended on the reformers' ability to wrest teaching from the hands of "amateurs," redefining
it as a life's work rather than an avocation. In 1886, they launched a campaign for a state-supported normal college that would train "an effective
and permanent teacher class" whose diplomas would signify their mastery
of the art and science of education. "We all know," the graded school men
explained, "that it is easier to prepare a new generation of employees in any
business than to break in old ones long accustomed to their own diverse
ways." Until the normal college was established, common school instructors would continue to "teach as they are taught, not as they are *taught to
teach.*"[1]

The reformers cultivated support for their crusade among a generation
of young white women who had already begun to take control of the state's
classrooms. For them, as for their brothers, the last quarter of the nineteenth century was a time of flux, a period when gender roles were open
to experimentation and redefinition. Teaching offered a new measure of

autonomy, an independent income, and the promise of admission to the male world of higher education. Men dominated teaching in 1878, outnumbering women three-to-one. By the turn of the century, the balance had shifted, with women claiming roughly half of the state's classroom jobs. Together with their graded school allies, these new recruits claimed teaching as their own, made it into a profession, and helped open the door to white women's participation in public life.[2]

The state first made provisions for teacher training in 1877 by establishing the university's Summer Normal School for whites and a similar program for blacks attached to the Howard Grammar School in Fayetteville. The black institution immediately ran into trouble. Republicans in the eastern part of the state denounced the school as a "Nursery for colored Democrats," designed to increase white authority over black education and community life. Principal Robert Harris dismissed those charges as the "silly tales of demagogues and pot-house politicians." But given the final collapse of Reconstruction just a year before the school's founding and the importance of politics in teacher hiring, that defense seemed particularly self-serving. Many black teachers shared the Republicans' suspicions; by 1879, the Fayetteville school had enrolled only ninety-three students.[3]

The university normal was, by contrast, an overnight success. More than four hundred teachers and interested citizens enrolled in its second six-week session. Impressed by those numbers, state superintendent Sidney Finger called on the legislature to establish additional normals placed strategically throughout the state. One institution for each race, he argued, could hardly meet the need for better teachers. The legislature of 1881 responded favorably, authorizing the state board of education to open eight new schools—four for whites, in Elizabeth City, Wilson, Newton, and Franklin, and four for blacks, in New Bern, Plymouth, Franklinton, and Salisbury. Lawmakers further expanded the teacher-training program for whites in 1885 by closing the normal in Chapel Hill and replacing it with schools in Boone, Asheville, Winston, and Washington. With the addition of a normal school for Native Americans in Pembroke two years later, the total number of teacher-training institutions rose to fourteen.[4]

The white normal schools began their work auspiciously, with fanfare and national attention, but ultimately they yielded disappointing results. Prominent educators from throughout the Northeast and Midwest traveled to North Carolina to train teachers in "the most approved and advanced methods of instruction known . . . in the country." Many of the graded school men also participated in the normals, sometimes as superintendents or as leaders of the "practice classes" that gave rural teachers hands-on experience with the new education. Enrollments in the white schools climbed steadily, reaching a total annual figure of more than 2,500 by 1886. A majority of the students, however, were curious townspeople rather than experienced or prospective teachers. Few of the men and women who labored in rural classrooms could afford to travel to one of the schools, much less devote a month without pay to improving their skills. In any case, they had little to gain by carrying newfangled practices back to schools whose patrons were perfectly satisfied with the old ways. By one estimate, the normals reached at most only one-fifth to one-fourth of the state's white public school teachers. "They did a great deal of good at first," the Raleigh *State Chronicle* editorialized in 1887, "but for the money they cannot be termed successes. The chief service they have rendered has been to stir up an increased interest in public education. If they had done nothing else their service is sufficient to gratify those who inaugurated them. But they must go. They have outlived their usefulness."[5]

Still, the "great question" remained: how could "a more exalted conception of professional excellence" be cultivated within the teaching corps? One answer was to establish full-time, degree-granting normal programs at several of the state's colleges. The university had opened a Normal Department in 1885, but the curriculum offered training only to men who were pursuing degrees in more traditional academic fields. Few of the department's students intended to pursue a career in education, and of those who did, the majority planned to work as administrators rather than as teachers. A year later, Charles McIver left his job at the Winston graded school to develop a "Normal Course" at Peace Institute, a Raleigh women's college. Like most private schools, however, Peace lacked the financial means to train more than a handful of teachers each year. As graduates of a church-supported college, its alumni also were unlikely to escape entanglement in the denominational conflicts that embroiled local school boards. The limitations of both experiments pointed in a single direction: only the creation of a state-supported teachers college would serve the needs of the classroom revolution. In the summer of 1886, McIver suggested to Edwin Alderman that they propose such a school to the next legislature.[6]

McIver's idea won enthusiastic support from the North Carolina Teachers Assembly, whose members desired the same respect accorded to lawyers, doctors, ministers, and politicians. "The office of the teacher is as old as civilization," they insisted. "It was a forerunner of all the professions; it was before law, before medicine and before statesmanship. Indeed, teaching was [the] soil out of which these grew and yet . . . it has never itself become a profession." A state normal college was the key to correcting that inequity. In an impassioned address before the assembly, Alderman exhorted his fellows to demand the honor that was rightfully theirs. "New aspirations, new thoughts and new ideals rule the teacher's mind," he exclaimed. "You have been . . . hewers of wood and drawers of water quite long enough. Suffering has been the badge of all your tribe, but the time has come to assert and not to suffer." Those words revealed a new aggressiveness among the graded school forces. No longer content to labor quietly in the classroom, they set out to make themselves into the standard-bearers of "true education [and] real teaching." The assembly closed its 1886 session by naming McIver to head a committee charged with petitioning the next legislature for "establishment of a 'North Carolina Teachers' Training School' " for whites.[7]

McIver and his associates produced a document that was quite unremarkable, with the exception of one provision: a demand that the new college provide coeducational instruction. The graded school men were gender reformers, committed to creating a society in which women could play expanded roles. They at once acknowledged the changing face of classroom teaching and demanded a reevaluation of established attitudes toward female education. "An army of bright young women" had already begun to preside over the state's schools; yet, unlike men who wished to teach, they had no place to prepare for their calling. "No just reason can be given for this," Alderman declared. "It is simply an inherited wrong in our state life." Playing on the consciences of fellow university men in the legislature, he argued that the time had come to make things right. "A century ago the women of our state gave of their time and money to [found] the University—our highest public school—[and] to train its long line of illustrious sons. Again, in 1875 the women gave of their time and money to rehabilitate its dismantled halls. It is the men's turn now."[8]

More was at stake, however, than simple fairness. The reformers also acted on motives grounded in persistent notions of sexual inequality and the needs of the new education. Women's entry into the classroom helped legitimate the hierarchical relations on which the graded schools were built.

Graded instruction, one skeptic explained, presupposed a new division of labor between administrators and teachers.

> Thirty years ago the leaders of thought in the teaching profession worked in school-rooms. To-day they work in offices. . . . The class teacher has lost . . . sovereignty and is become a private in the great army ruled by 'educators.' We witness a multiplication of positions filled by men who direct and supervise the work of teachers, but who do no teaching themselves. . . . The class teacher is given a course of study docked on all sides, with methods of teaching every subject, and a boss educator is on hand at intervals to see that all . . . class teachers keep in line.

Raised to obedience in patriarchal homes, women seemed well-suited to work as "servants of the State," employees rather than independent ped-agogues. Through the recruitment of vast numbers of female helpers, graded school men secured their own status as superintendents, principals, and guardians of professional knowledge.[9]

Women's entry into the classroom also facilitated expansion of the teaching corps and the lengthening of school terms. In 1886, when men still outnumbered women in the classroom by nearly two-to-one, male and female earnings were roughly comparable. Women received an average of $23.77 a month, or 90 percent of the $26.33 paid their male counterparts. That small differential remained relatively constant over the next decade in the aggregate figures for teachers throughout the state. But the gap widened in areas where graded schools stretched their terms to more than thirty-two weeks, nearly tripling the rural schools' three-month sessions. As teaching was transformed from a seasonal to a full-time occupation, men demanded higher wages, and in some cases the sex differential doubled in individual counties. That was an ominous development in a political environment where proposed increases in the school tax met with determined opposition from voters and lawmakers alike. Under such circumstances, the feminization of teaching was the key both to sustaining the graded schools and to spreading their influence beyond the borders of isolated towns and cities.[10]

These considerations of money and status, however, remained largely unspoken. Assumptions about women's subordination to men and the devaluation of their labor were so deeply embedded in the culture that they required little comment. Too frank a discussion of the savings offered by hiring women would also have undercut reformers' efforts to wean public officials from the notion that price rather than expertise was to be the first consideration in staffing a school. Even worse, such talk had the potential to provoke dissent within the graded school ranks. In 1887, for example, a small band of "lady members" broke from the leadership of the North Carolina Teachers Assembly, demanding parity with men and an end to the "universal injustice to us and our work." But they were outnumbered and outmaneuvered by their male colleagues, and their plea was quickly squelched.[11]

Perhaps the most important reason for the relative silence on matters of gender economics was the fact that graded school men looked to women as vital allies rather than as mere handmaidens of reform. That view was no less colored by familiar understandings of male-female differences, yet it signaled a convergence of the domestic realm of women and the public world of the new education. By virtue of their identity as mothers and caretakers, women appeared better prepared than men to implement the more nurturant pedagogy of the graded school. Proponents of the old education doubted women's ability to govern children. But if the common school, with its physical punishments and the stern discipline of memory work, seemed to require the presence of a patriarchal father, the graded school demanded a mother's care. "Woman is the only creature who is sympathetic enough to be a model teacher," one reformer explained. "The teacher must have the essence of tenderness developed in the highest degree, and no man has this."[12]

Women teachers also tended to demonstrate a greater interest in "educational progress." Most men who entered the classroom treated teaching as a stepping-stone to more lucrative employment. They relied on their superiors to get them into college or to open the doors to the worlds of business, law, and medicine. Male teachers took care not to offend local school committees by embracing unpopular innovations. Women, on the other hand, remained on the periphery of the political relationships that structured men's lives. They had less to lose by casting off tradition, and because of their marginal status, they received lighter punishments for their transgressions. As a result, argued advocates of the new education, female teachers were more "ready-witted and quick to catch ideas." Their increased presence in the classroom seemed to distance schooling from the politics of neighborhood life. That disentanglement was essential if the new education was to make inroads into the countryside.[13]

Unfortunately for the reformers, few lawmakers favored such a separation. Neither they nor local school committeemen were prepared to surrender control of the classroom to unelected, self-appointed arbiters of proper teaching. When Alderman and McIver took their normal college proposal to the legislature in 1887, they quickly realized that the initiative was "doomed." The bill never made it out of committee in the House of Representatives and was killed on second reading in the Senate. Two years later, prospects seemed to brighten. Augustus Leazar, a close personal friend of McIver, was elected Speaker of the House, and in defiance of his constituents, he promised to support the teacher-training bill if it passed the Senate. But even the power of Leazar's office failed to sway many votes. After McIver appeared before the House to plead for the school, one legislator urged his colleagues not to waste the state's money on a usurper who came before them "clothed in purple and fine linen." The attack struck home among lawmakers who saw the normal college proposal as an attempt to snatch authority over teaching out of the hands of parents and local communities. Despite Senate approval of the normal school bill, the House voted fifty-six to forty to reject the measure.[14]

State superintendent Sidney Finger had kept a low profile during both legislative sessions, but in the wake of the second rejection he moved quickly to keep the normal college idea alive. He proposed that the lawmakers abolish the summer normals for whites and use the money to hire two educators who would conduct week-long teaching institutes in each of North Carolina's ninety-six counties. Finger considered the plan a stopgap measure that would place basic "instruction in methods" within reach of every teacher in the state until a degree-granting normal school could be established. He also viewed the institutes as an ideal stage from which to arouse public support for a new professionalism in the classroom. The institute conductors would work as "deputy superintendent[s]," carrying the authority of Finger's office into even the most remote rural hamlets. Each man's task was to "'get down' to the county teachers and make himself familiar with [their problems] and 'get up' such interest as to command an audience of friends . . . of public schools." Given the close vote on the normal college proposal, dissident lawmakers were reluctant to hand Finger and his allies yet another defeat. The legislature quickly approved the institute program, authorizing the superintendent to implement it immediately.[15]

That small victory drew Alderman and McIver into an adventure they could never have imagined at the outset of the normal college campaign. When the state board of education met to consider candidates for the institute work, the two graded school men quickly rose to the top of the list. Alderman, twenty-eight, and McIver, twenty-nine, had already established themselves as leading advocates of the new education. They were just the sort of "missionaries" who might effect rural North Carolina's conversion to the graded school gospel. But the young reformers agonized over the decision to accept the assignments. Both men had recently married and begun families; it was hardly the time to take a job that would require "long absences from home." The institute positions also paid a tight-fisted salary of $2,000 a year, out of which the conductors would be expected to finance all of their expenses while on the road. Nevertheless, the work had "too broad a purpose and too wide a scope to be declined." For the architects of a new profession, the institute appointments offered an unparalleled opportunity for public recognition and acclaim. The enterprise also gave two friends a chance to rekindle the spirit of their undergraduate years in Chapel Hill. Alderman reveled in the news that McIver had agreed to join him as an institute conductor. "I am indeed glad that we are to work in harness," he wrote to his old classmate, "and I pray that we may sow some good work."[16]

The schoolmen traveled relentlessly over the next three years. Alderman reported that after six months in the field he had already journeyed "1745 miles, 1525 by railroad & 220 by private conveyance." During the busy summer season, a small band of graded school superintendents joined in the work. The group included the institute conductors' former classmates James Joyner and Marcus Noble, as well as Alexander Graham, whose lectures had inspired the graded school at Wilson. The superintendents usually labored in two-man teams, organizing as few as two institutes each or as many as eight. In purely statistical terms, the campaign was an immediate success. By the end of the first year, Alderman and McIver had lectured before 5,000 curious citizens and at least 4,000 teachers. McIver alone reached 1,500 of the teachers, more than double the combined annual attendance of the old normal schools. Those figures pleased Superintendent Finger. "I certainly made no mistake in selecting McIver and Alderman," he boasted to a friend. "They are men of large intelligence and with hearts in the work of public education."[17]

The young crusaders at first dismissed Finger's concern that they pace

One of the county institutes conducted by Charles McIver and Edwin Alderman. McIver is standing, third from the left, second row. (Courtesy of the University Archives, University of North Carolina at Greensboro)

themselves for the assignment. "You say take things easily," McIver protested. "How can I? Ignorance is so dense." But the demands of the work soon tempered that eagerness. Travel throughout much of North Carolina was slow and challenging, even by nineteenth-century standards. Many county seats lacked regular rail service, forcing the educators to rely on their own ingenuity and the kindness of strangers. Alderman once persuaded the residents of an Indian reservation to ferry him across a river in a dugout canoe. On another occasion, he hitched a ride with a moonshiner, enduring seven hours in "an ordinary springless wagon" to complete a twelve-mile trip across a high mountain pass. "This work," he confided to Superintendent Finger, "is not child's play."[18]

Rough weather could turn the shortest journey into a grueling trek. Even moderate rains forced streams beyond their banks and filled roads with deeply rutted mud. After struggling for two days to cover the twenty-two miles between Concord and Albemarle, McIver wrote home, "I've had one of those times you read about. Left Concord yesterday at 11:30 . . . struck a creek too full to cross & had to head it. Then struck another." With only a few hours of daylight remaining, he sought shelter in the home of a nearby farmer. The storm raged on into the morning, but McIver and his host decided to press ahead. "We had to ford creeks this a.m. that ran up to the seats in a high carriage & finally when we got within half a mile of [Albemarle] we had to walk over a log & leave the carriage on the other side."

Tired and soaked to the skin, McIver arrived at the courthouse only to discover that his institute had been postponed. Because of the weather, he told his wife, "nobody expected me."[19]

Hotel accommodations outside the largest cities and towns offered the weary traveler few comforts. In Troy, a village twenty miles east of Albemarle, McIver suffered the hospitality of an innkeeper named Allen, "a big fat dirty man [who] wore no coat nor vest. . . . About half a square foot of naked stomach was seen through a hole in his dirty shirt and a beautiful dimple . . . relieved the monotony of the smoothe surface." The hotel's cook looked like the proprietor's "twin brother," except that he was "dirtier and smells bad & wears a . . . greasy apron & has a snuff tooth brush in his mouth when he waits the table."[20]

McIver found his lodgings no better in Smithfield. "The proprietor's name is Gravely," he wrote to his wife Lula, and "just above the door is the sign—'Hotel de Gravely.' The whole thing is very much de Gravely—still it is a paradise when I think of Columbia." There, the schoolman had encountered a waiting boy who came to his room every morning to lay a fire and empty the chamber pot out the hotel window. "I stopped him as he was in the act," McIver reported, and "asked him if that's the way they empty chambers here. 'Yes sir,' says he innocently, 'when dere ain't noffin in der but piss.' . . . I saw that he would consider that I was depriving him of his right if I prevented his proceeding in the usual way, and so I told him 'to let her drop.'" The "pouring process" was "'plainly visible'" to passersby, who deftly avoided the splash. "I merely mention this," McIver concluded, "to show you that I'm not entirely without diversions."[21]

Such sardonic humor found its way into many of McIver's institute letters. Partly the product of what friends described as a sharp wit, it nevertheless had serious meaning. Mocking laughter revealed a deepening cultural rift in late-nineteenth-century North Carolina. McIver belonged to a new elite that believed passionately in progress and self-improvement. As he and other members of the town-dwelling middle class created new institutions of civic life and defined their own standards of refinement and decorum, the isolated communities in which many of them had grown up seemed increasingly backward and alien. The "old" North Carolina was at once to be feared, cherished, and reformed.

Laughter also helped ward off the loneliness that made physical hardships more difficult to bear. McIver often suffered "the blues"; on one occasion he wrote to Lula, "My sweetheart, I am getting so lonely without you that I feel like running away & going home. Since I have been in this work, I can appreciate the motives of the deserter from the army, who, tho' a brave soldier, got so homesick to see his wife & children that he could stand it no longer." The pain of separation was compounded by the fact that the schoolman's meager salary required postponing the purchase of a house for his growing family. While he traveled around the state, his wife worked first at Peace Institute in Raleigh and then at the Charlotte Female Institute, teaching and taking in boarders to help make ends meet. Although Charles "never doubted" his decision to become an institute conductor, he often apologized for denying Lula the security and comfort of owning a home. "I am mighty sorry that you have to work so hard and have so many things to worry you & make you grow old," he wrote shortly before Christmas 1890. "I wish I were able to make life easier for you & could at least give you a comfortable house. . . . You have not only been my sweet, good wife, but you have been my best friend, giving me hope, spirit & inspiration. I know it would help us both so much, if we could drop the tread mill of life for a little while & take a little genuine pleasure & recreation."[22]

Lula usually tried to soothe Charles's conscience by assuring him that his love was "worth more than anything that money can buy." But the strains of running a household alone occasionally got the better of her. She grumbled in response to one of Charles's letters, "I am so tired and disgusted I do not know what to do. . . . I want to yell or do something violent. When you read this you will thank your stars that you are in Asheville." McIver's travels also bore heavily on his children. "Poor little Charlie cried to see you this morning," Lula wrote, pleading with her husband to return as soon as possible. "He said he 'wanted his Papa to come home.' . . . Every morning the first question is how long before Papa comes home?"[23]

Alderman perhaps felt the pain of separation even more intensely. His second child and namesake died of a congenital obstruction of the bowels soon after the institutes began. The father's face revealed his grief, making him appear, in McIver's estimation, "five years older than when he began this work." Out of sympathy for his friend, McIver turned down assignments near Alderman's home in Chapel Hill. "I feel a deep sympathy for Alderman and his wife in their separation," he confided to Superintendent Finger, "and if . . . you can do so, make him such appointments as will best enable him to see his family often." Looking back on the institutes years later, McIver doubted that he and Alderman would have accepted the assignment had they been a few years older. But for men not yet in their thirties, the work's sacrifices were offset by ambition and the "untempered zeal of . . . youth."[24]

The South's educational past offered no precedent for the young men's crusade. Theirs was "a new and untried experiment." Rather than turning to other schoolmen for guidance, the institute conductors drew on their own evangelical heritage, modeling their work after the revivals they had known since childhood. They devoted the first three days of each gathering to instruction in classroom discipline and in graded school methods of teaching reading, writing, spelling, arithmetic, history, and geography. "Our work with the teachers," Alexander Graham explained, "was to arouse a desire to know more of what they teach and make a better use of their knowledge." On Thursday, teachers who felt they had mastered the lessons were invited to stand a public examination for a special three-year certificate that was good for employment in any school district in the state.[25]

The exercises concluded on Friday with "People's Day" ceremonies. Before an audience of teachers, county administrators, and ordinary citizens, the institute conductors expounded the "Gospel of Popular Education in all of its relations—the right of the matter, the necessity for universal training . . . and the feasibility of obtaining this great blessing." They especially stressed the need for teaching to join other professions in establishing new standards of expertise. "There is no dodging this issue," the reformers cried. "The Normal Training School is a necessity, and without it our schools must be what the bar, pulpit or medicine would be without their professional schools. Think of the matter in this phase . . . and if you would be willing to submit your litigation to shyster lawyers or your diseases to quack doctors, you may be content to submit your children to the instruction of the untrained teacher." Responsible parents had an obligation to keep step with progress; the ways of the past offered poor counsel for the future. The institute conductors turned aside their "earnest foes," insisting that it was "of no use to say to us now that *you* did so and so, and your fathers even went to paper-windowed cabin schools, where the pupils received more blows than lessons. We say that will not do now. Because we have ever been barbarians, is it said we must always remain so?"[26]

Like the evangelical ministers they emulated, the young men worked their audiences, hoping at once to inspire true believers and to "scoop up" new converts. But rural North Carolina proved to be more of a "missionary field" than the institute conductors had expected. Many country people simply did not share the ethic of ambition, progress, and accumulation embedded in the graded school curriculum. Alderman found the mountain counties of Ashe, Polk, and Transylvania blessed with "rich soil, perfect climate, exhaustless timber & minerals," but that wealth remained untapped because the inhabitants were "inert & work[ed] very little." From the schoolmen's perspective, the countryside seemed to be in a state of moral and economic decay. "The people—the masses—think more about fishing and duck hunting than about education," James Joyner complained. "*They need waking up.*"[27]

The institutes also brought the schoolmen face-to-face with "many sad & startling facts" concerning the practice of teaching in rural schools. Midway through his first tour of the state, Alderman lamented in his diary, "I have found the teachers, as a rule, utterly at sea as to methods & children learning in spite of, rather than by aid of them." In every community he found students who had "spelled through" Webster's Blue-Back Spelling Book but could not read a simple text, or who knew "more or less of Cube root & Duodecimals" but could not compute the value of a bale of cotton. "My work," he wrote in his diary, "has largely been to change these types."[28]

Only 12 percent of the teachers Alderman examined had ever studied a pedagogical text. A mere 8 percent subscribed to one of the state's fledgling educational journals, and virtually none had "used [or] heard of [the] Word Method" of teaching reading. "Our teachers . . . do not know books," the reformer complained. "The reading habit has not fastened itself upon them. . . . They teach an art which they do not practice." As a result, the prevailing "idea of education and teaching" was "knowing some thing or several things and telling about them." But rural teachers did not measure up even by that standard. When Alderman and McIver compiled the examination for the institutes' special three-year teaching certificate, they included many questions they had used before to test the knowledge of twelve- and thirteen-year-old students in the city graded schools. Only 6 percent of the rural teachers managed to obtain a passing score.[29]

As time went by, however, the institute conductors were less quick to condemn the men and women who labored in the country schools. During one of his early institutes, Alderman had his teachers write short autobiographies. Reading the essays left him "touched to the heart" by a "monotonous, sickening story" of poverty, inadequate education, and a general "lack of opportunity for mental development." Isolated from one another, "unable to compare methods, to discuss ways and means or to enkindle enthusiasm," most teachers perpetuated "the errors . . . of their own instruction." Their shortcomings, Alderman concluded, were "their misfortune, rather than their fault." Chastened by experience, the young reformer lowered his sights. Alderman tried in subsequent institutes to adopt a less critical tone and to focus his work on "pressing necessities" rather than "methods of ideal excellence." "I have realized," he confessed to Superintendent Finger, "that I must know [the teachers'] conditions, their limitations, their environment, and must apply my instruction in light of this knowledge."[30]

The institute conductors felt less compassion for "unprogressive" county officials. Alderman began the work expecting to be treated with deference and respect. "Would it not be best," he asked McIver shortly before starting his travels, "to see to it that the press thoroughly understand the matter and give it full dignity in their columns. Also, whatever good can be truthfully said of both you and myself ought to be expressed for the sake of the cause we espouse. . . . It behooves a great undertaking like this to be *more* than merely mentioned in 'items': the subject should be treated soberly . . . by the principal newspapers of the state." But such notices were not always forthcoming. In some cases, local officials simply did not understand the mechanics of a publicity campaign. Johnston County's school superintendent managed the only newspaper published in the county seat, but the paper carried "no notice or mention" of the institute work. "The Superintendent," McIver explained, "is a fairly well educated, soft easy going fellow 'who would like to be useful to a great cause but he doesn't know how.' " In other cases, a lack of advance publicity reflected outright hostility. The board of education and superintendent in Yancey County, for example, refused to appropriate money for an institute or to spread word of the event because they received no personal remuneration. In Cumberland County, officials worried that an institute would undermine the practice of trading teaching jobs for votes in local elections. Determined to keep attendance at a minimum, they publicly attacked the work "as a 'side show'—'a humbug' & 'a picnic.' "[31]

McIver was generally philosophical about such incidents. Drawing a lesson from his readings in English history, he consoled himself with the knowledge that "he who runs counter to the prejudices of mankind must expect rather obloquy than sympathy." Alderman, on the other hand, felt provoked to ridicule and biting sarcasm. After a disappointing institute in Mecklenburg County, he wrote to Sidney Finger, "The . . . superintendent here was badly wounded at Gettysburg. That is his only recommendation for office. He is undoubtedly the most superlatively incompetent man I have yet seen in office. He did not understand the law, had called no public meeting, had never seen any notices . . . or addresses on this work, and was hopelessly stupid." The young reformer used even harsher words to describe the superintendent in Ashe County. "Did me very little good," he scrawled in his diary—"a man of whiskey habits, with the conceit of ignorance, the courage of stupid convictions, large-red-faced-bulldogging-blundering, his civilities were obnoxious."[32]

Alderman encountered similar difficulties with the audiences who came to hear his People's Day lectures. He had distinguished himself as a public speaker at the university, winning the coveted Willie P. Mangum Medal for oratory in his senior year. Classmates described him as "polished and elegant," a man who was "graceful in delivery" and spoke with "beautiful diction." But those skills, so appreciated in the university's debating halls, only accentuated the social and cultural differences that set Alderman apart from ordinary rural folk. He often talked over their heads and seemed more condescending than concerned.[33]

Alderman's experiences with rural audiences left him frustrated and confused. He discovered in Ashe County that he was no match for the amusements offered by "crying babies, squealing pigs, badly behaved children, [and] 'Sam' the village idiot." By the same token, he found the inhabitants of Pamlico County to be "isolated, ignorant, [and] illiterate," hardly the sort of people he was accustomed to addressing. "What can I say to influence them!" he agonized in his diary. Sometimes there seemed to be no answer. When his institute in Montgomery County was "slim & not numerously attended," Alderman canceled the People's Day ceremonies and dismissed the audience. "I [only] tried to show them what an institute was," he advised McIver, "[and] urged them to prepare for your coming & make an effort at redemption."[34]

McIver surprised many of his old friends by succeeding where Alderman stumbled. As a student, he had shied away from public speaking. His classmates remembered his rare performances as "ponderous in argument, awkward in manner, and without special literary gift." Nevertheless, McIver had a way with rural audiences. When parents and teachers were distracted by a circus or revival, he joined the crowd and found some means of turning the event to his advantage. In one of his daily letters to Lula, Charles reported a "poor opening" due to a general lack of interest among town residents. But a postscript revealed his solution: "Have been to prayer meeting. The institute is advertised now."[35]

McIver also possessed a rustic talent for storytelling. He often captivated audiences with what Alderman described as "homely . . . illustration[s]." When the time came to explain the need for professional instruction in North Carolina's schools, McIver described teachers as "the seed corn of civilization," arguing that "none but the best is good enough to use." In similar fashion, the story of "Old Frog" made clear that reform would be achieved only through hard work and determination. "Two frogs," McIver told listeners, "were knocked into a crock of milk as the cover was set in place. One splashed around frantically for a few seconds, gave up, and drowned. But not Old Frog; he kept kicking. And the next morning when the housewife lifted the crock lid, there sat Old Frog safe and sound on a firm island of butter." Few country people recognized the classical references that littered Alderman's speeches, but everyone knew about churning butter and understood that quality seed corn was essential to a bountiful harvest.[36]

McIver reacted with surprise when newspapermen and school officials praised his lectures. After the close of one institute, he rushed to his hotel room to write Lula that "the Superintendent here . . . thinks I am 'as strong a man before the people as he ever saw.' " A lawyer in another town compared him favorably with Henry Grady, the Atlanta editor and nationally admired advocate of New South reforms. "Of course [these] are individual opinions," Charles admitted, "and others may think differently, but they are very pleasant to hear."[37]

Even more satisfying were reports that he was better liked than the other institute conductors. McIver wrote from Pitt County that he had met "a young teacher of a private school" who was "unenthusiastic over Alderman & especially over his Friday address. But he says he enjoyed my work most & that I put matters more strongly." The verdict was the same in Orange County, where school officials were "as pleased with [McIver's] work as an old maid is when courting & love is mentioned." In a letter to the state board of education, which Charles "accidentally saw," the county superintendent spoke glowingly of the work " 'McIver & others are doing,' " purposefully omitting any specific reference to the young man's co-laborers. "This is a small matter which I would not mention to anybody else," McIver bragged to Lula, "but I know it will interest you." He closed with instructions to "burn this letter," warning his wife, "you know chickens will come home to roost." McIver and his college friends had joined in pledging their lives to a common cause; he would never intentionally embarrass them. But in private, friendship stood as no obstacle to the desire for individual distinction. Years later, McIver celebrated quietly when a letter from an admirer pointed to the institute work as the beginning of his rise to fame as "the Crown Prince" of public education.[38]

In the short run, the institutes did more to enhance the reputations of the graded school men than to reform teaching. But that was not entirely a sign of failure. Personal accolades were easily translated into political clout. If the institutes effected few changes of heart among common school teachers, they nevertheless excited business and professional men who shared the educators' New South vision. "When Alderman and McIver had finished their round of the counties," wrote Josephus Daniels, a former University of North Carolina classmate, "they had left behind them an enduring enthusiasm. . . . In every county they effected an organization of young men, lawyers, editors, public officials, and others, who took up the torch." By 1891, those new champions of the graded school crusade had swelled the ranks of the North Carolina Teachers Assembly to more than four thousand members, enabling the association to build its own headquarters and meeting facilities on the beach near Morehead City. David F. St. Clair, editor of the *Sanford Central Express*, was in many ways typical of the sort of admirer the institute work attracted. He was a proud booster of Sanford's growing economy, having tied his own fortunes to the success of local ventures in manufacturing and commercial agriculture. At the close of the institute in neighboring Moore County, he wrote McIver, "I am in hearty accord with you in your revolution of education . . . and will do what I can in my humble way to help advance your ideas. . . . I am so anxious to see North Carolina get out of the woods."[39]

That kind of support effectively turned the political tide in favor of teacher training. Shortly before making his third pitch for a normal college to the legislature of 1891, McIver quipped to Superintendent Finger, "It is almost getting fashionable now to be for public education." But the graded school men were determined to take no chances. Seeking the broadest possible constituency, they agreed to join forces with the Woman's Christian Temperance Union (WCTU) and a smaller organization known as the King's Daughters, both of which had petitioned the lawmakers to establish a vocational school for poor white women. Together the two groups requested a single institution that would combine normal and vocational training. The proposal won quick approval in the Senate. As the day for the final vote in the House approached, McIver wrote Lula a hurried note, "We will win. I can't write. The excitement is too great. The galleries are full." A roll call on February 12 handed the graded school men a long-awaited victory. The legislature appropriated $10,000 for the new college, to be known officially as the North Carolina Normal and Industrial School for Women.[40]

Approval of the normal college bill touched off a firestorm of excitement. The legislature required that the institution be located in a community willing to provide the necessary land and buildings. Suddenly, a school that no one had wanted became the object of every town's desire. Bids poured in from across the state. Maxton's Floral College proposed surrendering its facilities; Morganton offered $5,000 and a one-hundred-acre farm; Thomasville and Graham each tendered $20,000 in bonds; Durham matched that offer and threw in a $10,000 construction site to boot.[41]

Each of the towns coveted the school as a badge of leadership in educational "progress," but they all eventually forfeited that honor to a latecomer. The normal college's board of directors visited Durham and Graham on June 10, then stopped over in Greensboro on their way to Thomasville. While they rested in the Benbow Hotel, a public rally of business and professional men secured pledges for $25,000. Officials in Thomasville and Durham sent urgent telegrams upping the ante to $30,000. But Greensboro's elite were determined not to lose the poker match. Another meeting brought pledges for an additional $5,000 as well as a large parcel of land. When the board accepted the offer, residents of Thomasville and Graham reacted with outrage at their neighbors' "sly and cunning" ways. But Durham spokesmen offered congratulations. Such competition was the lifeblood of the New South. "Greensboro was a winner sure enough," conceded the *Durham Weekly Globe*. "She had the boodle and she got the school. Greensboro will please shake."[42]

The board next moved to the delicate task of selecting the college's president. There had been talk for months that Charles McIver was the most likely candidate. In late February, George Winston, McIver's friend and undergraduate mentor, wrote, "I take it for granted that you are to be President. . . . I consider you well qualified for it; and I shall be glad to assist in securing your election. For ten years the success of the college will depend largely upon the very kind of zealous, missionary work that you are gifted at doing." But Alderman was also a contender, and he could claim a number of influential supporters on the board. Chief among them was Charles Brantley Aycock, a rising star in the Democratic Party and an old college classmate who had been chairman of the Goldsboro school board during Alderman's tenure as the town's graded school superintendent. Aycock confessed to Josephus Daniels that he would be hard-pressed not to support Alderman if a fight developed.[43]

Alderman's friends, however, seem to have dissuaded him from actively seeking the post. When word came of McIver's appointment, Alderman accepted the news gracefully. "I congratulate you most heartily, my friend, upon your elevation to the headship," he wrote. "I am not without the just ambitions of a young and vigorous man but I may say in simple truth, that miserable little petty rivalries and jealousies have not disturbed my sleep or come near to my mind or heart. I accept the wisdom of the Board." Alderman taught history and literature at the new normal college for a year, but in 1893 he left to take a position as professor of pedagogy in Chapel Hill. The job paid a higher salary, conferred greater prestige, and, perhaps most important, allowed him to escape his friend's lengthening shadow. Alderman's move also returned a handsome dividend. Three years later, he was made president of the university.[44]

Charles McIver had never known a year like 1891. Though he had yet to celebrate his thirty-first birthday, he faced the challenge of building a college from the ground up. He continued his regular schedule of county institutes while also supervising construction and the selection of faculty and students. A friend warned of the inevitable arm-twisting that would accompany staffing decisions. "I need barely say to you that you will make a fatal mistake if you do not begin with *trained* teachers, real, *live* teachers, experts," J. L. M. Curry wrote. "Confederate soldiers . . . daughters of the Hon. Mr. A. & the Rev. Mr. B. will be urged upon you . . . & it will require courage to resist but *you must do it* or Ichabod will be written over your door." George Winston also worried over the college's budget and the need to uphold a commitment to female education. Given McIver's limited resources, he advised hiring "a larger teaching corps of very talented and experienced women instead of a smaller corps of rather inferior men. . . . Besides, it is a woman's school, and it should emphasize the *woman idea*."[45]

McIver shared Winston's sentiments. With the exceptions of Alderman; Edward J. Forney, head of the commercial department; and Clarence

Faculty of the Normal School, 1893. By the time this picture was taken, there had been several changes in personnel. Shown here—starting at the back and reading from left to right—are Sue Mae Kirkland, lady principal; Dixie Lee Bryant, natural sciences; Gertrude W. Mendenhall, mathematics and German; Edward J. Forney, bookkeeping, stenography, typewriting, and telegraphy; Maude Broadaway, physical culture; James Yadkin Joyner (replacing Edwin Alderman), English literature and methods of teaching arithmetic; Melville V. Fort, industrial arts; Philander P. Claxton, pedagogics and German; Edith McIntyre, domestic science; Mary Petty, chemistry and physics; Anna M. Gove, M.D. (replacing Miriam Bitting), physiology and hygiene; Charles McIver, principles and history of education and the science and art of teaching; Lucy H. Robertson, history and reading; Viola Boddie, Latin and French; and Florence Stone, French. Clarence R. Brown, vocal culture, was not present. (Courtesy of the University Archives, University of North Carolina at Greensboro)

Brown, teacher of vocal music, he chose a faculty composed entirely of unmarried professional women. Dixie Lee Bryant, instructor of natural science, held a B.S. degree from the Massachusetts Institute of Technology. She was the first member of the faculty to obtain a Ph.D., studying geology at the Bavarian University of Erlangen from 1901 to 1904. Gertrude Mendenhall, who taught mathematics and German, was a North Carolina native who earned her A.B. degree from Wellesley College. Viola Boddie, also a North Carolinian, held a certificate from the Peabody Normal College in Nashville, where she had majored in ancient and modern languages. Melville Fort, an honors graduate from the Mississippi Industrial Institute and College, offered classes in art. Edith McIntyre, head of the domestic science department, came to the normal from the New York College for the Training of Teachers. And Miriam Bitting, college physician and instructor in physical culture, was an alumna of the Woman's Medical College in Philadelphia, where she had also established a private practice. This would have been an extraordinary assemblage regardless of location. But in a state where only four of every one hundred adult women were engaged in any sort of trade or profession, it signaled a radical departure. Supporters thought of the normal as their one best hope for educating "strong, self-reliant, intelligent women."[46]

Competition for admission to the school was fierce. Hundreds of applications flooded into McIver's home within a matter of months. Since Charles was still traveling with the county institutes, Lula did her best to forward the letters, sometimes sending them through five or six post offices before finally catching up with her husband. The process of sorting through the applications was made especially difficult by legislative constraints on the makeup of the student body. Each county was guaranteed representation in proportion to its white school-aged population. If a county had more applicants than allotted slots, its school superintendent was to administer an examination and forward the name of the winner to McIver. But some county officials were understandably hesitant to make such public choices, especially if the decision involved the daughters of politically powerful families. The Orange County superintendent begged McIver to relieve him of the duty. "I do not wish to shun any *work* connected with examining the [candidates]," he explained, "but I *do* wish to avoid saying who has won in this contest. They are, *all*, clever, and estimable young ladies, and are, *all*, my friends, and for this reason, I wish you to look over the manuscripts and decide according to your best knowledge who shall be appointed." McIver completed the work of reading, judging, and answering the applications only with last-minute help from the state superintendent's office. By the time of the normal's scheduled opening on October 5, 1892, he had selected an entering class of 223 students.[47]

The young women arrived at the Greensboro train depot throughout the day and made their way to the campus on hacks and wagons hired by McIver. What they found was not a very impressive sight. The two central buildings were "red and squat" and surrounded by construction debris. McIver's own house and part of the dormitory had no heat; many of the

The Normal School campus, ca. 1905. The McIvers' residence, a frame dormitory, the infirmary, the Students' Building, and a brick dormitory stand on the left side of College Avenue. On the right are the main classroom and administration building and the Curry Training School, a facility for hands-on teacher education. (Courtesy of the University Archives, University of North Carolina at Greensboro)

rooms were littered with wood shavings left behind by the carpenters, and some were not yet furnished. The grounds comprised ten treeless acres of sticky red mud that had once been a cornfield, and dried stalks from the last harvest still dotted the lawns. But none of the students complained; few, in fact, took much notice of the dreary surroundings. They were overwhelmed instead by the excitement of "entering upon a new way of life."[48]

Many paths led to Greensboro in the autumn of 1892. Each student's story was unique, but patterns do emerge out of the tangle of individual experiences. On average, the young women were nineteen years old. Most had grown up in middling households that provided the relative luxury of uninterrupted school attendance. In winning admission to the normal, they had proved their ability to "analyze ordinary arithmetic problem[s]," read an "English page fluently at sight," and "express [their] thoughts accurately in writing." But few had known truly privileged lives. A vast majority had no education beyond the common or graded schools. Between 60 and 70 percent of the women reported that they could not have afforded further training had they been denied a place in the normal. Women like these came to Greensboro seeking opportunity and firm footing in a turbulent and challenging world.[49]

Then and Now, a novel about school teaching in late-nineteenth-century North Carolina, opens in the home of a widow and her daughter, Hope. Hope's father had been a successful merchant, but his untimely death left the family in dire straits. The house itself revealed their plight. A "common, unpainted, rather dilapidated-looking" dwelling, it offered "nothing to please the eye nor gratify the taste. . . . Even the few flowers . . . growing on the sandy soil, served rather to evoke the sigh of pity than to give delight to the beholder." Hope enters the scene having just returned from the post office with an unexpected letter. Mr. Watkins, an old friend of her father, has written to offer her employment as a teacher. The letter could not have come at a better time. Hope had trusted that marriage would deliver her from poverty, but her romance with a neighborhood beau—"young, well-bred, and handsome"—had ended in disappointment. At twenty-one years of age, the young woman realizes that she can no longer look to her mother or to suitors for support; the time has come to make her own way in the world. Mr. Watkins's letter proposed only a "moderate" salary, "yet to Hope, who was very poor, and who had never earned five dollars in her life, the terms seemed quite *liberal*." After much soul-searching, she kisses her mother good-bye and heads off to become a teacher.[50]

Similar scenes, perhaps less tinged with melodrama, were played out countless times in real life. Between 1892 and 1900, roughly 25 percent of each entering class at the normal were orphans or the daughters of widows. In a society that denied married women basic property rights and offered them few opportunities for wage earning, the death of a husband had always made the lives of wives and children precarious. Mrs. J. C. Powell was one such widow "thrown upon [her] own resources by death and misfortune." When her husband passed away, she took a job as a matron in the State Hospital for the Insane. The work, she informed Charles McIver, provided a measure of basic security, but her daughters deserved better. For them, as for many others, teaching offered the only alternative to a life in domestic service or a hand-to-mouth existence taking in sewing.[51]

Mattie Gay saw the normal as salvation for both her mother and herself. "I am very desirous to enter The Industrial and Normal School," she wrote to McIver in August 1892, "but am so situated that I cannot leave my mother, who has been recently made a widow." Together with several other girls in her neighborhood, she devised a scheme that would take them all to Greensboro, despite the fact that their county's allotment had been filled. "We have decided on the plan of my mother's taking a house in G'boro and boarding the girls," Mattie informed McIver. "She is willing that her house shall be governed in harmon[y] and sympathy with your Institution." Gay's ploy failed; her application came in late, and McIver simply had no room for more students. But the dream came true for others. Mattie Albritton wrote in her application, "I am 18 years old. . . . I have a mother but no father and need all the help I can get to aid me in carrying out my plans of future usefulness, and I trust you will do what you can for me." That trust was well placed. A few months later, Mattie learned that she had been admitted to the normal's first freshman class.[52]

More than half of Albritton's classmates came from rural households, many of them dogged by debt and a market for cotton and tobacco that was headed steadily downward. As their hold on the land grew ever more tenuous, farm families began to rethink traditional notions of child-rearing and household economy. Parents who once would have jealously guarded the family labor supply showed a new willingness to send their children— particularly their daughters—out on their own. In some cases, that attitude reflected an effort to adapt old ways to new circumstances. Few parents seem to have laid claim to their daughters' earnings, but many did expect the young women to use their new skills to give other members of the household a leg up in life. The Sater family of Halifax, for example, thought that training one daughter as a teacher would be the best means of ensuring the advancement of all their children. We "have four girls to educate," Mrs. Sater reported to McIver, "and if I can get one of them through a Collegiate Course it will be a great help to me in educating the [remaining] three."[53]

Other parents broke more sharply with the past, encouraging their daughters, like their sons, to become self-supporting. They sent their children away to embrace an ethic of independence and upward mobility that they neither had known in their own lives nor yet fully comprehended. "My greatest desire has ever been to obtain an education!" confessed Pauline Harris of Sylva. "But as limited means have been the obsticle, it some times seems as far off as the stars. My father is very poor, and I am trying to climb the rough ladder alone." Katie Moore's father, too, was "a *farmer* and in debt." She, like so many others who traveled to Greensboro, left home expecting to survive "by my own exertions."[54]

The normal was for these self-described "poor girls" a "great blessing" and "kind Providence." They enrolled under the " 'promise to teach plan,' " taking advantage of the state's offer of free tuition for any woman who pledged to spend two years in the public schools after graduation. But even then they had to borrow money, take summer jobs, and perform domestic chores in the dormitory and dining hall to pay for room and board. Ada and Rebecca Vance promised, "We don't care how rough our board is, [we] will be willing to eat bread and water if we could go to school." Lottie Watkins offered "to do anything just so it is honorable in order to get an education." Still, such students' tenure at the normal was always uncertain. When a benefactor could no longer help with their expenses, they had little choice but to return home. Mabelle Pearce begged McIver to find a fellowship for her sister, explaining, "I am a [railroad] agent . . . & it will cost me a struggle to put her through four years at the cheapest rate." In Julia Pasmore's case, a brother's sudden change of employment spelled an end to her hopes of becoming a "professional" teacher. She wrote to McIver at the close of her first semester, "I deeply regret to tell you that I can not return after Xmas. My brother, who has been paying my expenses, has made other arrangements for next year, so that he can not pay them any longer and I have no other source to look to for means." McIver occasionally offered personal loans to promising students who fell on hard times, but his charity was seldom sufficient to meet their needs.[55]

The New South also buffeted the daughters of more prosperous families, affecting not so much their economic security as their sense of place in life. These young women grew up in a society taken with money-making and individual ambition, one that abhorred dependency. They were taught to view "idleness [as] a crime" and to think of "any healthy person who does not create more than he consumes" as a "contemptible drone and moral vagrant." In their own lives, however, those same women experienced new forms of dependency on fathers and husbands.[56]

As farm families grew less for themselves and more for the marketplace, power relationships within households shifted in subtle but disturbing ways. Men traveled to town to sell their crops, bargain for credit, and purchase supplies, leaving their wives at home in relative isolation. They also served as family bankers, diminishing women's voice in economic decisions. Husbands, not wives, handled the money that was becoming an ever more vital part of day-to-day existence. Town-dwelling women experienced similar changes. As merchant and professional families withdrew behind manicured lawns and walls of Victorian gingerbread, wives took on new identities as consumers and symbols of their husbands' success. Because domestic labor generated no income, their heavy burden of chores was often dismissed as mere "housework," devalued in an age that took the ability to earn money as its standard of worth. That tilt of household relationships further toward the advantage of men helped explain the inter-

Charles and Lula Martin McIver with their children, Charles Jr., Annie, Verlinda (who died in 1908, two years after her father), and Lula Martin. This photograph was taken in September 1900, on the occasion of Charles's fortieth birthday. (Courtesy of the University Archives, University of North Carolina at Greensboro)

est of the Woman's Christian Temperance Union in establishing the normal. Members of the WCTU campaigned for more than prohibition; they sought to redress women's powerlessness, whether in the form of subjection to a drunken husband or denial of access to the family's purse strings. The normal offered one means to that end. In the eyes of its founders, the school embodied the notion that women were "not mere onlookers in life" but, like men, had "a great part to play."[57]

Charles McIver's devotion to that precept both shaped and drew reinforcement from his unconventional marriage. Lula Martin McIver was the daughter of a prominent Winston physician. Raised in the Moravian Church, she abandoned her family's faith and converted to Methodism when she discovered that some of her ancestors had chosen their wives by lot. Disappointment in her childhood determination to study medicine, however, was not so easily remedied. Only a few medical schools in the country accepted women; none of them were located in North Carolina or the South. Lula eventually had to settle for teaching, one of the few occupations in which an ambitious young woman could find some measure of intellectual and economic independence. She and Charles met and married while she was working at the Winston graded school and he was serving as its superintendent.

Lula did not give up her career or her dreams on her wedding day. She read law with her new husband and pursued her interest in medicine through a close friendship with Dr. Annie Laurie Alexander, one of the state's first female physicians. When Charles left to conduct his institutes, Lula's teaching job paid most of the household accounts. Shortly after accepting the normal school presidency, Charles acknowledged the unusual partnership they had formed. He sent Lula a copy of Harriet Beecher Stowe's *My Wife and I*, a novel advocating domestic equality, with a note attached.

> You know . . . I have always regretted that I was not able to have a house for you & hardly able to furnish you with the money absolutely necessary to live on, yet this book and the domestic lesson running through it, has somewhat compensated for what I have regretted. The fact is when we do get a house and a competency you will have done at least as much to earn it as I have. It will be ours to use. I think I see more clearly than ever how galling dependence must be to a sensible woman, and while I wish I could give you all you want & deserve & ought to have now, it is a pleasant thing for me to contemplate you and me in a house that is really *ours* & not mine. Some sarcastic cynic might smile at my generosity in allowing you to work for your house, but I know you will understand me.

The note was a concession to Lula's claim to authority in the marriage as well as a statement of Charles's New South faith in the necessity of earning one's way in life. An ideology of bourgeois individualism became the seedbed for a broadening conception of woman's sphere. For women no less than men, Charles declared, "dependence [was] worse than almost any other form of slavery."[58]

Charles's sister, Elizabeth, resembled Lula in her aspirations and was precisely the sort of woman McIver most wanted his school to benefit. When Charles took charge of the normal, Elizabeth was living at home, caring for her two younger brothers in return for a small allowance from the till at her father's store. She had no intention of ever marrying, but she was determined not to live out her life relying on the charity of her brothers. Elizabeth asked Charles to reserve her a place in the first freshman class. "I need it," she explained. "It is an opportunity for improvement. . . . Sooner or later it will be necessary for me to teach or do something to take care of myself and if I teach, I want to know how to do it well enough to be proud of my work. . . . I know, dear Brother Charlie, that you and Brother Will will take care of me, if necessary, as long as you are able, but I can't stand to think of myself at thirty-five or forty years old not able to earn my salt." When Elizabeth arrived in Greensboro, she met other students who shared her purpose. "I want to educate myself," insisted Maggie Harrison. "I have been teaching school for three years and must confess that I like it much better than anything else, and I expect to teach as long as I live." Like Lizzie McDuffie, another of her classmates, Harrison would settle for nothing less than making herself into a "self-sustaining woman."[59]

Such pronouncements expressed hope and desire as much as need. The student letters that spoke of misfortune and self-doubt also bristled with excitement and expectation. Young women viewed the normal less as a refuge than as an " 'open sesame' to a region of enchantment." The school introduced its students to wage-earning work and the world of ideas, educating "for usefulness . . . and not for ornament." It was first of all a vocational college that sought to prepare young women for teaching as well as careers in "telegraphy, typewriting, stenography, and such other industrial arts as may be suitable to their sex and conducive to their support." That training, however, was offered "*in addition to* genuine literary culture." Female colleges and seminaries in North Carolina had been educating young women since the antebellum era, but they seldom offered more than a year or two of coursework and a smattering of languages, music, and drawing. The normal broke with that pattern by providing a thorough, four-year course in the liberal arts. "I am trying to develop a great institution for women of the white race," McIver explained to a friend, "which shall combine . . . industrial and normal features . . . with the work of a high class college like Vassar or Smith."[60]

McIver's dreams were grandiose. But his institution did come closer than other North Carolina women's colleges to offering its students the same sort of education enjoyed by their brothers at the university. The young women read widely in English, German, and French literature as well as world and American history. They formed two competing academic societies, the Adelphian and the Cornelian, and published original poetry along with literary criticism and historical essays in a student-run journal. In their science courses, they studied analytic and organic chemistry, physics, zoology, geology, and comparative anatomy. That work was supplemented with independent laboratory investigations and a thorough grounding in mathematics, including trigonometry and analytic geometry. In the Department of Physiology, the students were encouraged to exercise in the gymnasium and to pursue sports such as basketball, which were generally thought to be the province of men. Dr. Miriam Bitting, the college physician, championed reform in women's dress. After she explained the ill effects of lacing on health, more than two-thirds of the girls gave up their corsets. McIver and other observers believed that increased physical activity and less restrictive dress wrought an immediate transformation. "Many chests increased in girth, shoulders straightened, arms became stronger," the president reported in the *First Annual Catalogue*. The "Normal Girl" seemed to carry herself with a new bearing, which one writer tried to capture in verse.

> You can tell her by her manner
> When you meet her on the street,
> For she walks as if she meant it,
> Treading squarely on both feet.
>
> If some friend should introduce you,
> You would know her by her talk,
> Which is fully as decided
> As the manner of her walk.
>
> She is versed in many matters,
> And she always has a view
> Which she clings to in a manner
> That would shame the strongest glue.[61]

Students, as well as many teachers who never made it to the normal, heralded the school as a bright "morning star" for womanhood. Graduates developed lifelong attachments to the institution. Sallie Wellford had to leave school early, but she prized her single year at the normal far above the time she had spent in an assortment of other female colleges. "I am determined that if I live long enough," she wrote McIver, "I will teach and make the money to finish my course at the place, which after my home, must ever be the most loved. I can hardly tell you of the good that I feel that it has done for me. . . . I would give up, gladly, my other four years, rather than part with the strength mental, moral and physical gained there in that

Edwin Alderman, Charles McIver, and the Normal School's first graduating class, May 1893. All of these students entered with course credit from other institutions; several, in fact, served as assistants to the faculty. They are, from left to right and back to front, Maggie McIver, Lizzie Lee Williams, Maggie Burke, Carrie Mullins, Annie Page, Mattie Bolton, Bertha Lee, Minnie Hampton, Maude Broadaway, and Zella McCulloch. (Courtesy of the University Archives, University of North Carolina at Greensboro)

one. . . . I will ever be thankful for the influence it has had on my life." Mary Wiley put the same thoughts more succinctly. "Coming here," she confided to her diary, "has been the very making of me."[62]

For other students, McIver himself became an exalted figure. "Our whole state," one teacher declared, "especially the young women, have something indeed to be proud of, and in that Great Day there will be many to rise up and call you *blessed*." Another wrote asking for a memento of her years in Greensboro. "Will you be so kind as to send me a pen or bit of pencil which you have used your very own self," she pleaded. "I wish it to place in a 'Memory Jug.'" She closed by asking McIver's pardon for the imposition, confessing, "I have no excuse to offer, except my deep love and admiration for you and the Normal." When McIver died suddenly in 1906, that devotion moved his students to organize a special fund-raising campaign. They erected a statue on the state capitol grounds in Raleigh to the man they credited with the "beginning of woman's freedom."[63]

Passage into that freedom was not always easy, either for the students or for the people they left at home. Some parents fretted over their children's ability to handle money. Mrs. R. M. Middleton wrote in advance of her daughter's arrival, advising McIver that she was sending the girl with seventy dollars in cash. "Will you please take the money and pay her bills your self," Middleton asked. "Girls are sometimes careless about business matters." Others were anxious that their daughters not be frightened by their "first experience among strangers." "Mary is a timid backwoods girl," J. D. Currie admitted of his niece, Mary Singletary, "[and] any favor you may do her in the way of setting her up and making her feel easy will be duly appreciated." But above all, parents worried about the moral perils of college and city life. John Coke, like other guardians, wanted to ensure that his niece got a place in the dormitory "as close to Mrs. McIver" as possible. "A girl of the tender age of 16 years who has never been from home," he advised the president, "needs to be guided and directed, and therefore I would like her to be surrounded by those influences which tend to her best moral development."[64]

McIver tried to assuage parental concerns by swearing his students to a strict "contract" governing dress and behavior. He also hired Sue May Kirkland to serve as "Lady Principal" and "referee in all matters social and domestic." Kirkland lived in the dormitory and kept tabs on every aspect of the students' private lives. "She is just as dignified & and strict as she can be," one student observed, "& we all are scared to death of her." But neither Kirkland nor McIver could maintain a constant vigil. The students were indeed among "strangers," and they enjoyed the liberty that situation afforded them. They smoked cigarettes in their rooms late at night, traveled into town without a chaperone, and devised ways of slipping out of the dormitory "to entertain [a] special beau."[65]

Distance from the prying gaze of parents and neighbors nurtured new patterns of romance and courtship. Students no longer had to share their affections with boys they had known since childhood; they could experience the danger and excitement of seeking "attention from young gentlemen" they had never met before. "Right in front of our building," Mary Wiley wrote in her diary, "is Moore's Springs and since school opened it has become quite a resort for the Greensboro boys." The men purportedly came to take the mineral waters for their health, but they had the habit of sitting on the banks and staring expectantly at the dormitory.[66]

Wiley never visited the spring. She was determined "to avoid all complications & associations by which the fleshy forces [would] be increased."

Instead, she satisfied her need for intimacy and affection through friend-ships with other students. Mary and her roommates treated one another with "spreads" of cakes, jam, and fruit; swapped stories in their "Anti-Gossiping Society"; filled their diaries with "character sketches" of one another; and pledged their devotion in a "Circle of Sisterly Charity." They were bound by qualities one saw in another and wished for herself. Mary especially admired Bertha Lee. She wrote in her diary, "[Bertha] is cer-tainly a lovely girl, such a devoted Christian. I wish I was as good as she is. I certainly do *love* her. She is not one of your goody-goody saints, but she is as human as the rest of us, and has a temper too. Not that she flies into passions. I don't mean anything like that. She's just got *spunk*—that's the word." Mary viewed Bertha's Christian virtue and personal fortitude as flip sides of the same coin. In her eyes, personal strength depended on self-denial.[67]

Many of Wiley's classmates, however, had no taste for such discipline. They would "go to walk every evening, and meet with the men [at the spring], whom they [would] leave when they [got back] in sight of the Normal." When chastised for breaking college rules, the young women sometimes became defiant. Della Stikelether informed McIver that she kept company with the Greensboro boys only because she had heard it said " 'that *you* thought every young lady . . . ought to have gentleman callers *at least twice a week.*' " McIver asked her not to return the next year. He admitted privately that more than a few of his charges seemed "too much inclined to have a good time" and were "unwilling to submit to restraints which interfered with . . . forbidden pleasures."[68]

McIver's sternness was rooted in his own moral code and fears for his school's reputation. He understood that his students' brashness, public self-confidence, and demand for the sort of professional respect usually reserved for men could stir fears about women's sexuality. That point was driven home by a letter of inquiry about Bessie Watkins, a student from Lawrenceville, Virginia. "Previous to going to your school," explained Carson Watson, one of her former neighbors, she "was employed in a store in Lawrenceville conducted by a young gentleman as reputable as any I know. . . . Recently, however, reports have been started, *somewhere*, by *somebody*, derogatory to the moral character of [Miss Watkins] and this young man. . . . The report is that, there having been improper relations between them, he gave her $2,000, and sent her away [to Greensboro], that she might be confined." Watson demanded that McIver tell what he knew, insisting that "if there be any truth in this report, some knowledge of it must have come to you through your own observation, or that of your teachers or matron."

The rumors were unfounded; they revealed less about Bessie Watkins than about the challenge that she and other "Normal Girls" posed to conventional notions of sexual hierarchy. Neighbors who had recommended their friends' daughters to McIver as "amiable and genteel in disposition and lady-like in deportment" were startled when the students returned home willful and self-sure. An independent spirit threatened to place the young women beyond the gaze of family and community, tempting them with the possibility of a new sexual autonomy and at the same time leaving them unprotected and susceptible to victimization.[69]

Even some of the normal's most ardent supporters voiced concern that the school was undermining a gender system in which chastity before marriage, motherhood, and male authority were closely intertwined. "Long may you enjoy the proud position you have won . . . & may you . . . be spared to carry on the good work you have begun," P. L. Murphy, superintendent of the State Hospital for the Insane, wrote to McIver, "but don't forget that women are women & that their place in the great economy of nature is to love children & raise them." Fodie Buie's neighbors were even more straightforward. Before she left to enroll in the normal, one of them cornered her in the post office, exclaiming, "I don't approve of your going to college. . . . All you gals will come back from there a pack of infidels and the whole world will go to the dogs."[70]

Such fears were exaggerated. Normal School graduates had little chance of tearing the world asunder, but they did author new images of womanhood and teaching. By the late 1890s, the normal had more than one thousand alumnae "scattered over the State." The sheer weight of their numbers redefined teaching as women's work, while their activism cleared a path for female participation in public life. "Normal Girls" became the foot soldiers of the graded school movement. They learned in Greensboro to hitch "high ambition" to a commitment to "public service." As teachers, they were not satisfied to work as mere "instructor[s] of youth"; instead, they sought to become "influential adviser[s] on all matters . . . pertaining to schools." They visited in their students' homes to improve attendance, lobbied for the election of "progressive" county officials, and, by 1913, won seats for themselves on county school boards, despite the fact that they were still denied the right to vote.[71]

In gaining even limited access to the male world of politics, normal school graduates remapped the terrain of gender relations. *Then and Now* concludes with an admission by Rodney, Hope's husband, that life with a teacher had changed his thinking about woman's place. " 'Do you know,' " he said, " 'I have sometimes thought that a man might run a great risk in marrying a talented and ambitious woman; but I see now that I was in error.' " Hope's strength and independence were attractive qualities that had enabled her to steal Rodney's affections from Amelia, a rival of great charm but little substance. Public fears aside, the "good wife" and the "citizen woman" could be one and the same.[72]

Women sought out teaching and were welcomed into the classroom because the new education demanded qualities they were assumed to possess. Belief in women's special qualifications for the job provided ammunition in the battle to make teaching into a profession complete with its own credentials and unique body of expert knowledge. But as "women's work," teaching was destined to remain a "shadowed" profession. In the graded schools and in the countryside, women teachers ultimately looked to male administrators for guidance; women taught and men managed. A graduate of the normal school revealed the ambiguities of her life's work as she hesitated in describing her relationship to McIver and the graded school movement. Recalling her years in Greensboro, she wrote, "We were ever in awe of [Charles McIver]. He had a vision and we were following him. No, we weren't following him. We were all going along together." The feminization of teaching reaffirmed old sexual hierarchies even as it changed them into something new.[73]

Voices of Dissent

I am for a public school and I will do all I can for it, but I'll
be blamed if I'll ever vote for a Graded School.
—Unidentified parent quoted in the *State Chronicle,*

April 14, 1887

The late 1880s and early 1890s were flush times for the new education. Graded schools were taking root in most of North Carolina's towns and cities, the university had embraced a bold new curriculum, and the Normal School was beginning to train a generation of classroom evangelists. But despite those successes some reformers worried about the future. In March 1891, George Winston, president of the university, wrote to Charles McIver describing a "vague feeling" that their "entire educational struggle" was about to confront a crisis. Six months later, Edwin Alderman reported from an institute in Franklin County that the people there were "theoretically sound on popular education" but that "practically" they did not "recognize its benefits." What he took for a lack of understanding was actually a sign of growing disagreement over the course of New South development and the purposes of schooling. Within four years, Alderman and his colleagues would be swept up in a bitter contest that pitted reformers against men and women who questioned the New South vision of a society governed less by the authority of persons than by that of the marketplace.[1]

By the late 1880s the ways of commerce were closing in on many North Carolinians. Shifting crop mix and land tenure patterns told the story of a virtual assault on a semisubsistence way of life. The 145,000 bales of cotton raised in 1860 soared to 336,000 three decades later, while tobacco production increased from 32,000,000 to 36,000,000 pounds. During that same period, production of corn, wheat, sweet potatoes, milk cows, and swine all plummeted. Tenancy rates reflected the effects of these developments on farm families. Even in areas without a legacy of plantation agriculture, one-third more farmers tended someone else's land in 1900 than in 1880. Counties that surrounded major trading centers registered particularly dramatic increases: by 1900, for instance, more than half of the farmers in Charlotte's hinterland were tenants.[2]

As more farm families committed themselves to the market, prices for cash crops tumbled. Cotton prices dropped from twenty-five cents a pound in 1868 to only seven cents by the early 1890s. But farmers' costs for fertilizer, bagging, and machinery remained substantially unchanged, while collusion among the railroads made it ever more expensive for farmers to carry their goods to sale. The deflation sparked by collapsing prices also raised the real value of farmers' debts; by one calculation, that burden rose 16 percent every five years between 1875 and 1900. Many producers found themselves trapped in a vicious cycle, falling farther behind even as they gambled more heavily on cash crops in hopes of getting ahead.[3]

Farmers fought back through the Southern Farmers Alliance, organized in Texas in 1886 and transplanted by means of local chapters throughout the region. By 1890 membership in North Carolina had grown to more than ninety thousand. The economic hardships rural folk struggled against reached into most households in nearly every neighborhood. As a result, the alliance appealed to a broad and sometimes fractious cross-section of rural society. Tenants, sharecroppers, landowners, and even small-time merchants worked toward common goals. The alliance operated sawmills, tanneries, and shoe factories that enabled farmers to process lumber and hides for their own use. It also established agricultural exchanges, institutionalizing an ideal of neighborliness that linked independence and mutual aid. Members sold their cotton and tobacco through alliance warehouses and bought their supplies in alliance stores, cutting out the profits of middlemen.[4]

The alliance became a powerful political force by the early 1890s. Under the leadership of Leonidas L. Polk, a North Carolinian elected president of the National Alliance in 1889, farmers throughout the South and Middle West broke from the Democratic fold and formed a new People's Party. In 1892, they ran a campaign demanding nationalization of the railroads, government control over the banking system, public warehouses for farmers' crops, and federal loans at an interest rate of 1 percent a year. The Populist ticket in North Carolina was defeated, but it drew enough votes to threaten conservative Democrats' hold on power. In retaliation, the Democratic legislature amended the alliance's charter so as to prohibit its business activities and close the cooperatives. Then, in what could have been seen only as an act of vengeance, the new governor, Elias Carr, himself a wealthy landowner and one-time alliance member, leased the state-owned North Carolina Railroad to banking magnate J. P. Morgan's Southern Railway for ninety-nine years. Turning his back on his former allies, Carr abided by his campaign promise to "listen to no revolutionary sentiments . . . of reform, but, on the contrary, [to] let conservatism dictate . . . every policy."[5]

Stung by those reprisals, Populist leaders searched for a winning electoral strategy. Together, the Republican and Populist candidates had received a majority of the votes in the 1892 gubernatorial race, but Carr won the office. Clearly, a fusion of the two parties could defeat the Democrats in the next off-year legislative contest. Populists and Republicans, black farmers and white, reached beyond their differences and distrust to field a joint ticket in 1894. A white Democrat preparing to bolt to the Populists explained his decision forthrightly: "The issue confronting the American people to-day is the liberty of the laboring people, both white and black, an issue of vastly more importance than the enslavement of the negro ever was." The 1894 election gave vent to years of anger and suffering. Fusionists won 116 seats, compared to the Democrats' fifty-four, effecting "a virtual revolution in North Carolina politics." The new legislators immediately set about regulating railroads, limiting interest rates, and democratizing election laws and local government. They also had schooling on their minds. Many of the Fusionists were Baptists ministers and laymen determined to halt the spreading influence of the new education. In 1895, they spearheaded an all-out attack on the university and the Normal School.[6]

Hard-line Democrats and friends of the new education publicly dismissed the church activists as misguided rubes. Josephus Daniels, editor of the *Raleigh News and Observer* and an old classmate of Edwin Alderman and Charles McIver, hurled insults at two Populist preachers elected to the legislature. Although he never offered proof of his charges, Daniels reported that the men were known "to walk rather unsteady, and to have an unnatural thickness of tongue, and irreverent breaths." With a similar lack of restraint, the *Charlotte Observer* heaped ridicule on the Reverend Mr. Martin, a Baptist legislator from Mecklenburg County. It described him as a "Pop[ulist] of the rankest order . . . a man of profound ignorance, very nervous and excitable . . . with an Elgin-movement-clockworks system in the place where brains ordinarily are." But reformers admitted in the privacy of their letters that the Baptists would be formidable opponents. Charles McIver's brother wrote in early 1895 with a warning about Alexander W. Wicker, a Fusionist from Chatham County: "Wicker is a poor fellow of slight education, though, if I am not mistaken, he was at one time a free school teacher. He is a fellow of not much principle nor stability, still of considerable pride with people of his class; has always been recognized among them and in his neighborhood as a leader."[7]

When the legislature convened in January, both sides were poised for battle. Baptist lawmakers introduced a number of bills aimed at the university and the normal, including one to reduce the salaries of the officers and teachers by 20 percent, another to abolish free tuition and scholarships, and another demanding information on alleged budgetary abuses. Most of the bills died in committee, but one provoked a battle royal. Introduced by Senator J. B. Fortune of Cleveland County, it called for an end to all state funding for both schools. With Baptists occupying over a hundred of the legislature's 170 seats, and Populists and Republicans outnumbering Democrats by more than two to one, Fortune and his allies were confident of an easy victory. Friends of the state institutions feared the worst. Edwin Alderman, who had returned to the university as a professor of pedagogy in 1893, confided to Cornelia Phillips Spencer that the school was "in grave danger" as a result of the "political revolution" and "denominational crusade. . . . A false step, an ill-considered word, an impolitic act and we are seriously crippled."[8]

The attack on the university and the normal arose partly from the economic crisis of the early 1890s. By late 1891, state superintendent Sidney Finger had spotted trouble on the horizon. He wrote Charles McIver that the next year would "be one of very great dissatisfaction and unrest among our people. The evidence seems to be pretty plain that the receipts of this year's cotton crop in North Carolina will fall short of last year at least ten million dollars. . . . From what I can gather there will be actual suffering, and much of it, in our state this winter." As hard times set in, the faithful dropped fewer coins into collection plates, and enrollments at denominational colleges dwindled. Wake Forest, the state's leading white Baptist college, had 233 students in 1890–91, but by the winter of 1892 the ranks had thinned to 185. At the same time, the university's student body swelled from 198 in 1891 to 316 in 1893 and 389 by 1894. Church leaders blamed their declining fortunes on the university's use of free tuition and scholarships to attract "many boys from Baptist homes . . . preventing the numerical growth which justly belongs to the Baptist college." To make matters worse, the legislature had increased the university's annual appropriation from $5,000 to $20,000 and had created two new institutions certain to compete with sectarian schools: the Agricultural and Mechanical College, chartered in Raleigh in 1887, and the normal, which promised to draw young women away from the Baptist-funded Chowan Female Institute.[9]

Frustration and fear for their institutions' survival spurred Baptist educators to abandon the classroom and the pulpit for the world of politics. They made the state-aid question a central issue in the 1894 campaign. "Keep 'Christian and Popular Education' prominent in your own and your neighbor's and your candidate's mind," advised the *Biblical Recorder*, North Carolina's leading Baptist newspaper. "Know that State-aid means the crippling of the best institutions of higher learning in the State; know that [the university] now waxes fat while the common schools are suffering; know that it is taking all it can get and crying for more of the taxes you pay,—know these things, and let it not be your fault that your neighbor and your candidate don't know them." Such appeals touched a nerve among hard-pressed farmers, who considered a dollar "a very great thing." To many rural folk, the $500 annual salary of professors at the university and the normal must have seemed like a fortune.[10]

Bickering among the graded school men only worsened the problem. Since the Normal School's opening in 1892, Eugene G. Harrell, editor of the *North Carolina Teacher*, had hurled charges of financial misconduct at Charles McIver. Harrell was a senior partner in Alfred Williams and Company, a Raleigh stationer and bookseller. He had established the *North Carolina Teacher* in 1883 partly out of devotion to school reform and partly in hopes of profiting from enthusiasm for the new education. When Charles McIver overlooked his firm in placing book orders for the normal, Harrell was outraged. In November 1892, he sent McIver the first payment for a scholarship sponsored by his magazine and issued a direct threat. "Would have sent it before," Harrell wrote, "but really did not know the school was open. . . . Our house has not even received an order for books or stationery from the institution and I learn from friends at Greensboro that about all supplies for the State Normal and Industrial School are purchased direct from the *north!* If this be true perhaps the taxpayers may not feel the same interests in the institution in future." Several months later, Harrell published two articles charging that the normal's first annual report failed to account for $9,000 in cash income and fees. He insinuated that McIver was lining his own pockets through a "reckless waste of the state's money."[11]

McIver's friends encouraged him to strike back before Harrell's allegations had time to "sink into and poison the minds of the people." "In my humble judgment," his brother wrote, "the war is on, and you must crush Harrell, or he will crush you." McIver demanded a public apology and rallied his allies in the press to spread the word that the Normal School's funds, handled by a state-appointed bursar, never passed through his hands. Students at the school also issued a statement of confidence in McIver and renounced their scholarships from the *North Carolina Teacher*. One young woman wrote to Harrell, "I wish to thank you for your fellowship and to say that, under the existing circumstances, I care for it no longer. . . . Possibly you will never know what a great change your assistance has wrought in my life, for which I am truly thankful, but I think you are going very wrong . . . and I cannot eat of your food and fight you at the same time." In June, Harrell withdrew from the public arena, advising readers of the *North Carolina Teacher* that "we have closed our discussion of the Normal and Industrial School for the present, and our friends on the other side may now pile the abuse on us. We don't mind it at all."[12]

But Harrell did not give up the fight. He continued to question McIver's integrity in private discussions with legislators and other state officials. By 1895, he had gained the ear of Edward Moses, superintendent of the Raleigh graded school. Moses had come from Tennessee in 1881 and had quickly established a reputation as the "Pestalozzi of North Carolina." He gave Edwin Alderman his first teaching job in Goldsboro in 1882 and served as a mentor for many of the other young graded school superintendents. But Moses soon became a bitter man. When Charles McIver was named president of the normal, Moses felt that he had been robbed of an honor that was rightfully his. The Fusionist victory in 1894 offered him a chance to settle the score. Moses joined Harrell's rumor-mongering, hoping to gain a place on the normal's board of trustees and thus position himself for nomination, at the next Fusion convention, as the state superintendent of public instruction. Friends of the new education considered such behavior beneath contempt. J. A. Holmes, the state geologist, dismissed Moses as "a little fice which is trotting around, barking at the Normal School . . . even wet[ting] on the doorstep." He advised McIver to ignore the pest, but the anger behind those words suggested just how much damage Moses and Harrell could do if left to carry on their campaign.[13]

The contest over state aid, however, ran deeper than denominational self-interest and personal pique. At the most fundamental level it spoke to conflicting ideas about the proper distribution of social authority. By the 1890s, university administrators had grown fond of describing their institution as "a mighty piece of social machinery" capable of forging a new North Carolina. "The university is the dynamo, the public school the incandescent light," exclaimed Edwin Alderman. Together with the normal, the university and the graded schools promised to train "a grand army" of young people who would nationalize southern thought and commercialize southern life. For friends of the state institutions, word of the new education's expanding influence was cause for rejoicing. But such news fell less easily on other ears. Many North Carolinians, wary of the growing power of distant monopolies in other areas of their lives, feared the emergence of an "educational ring" that would eventually deny them control over their own children.[14]

Charles Elisha Taylor, president of Wake Forest College, laid out the dangers of state-supported higher education in a series of essays that first appeared in the *Biblical Recorder* in April and May 1894. Hoping to reach beyond an audience of regular churchgoers, Baptist leaders had the articles reprinted as a pamphlet titled *How Far Should a State Undertake to Educate? or, A Plea for the Voluntary System in the Higher Education.* By election day, more than 25,000 copies had been circulated throughout the state. Seeking to distance himself from the tactics employed by Harrell and Moses, Taylor offered "to discuss in a calm and good-mannered way some grave and practicable questions of public policy." He asked his rivals to return the courtesy. Since his views were shared "by very many thoughtful men in many parts of our country," he believed "that they should not be treated with ridicule or answered with epithets."[15]

Taylor argued that despite honorable intentions the new education threatened to "sap the foundations of public liberty." The university, the normal, and the graded schools fed off of one another, quietly spreading their dominion over everyday life. "A large portion of those who seek higher education expect to teach," Taylor wrote.

Charles E. Taylor, president of Wake Forest College and opponent of the new education, seated (left) in his library and surrounded by his extended family (Courtesy of the North Carolina Division of Archives and History, Raleigh)

[A] monopoly of influence for appointment to positions in the graded schools will naturally draw the great majority of this numerous class to the State institutions. . . . These and other motives will largely increase the numbers of students at [those schools]. This increase will be made a plea for larger appropriations from the State Treasury. These, when granted, will multiply attractions. Then as soon as it can be enacted by a Legislature, unlimited free tuition will be granted to all State students. On the other hand, the patronage of the other colleges will continue to decrease. Their incomes from students' fees will gradually cease entirely[,] . . . buildings will cease to be erected, and endowments to be enlarged. Their corps of professors will be cut [until] a melancholy silence will reign in halls of learning [once] dedicated to higher education under Christian influence.

The demise of the denominational colleges might give little reason for concern, except that it would make way for a "vast and complicated system under State control." Along with the church schools, the principle of educational voluntarism would die, as would the American idea that an individual, "in conjunction with his fellow citizens," should employ "social forms which he can modify at pleasure, instead of being employed and moulded by them."[16]

A clause in the Normal School's charter granting its alumnae lifetime certificates to teach anywhere in the state stood as one of the most glaring examples of the sort of subordination to bureaucratic control the Baptists most feared. By denying local officials the right to examine and certify Normal School graduates, the provision effectively separated the classroom from the community and empowered teachers to run their schools according to professional standards rather than parental desires. Josiah Bailey, the young editor of the *Biblical Recorder*, railed against this substitution of expertise for more personal assessments of character. In his view, a teacher was to be judged not by the formal criteria of the college classroom but by the "knowledge of men" acquired through face-to-face encounters. To do otherwise would destroy the patterns of connectedness and community responsibility that made authority approachable and gave power a human face.[17]

The Baptists embraced a vision of democratic localism championed by the Farmers Alliance, the Knights of Labor, and other late-nineteenth-century insurgents who were alarmed at the widening gulf between individuals and the institutional and economic forces that shaped their lives. Such a political commitment came easily to the churchmen, whose own faith was based on the rejection of centralized ecclesiastical governance in favor of the autonomy of local congregations. At its worst, democratic localism could give voice to a tyrannical majority that might impose its own narrow, sectarian views on the classroom. At its best, such a system acknowledged the authority of ordinary people and accepted their desire to establish institutions that served their own needs and aspirations.[18]

Before a gathering of county school superintendents, Josiah Bailey rebuked the New South and a conception of progress that subordinated local interests to material development.

I am no dreamer, but I believe in visions. I have a vision of my North Carolina; it is not of her matchless resources—I am content to let them await the inevitable fruition of time. It is not of her gracious rivers rolling their mighty waters unused, but not wasted, into the Atlantic. I am content with their beauty as they are. It is not of her mountains so rich in mineral wealth, so marvelous in their majesty. I am content that I may stand upon her heights sometimes and breathe the incense of heaven and worship God in the grandeur of His tabernacle. No, no, it is not of North Carolina's material blessings: My vision is of her children to-day, herself to-morrow. . . . I shall be content to depart without entering but having seen the era in which . . . men and women, 'diviner but still human' . . . [shall] serve each other as brothers, seeking the common good of all . . . and exact justice between man and man.

Justice, of course, did not necessarily imply equality. Bailey's own church recognized hierarchies of wealth, class, race, and gender. But his evangelical faith also embodied a commitment to a world where individual ambition and the exercise of power remained checked by a sense of responsibility to neighbors and kin.[19]

Critics charged that opponents of state aid secretly wished to destroy all public education, not just the university and the Normal School. Sidney Finger instructed Charles McIver in 1894, "write me . . . what you gather about . . . the denominational fight against Higher State Education. I think behind it all is a real opposition to *lower state education also*. I am much inclined to the opinion that the leaders would have nothing unless possibly the three R's." But Finger misrepresented his challengers' position. The Baptists cherished public education; they viewed it as a positive good so long as control over the schools remained in local hands. In their attack on the university and the normal, they argued that the money spent on those institutions could be put to better use improving schoolhouses and lengthening the school term for the vast majority of children who would never go to college.[20]

Like other turn-of-the-century dissidents, the Baptist challengers were complicated figures who tried to adopt the favorable aspects of development while avoiding those that threatened harm. They welcomed improved school facilities, just as they enjoyed the new comforts money and markets could bring. They were ready to embrace the modern world but demanded a voice in the direction of social and economic change. Opponents of state aid attacked the university and the normal because those institutions had become the seedbeds of a school movement that emphasized bureaucratic management and expert knowledge above local accountability.

When Senator Fortune's bill to abolish state aid finally came before the legislature's joint committee on education in March 1895, feelings on both sides of the issue had reached "fever heat." The Reverend Christopher Columbus Durham, corresponding secretary for the North Carolina Baptist State Convention, spoke for the opposition. Unlike Charles Taylor, who preferred intellectual appeals over "a tussle on the hustings," Durham was prepared to wage holy war. Observers described him as a martyr, a man without "the least shadow of humor" who "asked no quarter and gave none." Before a packed audience in the State Library, Durham played relentlessly on issues of class and racial resentment. He charged that the university enticed poor boys away from the denominational colleges with promises of free tuition, then welshed on the deal by giving the money to "sons of the most well-to-do citizens of the State." Those young men enjoyed a life of luxury, housed in dormitory rooms "with service . . . provided free." "That means," Durham exclaimed, "a nigger to wait on you." Stunned by such demagoguery, Durham's closest friends admitted privately that he had momentarily "lost his head." Supporters of the university and the normal were less kind. They accused the minister of "bigotry and ignorance and hatred and falsehood and stupidity and envy and selfishness and . . . jealousy and folly and all uncharitableness."[21]

George Winston, president of the university, countered Durham's attack with a combined strategy of behind-the-scenes maneuvering and public confrontation. He had worked quietly since the state-aid issue first broke, building bridges into the Fusion camp. "My idea," he confided to Charles McIver, "is to yield not an inch to the denominations, but *personally* to cultivate their *leading men*." Winston found support for that tactic among the university's alumni, many of whom wielded considerable political power. The presiding officer of the state Senate, a Democrat, and the speaker of the House of Representatives, a Republican, were both Chapel Hill graduates. As a younger institution devoted to women's education, the normal had fewer influential allies. McIver's associates encouraged him to "say nothing and . . . let other folks do the talking." Heeding that advice, he relied on the university's friends to barter political favors and privileges for votes in support of both schools. In February, university alumnus Marion Butler, the Populist state chairman and U.S. senator, publicly endorsed state aid, signaling his subordinates to fall in line.[22]

Winston pulled no punches during the joint committee's hearings. First, he tried to split the Fusion alliance along racial lines by recruiting a black minister to defend the university and convince black Republicans that the

George T. Winston, professor of Latin and German, and president of the University of North Carolina during the funding crisis of 1895 (Courtesy of the North Carolina Collection, University of North Carolina at Chapel Hill)

state-aid issue was a "white folkses' fight." What exactly the preacher meant by that remark newspaper accounts never fully explained, but his point seems easy enough to infer. From the beginning, black Republicans had been cautious in estimating their white allies' true sympathies and intentions. In 1894, for instance, the *Star of Zion*, an influential black newspaper published in Salisbury, had advised its readers to enter the Fusion alliance with their eyes open. On matters of race, the editors observed, many Populist leaders had records that were indistinguishable from those of hard-line Democrats. Consider the case of Marion Butler, by all rights one of the most influential members of the Populists' inner circle. As a student at the university in 1883, he had argued in the halls of the Dialectic Society for the "subjection of the negro to the Anglo-Saxon." Nearly a decade later, as editor of a Populist newspaper called the *Caucasian*, Butler was unreconstructed in his views. He defended lynching as a legitimate instrument of justice sanctioned by "public sentiment, if not by law," and warned of the Negro's tendency, once freed from the restraints of slavery, to sink back "to the conditions of barbaric Africa." In the context of such behavior on the part of their white "friends," black lawmakers had little need for the minister to elaborate on his remarks. Suppose that the legislature succeeded in defunding the university and the Normal School; even then, could blacks realistically expect that their schools would reap the rewards?[23]

Having planted the seeds of racial doubt and suspicion, Winston next challenged the integrity of his Baptist opponents. How could they explain the fact that their colleges accepted donations from Standard Oil, one of the late nineteenth century's most notorious monopolies? And what of their own political loyalties? Hamilton Ewart, a Republican maverick and ardent defender of state aid, delivered the killing blow. "Were not the Democrats understood to favor the appropriations [to the university and the normal] and the fusionists to oppose [them]?" he asked the Reverend Durham. "I believe so," Durham answered. "How did you vote [in the last election]?" Ewart pressed. Flustered, but determined to stand his ground, Durham admitted the truth: "The straight Democratic ticket, as I always have done." "Then you didn't vote as you shot!" Ewart retorted in triumph. Many in the gallery roared with laughter; others shook their heads, one black Republican mumbling to himself "that the white Baptists did just as the Democrats always did: talked one way and voted another." Durham's apostasy revealed just how brittle the alliance among Populists, black Republicans, and Baptists could be.[24]

When the roll was called, the joint committee voted thirty-eight to two against the Baptist challenge. But that margin belied how narrowly the graded school men had escaped defeat. George Winston advised an old friend that even with the help of university alumni, "we came near destruction. The Baptist flood roared and surged and threatened us. . . . Could they have gotten a vote [earlier in the legislative session], we [would have] been abolished root and branch."[25]

In Greensboro, news of the victory sparked a celebration on Charles McIver's front lawn. Lula McIver wrote to her husband that "four hundred boys could not have made more fuss. [The girls] came by here and stopped, giving three cheers for you and three cheers for a member of the faculty . . . until they had gone through . . . everyone connected with the institution.

Then they took [three of the professors] and I do not know who else up and *carried* them all around and . . . demanded speeches." Later that evening, local townspeople joined the festivities by turning out to serenade the students and their instructors.[26]

The rejoicing was premature. Advocates of the new education had only won a skirmish in a much larger war. When the public school law came up for review several weeks later, state superintendent John C. Scarborough begged the legislature to steer clear of any "violent changes." But the embittered Fusionists ignored his pleas. They struck back at the encroachments of reformers and incipient bureaucrats by abolishing the office of county superintendent, dismantling the boards of education created in 1885, and handing full authority over the common schools to neighborhood committees appointed by county commissioners. From across the state, letters from school reformers poured into Scarborough's office deploring the new law. One schoolman ridiculed the Fusionists, describing them as "Asses who . . . evidently knew nothing of the law they were changing, but like children wanted to do something for variety sake." Another viewed the legislature's changes as "nothing short of an outrage," signing his letter, "Yours in sorrow for the children of our state." Having spearheaded the effort to professionalize school management in the early 1880s, Scarborough himself found the setback demoralizing. "I have lost heart and interest in the work," he wrote to close friends. "No one could teach these men anything. I besought them not to go backwards. But go they would. . . . We are left just where we were when I took charge of this office in January 1877."[27]

The Fusionists embraced old ways, but they were something more than backward-looking obstructionists. Revision of the school law grew partly from a hard-fought battle to democratize county government. After the Democrats overthrew Reconstruction and returned to power in the mid-1870s, they moved quickly to stifle the voices of black Republicans and poor whites by abolishing elections for county commissioners. Under Democratic rule, commissioners were appointed by local justices of the peace, who were in turn named by the legislature. The Redeemers further safeguarded their counter-revolution by enacting a series of election laws that gave Democratic registrars the ability to disfranchise voters "on the flimsiest pretext." Having suffered these constraints on political participation for nearly twenty years, the Fusionists acted decisively to set things right. They restored the power of popularly elected county officials and adopted what one historian has described as "probably the fairest and most democratic election law in the post-Reconstruction South." The new law permitted one precinct judge from each party to be present when the ballots were counted, limited the registrars' powers to disqualify voters capriciously, and assisted illiterate voters by allowing the use of color-coded ballots marked with party insignia. Placing school administration fully in the hands of elected county commissioners and local trustees thus completed a long-sought plan of home rule.[28]

The effort to safeguard traditional forms of educational management also spoke to simmering schoolhouse grievances. For years, black North Carolinians had found themselves pushed to the margins of the school reform movement. Following their return to power in the mid-1870s, Democrats promised to safeguard the rights of black citizens and students. As proof of his party's good intentions, Governor Zebulon B. Vance called on the legislature to "make no discrimination in the matter of public education." But black people had every reason to distrust the Redeemers, many of whom preached the maxim that "when you 'educate a negro you spoil a field hand.'" In 1880 and again in 1881, Democratic lawmakers authorized Goldsboro to operate its graded schools with racially divided tax funds, using the levies paid by whites to finance the white school and forcing the black school to rely on the smaller revenues paid by a poorer black population. Obviously, this method of financing stood to cripple black education. In 1883, the legislature extended the provision to every school district in the state. Authored by Senator William T. Dortch, a Goldsboro lawyer and Democratic Party leader, the new law enabled district residents to force a vote on the racial division of school funds by obtaining the signatures of only ten white petitioners.[29]

The *Star of Zion* condemned the Dortch law as a "monstrous enactment—a disgrace to the State." Black voters in a few communities managed to forestall its implementation. In the eastern cotton-belt town of Tarboro, for example, blacks defeated a bid to establish graded schools based on a segregated financial scheme. There were 884 black children of school age in the community and only 374 whites; yet if the measure had been approved, the black school would have received $1,942 a year, compared to the white school's $5,650. Nevertheless, the editor of the *Tarboro Southerner* saw the black vote as an affront to white generosity. "The vote against [the graded schools]," he chided black readers, showed "a degree of ingratitude that should instill disgust and contempt" in the heart of every white citizen. "Race prejudice defeated the bill, and the color line was drawn by the black ingrate."[30]

But not all whites shared the editor's high opinion of the Dortch law. In 1886, James C. Pruitt and Eli Pasour, white merchants from the small Gaston County town of Dallas, joined with black neighbors to challenge the law before the North Carolina Supreme Court. To the surprise of many observers, the Democratic court ruled that a racial division of school funds violated Article IX of the state constitution, which forbade "discrimination in favor of or to the prejudice of either race." Writing for the majority, Chief Justice William N. H. Smith also cited fundamental principles of fairness and equity. In his view, the court could not shut its eyes "to the fact that the vast bulk of property yielding the fruits of taxation belongs to the white people of the State, and very little is held by the emancipated race; and yet the needs of the latter for free tuition, in proportion to its numbers are as great, or greater than the needs of the former." Many local officials saw things differently. A year after the court's ruling, state superintendent Sidney Finger was still trying to enforce compliance. The school board in Person County, for instance, continued to divide school funds along racial lines. C. Jeffers, a black parent, explained that "in one district particularly" the action "deprive[d] the children of the freedmen of School privileges as they are so largely in the minority it would take several years apportionment to run even a two months school." Demanding that Finger correct the situation, Jeffers reminded him, "It is not law."[31]

The supreme court's decision signaled a rare triumph for color-blind justice, but it left untouched the more insidious consequences of the school law of 1885. Anticipating trouble with the Dortch provision, Democratic legislators gave county officials broad discretion over one-third of their school funds. On its surface, the measure seemed innocent enough. It stated simply that after the per capita distribution of two-thirds of the school revenues, the remainder was to be spent "in such manner as to equalize school facilities to all districts of the county, as far as may be practicable and just to all concerned." But since the money did not have to be distributed in proportion to enrollment, it could be used in a variety of ways, limited only by the school boards' imaginative definitions of equity.[32]

The results were often devastating for black education. In Duplin County, a relatively poor area in eastern North Carolina, blacks and whites alike would have been entitled to no more than six cents for every school-aged child under a strictly color-blind per capita financing plan, but as one angry parent pointed out, "the ⅔ distribution does not give the negro even this small sum." So long as such discrimination prevailed, blacks had everything to gain by supporting the abolition of county school boards. With the return of educational authority to elected county commissioners, they could add the power of the ballot to their demand for a greater measure of schoolhouse justice.[33]

White yeomen also had reason to celebrate the revival of traditional school governance. By the late 1880s, reform-minded school boards had begun consolidating local districts in the name of efficiency. Their object, one administrator explained, was "to put schools on a strictly business basis," expecting them to succeed "solely because of intrinsic merit—that merit which makes a neighborhood dependent upon a school, rather than the reverse." Outraged by this violation of established prerogatives, parents flooded the state superintendent's office with angry letters. Typical was R. R. King's complaint that the redistricting effort in Mecklenburg County ran "greatly against the wishes of the citizens." Seeking to regularize district sizes and enrollments, the Mecklenburg school board laid out new boundaries four miles square, ignoring local terrain and neighborhood attachments. King argued that "these large districts [would] be inconvenient. . . . There will be many children so far from the school house they will not do any good going to school." Pleading for the superintendent's intervention, he insisted that "every neighborhood" knew best its own "wants and conveniences."[34]

Other parents protested the adoption of graded school methods without their approval. They valued education, especially in a world increasingly shaped by the manipulation of money and credit. "Let me tell you," one man exclaimed, "the experience of the past twenty years teaches that no man is so likely to die poor as the son who was left a fortune without an education! And this will grow more and more manifest as the world becomes more . . . filled with sharpers!" Nevertheless, many parents resented the "insolent" and "dictatorial . . . tone" of Normal School graduates who claimed that they knew best how to educate children. In Wilson, an angry father compared the standardization imposed by the new education to the effects of fence laws, which abridged small farmers' access to common range and thus denied them the resources necessary to sustain their semi-subsistence way of life.[35]

From the mountains of western North Carolina, another father wrote to the state superintendent with biting sarcasm:

As there has quite a dissension arisen in our district I write you for your opinion. . . . The case is just about this: A few years ago the people here built a frame school house 18 × 28 feet & in it placed 12 substantial benches, some 8 or 9 feet long, its only furniture barring a B[lack] board 3 by 3. They have had several schools taught in the house, and no complaint till now a [new teacher] has come along and right away he wants an alteration. He wants to paint part of the ceiling at one end black and use it as a black board, and cut the seats into three each and face them in three rows through the house with a writing table on the top and back of each, so he claims that each student will have a place for his or her books & papers. . . . Again he claims that [the students] can spend their time more profitably than in long spelling exercises in the dictionary without defining. Now as your stand point is out E[ast] where you get the light of the sun a few hours sooner in the morning, and retain it as much longer in the evening than some of us who live in the mountain gorges, we expect you to have opinions different from ours. . . . [W]hich of the twain the teacher or the populace are right[?]

These parents were content to muddle along with what state superintendent John Scarborough once described as an "old inefficient system" of schooling. They would train their children for "the duties of Life and Citizenship" without abandoning the ways of tradition.[36]

The election of 1896 seemed to promise even further setbacks for the new education. Fusionist candidates bested their earlier victory, this time filling all of the major state offices and capturing the governorship. Compared to the legislature of 1895, the new assembly had sixteen more Republicans, four more Populists, and twenty-one fewer Democrats. Baptists also returned in large numbers, still committed to agitating the state-aid question. This time they had the support of influential Methodists, including John C. Kilgo, president of Trinity College (later named Duke University). "The Baptists are not quitters," Josiah Bailey proclaimed shortly after election day. "In the same spirit that our fathers bore stripes and imprisonment and infamy and death for religious freedom, the separation of Church and State, the Baptists of North Carolina are called to stand for the voluntary principle in higher education."[37]

Given the odds stacked against them, school reformers feared the final destruction of all that they had worked for. J. M. Spainhour, a Normal School trustee, wrote Charles McIver, "I must have consolation in this the darkest era of our existence. . . . The majority of the legislature is an incongruous mass of odiousness that will . . . pander to the lowest and meanest element to disgrace us. With such a conglomeration, the governor and his advisors, the legislature which is said to have one hundred of the Baptist Church, with the most of them pledged against higher education . . . what is to become of our schools? What is our hope for the future? I tremble at the thought. . . . Everything proposed . . . for the good of the people will be voted down."[38]

Such dire predictions failed to come true. Despite their victory in the state elections, realignments at the national level had thrown the Fusionists into disarray. In 1896, national leaders of the Populist Party, more interested in office holding than in establishing a cooperative commonwealth, allied themselves with the Democrats and their presidential candidate, William Jennings Bryan. That move effectively narrowed the Populist agenda to debt relief through the free coinage of silver and monetary inflation, a platform that thrust the People's Party in North Carolina into head-on conflict with its Republican allies, whose candidate, William McKinley, a staunch defender of the gold standard and hard money, won the White House.

A deep rift opened between factions of the People's Party early in the legislature of 1897. The dispute centered on the election of a U.S. senator. In 1895, Jeter C. Pritchard, a conservative white Republican, had been selected to fill an unexpired term left vacant by the death of Democratic senator Zebulon Vance. He entered the office with assurances that he would have Fusion support for reappointment in 1897. By 1896, however, Pritchard had fallen in line with the national Republican Party by abandoning free silver for the gold standard. Populist senator Marion Butler consequently urged his defeat, but Harry Skinner, a Populist congressman and Butler's successor as chairman of the state executive committee of the People's Party, insisted that old pledges be honored, despite changed circumstances. When the legislature reelected Pritchard, both Fusion and the Populist movement in North Carolina began to fall apart.[39]

Dissension among the Populists provided an opening for advocates of the new education. Ironically, their cause was championed by the Populist state superintendent, Charles H. Mebane. J. M. Spainhour and other Democrats often dismissed Mebane as "a little puke," but the superinten-

Charles H. Mebane, elected state superintendent of public instruction on the Fusion ticket (Courtesy of the North Carolina Division of Archives and History, Raleigh)

dent was in fact a devoted proponent of reform. His affiliation with the Populists was more a matter of expediency than a sign of ideological commitment. Born in 1862, Mebane, like the graded school advocates, was a young man who had come of age in the New South. But because he attended Catawba College rather than the university, he always felt locked out of the cadre he once referred to as the "University Gang." His only chance of fulfilling his ambition for high office and leadership in the educational crusade was to abandon his Democratic roots and make a name for himself as a Fusionist.[40]

With the skill of a seasoned politician, Mebane played warring factions within the legislature against one another, and ultimately he won approval of a far-reaching school law. The measure took a bold step toward reorganizing the common schools on a graded school model, effectively divorcing education from what Mebane derisively called courthouse "politics and mere local selfishness." At the county level, commissioners regained the authority to appoint boards of education, which in turn selected county school superintendents. To ensure reformers' claim on that office, the law gave board members no choice but to fill the position with a "practical teacher." To appoint anyone else, Mebane argued, was to ignore the standards of professionalism that had come to govern much of public life. "Would the physician think of calling on a teacher to examine medical students for license?" he asked. "Would the lawyer of North Carolina call on a school teacher for legal advice? Would the merchant ask the advice and guidance of the teacher in his business transactions?" Of course not. The late nineteenth century was "the age of the specialist . . . the time of the smatterer [was] past."[41]

The new school law introduced even more drastic changes at the neighborhood level. In what reformers heralded as "the most signal advance . . . made during recent years," Mebane's bill did away with neighborhood school districts, consolidating them into larger township units. In each township, control over the common schools passed from as many as thirty district officials to a five-man committee named by the school board. That reduction in the number of local officials marked a victory for bureaucratic management. Many North Carolinians prized the neighborhood school district as an embodiment of "home rule and self-government"; they "loved its exclusiveness, its direct and positive management." But in the end, argued the reformers, "the old district system . . . was not liberty, but chaos . . . democracy gone to seed."[42]

Township committees assumed the authority neighbors had once exercised over the building and location of schoolhouses. Under the new law, committeemen were required to close small schools with low enrollments and irregular attendance and to replace them with larger, centralized facilities averaging no fewer than sixty-five pupils. Mebane realized that consolidation would stir considerable opposition among parents whose children were forced to attend what someone else defined as a "good, strong school." Ultimately, however, the superiority of the township system was "not a debatable question." Addressing a gathering of county officials in 1898, the superintendent donned the mantle of a pedagogical savior. "Does this opposition mean that I have asked you to do something wrong," he exclaimed, "or when your people oppose your own efforts in this work, does this mean that your work is wrong? Most assuredly it does not. The majority of the people opposed Christ and His work while on earth. A great many people oppose the Gospel to-day, but that is not evidence of its being wrong."[43]

Winning the favor of ordinary citizens required "courage, patience and persistence." Mebane combined traditional ideals of neighborliness with a businesslike concern for efficiency, urging parents to "lay aside personal preference and join in hearty cooperation for the greatest good to the greatest number." He promised that the township system would deliver better education to all by standardizing the curriculum, improving teaching, and equalizing school facilities. Instead of arranging individual school terms to suit "relatives and special friends," township committeemen would adopt uniform calendars. Rather than forcing children to master their lessons in widely scattered "huts," the township system would provide "*one good school-house*" serving several neighborhoods. And instead of suffering the incompetence of "$15 teachers," each school would benefit from the work of a "$50 man or woman" capable of doing "more for the school children in four months than under the old system in two or three years."[44]

Those assurances rang hollow to many parents who lost their voice in determining how and by whom their children were taught. Mebane and his allies took offense when mothers and fathers insisted that they knew "just how to teach and just how to manage schools." Under the new school law, such "meddling" became largely ineffective. Township committeemen served broader constituencies than their counterparts in the old district system and were therefore less responsive to the demands of particular neighborhoods. When a township official interviewed prospective teachers, he was more likely to hire the person who was "best prepared for the work, without any thought of whose son or daughter he or she may be, without any special concern of where the teacher comes from."[45]

Mebane's school law further encouraged that attitude by reaching deep into the classroom, establishing new standards of professional conduct. It created a state Board of Examiners responsible for compiling and dis-

tributing a recommended course of professional study along with guidelines for school management. The board also administered the examination for a new lifetime teaching certificate that was similar to the one held
by Normal School alumnae. Together, those measures were designed to
bid up the competition for classroom employment and purge schools of the
"accidental teachers" who sought only temporary or seasonal employment. In a widely circulated broadside, the Board of Examiners made its
message clear: teachers who wished to hold on to their jobs could either
"*study* and keep up . . . or fall out by the way and make room for those who
are progressive." To drive the point home, the new school law abolished the
third-grade teaching certificate, which until 1897 had been available to
anyone who could demonstrate a basic knowledge of reading, spelling, and
"the four rules of arithmetic." That move made it virtually impossible for a
young person to advance directly from the common school classroom to a
teacher's desk and, in turn, severely constrained the dispensing of teaching
jobs as a form of public charity.[46]

A special election called for August 10, 1897, served as a public referen-
dum on Mebane's reforms. Under the new school law, every township in
the state was required to vote on levying a special tax that would raise up to
$1,500 annually to finance the new administrative apparatus and fund
school improvements. As an incentive to adopt the tax, the State Board of
Education promised matching grants of up to $500 a year for three years to
any township that voted in the affirmative. Charles Mebane laid out the
arithmetic. With a minimal increase in the ordinary taxpayer's burden, a
township that operated eight schools could instantly obtain an extra $250 a
year for each facility, enough money to attract a "professional teacher."
Mebane and his allies realized that "all communities are not ready to vote
an increase of tax," but they expected that once a handful had done so,
enthusiasm for the measure would spread "like a blessed contagion from
county to county." For those townships that required special persuasion,
the law required a new election every two years until the school tax was
approved.[47]

Late in the spring, Mebane began to put together a last-minute campaign for the upcoming vote. He created a special committee of well-
known politicians and civic leaders to rouse public opinion and fired off a
volley of letters to the county superintendents, encouraging them to "send

out . . . workers and literature" to "show the people . . . what great things [the tax] will do for them." From across the state, the superintendents replied, asking Mebane to lend them his "biggest speakers—Alderman and McIver." But there was no money to take the issue to the hustings. The legislature refused to fund campaign materials for the local tax election, and the first public donation—an anonymous gift of five dollars—came in only ten days before voters went to the polls.[48]

Unable to canvass the state, supporters of the local tax injected the issue into every public occasion. Charles McIver invited his close friend Walter Hines Page to address the topic at the Normal School commencement in May. Page was born in 1855 in a tiny settlement just eight miles west of Raleigh. The crossroads had no official name, but it appeared on railroad maps as "Page's Station." Although Walter's father owned four slaves in 1860 and listed himself in the census as a farmer, he made his living by distilling turpentine and cutting plentiful pines into lumber. In 1871, Walter studied briefly at Trinity College, where he was disappointed by his fellow students' cavalier attitude toward book-learning. Good grades, he complained to his mother, gave "grounds for suspicion, of being a professor's pet, a boot-lick, or a scoundrel [with] no sense of honor." At the end of the first term, Page transferred to Randolph-Macon College, where he thrived. In 1876, his academic achievements won him one of the first fellowships to the newly established Johns Hopkins University. But by the time Page arrived in Baltimore, he had become impatient with college life. He had taken up the New South creed and was eager to make a place for himself as a reformer and writer. Between 1878 and 1882, Page worked as a journalist in Louisville, St. Louis, and New York. Then, in 1883, he returned to Raleigh, where for just over a year he edited the *State Chronicle*, making the paper into a champion of "education, material development, money making, and hearty living." His homeland's conservatism, however, soon disillusioned him. In 1885, Page moved to New York, where as editor of *Forum*, *Atlantic Monthly*, and *World's Work* he continued to preach the gospel of progress and to introduce northern philanthropists to the New South cause.[49]

Page greeted his audience in Greensboro with a confession of his undiminished devotion to North Carolina, comparing himself to "old-time wanderers" who carried a pot of native earth wherever they roamed. Then he launched into the heart of his message: a call for the state to uplift its common people and for rural and working-class whites to return to the

Walter Hines Page, North Carolina expatriate, outspoken critic of the Old South, and leading advocate of the new education (Courtesy of the North Carolina Division of Archives and History, Raleigh)

Democratic fold. To ensure its future, North Carolina had to cultivate "one undeveloped resource more valuable" than all others, "and that is the people themselves," particularly "forgotten and neglected men." Those citizens were important because they formed society's underpinning. "When you build a house," Page explained, "you make the foundation the strongest part of it, and the house, however ornate its architecture, can be no stronger than its foundation." The same principles governed human civilization. "Its few rich men, or its few cultivated men," did not "really make the community what it is" or determine "the soundness of its social structure, its economic value and its level of life. The security and soundness of the whole body are measured at last by the condition of its weakest part."

In Page's view, both the common schools and ecclesiastical education had failed in the task of proper social development. "In 1890," he told the crowd, "twenty-six per cent of the white persons of the State were unable to read or write. One in four was wholly forgotten." But illiteracy was only the outward sign of a much deeper problem: a "stationary social condition" and a lack of ambition. "The forgotten man," Page exclaimed, "was content to stay forgotten." He not only became "a dead weight" on social progress; he also served as the willing "dupe" of preachers and politicians who opposed every new idea. "What was good enough for his fathers was good enough for him." The "forgotten woman" was even worse off. Page conjured an image of her kind as "thin and wrinkled in youth from ill prepared food, clad without warmth or grace, living in untidy houses, working from daylight till bedtime at the dull round of weary duties, the slaves of men of equal slovenliness, the mothers of joyless children—all uneducated if not illiterate." Unlike her husband or brother, the forgotten woman could not even hope for a better life. "Some *men* who are born under these conditions may escape from them," Page explained. "A *man* may go away, go where life offers opportunities, but the women are forever hopeless." These were the people whom "both the politician and the preacher have failed to lift." Clearly, the time had come "for a wiser statesmanship and a more certain means of grace." For their own sake, North Carolina's "forgotten" whites should rise up, embrace again their Democratic friends, and rally behind the "new educational progress."[50]

Echoes of Page's speech bounced through the state press for weeks. Newspaper editors reprinted his remarks word-for-word, commending it to readers as "the product of an honest heart and an honest brain." But few voters were swayed. While middle-class townspeople heard the ring of truth, many rural folk winced at the discordant sound of condescension mixed with genuine concern. When the ballots were counted, the local-tax proposition went down to defeat. Only twelve townships in nine of the state's ninety-six counties approved supplementary taxation. Less than half of the qualified voters went to the polls, and of those who did, four out of five made the trip to say no to school reform and the new education.[51]

Observers gave a variety of reasons for the local tax's defeat. Charles Lee Coon, a young graded school teacher and county institute conductor, viewed it as yet another expression of North Carolina's backwardness. "Oh, but the *apathy*, that is among us on this question of the schools!" he wrote to Charles McIver. Others blamed dirty politics. Shortly before the election, rumors about the local tax abounded. Some people claimed that it was unconstitutional because the legislative journal contained no record of a vote on the local tax law; others held that the state would be unable to pay its share of the matching funds. In one eastern county, officials tried to conceal the election from the black community and told whites that they were voting on the consolidation of school districts. Apathy, rumors, and trickery—all of these pointed to the same conclusion. The local tax failed because, as one man put it, "so many voters oppose[d] the new order of things."[52]

The loss might have been softened had the school reformers' Democratic allies not abandoned the cause. But the Democrats were looking ahead to the election of 1898, plotting a strategy for recapturing the legislature and breaking the back of the Populist-Republican insurgency. Targeting Fusion's weakest link, they began laying plans for a campaign that would subordinate every issue to the volatile question of white supremacy. Black-white cooperation under Fusion had always represented an uneasy alliance. After the turmoil of 1896, neither the Populists nor the Republicans had the wherewithal to fend off a direct racial attack.

Josephus Daniels, editor of the *Raleigh News and Observer* and an old classmate of the graded school men, apologized to Charles McIver for giving the local tax only half-hearted support. "I am unwilling to go any further in the matter of the local tax than I have gone," he wrote to his friend. "The only hope for public education in North Carolina is in restoring the state into the hands of the white people." In Daniels's view, it seemed best to let opponents of the new education defeat the tax and then present the loss as a vote against the handful of black county commissioners and school officials who had come to power under Fusion. Regardless of the reformers' efforts, the tax would be approved "in very few places." When "it is voted down," Daniels argued, "it is much better for the cause for those of us who believe in education to show that the people voted against it because of the character of the public officers than because they do not believe in being taxed for education."[53]

By the fall of 1898, Daniels and the Democrats had fanned the fires of racial hatred with charges of "negro rule." Furnifold Simmons, chairman of the Democratic Party's executive committee, set the tone for the cam-

Furnifold Simmons, state chairman of the Democratic Party and architect of the white supremacy campaigns of 1898 and 1900 (Courtesy of the North Carolina Division of Archives and History, Raleigh)

paign with his "Appeal to the Voters of North Carolina." Beseeching them to "restore the state to the white people," he portrayed a handful of black officials as an army of racial domination: "NEGRO CONGRESSMEN, NEGRO SOLICITORS, NEGRO REVENUE OFFICERS, NEGRO COLLECTORS OF CUSTOMS, NEGROES in charge of white institutions . . . NEGROES holding inquests over white dead. NEGROES controlling the finances of great cities, NEGROES in control of the sanitation and police of cities, NEGRO CONSTABLES arresting white women and men, NEGRO MAGISTRATES trying white women and white men." Simmons took special offense at the small number of blacks who won seats on Mebane's new township school committees, insisting that they exercised "authority over white . . . schools." The charge was pure demagoguery. No township committee contained more than a single black officer, and, as one parent pointed out, the dismantling of the old district committees actually reduced black participation in school affairs. In his view, Mebane's school law "might have been entitled an act to take from the colored people the control of their public schools." But Simmons cared more for appearances than reality. He closed his broadside with a promise to "crush the party of negro domination beneath a majority so overwhelming that no other party will ever again dare to establish negro rule."[54]

Racism was a potent political weapon, but it alone could not ensure a Democratic victory. Recognizing that fact, Simmons and other party leaders turned to brutality and fraud. They organized White-Government Unions throughout the state, and in heavily black counties in the east and along the South Carolina border, they encouraged the party faithful to strip down to their red undershirts, the late-nineteenth-century equivalent of the white-hooded robes worn by the Ku Klux Klan during Reconstruction. According to historian J. G. de Roulhac Hamilton, an ardent defender of white supremacy, the "Red Shirts" were not poor whites acting on a need to assert their superiority over black neighbors; rather, they were leading citizens of the New South, "respectable and well-to-do farmers, bankers, school teachers, and merchants." In Wilmington, elite Democrats considered victory worth any price. Under the guidance of former congressman Alfred Moore Waddell, they rioted against the city's Republican aldermen, leaving between eleven and thirty black citizens dead.[55]

Democrats won the 1898 election by only 52.8 percent of the vote, but that was enough to oust the Fusionists from the legislature. The victors moved immediately to silence black and white dissenters. Under a new election law, the reforms of 1895 were rescinded; all voters were required to re-register before Democratic precinct officials, and the date for state elections was moved from November to August to avoid possible federal enforcement of voting rights. Democratic lawmakers also restructured county government. The changes were complex and varied from one county to the next, depending on local Republican and Populist strength. The number of commissioners in some counties was increased to dilute Fusion majorities, while in others the office was once again made appointive. In addition, county boards of education were renamed boards of school directors. The legislature appointed new school officials for each county and empowered them to take office immediately, but many Fusionist boards refused to relinquish their authority. Until December 1900, when the law required that the new directors stand for election, administration of the state's schools was in chaos. In many cases, county treasurers ended up arbitrating local disputes. The school board of the treasurer's own political persuasion got paid; the opposing board did not.[56]

The Democrats came to power promising not to adopt measures that would disfranchise illiterate black and white voters, as their counterparts in Mississippi, South Carolina, and Louisiana had done. But disfranchisement was the surest means of destroying "once and forever" the coalition of blacks and disaffected white farmers that had challenged the direction of New South development. According to the *Charlotte Observer*, it would ensure that poor whites who had been "saved again by the Democratic Party" would "stay with it hereafter" and not "run off after Farmers' Alliances and populism." As soon as the election was over, Furnifold Simmons and the party bosses sent Josephus Daniels out to study disfranchisement measures in other southern states and bring back recommendations for North Carolina.[57]

Disfranchisement also appealed to the advocates of school reform. For several years, Charles McIver had been privately talking up the idea of an educational requirement for voting. He viewed it as "the mildest form of compulsory education," a move that would force reluctant parents to support the new education. "I recommend," he wrote in an unpublished essay, "that the State enact into law that no man coming to the age of 21 after the year 1905 shall be permitted to vote in North Carolina if he cannot read & write from dictation the Constitution of the State and of the United States." Such a law would make parents understand "that if they do not send their children to public schools . . . they themselves are disfranchising their own offspring." And as an added benefit, it would increase "the number of people feeling a personal interest in the public schools," causing great "improvements in our entire school system."[58]

People who knew McIver well were probably not surprised that his good friend Francis D. Winston, a younger brother of university president George Winston, became the "chief engineer" of disfranchisement in North Carolina. Together with George Rountree, a leader of the Wilmington uprising and chairman of the Constitutional Amendments Committee in the state house, Winston won legislative approval to put a suffrage amendment on the ballot in 1900. Like the measure outlined by McIver, it required that anyone seeking to vote first pass a literacy test administered by precinct officials, who would almost certainly be Democratic loyalists. The only difference between the two proposals was that Winston's bill extended the "grandfather clause" to 1908. Under that provision, anyone whose father or grandfather was entitled to vote on or before January 1, 1867—the date Congress made its first effort to extend the franchise to freedmen—could continue to exercise that right so long as he registered before December 1, 1908. The grandfather clause was designed to reassure poor whites who feared that the Democrats intended to close the polls to them as well as blacks. As many former Populists pointed out, however, the gesture gave little comfort. The broad discretionary powers handed to registrars under the Democrats' new election law provided numerous other means of turning away "disloyal" white voters.[59]

The 1899 legislature also adopted North Carolina's first significant Jim Crow law—a measure requiring separate seating on trains and steamboats. Its aim was to discourage interracial cooperation by setting blacks apart as a pariah caste, a goal that white supremacist rhetoric alone had failed to achieve. Furnifold Simmons admitted as much, indicating that without some sort of legal compulsion, "the white people will not always stand together and vote together." Along with disfranchisement, segregation would erect a nearly insurmountable wall between the blacks and poor whites who had risen up to challenge Democratic power.[60]

In 1900, gubernatorial candidate Charles Brantley Aycock built his campaign around disfranchisement, education, and economic development. Aycock hailed from Goldsboro, home of one of the state's first graded schools, and had been a university classmate of Alderman, McIver, Joyner, and Daniels. Outlining a new "era of good feeling," he promised white voters an end to violence at the polls and an education that would not only qualify their children to vote but would also make them full partners in the New South. The hour's need, Aycock declared, was "to form a genuine white man's party":

Then we shall have no more revolutions in Wilmington; we shall have no more dead and wounded negroes on the streets, because we shall have good government in the State, and peace everywhere. . . . Life and property and liberty from the mountains to the sea shall rest secure in the guardianship of the law. But to do this, we must disfranchise the negro. This movement comes from the people. . . . To do so is both desirable and necessary—desirable because it sets the white man free to move along faster than he can go when retarded by the slower movement of the negro—necessary because we must have good order and peace while we work out the industrial, commercial, intellectual and moral development of the State. . . . In coming together for the common good we shall forget the asperities of the past, and shall go forward into the twentieth century a united people, striving in zeal for the . . . upbuilding of the State.

In the end, Aycock argued, white supremacy and the new education offered more certain rewards than political insurgency.[61]

That appeal apparently convinced many voters. Weary of years of conflict, in which "the sound of the pistol was more frequent than the song of the mocking-bird," they must have longed for an end to the killing and intimidation. "We have ruled by force, we can rule by fraud, but we want to rule by law," Aycock assured a restless crowd in Snow Hill. For those who still harbored doubts about supporting a Democratic candidate, however, the Red Shirts provided a familiar brand of persuasion. On election eve, Alfred Moore Waddell encouraged a rowdy crowd in Wilmington to "go to the polls tomorrow and if you find the Negro out voting, tell him to leave the polls and if he refuses, kill him, shoot him down in his tracks." The tattered remnants of the Populist and Republican opposition could hardly counter such tactics. With a turnout of nearly 75 percent of the qualified voters, Aycock and disfranchisement won by a 59 to 41 percent margin.[62]

The graded school men greeted Aycock's victory with both jubilation and a keen awareness of the challenges that lay ahead. They rejoiced that disfranchisement had at last removed African Americans from politics; no longer would they confront what Democrats described as "multitudes of ignorant voters controlled by a few wicked demagogues." But the "negro problem" and its potential for social disruption remained. Although they offered no apologies for the resort to terror, the graded school men worried over the events that they had helped to set in motion. Even Charles Aycock conceded that the campaign for white supremacy might have gone "too

Charles Brantley Aycock, elected governor in 1900 on a school reform and white supremacy platform (Courtesy of the North Carolina Division of Archives and History, Raleigh)

far" in unleashing forces that could easily spin out of control. "It is a glorious victory we have won," he exclaimed, "and the extent of it frightens me." What alarmed Aycock and others was the fact that many whites seemed to move far too easily "from the contention that no negro shall vote, to the contention that no negro shall learn, that no negro shall labor, and (by implication) that no negro shall live." Such reasoning offered a certain prescription for race war. By contrast, promoters of the new education insisted that North Carolina's true need was for a more flexible, adaptable system of race relations, one that would discipline behavior on both sides of the color bar. "Let the Negro learn . . . that there is unending separation of the races," Aycock pleaded; "let the white man determine that no man shall by act or thought or speech cross this line, and the race problem will be at an end." Such a "peace," grounded in civility and accommodation rather than violence and fanaticism, seemed, in the new governor's view, to hold out the only hope for continued economic development and regional progress.[63]

The graded school men also worried over what many in the South described as the "other half of the race peril." Although Populism had been crushed, the countryside still harbored vast numbers of "untrained" whites, men and women who were perhaps attracted to the material rewards of the New South but who remained wary of the notions of power, self, and authority on which that world rested. With his usual flair for drama, Walter Hines Page proposed a solution. "In an ideal economic state," he mused, "we should kill every untrained man; for he is in the way. He is a burden, and he brings down the level of the economic efficiency of the whole community." Such ruthlessness was, by Page's own admission, impractical, but it did point to what the graded school men perceived as a serious problem of social development. Reform-minded observers across the South complained that a majority of rural whites still lived in conditions of "ignorance, poverty, and irresponsibility"; they had not yet been raised "to a safe level of civilization." Efforts to reclaim adults proved futile, "for the grown folks [were] usually past saving." But children were another matter altogether. With proper instruction, they could be made into "the right kind of revolutionists." Only in the lives of children, explained Edwin Alderman, could North Carolina find its redemption. For that reason, an enlightened social policy would spare no effort in making "out of them, for their own sake and for the State's sake, everything that can be made."[64]

The work of the new century seemed clear. In the years to come, the graded school men would wage yet another campaign to win hearts and minds, this time among blacks and whites alike. As always, they stood firm in their conviction that schooling held the keys to a new age of "material prosperity and social quiet." "The right training of all the people," Walter Hines Page predicted, "would come pretty close to ending all our troubles—to removing our difficulties, economic, political, and ethnological." The reformers' task was daunting, but few among them doubted the certainty of success. "The world lies before us," Page crowed to an associate. "It'll not be the same world when we get done with it. . . . [You may] bet your last penny on that!" Even friends with no taste for gambling knew better than to decline the wager.[65]

Rubes and Redeemers

The people must be given a new spirit, a new way
of thinking and doing . . . in order to save the rural
part of the country. And we must look to our educational system to give [them] these.

—George S. Dickerman, *Proceedings of the Third
Capon Springs Conference*, 1900

When Charles Aycock took office in January 1901,
he had great promises to keep and only limited
resources with which to pursue them. In his inaugural address, the new
governor reminded fellow Democrats of the bargain that they had made
with the state's "poor and unlettered" white voters. Many of those men had
cast their ballots for "the Democracy" and black disfranchisement in exchange for assurances that their children would be given an education and
new opportunities in life. Now the time had come to deliver on that "most
solemn of all . . . pledges." "Let [the countryside] be bright with the shining of ten thousand lights emanating from as many schools," Aycock exclaimed. "Our industries will be benefitted; our commerce will expand . . .
when we shall have educated all the children of the State." Graded school
men applauded the governor's rhetoric, but in private they doubted their
old classmate's ability to turn words into action.[1]

Aycock faced resistance and foot-dragging at every turn. Business leaders and wealthy landowners objected to the taxes necessary to build new
schoolhouses, and many influential Democrats—perhaps the majority—
were only lukewarm in their commitment to improved education. The
governor's troubles had in fact been apparent since the outset of his cam-

143

paign. When the time came to choose a candidate for the office of state superintendent of public instruction, Furnifold Simmons and party strategists passed over Charles McIver, James Joyner, and the entire generation of young school crusaders. Instead, they named Thomas Fentress Toon, a devout Baptist and one-time teacher whose chief qualification was his service as a brigadier general in the Confederate army. Certain of a tight election, Simmons and his lieutenants had no intention of alienating county loyalists whose hold on power depended in part on their ability to dispense favors in the form of teaching jobs and redrawn district lines. The message of Toon's selection was clear. For the time being, control over schoolhouse matters would remain firmly in what reformers called the *"galling grasp"* of courthouse rings.[2]

The young governor and his elderly superintendent spent their first year in office repeating the Democratic campaign promise that no white child would be denied an education and thus subjected to disfranchisement. Their speeches, however, were largely ineffective. Members of the new legislature answered calls to show what they had done for education by pointing to a bill that required observance of a four-month term in every school district. But when railroad interests refused to pay the taxes that would have helped to fund the measure, even Aycock found himself cornered by the realities of political life. He and his council of state had little choice but to make quick concessions; after all, the railroads had been major contributors to the Democratic Party's war chest during the campaigns of 1898 and 1900. Lawmakers also bragged of the appointment of a state "Educational Agitator." His job was to hold five rallies a week, opening each by "singing as loud" as he could North Carolina's anthem, "The Old North State." If he should "at any time become luke-warm or cease to agitate with full force," a legislative spokesman proclaimed, "he shall be arrested, brought before the State Board of Education and there be dealt with as they may direct." Many lawmakers found great satisfaction in that sort of posturing. Indeed, John Wilber Jenkins, a Democratic representative from Granville County, offered it to the public as ample proof that he and his fellows had "done [their] duty."[3]

Such antics raised a storm of protest among disappointed voters across the state. "You promised us a four-months term," they scolded, but the money to fulfill that commitment was "neither in hand nor in sight." "Where lies the fault?" newspaper editors demanded, "who is to blame?" Government inaction also reaffirmed the graded school men's distaste for electoral politics. The moment was ripe for consolidation of North Carolina's classroom revolution, yet lawmakers and politicians could be trusted only to perpetuate the forces of localism. Once again, advocates of the new education took matters into their own hands. During the early years of Aycock's administration, they broadened their existing ties to reform-minded, middle-class white women and reached out beyond the borders of the state to make new contacts with northern businessmen and philanthropists. Politicians, the reformers charged, had failed to cultivate the New South dream; now they would mount a "seed sowing campaign" of their own.[4]

At first sight, the alliance that sprang from those efforts seemed quite improbable, but it actually drew its strength from a remarkable affinity of interests. The reformers' appeals to educational efficiency and expert management echoed the principles of businessmen who were reorganizing vast sectors of the American economy along corporate lines. The new education also seemed to offer a way of integrating the South into a national market that was rapidly swallowing up regional distinctions. "The South with its varied resources and products," one northern observer explained, "has immense industrial potentialities, and its prosperous future will be assured with the right kind of [schooling]."[5]

For women, the new educational alliance presented enticements of similar consequence. Like the teachers who had entered the classroom before them, female school activists of the early twentieth century recognized in the reform movement an unprecedented opportunity to take part in public life. Women who were denied formal authority in the exclusively male world of politics learned to wield considerable influence by making their responsibilities for child-rearing the basis of social policy. Indeed, the new education owed its final triumph to a convergence of male and female reform cultures, both of which were born of a rejection of nineteenth-century partisanship and patronage politics.[6]

Southern school reformers and northern philanthropists first met at the Conference for Education in the South. Begun in 1898 at Capon Springs, West Virginia, the gathering had its roots in the freedmen's aid societies founded during Reconstruction by white churchmen from the North. The first conference appealed primarily to religious leaders interested in church-supported higher education for blacks and poor relief among the white inhabitants of Appalachia. But under the influence of Robert Curtis Ogden, a New York retail merchant and associate of department store magnate John Wanamaker, that missionary agenda quickly gave way to a more calculating attitude toward southern educational and economic development. Ogden represented a generation of reformers—in both the North and the South—who had little patience for the radical humanitarianism of an earlier era. They longed instead for regional reconciliation and the South's inclusion in a burgeoning national economy. "As I see the situation confronting those who wish to do something for the South," one of Ogden's associates explained, "the work must be thorough-going, because we wish gradually to change . . . an outworn system of society. To work effectively it is necessary not merely to give the children of the South an acquaintance with a certain body of knowledge, which we call an 'education,' but to beget in them a national mind [and] a progressive energy, in a word, complete reintegration with the world-forces from which [they] have so long been isolated." Southern thought needed to be "nationalized; [southern] life to be industrialized, and the whole process was one of education."[7]

In 1900, conference participants resolved to carry that message to a broader audience by convening "in more central places." Over the next fifteen years, they traveled to every corner of the South, meeting in a different city each spring. The 1901 gathering took place in Winston, North Carolina, at the invitation of Henry E. Fries, a local industrialist, and William A. Blair, editor of the *Schoolteacher*, a widely circulated journal committed to educational reform. In an effort to draw attention to the conference, Ogden invited more than seventy special guests from the North to accompany him on a lavish private train hired at a daily cost of more than $2,500. The passengers included the southern reformers' old friend Walter Hines Page; William H. Baldwin Jr., president of the Long Island Railroad and one-time manager of the Southern Railway; Lyman Abbott, editor of the *Outlook*, a magazine of liberal reform; George Foster Peabody, a Georgia-born investment banker from New York; Albert Shaw, publisher of the *Review of Reviews*; and John D. Rockefeller Jr., heir to the elder Rockefeller's oil and transportation empire. The travelers received an enthusiastic welcome from Governor Aycock, Charles McIver, and Josephus Daniels, along with a host of county and city superintendents, teachers, and Normal School students. Ogden and his guests also enjoyed the hospitality of Winston residents, who arranged private tours to show off the

On April 18, 1901, Robert Curtis Ogden's private train, on its way to Winston, stopped in Greensboro to be greeted by students from the Normal School and to take Charles and Lula McIver on board. (Courtesy of the University Archives, University of North Carolina at Greensboro)

tobacco factories and cotton mills that bore witness to their community's New South spirit.[8]

Charles William Dabney, a former professor of chemistry at Chapel Hill and president of the University of Tennessee, opened the meeting with a bleak statistical portrait of southern education. "Dr. Dabney's position was not pessimistic; it was simply business-like," Albert Shaw recalled. "Like the skillful surgeon, he laid bare the difficult and distressing situation, not to pronounce it hopeless, but as the necessary preliminary to remedial measures." Dabney used specially prepared charts to demonstrate "the wretched condition of the public schools—shacks for schoolhouses; young, untrained, and indifferent teachers[;] . . . school terms of from three to five months." The performance was calculated to prod the conference away from abstract discussion toward some concrete plan of action.[9]

Dabney closed his speech with a call for the union of northern beneficence and southern self-help in a coordinated, regionwide campaign for "better public schools." His associates embraced the idea at once. They ordered a committee led by Charles McIver to turn the proposal into a detailed public relations strategy. Two days later, the conferees endorsed the panel's recommendations: they voted to appoint from within their ranks a new executive body known as the Southern Education Board (SEB) and to establish a Bureau of Information and Investigation in Knoxville, Tennessee, under Dabney's direction. Philander Priestley Claxton, former superintendent of the Asheville graded schools and a member of McIver's faculty at the Normal School, served as research chief, assisted by Joseph DuPuy Eggleston, who had replaced Claxton after his move from Asheville to Greensboro. When Eggleston left the bureau in 1903 to take charge of the schools in Virginia's Prince Edward County, Charles Lee Coon, superintendent of the Salisbury graded schools, assumed his responsibilities as secretary and editor. The bureau's staff undertook the monumental task of documenting educational conditions in each of the southern states. They prepared detailed county-by-county reports and outlines of model school legislation, which the SEB, operating as "a central propaganda . . . agency," used to lobby for reform. The board spread word of the bureau's findings and of schoolhouse needs through newspaper and magazine articles, broadsides, and personal correspondence with businessmen, educators, and church leaders.[10]

From the outset, northern board members made it clear that they had no desire to challenge the racial views of their southern co-workers. Ogden announced to the Winston assemblage that "while we were [initially] interested in the South through Negro education, our impulses have risen . . . to the question of the entire burden of educational responsibility." Unlike the churchmen who pioneered educational opportunities for blacks after the Civil War, he and other industrial philanthropists had little interest in issues of political and economic equality. As a trustee of both the Hampton Institute in Virginia and its most important offspring, Booker T. Washington's Tuskegee Institute in Alabama, Ogden had become involved in black schooling out of a desire to make southern society more efficient, not more democratic. William Baldwin, another Hampton and Tuskegee trustee, explained that both institutes operated on the assumption that freedmen and their descendants would "willingly fill the more menial positions, and do the heavy work, at less wages." While missionary colleges offered liberal arts courses and preparation for the professions, Hampton and Tuskegee followed a vocational curriculum designed to raise up a new generation of hard-working farmers, laundresses, and tradesmen.[11] That approach to black education made it easy for Ogden and Baldwin to accept the southern argument that white school improvement should be their first priority. "The white people are to be the leaders, to take the initiative, to have the directive control in all matters pertaining to civilization and the highest interests of our beloved land," proclaimed J. L. M. Curry, a former Confederate general and longtime proponent of the new education. "This white supremacy does not mean hostility to the Negro, but friendship to him."[12]

Other members of the northern entourage were equally quick to endorse their hosts' racial mores. The trip to Winston gave the Reverend Dr.

Charles H. Parkhurst, Ogden's pastor and a leading New York moral reformer, his first glimpse of black life in the South. He was moved to tears by the poverty and suffering he witnessed when Dabney took him to visit the city's black inhabitants at their jobs in the tobacco factories and in their homes, schools, and churches. But rather than exciting Parkhurst's moral sensibilities, the experience convinced him of the wisdom of disfranchisement and segregation. "I never had a right conception of the southern Negroes before," he reported. "This visit changes my whole view. . . . Now I see that the southern people know far better than I how to train and prepare them for American citizenship. I understand now why they should never have been made full citizens before they were trained."

Parkhurst's sentiments reflected a broadening national acceptance of white southern attitudes. Faced with the challenge of assimilating a growing population of Eastern European immigrants, and eager for dominion over foreign territories recently acquired in the Spanish-American War, white northerners displayed a new tolerance for their kinsmen's prejudices. Upon his return from Winston, Lyman Abbott shared what he had learned in the South. Future prosperity and social stability, he advised readers of the *New York World*, depended on getting "rid of our more or less vague ideas that all men are created free and equal and that every man has an equal right to stand where everybody [else] does."[13]

The graded school men and their allies greeted such pronouncements with a feeling of vindication. Since Reconstruction, they had watched jealously as private black colleges became—to their way of seeing—"inexhaustible mines" of charitable giving. Now the tables had been turned. "Thus far the color of [northern] fortunes & riches has been *black*," exclaimed Robert Bingham, a leading Democrat and headmaster of a private academy near the university at Chapel Hill. "The Ethiopian cannot change his skin, but the Yankee has changed *his* color & the winnings are *ours*." Bingham advised Charles McIver to "work the awakened Yankee conscience for every cent it is worth. . . . [Y]ou are our Mogul Engine along this line. . . . We must be making progress if we can get a [Yankee] to admit that *we* are right in any thing & that *he* is wrong in any thing. And if we can make enough of them think this we can get all the money we need, tho' we shall never get what they really *owe* us."[14]

The SEB opened its Knoxville office with a guarantee of $40,000 a year for two years from George Foster Peabody. But vastly larger amounts were soon forthcoming from John D. Rockefeller Sr. Rockefeller's son John Jr.

considered his trip to Winston "one of the most outstanding events of my life." Impressed by the SEB's objectives, he returned home to discuss the issue of southern school improvement with his father and two of the family's trusted advisers, the Reverends Frederick Taylor Gates and Wallace Buttrick. In January, the four men drew up an outline for one of the largest of the Rockefellers' many philanthropic ventures, and in February, John Jr. announced the formal chartering of the General Education Board (GEB), financed by an initial gift of $1 million. The board's purpose, the younger Rockefeller explained, was to systematize educational philanthropy throughout the nation, with a special emphasis on developing a "comprehensive educational policy" in the South. Over the next two decades, his father contributed an additional $128 million to that cause.[15]

The General Education Board practiced what its directors described as "scientific philanthropy." By the 1890s, the elder Rockefeller had begun to grow weary of "the haphazard fashion of giving here and there as appeals presented themselves." That approach to beneficence, he wrote, drove him "almost to a nervous break-down" as he tried to grapple with the hundreds of pleas for assistance that crossed his desk. Even worse, a system of "distribution by chance" provided no way of gauging the value of his kindness. Rockefeller created the GEB and a number of other foundations to remedy those problems by shaping his fortune into purposeful programs, directing it along the same "distinct lines of progress" that guided his business affairs. Rather than indulging in "superficial remedies, palliatives, [and] artificial reliefs," the Rockefeller charities employed statistics and the research methods of the new social sciences to identify "underlying causes [of] 'backwardness'" and to plan investment programs that would yield broad structural changes. In the case of public education, the GEB's mission was to rationalize schooling under the supervision of expert managers in the same way that Rockefeller had reorganized production in the oil industry. The board was to operate as a mighty social engine, "rehabilitating the South" by promoting its absorption into "the great stream of modern life."[16]

Rockefeller ensured cooperation between the GEB and the SEB by choosing seven of his directors from the southern board. North Carolinians Walter Hines Page and Edwin Alderman, for example, divided their time between the two agencies. Rockefeller also included administrators of the George Peabody and John F. Slater Funds, forming a powerful "community of interests" among the other influential charities active in southern school reform. "The purpose of this association," a press release explained, "is to provide a vehicle through which capitalists of the North who sincerely desire to assist in the great work of Southern education may act with assurance that their money will be wisely used." Backed by such potent resources, the SEB and GEB quickly established themselves as the arbiters of educational policy throughout the region, deftly shaping the actions of state lawmakers and local school officials. "The Southern Conference and Board were the propaganda agents," Charles Dabney later recalled with the joy of a proud parent, while members of "the General Board" served as "constructive workers in the field," busily establishing model programs in school supervision, teacher training, curriculum design, and student health.[17]

The two boards chose to begin their work in North Carolina because of the state's reputation for regional leadership in school reform. Late in 1901, the SEB appropriated $5,000 annually for two years to support a "vigorous educational campaign" under the direction of Governor Aycock, state superintendent Toon, and Charles McIver. The three men invited leading advocates of the new education to an organizational conference in Raleigh "to discuss the best methods by which the rural schools can be strengthened." Gathered in the governor's office on February 13, 1902, the reformers dubbed themselves the Central Campaign Committee for the Promotion of Public Education and devised a strategy for convincing county leaders to consolidate small school districts, levy supplemental school taxes, and repair or replace dilapidated schoolhouses.[18]

The committee opened its campaign with a public "Declaration against Illiteracy." Citing statistics collected by the U.S. commissioner of education, the document sought to "arouse [state] pride and . . . patriotism" by revealing North Carolina's poor showing on the national stage. The country's average per capita expenditure for education was $2.83 a year, more than four times the $0.67 spent in the reformers' home state. When calculated as annual funding per school-aged child, those figures translated into "$3 or $4" for white North Carolina students, compared to $20.29 for their counterparts throughout the rest of the nation. "We believe the future will hold us responsible for perpetuating these unfavorable conditions," the committee exclaimed, "and, therefore, we conceive it to be the patriotic, moral and religious duty of this generation . . . to find the means by which all our children can receive . . . more efficient training for the duties of life." The declaration closed with an appeal for "men and women, who love their

State . . . to band themselves together . . . aided by the Southern Education Board, to carry forward the work of local taxation and better schools."[19]

While most of the state's newspapers applauded the declaration, Josiah Bailey tried to fan the dying embers of opposition. He attacked the educators who met in Raleigh, snarling, "We shall not be surprised if they 'meet' in behalf of the free schools and 'scheme' in behalf of themselves." The public school campaign, the *Biblical Recorder* charged, was "wholly in the hands of a clique, a very small clique," serving as "a mere base of operations for Messrs. McIver and Dabney." The paper insisted that Dabney wanted to make himself the educational spokesman for the entire South, while McIver had his eye on the state superintendency. Worse still, the two men aimed to purge schooling of all denominational influences and to deliver a death blow to the particularistic structures of neighborhood life. "If we wish our children to be . . . Baptists from conviction, and Baptists of power, we must educate them," the *Recorder* exclaimed in a last-ditch effort to rally the faithful. "There rests upon us a responsibility that we can neither evade nor transfer to the state." But local Baptist associations had in fact already begun to surrender that responsibility by withdrawing from public school battles and selling or giving their privately held school facilities to county boards of education. Church leaders who felt embarrassed by Bailey's vitriol forced him to issue a formal apology. Chastened but not silenced, the editor turned his attention away from schoolhouse issues toward a career in politics and the battle for prohibition.[20]

On February 19, less than one week after the Central Campaign Committee was organized, Superintendent Toon died. Governor Aycock turned immediately to his old college classmate James Joyner to fill the post. When Alderman left the Normal School for the university in 1893, Joyner had resigned his position as superintendent of the Goldsboro graded schools to take Alderman's place as professor of English and dean of the faculty. He was reluctant to give up that job for the state superintendency, citing a cut in pay and the future uncertainties of political life. But Joyner's friends convinced him to make the move for strategic reasons: he would become the first professional educator ever to occupy the office.[21]

Once in Raleigh, Joyner moved quickly to change the public perception of the superintendency as a political sinecure. He courted the press and sought to surround himself with other young men who had made education their life's work. With money from the SEB, Joyner appointed Eugene

Clyde Brooks, the thirty-year-old administrator of the Monroe graded schools, to serve as secretary of the Central Campaign Committee and charged him with putting the committee's work on a sound professional footing. Brooks coordinated an effort to place educational essays in each of the state's newspapers, wrote letters to clergymen requesting that they preach a sermon on improved schooling at least once a year, and secured speakers for a series of educational rallies during the spring and summer months.[22]

The first rally, held in Greensboro on April 3 and 4, brought heartening results. A local merchant challenged the crowd to raise a fund to aid surrounding rural districts that voted a supplemental tax to improve their schools. "It is high time that we, the business men, come to their aid," he declared. "If you and I take one hundred or one thousand dollars from our surplus funds for this cause, what does it mean to us. Simply that we have reduced our incomes a little by the loss of interest on the amount given. . . . But what does it mean to the State. It means that for every school house built in a needy district, sixty or eighty children have been given an opportunity to escape from the bondage of ignorance and to become intelligent, well trained . . . workers for her future development." The merchant then presented a letter from the GEB, which had just opened its office in Washington, D.C.; in this letter, the board promised to match the money raised by Greensboro residents up to a maximum of $4,000. His audience cheered with delight. Officials of the city's new street railway pledged half of the receipts from car fare on the company's opening day. The mayor made a contribution of $125, and citizens lined up one by one to add their five- and ten-dollar donations until the entire $4,000 had been collected.[23]

One month later, a rally in Charlotte that was led by a member of the city's Board of Trade raised an even larger fund of $6,000, which the GEB again matched. An anonymous "friend" of education gave $2,000, and an enterprising merchant, eager to help the schools and to cash in on the excitement, promised a percentage of his profits from a special "educational sale." Two-thirds of the money was divided among rural districts near Charlotte, while the remainder was given to poor mountain schools in Henderson County, located one hundred miles west. As news of the Greensboro and Charlotte rallies spread, civic leaders in Oxford, Washington, Hickory, Fayetteville, and Goldsboro wrote to the state superintendent requesting that similar events be staged in their towns.[24]

Such success was to be expected in the state's urban areas. After all, Greensboro was home to the Normal School, and like Charlotte and other towns, it had shown a long-standing enthusiasm for the new education. But old ways persisted in the countryside. After surveying the state for the Central Campaign Committee, Charles McIver reported that rural schools remained captive to the male world of courthouse politics, where teaching jobs were traded as personal favors and where decisions about school funding and location reflected the reputation, family connections, and economic clout of powerful individuals. "Men largely have the exclusive management of school houses," McIver complained, "and the marks of masculinity and neglect are plainly visible."[25]

The young crusader once again turned to white middle-class women for a cure. Beginning in the early 1880s, dozens of female voluntary societies and social service organizations had sprung up across the state. They drew their membership primarily from the same generation of New South women that had lobbied for the Normal School and had begun to take command of the classroom. McIver praised the club women's civic-mindedness but warned that their energies could easily be misdirected. "We have Daughters of the Revolution and Daughters of the Confederacy and daughters of everything in the past," he scolded an audience in eastern North Carolina, "but it is time for the daughters of somebody to make it their mission to take care of the future. Shining in the social functions the 'daughters' do so revel in, may look well in the newspapers, but it is not worth a copper cent to humanity." Rallying behind the cause of education, McIver concluded, would best serve women's aspirations and the needs of the state. "It is to the interest of all of us," he explained, "that their great tact, enthusiasm and power should not exhaust itself upon chimerical schemes and foolish crusades as has often been the case . . . [with] women of the noblest impulses."[26]

McIver appeared before a gathering of more than two hundred Normal School students and interested townspeople on March 20, 1902, to share his conviction "that the present hard conditions as to schoolhouses . . . can be remedied, and that they can be remedied best by women." He implored his audience to take up the work of school improvement with the same energy they devoted to keeping their homes and churches "neat and attractive." "I appeal to mothers of little children in behalf of the children of all women," McIver roared.

I appeal to those who in every great battle against a powerful enemy have furnished enthusiasm and courage to your husbands and sweethearts and sons and fathers, and nerved them for struggle. . . . [I]f five or ten women around each public school house will organize themselves into a voluntary association to visit that school house, to co-operate with the teacher and see that the yard is swept, that a tree or a flower is planted here and there, and that occasionally an inspiring picture be placed upon the walls, it will not be long before there will be a revolution in the character of the school houses men will erect for their children, and the ability of teachers they will employ to teach their children.

Though such educational "housekeeping" may seem tame as a revolutionary act, it nonetheless inspired McIver's audience. After his speech, they founded the Woman's Association for the Betterment of Public School Houses (WABPS) and urged the press to spread word of their organization across North Carolina.[27]

With permission from the state Board of Education, the Teachers Assembly sponsored the association's first annual conference in June 1902 for the purpose of launching a membership drive. During the meeting, ten of McIver's students volunteered to stump the state and organize local auxiliaries. They spent the summer lecturing at church socials, community picnics, and small gatherings in private homes. Their labor brought in a bountiful harvest, particularly from urban areas. The young women recruited more than two thousand members by September 1902, and over the next four years they established branch associations in seventy of the state's ninety-seven counties. Never before, except through the church, had so many white North Carolina women been brought together in a single organization.[28]

From the outset, leaders of the WABPS employed well-worn images of women as housekeepers, guardians of virtue, and counselors of youth to justify their involvement in school affairs. Elvira Evelyna Moffitt, president of the Wake County chapter, explained that she and her co-workers meant not to "invade the kingdom of men" but only to assist local school committees. Fathers, she argued, were unfamiliar with the basic elements of childrearing because they worked away from home and left their wives to take charge of the children. As a result, male school officials often became so involved in "larger undertakings"—such as hiring teachers and managing budgets—that they lost sight of the " 'little things' that in reality make the sum and substance of educational success." Association women desired to remedy that neglect by using their domestic skills to make schoolhouses into "school homes."[29]

Behind the rhetoric of womanly self-sacrifice, however, lurked an unprecedented claim to social authority. That blend of old and new values shaped the association's constitution. Women who joined the WABPS paid no dues but were expected to participate regularly in school-improvement projects and to vote in the annual election of officers. Men, on the other hand, paid one dollar a year to join as "associate members" with no voting privileges. The WABPS requested that its male patrons limit their services to the provision of money and manual labor. As Sue Hollowell, a state officer, explained to a gathering of philanthropists, educational leaders, and politicians, the organization was "purely feminine." "We allow the men to pay the money to carry on this work," she boasted. "We do not pay one cent, but every man that becomes an associate member gives one dollar and then he does the work we ask him to do. When we come to our election of [officers] . . . we never let him vote. The women do all the voting in this Association and the men pay all the money—taxation without representation, if you please." Perhaps Hollowell felt that a touch of humor was necessary to diffuse potential criticism of women's forays into the male domain of public affairs; nevertheless, her tone revealed a longing for release from traditional restraints. Even as they clung to familiar notions of womanhood, association members defined new and challenging standards of feminine conduct.[30]

The WABPS mobilized women in its school-improvement programs through a hierarchy of state, county, and district associations that mirrored the political organizations that had traditionally structured men's public lives. Groups at each level held specific responsibilities. The state association was an umbrella organization that included members of all the county and district branches. Delegates from the local chapters met in annual conventions and elected five executive officers and five field agents, all of whom worked out of a central office in Greensboro that was financed by funds from the SEB. The executive officers dealt primarily with matters of planning. They consulted with the state's Departments of Public Instruction, Agriculture, and Health on the development of improvement programs; issued regular advisory bulletins; and sent the field agents on lecture tours intended to create a sense of urgency and opportunity among local

Unidentified group of students gathered to clean the yard around their rural school, ca. 1905 (Courtesy of the North Carolina Division of Archives and History, Raleigh)

women. In turn, officers of the county associations used information from the state headquarters to establish improvement priorities in their communities and to direct the work of subordinate district associations. Together, those management activities shaped the efforts of individual members into a unified campaign.[31]

District associations were the workhorses of the WABPS. Women organized themselves around individual schools and strove to cultivate local enthusiasm for reform through a wide range of improvement projects.[32] Outside the buildings, they mobilized neighborhood men and boys to cart away rubbish, clean wells, clear stumps and underbrush, and lay out grassy plots for children to use as playgrounds. Inside, the women installed window shades, painted walls, polished stoves, hung maps and pictures, and arranged bookcases and display shelves. District associations generally financed their work with money solicited from students and their families at school picnics and plays. A teacher in Edgecombe County, for instance, raised more than thirty dollars by having her students bring lunch baskets for a class auction. On occasion, district organizations also sponsored larger events. In 1906, women in Raleigh directed a performance of "Cinderella in Flowerland" with a cast and crew of children from all of the city's schools. The operetta drew a large crowd and raised more than enough money to support the Raleigh Township association during the following year.[33]

The neat division of labor within the association enabled it to accommodate the various motives that brought women to the work. Sue Hollowell explained that she and her friends in Wayne County assumed the responsibility of "those who are more fortunate . . . to make bright, beautiful spots in the lives of those who know not what sunshine and brightness is." For Hollowell, school reform represented an effort to "raise the masses to a higher plane of life." Others shared that sense of duty but expressed it in terms of maternal rather than class obligations. At the district level in particular, they often described themselves as "school mothers." Local women adopted neighborhood children as their own and labored to nurture their new charges by carefully monitoring the details of school life. Hortense Rose Turlington of Smithfield found that her participation in the WABPS helped ease the loneliness of an empty nest. "I miss my own children less," she declared, "because of the love I give the school children and the love they give me in return. It is a better solace than fancy work, bridge whist, or transcendentalism."[34]

School improvement also provided an avenue of escape from the confines of rural life. It allowed women who dreamed of something better for themselves and their families to share in the get-ahead spirit that animated neighboring towns. Mrs. Gordon Wilfong served as secretary of the WABPS chapter in the Pleasant Grove school district outside Newton, a bustling Catawba County trading center and cotton mill community. To one of state superintendent Joyner's assistants, she bragged, "We are forty country women" who "have cooperated in trying to better conditions in our schools as well as our neighborhood and County at large." Her husband was a successful commercial farmer whose stationery boldly announced his standing as the leading local "Grower of Sweet Potatoes and Blount's Prolific Seed Corn." Mrs. Wilfong and her neighbors saw school improvement as a way of expanding the renovation of the countryside that Mr. Wilfong had begun in his fields. Acutely aware of outside perceptions that "we were not given the training . . . we could and should have had in our country schools," they set out to make themselves into moderns and to create "a better rural civilization."[35]

Still other women were drawn by the leadership opportunities the WABPS offered. Elvira Moffitt and Lucy Bramlette Patterson, for example, hungered for recognition as figures of strength and influence. Both women had come of age in the shadow of power. Born in 1836, Moffitt was the daughter of Jonathan Worth, a distinguished antebellum Whig politician and governor of North Carolina from 1865 to 1868. She had been thrice married and widowed by the time she helped to organize the WABPS. All three of her husbands were men of wealth who left behind "large estates with varied complications and investments." Moffitt acquired her first knowledge of the male world of law and finance as she learned to administer those inheritances, and through these experiences she developed considerable "executive ability."[36]

Lucy Patterson, born in 1865 to a family of plantation owners and merchants from Tennessee and Pennsylvania, was much younger than Moffitt, yet the two women maintained a close friendship. In the late 1880s, Lucy's parents sent her to Salem, North Carolina, a Moravian settlement outside Winston, to study at Salem Academy, her mother's alma mater and one of the few outstanding women's colleges in the South. While there, she met and married a young lawyer named Lindsay Patterson, the son of Rufus Lenoir Patterson, a prominent textile manufacturer, and Louise Morehead Patterson, the daughter of Governor John Motley Morehead, also an industrialist and railroad builder. Lindsay Patterson later distinguished himself as one of the "ablest lawyers of the State."[37]

The WABPS gave Moffitt and Patterson a chance to win respect and exercise authority on their own terms, not as surrogates for their fathers and husbands. They each spent their later years as executive officers of the association and satisfied their ambitions by managing its statewide programs.[38] The women found openings for personal growth in the travel and speaking engagements connected with executive work. Patterson was extremely shy and had always succumbed to "stage-fright" whenever she appeared before more than a small group of friends. Several months of work as a state organizer, however, helped her to cultivate new self-confidence. In August 1903, she reported with pride that she had addressed "a big crowd for fifteen minutes and didn't get frightened!" Involvement in the WABPS campaign taught Patterson that she could conquer her inhibitions and express her views in public with poise and persuasive force.[39]

Such discoveries often had an acute effect on women's perceptions of themselves. Organizers who felt "unwomanly" when they began their work quickly came to accept public agitation as a respectable female activity. After lecturing before several rural audiences, Leah D. Jones no longer found herself "embarrassed and frightened" by seeing her name "posted quite publicly on trees and houses as a lecturer." "I felt that I was certainly doing nothing unwomanly," she wrote, "when I sat in some school house, with women and children close around me . . . [or] stood in front under the trees and discussed with fathers as well as mothers the need to have the school attractive." Association work confirmed what Jones and other women thought privately about themselves: they were competent and resourceful individuals capable of succeeding in what most people would have considered strictly male undertakings.[40]

Turn-of-the-century elections for supplemental school taxes proved just how influential the association could be. In counties where the WABPS was most active in stirring up support for school reform, voters granted overwhelming approval of higher educational levies. The number of special tax districts mushroomed from only seven in 1899 to 406 by August 1906. In the first year of their campaign, the WABPS women also helped to abolish more than three hundred school districts through consolidation and to win community backing for the construction of 676 up-to-date schoolhouses. That record contrasted sharply with the inaction in other southern states, where the SEB had not organized at the local level but had simply concentrated on investigating and publicizing the conditions of rural schools.[41]

The board's work generated little more than public hostility outside of North Carolina. In the spring of 1904, Richard Hathaway Edmonds, editor of the Baltimore-based *Manufacturer's Record*, orchestrated a region-wide attack on the SEB. Edmonds spoke for conservative industrialists who feared, quite correctly, that agitation for school improvement would quickly evolve into a campaign for child labor restrictions and compulsory attendance laws. He denounced the board's work as an expression of northern arrogance and condescension toward the South. How would northerners react, the *Manufacturer's Record* wondered, "to the proposition that a small group of genial, self-appointed busybodies at the South, posing as philanthropists and educators, should come on a special train, advertised as widely and freely as a circus, to help Mr. Ogden's partner, Wanamaker, to overcome the terrible political and moral plight of Philadelphia. . . . Imagine 'the best' New England turning itself loose to welcome such excursions. Imagine the people of New York . . . giving any special heed to it."[42]

Edmonds and his supporters skillfully worked both sides of the class divide. Acknowledging elite interests in maintaining existing relationships of power and authority, they cautioned that too much education would breed radical ideas and popular rebellion. "The great crazes, isms, and fads, which have afflicted the American people during the past century, such as Abolitionism, Bloomerism, Female Suffragism, Mormonism, Oneidaism, Spiritualism, Emersonianism, Walt Whitmanism, Greenbackism, Grangerism, and Populism," the editor cried, "were directly originated or have found their fertile soil in those parts of the country which have been especially equipped as to 'education.'" Then, with a quick about-face, Edmonds attempted to revive Populist fears of monopolistic power, in education as well as economics. One of his supporters, Bishop Warren A. Candler of the Methodist Episcopal Church, South, pointed to John Rockefeller's prominent role in the SEB, warning that the board would hand the great robber baron the same sort of control over schooling that he enjoyed over the oil industry. "It has been by some considered unfortunate (to state the case mildly) that Mr. Rockefeller's 'Standard Oil Company' controls the character and cost of the light for the poor man's body," the bishop growled, "but this is nothing compared with an effort to control the education of the country, which is the light for the minds of both the present and future generations. . . . Let us beware of Greeks when they are bearing gifts."[43]

The WABPS's focus on local schools and neighborhoods made North Carolina largely immune to such attacks. A decentralized approach to reform, modeled in part on Alderman and McIver's work with the county institutes more than a decade earlier, seldom provoked opposition, because it enabled campaigners to adjust the SEB's objectives to the wants and circumstances of diverse communities. That strategy also made the psychic rewards of reform both personal and immediate. At the district level, WABPS women acquired certain knowledge that they were "doing some real sure enough good" by observing directly the results of their handiwork, an experience few would have enjoyed in a more single-minded public relations effort to upgrade the entire school system at once. That high rate of return on investments of time and labor was crucial to the association's survival, for it sustained women through terms of membership that commonly ranged between five and ten years. Such devotion marked the WABPS's success in fitting the benefits of betterment work to the needs of individual lives and neighborhoods.[44]

Leaders of the SEB learned a vital lesson from the North Carolina experience. As one worker explained, "No matter how earnest and enthusiastic the reformer, he who goes directly to the country [people] and tells [them] that their entire . . . system is wrong and that they ought to change, will meet with failure and even well merited opposition. Under such circumstances it will be an affront and almost an insult." The Bureau of Information's publicity efforts, another observed, suffered from just such a " 'crusade' trademark." By 1904, the board's directors had begun to embrace the WABPS approach as a more effective route to reform. Rather than prodding reluctant citizens to action by denouncing their educational deficiencies, the schoolmen chose to enlist ordinary people in reshaping their own lives.

In 1905, teachers attending the Summer School of the South in Knoxville, Tennessee, laid plans for transforming the WABPS into a regional enterprise. They organized the Interstate Association for the Betterment of Public School Houses and elected delegates to establish state chapters modeled after the North Carolina body. Within two years the delegates had rallied volunteers in Alabama, Arkansas, Georgia, Kentucky, South Carolina, Tennessee, Texas, and Virginia. The SEB commended the women's initiative. "The one most hopeful factor in our . . . situation today," boasted board secretary Edgar Gardner Murphy, "is the 'School Improvement' organization of our women. . . . [T]hey represent the very *best* life and organization of the South."[45]

Over the next decade, women's work served as the reform movement's passport into the otherwise insular world of the neighborhood school. In some cases, the WABPS conceived projects that were eventually implemented as official policy through the office of the state superintendent. At other times, association women prepared the way for large-scale interventions by the GEB and its affiliated agencies. All of those efforts, however, were linked by a common purpose. They were meant to remake the countryside in the image of the town. "[Our] most pressing and most important task," reformers explained, "is the economic organization of our country people. The town *is* organization; the country is unorganized. That's the essential difference. . . . [P]rogress . . . hangs on the obliteration of that difference."[46]

The women continued to concern themselves above all with the physical condition of rural schoolhouses. When the WABPS began its work in 1902, the average value of the buildings, furnishings, and grounds in North Carolina's 5,653 white rural districts was $206—less, explained state superintendent Joyner, "than the value of almost the poorest house in any city or town." In 625 white communities there were no school buildings of any kind, while another 484 used "rude log houses," many of which had endured decades of wear and deterioration. Children in a majority of the remaining districts attended school in what Charles Coon described as "shabbily built board structures." The typical rural schoolhouse consisted of a single room with six windows, none of which had curtains or blinds. The students sat on homemade benches facing a teacher who had a chair but no desk. A "dilapidated wood stove . . . red with rust and dirt" stood in the center of the room. In winter, it barely compensated for the cold winds that blew through cracks in the walls, so parents were sometimes forced to keep their children at home "because [they] could not be kept warm." The building had an inclined plane of dirt rather than steps leading to its door. The yard was always muddy, and the general appearance of the surroundings was "anything but attractive."[47]

Association women labored to transform these "cheerless schools" into "places of beauty and refinement" by modeling them after the ideal schoolhouse depicted in the photographs that adorned the WABPS's annual reports. That school was a one- or two-room structure nestled in a grove of trees and surrounded by flowers. A small steeple or cupola sat atop its roof and housed the school bell. The building possessed all the charm of a modest Victorian cottage and represented the transfer of woman's aesthetic talents and motherly skills from the domestic sphere into the public realm. Through the model school, association women gave substance to their idea of the surroundings required in rearing children to responsible adulthood. That image emerged from a combination of their personal experiences as mothers and the cultural conventions of middle-class life.[48]

The physical improvement of schoolhouses was partly a public relations strategy designed to win neighborhood acceptance of the new education and the changes it wrought in teacher hiring and the curriculum. "A respectable school house," argued Superintendent Joyner, "is not only necessary for conducting successfully the business of public education, but is absolutely essential for commanding the respect of the community for that business." With help from the WABPS, the school would come to share the reverence once reserved for the church and the courthouse as symbols of community pride and authority. But even more compelling was the notion

Women reformers worked to replace one-room rural schoolhouses with two- and three-room structures that allowed for graded instruction. The examples here are from Harnett County (above) and Rockingham County (below), ca. 1905. (Courtesy of the North Carolina Division of Archives and History, Raleigh)

of creating a setting in which children and "the plain people" of rural districts could learn "right ideals of living and of life." Joyner waxed poetic in explaining that aspect of the women's work to the state legislature. "What is the character of this strange business that men call education?" he mused. "It has to do with mind and soul and body. It has to do with the formation of habit, with the shaping of character." What children learned of such matters, Joyner insisted, derived as much from their surroundings as from the "study of books . . . and formal lesson teaching." Efforts to "transform uncleanness into cleanness, discomfort into comfort, ugliness into beauty" amounted to more than mere public housekeeping; they were the prerequisites for a sweeping moral regeneration of the countryside.[49]

Like progressive reformers elsewhere, association women had come to view the perceived "backwardness" of rural life as the product of a deficient "social environment" rather than personal failings. They turned accordingly from sentiment to science, abandoning nineteenth-century strategies of individual uplift for broader programs of social management. In the small towns of the South, as in the cities of the urban Northeast, those changes reflected the realities of life in a world where face-to-face encounters and family ties were diminishing in importance. Social reform became a matter of planning and design rather than persuasion. Future citizens of the New South would be trained less through personal influence than through the benevolent manipulation of their physical and social surroundings.[50] The WABPS summed up the new environmentalism in a paraphrase of an old-time adage: "As a child's surroundings are, so is he liable to be." Elvira Moffitt explained to members of the Raleigh Township association that "there is an embryo" of a productive citizen "in every human being that grows to good or evil, governed by circumstances." In country youngsters, that embryo too often withered and died simply "for the want of direction."[51]

Association women envisioned the model schoolhouse as an architectural complement to the new education, inculcating the same ambition and individualism that were embedded in reading and arithmetic lessons. Beautiful buildings and yards, they promised, would overcome rural idleness and economic inertia by altering children's perceptions of themselves and the world. "A child seeing the pleasant school house and its attractive surroundings gets a new impulse," Moffitt declared, and "new hope springs up in his breast and a new life opens to his view." Each aspect of the setting contributed to that awakening. The pictures of famous men that decorated the walls provided students with role models, fostering in them "a spirit of self-reliance" and a thirst for "high and noble endeavor," while the pleasing atmosphere created by freshly painted walls, clean window shades, and landscaped lawns cultivated contempt for the "low, groveling, canine conditions of life" pupils experienced at home. Taken together, those effects imparted to schoolchildren both the desire and the self-confidence "to be somebody and to do something in the world."[52]

That ambition would count for little, however, unless children were also made familiar with the ways of the marketplace. Taking their cue from the North Carolina Department of Agriculture and from journals such as the *Progressive Farmer*, edited in Raleigh by New South advocate Clarence Hamilton Poe, WABPS women planted school gardens to give students serviceable experience with commercial agriculture and the handling of money. Association field agents explained that rural children often learned from their parents "the practical part of tilling the soil, but not the science of it." As a result, the "inefficient" agricultural practices of the past became habitual with them even before they reached adulthood. School gardens were meant to break that cycle of ignorance by exposing pupils to the "fundamental principles of farming," just as classroom lessons taught the "fundamental truths of arithmetic, geography, or grammar." Association women looked to their patches of cotton, tobacco, and vegetables to produce not only the cash they needed to finance school improvement but also a crop of young farmers eager to adopt "new discoveries" and to work their land in accordance with "well-tried experiments made at the A[gricultural] and M[echanical] College." A bountiful harvest was essential to fulfillment of the New South vision. "With 80 percent of our people engaged in agriculture," one advocate of commercial farming explained, "it can be seen at a glance that the farmer must be prosperous in order that all classes may prosper."[53]

The association's school garden work took a dramatic turn in 1906, when the GEB decided to place it on a permanent footing. Board officials were inspired by the experiments of Seaman A. Knapp, a former professor at the Iowa State College of Agriculture. In 1903, while working as a special agent for the federal government in Texas and Louisiana, Knapp developed a "demonstration" strategy for spreading the practice of "scientific" farming. His approach closely resembled that of the WABPS. Knapp went directly to farmers, asking them to adopt new cultivation techniques, better seeds, and improved implements. Those who agreed kept all the profits from the venture and were insured against losses by a committee of neighbors interested in observing the work. The results were usually dramatic. After the first harvest, doubters clamored to join the program, touching off what Knapp described as a "revolution" in attitudes that promised to create a new "standard of excellence for farming and for living."[54]

In 1904, the U.S. Department of Agriculture (USDA) adapted Knapp's demonstration technique to fight a growing boll weevil infestation in the Deep South, but the agency refused to finance the work throughout the rest of the region. Federal officials insisted that the government could provide funds only to combat the insect's threat to interstate commerce. The GEB, however, was convinced that Knapp had discovered the answer to developing a "great rural civilization." Two years later, the board won permission from the USDA to carry Knapp's ideas to Mississippi, Alabama, Georgia, North Carolina, South Carolina, and Virginia. "If these... people in the South could have in some practical way the facts of the science and art of agriculture," proclaimed Wallace Buttrick, the board's secretary, "there would be no limit to the value of the crops they might raise, no limit to their productive efficiency."[55]

Over the next nine years, the GEB spearheaded a regional campaign to organize corn clubs for boys and tomato clubs for girls. The work in North Carolina was orchestrated by agents of the North Carolina Department of Agriculture (whose salaries were paid by the board) and local chapters of the WABPS. The state representatives made personal appearances in fields, schoolhouses, and churches to kindle enthusiasm for the club idea among children and their parents, then turned day-to-day operations over to teachers and local women who served as county supervisors and subagents. By 1914, the clubs had enrolled more than six thousand students, drawn from all but ten of the state's one hundred counties.[56]

The corn clubs taught boys to become "business farmers." Each member planted and tended his own acre of land with guidance from USDA bulletins on seed selection, tillage, and cultivation. Throughout the growing season, the boys kept detailed records of their expenses, and at harvest time, they balanced those accounts against their market earnings. On average, the corn clubs more than tripled the productivity of ordinary farmers. But yield was not the sole measure of success; organizers of the clubs were also interested in evidence that the boys were learning proper lessons of acquisitiveness, competition, and hard work. In the determination of county, state, and regional champions, they awarded thirty points for yield, thirty

Members of the Buncombe County Corn Club (Courtesy of the North Carolina Division of Archives and History, Raleigh)

points for profit, twenty points for the best ten ears of corn, and twenty points for written accounts of the year's work and the motives behind it. The corn clubs' purpose was not simply to reform agricultural practices but to make each young man into "an effective economic unit."[57]

Tomato clubs promised to do much the same for girls. Club members learned "to select and prepare the soil, fertilize it, study the plants, cultivate and prune them, and finally to harvest the crop and can it according to . . . scientific methods." In most counties, the local WABPS chapter helped provide the necessary stoves, canners, jars, and tins, which were carried from one neighborhood to the next until all of the tomatoes had been put away. A club member in each community usually served as a "hostess," inviting her friends into her home to share the work and to celebrate their accomplishments with a picnic prepared by parents and teachers. The girls then took turns selling their produce in special markets established by the boards of trade in neighboring towns and cities, an "opportunity . . . eagerly sought . . . for recreation and pleasure." Some of the best tomatoes were even shipped north for distribution by grocery wholesalers.[58]

Tomato clubs introduced young women to the mysteries of the marketplace and enabled them to earn money that they could control themselves rather than turn over to their fathers or brothers. The average club member realized an annual profit of $20 to $50, a handsome sum in a world where cash was often scarce. Club work also gave reformers access to country homes. "Through the tomato plant," Seaman Knapp advised club agents, "you will get into the home garden and by means of canning you will get into the farmer's kitchen." Once there, teachers, WABPS women, and tomato club organizers sought to impart lessons on thrift, orderliness, and especially sanitation. They encouraged farm girls to use their earnings to purchase curtains, furniture, and pictures that would make their homes neat and attractive—rural replicas of the middle-class urban households that had become refuges from the workaday world. Club officials also urged the installation of window screens and the digging of sanitary wells and privies to protect families against the diseases that robbed them of health and fitness. The tomato clubs taught school girls to produce and consume more—to become full participants in a market economy—and at the same time made them into missionaries for the "reconstruction and reorganization and cleaning up of country life in general."[59]

The clubs' sanitation work dovetailed with the WABPS's concern for school health. At the turn of the century, North Carolina children suffered alarming rates of sickness and death. Malaria and yellow fever ran rampant in coastal counties, while tuberculosis, smallpox, hookworm, typhoid, diphtheria, and a host of gastrointestinal ailments struck young people down regardless of where they lived. Physicians and educators blamed much of that suffering on "ignorance" and on "filthy" habits of personal hygiene. They pointed especially to the failure of rural families to build and use outdoor toilets. "Although the privy was in old times called a 'necessary,'" exclaimed a contributor to the state health bulletin, "it is startling to find how many persons do not consider such a structure to be a necessary adjunct to the human dwelling. The absence of a privy can fairly be called uncivilized. . . . It ought to go without saying that every person should have the opportunity to use a properly constructed privy at all times, and should also be compelled to use it, and never under any circumstances be allowed to deposit his discharges in any other place." Reformers' interest in policing such intimate matters was a response to both the tragedy of wasted lives and the economic costs of a population that was "not as [productive] as [it] ought to be." The "loss of efficiency" due to preventable illness, they argued, presented a "cumulative handicap to the development of . . . all things that make for civilization."[60]

Association women shared health workers' belief that intellectual and physical development went hand in hand. The school's duty, charged Elvira Moffitt, was to educate the "whole child." Dr. Watson S. Rankin, secretary of the North Carolina Board of Health, explained what that meant in an address before the Teachers Assembly in 1910. "Education," he observed, "is rapidly passing through three evolutionary stages."

The first stage, now past, had for its dominant idea to teach the child to read, write, and figure. . . . Having prepared the soil of the mind, it was left to receive the grains of knowledge that fall perchance as seed are strewn haphazard over the field by the wind. The second stage, developing now very rapidly, is characterized by the dominant idea of equipping the cultivated mind with practical knowledge of everyday use—sanitary, domestic, and agricultural science. More attention is being given to seed selection and the time of planting. The third and final stage . . . is characterized by the dominant idea of assured usefulness; and assured usefulness means a healthy body. . . . Education that takes no account of the health of the children is like the proverbial house upon the sand.

Thus the ideal school was to cultivate in students not only new values but also the capacity to act on them. To that end, the WABPS undertook a variety of programs aimed at making sick and feeble students into robust adults. "[E]verything should be done for children to make them good physical machines," advised Dr. Paul Anderson, director of the state's Western Insane Asylum at Morganton. "This is an age of commercialism when everything is counted in dollars and cents . . . [and] only so far as manhood is developed will our nation prosper."[61]

Public health work had first begun in North Carolina during the late 1870s. Interest in the subject was largely a product of the Civil War. Troop movements across the South and unsanitary conditions in military camps and prisons touched off epidemics of typhoid, yellow fever, and small-pox that ravaged the state in 1865. The problems grew even worse in later years, as burgeoning towns and an expanding transportation system brought people into closer contact without the benefit of water purification and sewerage facilities. In 1888, thousands of North Carolinians fell prey to smallpox, measles, and meningitis, and an outbreak of yellow fever nearly brought railroad travel to a halt and "hampered or ruined . . . trade of all sorts." But the late nineteenth century also offered reasons for hope. The germ theory of disease won virtually universal acceptance by the mid-1890s; water filtration was shown to be an effective preventative for cholera in 1892; Italian and English physicians identified the cause of malaria in 1898; and in 1899, Walter Reed, working with the army on the Panama Canal, identified the source of yellow fever. By the first decade of the twentieth century, doctors and civic leaders across the state had begun using the new medical knowledge in tentative local efforts at eradicating "unnecessary sickness . . . physical and mental lassitude . . . thriftlessness and poverty."[62]

Association women joined heartily in that enterprise. They invited physicians to attend their meetings and lecture on the proper care of children's eyes, the best methods of draining swampy schoolyards, and the most up-to-date privy designs. In Raleigh, Elvira Moffitt and her friends waged war on customary notions that " 'running water purifies itself' " and that water that looked fresh and tasted sweet was undoubtedly pure. The women worked in schools throughout Wake County to replace the ubiquitous water bucket and tin cup with gravity-fed coolers. Moffitt explained, "Children are often careless to put the dipper back into the bucket with water in it," thus contaminating the entire supply with the "germs of disease." Coolers removed that hazard by simultaneously providing "unpolluted water" and flushing waste safely down a drain.[63]

Through education and sanitary engineering, the women sought to teach students that control of their bodies was more than a matter of personal choice and comfort. It also defined the very core of citizenship. "The essential difference between the citizen and the savage," they and public officials argued, "is the expression in his daily routine by the former of the principle, 'No man liveth unto himself.' " Children who ignored the lessons of clean living not only risked their own well-being but were also "partisan[s] to the criminal destruction" of the lives of others.[64]

The WABPS made health and personal hygiene a central element of the public school curriculum. But as with farm demonstration work, the resources of the General Education Board were necessary to institutionalize the innovation. In 1902, Dr. Charles Wardell Stiles, a researcher for the federal Bureau of Animal Industry, announced that he had discovered the source of "the proverbial laziness of the poorer classes" of the rural South: widespread infection with hookworm, an intestinal parasite spread by the improper disposal of human waste. The worm robbed its hosts of nutrition and sapped their strength through anemia. Six years later, Walter Hines Page discovered Stiles while the two were serving together on President Theodore Roosevelt's Country Life Commission. Certain that the doctor held the key to setting rural inhabitants on a course of "progress and efficiency," Page reported Stiles's work to the Rockefeller advisers on the GEB, who were equally excited by the news.

Hookworm was a disease made to order for philanthropy. Easily diagnosed with simple equipment and cured by the administration of thymol, a crystalline phenol found in thyme oil, it offered an ideal vehicle for convincing ordinary citizens of the benefits of public health work. In 1909, John D. Rockefeller Sr. provided a gift of $1 million to establish the Rockefeller Sanitary Commission (RSC) for the purpose of stamping out the illness and making "inefficient lives . . . efficient." The commission's directors, many of whom also served on the GEB and SEB, offered James Joyner the job of overseeing the work, but Joyner declined, insisting that he could "be of more service as Superintendent of Public Instruction," promoting the effort locally through his office in Raleigh. The post eventually went to Wickliffe Rose, dean of the George Peabody College for Teachers and executive director of the SEB.[65]

The RSC began its work in North Carolina with an epidemiological survey that revealed startling results: at least 43 percent of the state's people were infected to some degree. Treating such a large number of patients demanded an imaginative strategy. In 1911, the commission implemented a dispensary program aimed at " 'de-hookworming' and 'thymolizing' the people; and 'privyizing' their premises as rapidly as possible." Teams of physicians, microscopists, and record-keepers traveled from one community to the next, talking first to editors, ministers, and politicians to secure promises of support and local funding. They then pitched their tents and invited citizens to come for diagnosis and a cure. Most of the dispensaries operated on the grounds of local schoolhouses. But in some cases the schools served better as object lessons on improper sanitation than as treatment centers. In August 1912, Charles Stiles visited Tabor City and discovered that its schoolhouse had been left unattended throughout the summer recess. "The place is unlocked," he reported, "one door is entirely off its hinges, and a number of windows are broken. As there is no privy in the school yard, the school building has been used as a privy by the general public." Stiles was scheduled to speak before a neighborhood audience in one of the building's four rooms, but "the odor from the defecations was [too] horrible" to stomach. "On account of the ladies," he reported the trouble to his local hosts and asked that the gathering be moved to another location.[66]

Women from the WABPS played a critical role in the Rockefeller Sanitary Commission's work. Wickliffe Rose was eager to downplay the hookworm campaign's connection to northern wealth. Remembering the SEB's early troubles, he warned his lieutenants to let local people in the South do "all the talking and writing." The commission's representatives in North

Parents and children gathered for a hookworm clinic, Lawndale (Cleveland County), 1912 (Courtesy of the Rockefeller Archive Center)

Carolina looked especially to teachers and association women, requesting that they raise funds for the treatment of indigents and, more important, that they help make the idea of seeking diagnosis "fashionable." Members of the WABPS organized special committees in rural schools. Consisting of two boys, two girls, and a teacher, these committees made certain that every child was examined, conducted routine inspections of school wells and privies, and sent students home with the "Catechism of Public Health" and outhouse plans. Schools that reported the highest rates of participation were rewarded with prizes. Association women also brought their own children forward to be the first in line for examination. "What you do," one dispensary worker advised the women, "the masses will do." By submitting themselves and their families, the women publicly affirmed their "progressive spirit" and claimed their place "among the better class of people."[67]

Those strategies proved to be remarkably effective. People streamed into the dispensaries on foot and horseback, by train and mule-drawn wagon. Dr. Benjamin Washburn, a North Carolina fieldworker, recalled the scene in the mountain community of Mills' Spring. "It was early June and the weather was warm and fair," he wrote. "By the time we arrived a great crowd, probably upwards of two hundred men, women, and children had gathered on the schoolhouse grounds . . . and more than a hundred [fecal] specimens had already been brought in." Washburn's companion, Dr. Platt W. Covington, knew the ways of the revivalist and was "a master at handling a crowd of this kind." After setting his microscopists to work on the stool samples, he called up people who had received treatment during his previous visits and asked them to testify to their improved condition. Covington then made a great show of listening to each patient's chest with his stethoscope. The procedure fascinated the locals, who referred to it as "sounding" the body's inner workings.

Covington closed the day's activities with a heart-wrenching lecture. When he "explained the effects of hookworm disease on children, how it stunted their growth mentally and physically and left them ignorant and incapable of earning a decent living," two "rather old rather large ladies" sitting in the front row "got out their handkerchiefs and began wiping their eyes. This was soon followed by subdued sobs and finally copious tears." Then, with the lecture completed, Covington asked "if a Sunday School singing leader was present. There was; and a lean tall man came forward with a tuning fork. After sounding a few 'do do re re's,' " he led the crowd in a rousing chorus of "Onward Christian Soldiers." Covington had of course modeled his appeal on the evangelical ritual of conversion and salvation, a tactic that struck a chord among even the most sophisticated observers. " 'To see the crowds, to witness their transformation from invalidism, wasted ambition and poverty to health, happiness, activity and prosperity,' " another medical worker confided to Wickliffe Rose, " 'brings to one's mind the miracles of the New Testament, and the healing of the multitudes. . . . It looks like the days of Galilee.' "[68]

The hookworm cure brought immediate and dramatic results. Within a matter of weeks, emaciated patients began to regain their strength and vigor. But reformers thought they recognized other changes as well. Benjamin Washburn recalled receiving stool samples collected by the father of a family of fourteen. "A more dirty, ignorant, and uncivilized specimen of humanity you will seldom see!" he wrote to a friend. Washburn gave the man treatments for the entire clan and asked him to return for a second examination. "The next week he brought several of his children with him and a happier man you will seldom see. He was washed, shaved, and wearing clean clothes, and the remarkable tales he told of his improved health and of the numbers, kinds, and sizes of worms removed was beyond belief." Another farmer made the significance of that conversion explicit. " 'Aside from saving my son,' " he told one of Washburn's co-workers, the hookworm cure " 'means money in my pocket. . . . Before I saw you I had to feed and clothe [my boy] and care for him at a dead expense, and with no hope that it would ever be different. . . . Now I . . . am not only saved the dead expense of his doctor's bills and medicine, and all like that, but I am saved the price of the hand which I have discharged, which is $1 a day, not for a day or two, not for one or two years, but for many years, until [my son] is grown and leaves me to make his own way. . . . I consider that this is the darndest best investment I ever made,'" the old man concluded. When hookworm crusaders looked into the eyes of the cured, they found satisfaction in their own reflections.[69]

In early 1914, the sanitary commission began to plan for its disbanding a year later. Leaders of the work had always viewed the dispensary work as a temporary "rallying-point" designed to relieve the worst suffering and to convince individual communities to begin caring for their own needs. Guilford County, home of the Normal School and of early support for the new education, led the way by establishing one of the nation's first county boards of health. Hoping to spur similar initiatives in other areas and to pull together the disparate strands of the school-improvement campaign, GEB and RSC officials helped state authorities establish "ideal communities" in the white hamlets of Salemburg, Philadelphus, Red Oak, and Hallsboro. Schoolhouses in those districts served as social centers where parents and children gathered for instruction in domestic economy, mastered the techniques of scientific agriculture, developed marketing strategies for their produce, and underwent routine medical examinations. The four neighborhoods provided blueprints of progressive country life for all in the state to copy.[70]

Creation of the model communities marked the climax of North Carolina's schoolhouse crusade. For Frederick Gates, chairman of the GEB, they represented "a beautiful dream" come true. The people, he explained to fellow board members, "yield themselves with perfect docility to our moulding hand. . . . [U]nhampered by tradition, we work our own good will upon a grateful and responsive rural folk." In Salemburg, school children greeted visitors with a chant that neatly captured the reformers' vision:

Brushing, brushing, till we're fainting,
  washing, scrubbing, rubbing, painting.
See we're cleaning, what's the meaning?
  Opportunity!! Model community!!

Perhaps many older listeners heard in that jingle echoes of a familiar world of neighborhood school raisings and turnings out. But the dominant tones were surely those of a much different South. Salemburg's youngsters belonged to a generation of "new" North Carolinians who had learned to think of themselves in the likeness of commodities, and theirs was a community polished and shined, ready for display, and eager to compete in the marketplace of "progress." For those children, schooling had taken on a decidedly modern purpose. It represented not so much an initiation into the local ways of family, community, and neighborhood as a port of entry into the much larger world beyond.[71]

The Riddle of Race

Take hold on instruction, leave it not; keep it because it
is thy life.—Proverbs 4:13, Douay-Rheims, adapted by
Bertha Maye Edwards, *The Little Place, and the Little Girl*

Look where you may," a troubled white citizen wrote to
the *Charlotte Observer* in 1903, "you cannot avoid . . .
the race question. The negro as an unsolved problem faces us daily." Although white supremacy had triumphed in 1900, nervous uncertainty still characterized most discussions of race matters. The politics of the 1890s had poisoned the affairs of daily life with "more hatred of whites for blacks and of blacks for whites than ever before." On both sides of the color bar, adversaries seemed swept up in a "torrent of passion." Education, too, figured prominently in this expanding crisis. But was it, like politics, part of the problem, or was it the key to peace, prosperity, and a new racial order? During the opening years of the twentieth century, that question became crucial to North Carolina's racial future.[1]

The state's white leadership was deeply divided over the issue of African American schooling. At one extreme stood racial exclusionists—men like Alfred Moore Waddell, who argued that whites should abandon black instruction altogether. Waddell openly condemned universal education. In a commencement address delivered at South Carolina's Newberry College, he mocked reformers who embraced schooling as "the panacea for all social and political evils." "Thousands of enlightened persons" rejected that idea, he exclaimed. "They do not believe it even when applied to the dominant race . . . and much less so when applied to both races indiscriminately."[2]

Many Democrats in the state legislature counted themselves among those thousands and encouraged the translation of Waddell's sentiments into law. In 1901 they championed two bills that were intended to limit the funding of black schools. The first bill sought to resurrect the Dortch law of the 1880s by proposing a constitutional amendment that would have required that all educational appropriations be divided according to the amount of taxes paid by each race. The second took a more subtle approach, calling for an amendment that would authorize citizens to vote on school taxes in single-race elections. Under either provision, whites would have enjoyed a new freedom to levy taxes for the benefit of their schools alone.[3]

In defense of the proposed amendments, racial exclusionists pointed to what they described as black education's dismal record of failure. Schooling, they charged, had "spoil[ed] the negro as a laborer" and had cultivated among the young an especially "vicious attitude" of assertiveness and criminal irresponsibility. To white observers, North Carolina's courts seemed to be awash in a "sea of black faces," evidence that the "old-time Negro," who had once been "both servant and friend to the white man," was "rapidly passing away" in favor of a new generation of blacks who were "indifferent, unreliable, untrained, and indolent." More than a quarter century of "experimentation" designed "to make [the Negro] a white man in character and capabilities," one leading Democrat exclaimed, had done little more than cultivate false ambitions and base temptations.[4]

Advocates of universal education found no fault with that indictment of black schooling, but they did challenge the way that it framed the issue. The appropriate question, they insisted, was not whether blacks should be educated "but rather who shall do it and how it shall be done." In his first annual report, state superintendent James Joyner spelled out the argument for universal instruction. "We have made many grievous mistakes in the education of the negro," he conceded. "We have too often flung him the part of the money that the Constitution required us to give, and then left him without direction to waste it at his will. . . . What wonder if his head has often been filled with false notions and the results have been . . . discouraging to us?" But those mistakes could not be set right by further abdication of responsibility. Turning the logic of exclusion on its head, Joyner warned that to deny black children access to the classroom would only hasten the chaos that Waddell and his allies feared most. "Who can estimate the danger that lurks in such a mass of ignorance, if these negroes be left uneducated?" he asked. "The rapidity with which any race will lapse into a state of savagery and brutality through ignorance depends upon the years and generations of education and civilization that lie behind that race. . . . If this be true, does it not follow that the decline of the negro race . . . would be more rapid than that of the white race, and that there is even more danger in black ignorance than there is in white ignorance?" Superintendent Joyner saw only one alternative to race war. Instead of abandoning black instruction, white North Carolinians should engage it more vigorously than ever before. "With the negro," Joyner concluded, "it must be elevation through proper education or extermination."[5]

Charles Aycock used similar arguments to hold exclusionists at bay in both the state legislature and the inner circles of the Democratic Party. In 1901, he threatened to resign unless the proposals for school-tax amendments were defeated, and two years later, when the issue surfaced again at the Democrats' state convention, he convinced restive delegates to reject an exclusionist plank in the party platform. Aycock insisted that "permanent white supremacy" could never be established on a basis of force and repression alone. Such a policy would surely set in motion a black exodus from North Carolina, and it might also provoke federal meddling with the literacy test on which disfranchisement and white political authority depended. Most important of all, whites simply could not afford the risk of "leaving [the Negro] to his own devices." The problem with the exclusionists, Aycock insisted, was that they were content to look the other way while the next generation of black children were trained "out of harmony and in enmity to the people among whom [they] live[d]." To the governor's way of thinking, the state's real need was for a more flexible and adroit racial policy—one that joined the active subordination of blacks with an effort to cultivate among them some measure of collaboration and consent. He warned fellow Democrats, "We are confronted with a condition which demands statesmanship and not passion and prejudice."[6]

Aycock also took his message of accommodation and reconciliation directly to black parents and teachers. In the fall of 1901, less than a year after his inauguration, he delivered the opening address at the Negro State Fair in Raleigh. Aycock urged his listeners to abandon their attachment to politics and abstract notions of equality. The social separation of the races was now a settled issue in the South, he explained, and its "violation" would lead only to black "destruction as well as to the injury of the Whites." Under such circumstances, the preferable course was for African Americans to turn inward and establish among themselves "a society founded upon culture, intelligence, and virtue." Separate development, Aycock advised, "is well for you; it is well for us; it is necessary for the peace of our section."[7]

The black men and women in the governor's audience must surely have felt trapped. Aycock's allusions to "destruction" and "injury" made clear the price to be paid for any continued effort at challenging disfranchisement and segregation head-on. At the same time, blacks were also being abandoned by the whites they had once counted as political allies. In an effort to refurbish its image and maintain sectional goodwill, the Republican Party at both the state and national levels had embraced a "lily-white" platform aimed at purging its ranks of the handful of remaining black voters. What alternative was left but to accept Aycock's offer of civility, even if it meant rethinking the meaning of something so fundamental as freedom itself? In 1903, James Edward Shepard, a Durham educator and later founder of the North Carolina College for Negroes, offered solace to fellow blacks who had grown discouraged. "Citizenship is not in constitutions but in the mind," he proclaimed. "My mind, my soul, and my virtue are ever free."[8]

Accommodation was not to be misread as acquiescence, however. For most African Americans, the choice at hand was never a simple matter of agitation versus passivity. Instead, they adopted a more subtle strategy of survival, one that acknowledged the reality of white rule but at the same time searched the crevices of white supremacy for every opportunity for black power and self-determination. In the affairs of daily life, resistance and collaboration were not so much at odds as tightly interwoven.

That fact was perhaps best illustrated by the black women teachers from North Carolina and across the South who in later years traveled at public expense to Virginia's Hampton Institute. There they received instruction in the philosophy of racial self-help expounded by Booker T. Washington, Hampton's most celebrated alumnus. Like Washington, the women had devoted their lives to a project of uplift in their home communities and were willing to cast their lot with the white South. Yet many of them also carried in their satchels copies of *The Crisis*, the journal W. E. B. Du Bois edited for the National Association for the Advancement of Colored People. Even as they worked within the constraints of segregation, the women refused to "grow indifferent or discouraged to any of [their] rights."[9]

Those teachers, and countless others like them, ensured that the debate over black schooling would never rest in white hands alone. Through classroom lessons and now-forgotten acts of quiet advocacy, they helped to place education at the center of a much broader contest over race, justice, and citizenship in a democratic society. There the classroom has remained, of course, well into our own time.

North Carolina's white school leaders found ready support for their views among the northern philanthropists who participated in the Conference for Education in the South and whose money financed the work of the Southern and General Education Boards. Together they framed a diagnosis of the South's racial ills which was grounded in the theories of scientific racism that had gained credence during the 1880s and 1890s. The reformers started from an assumption that "the negro [was] a child-race . . . grown up in body and physical passions, weak in judgment, foresight, self-control and character." They argued that slavery had tempered those traits and advanced blacks rapidly toward civilization, thanks largely to harsh lessons in the "discipline of work." Indeed, the results appeared so striking that reformers described slavery as "the first [and] most fruitful chapter in the history of negro education." But with emancipation, that instruction ceased, and whites worried that much of what had been gained was quickly being lost. Railroad magnate William Baldwin explained, "As a child who during his period of infancy is kept under careful restraint, and then is turned suddenly out into the world, is inclined to lack the power of self control . . . so the Negro, when his shackles were loosened, aimed to enjoy to the fullest extent freedom from his point of view. . . . He had no outside control; no guidance; no aim. . . . The negro artisan gradually disappeared; the negro politician took his place." The result, Baldwin concluded, was nearly a quarter century of social and economic turmoil that divided the nation and stood like a "lion in the path" of New South dreams.[10]

Baldwin and other Conference participants felt no fondness for slavery, but they did find guidance for the future in the experiences of the past. Southern prosperity, as well as the very survival of the Negro race, demanded that the old "tutelage of slavery" should not be rejected but instead should be adapted to the new circumstances of freedom. "The southern white people among whom the negro lives . . . must be his teacher and guardian," insisted George Winston, former president of the University of North Carolina. "The old relationship, not of owner and slave, but of master and servant, of guardian and ward, of superior and inferior, with the old time friendship, sympathy, and affection, must be restored." Otherwise, there was little hope for either black survival or social peace. "A continuance of the relations now existing between blacks and whites in the South, with ever increasing neglect and oppression, passion and prejudice," Winston predicted, "must inevitably push the negro to the wall and grind him to powder."[11]

The means of restoration seemed to be readily at hand. It took the form of "industrial education," pioneered at Hampton Institute by Samuel C. Armstrong, a white military officer and the son of Hawaiian missionaries, and later transplanted to the Deep South by Booker T. Washington, Armstrong's protégé and the founder of Alabama's Tuskegee Institute. Armstrong opened his school in 1868 as a counterweight to what he viewed as the overly politicized education offered to ex-slaves by northern church workers and the freedmen's own subscription schools. He advised African Americans to "leave politics severely alone" and to concentrate instead on cultivating what one of his admirers later described as "the virtues of order, fidelity, temperance, and obedience." To that end, Armstrong structured the Hampton curriculum around vocational instruction in domestic science, agriculture, and the building trades. His idea was not only to train black students in particular skills but also to produce a new generation of conservative race leaders, most of them teachers, who would work to adjust the black population to its subordinate position in the emergent New South. Armstrong expected those men and women to provide object lessons in what he called the "right ideas of life and duty."[12]

Industrial education offered southern schoolmen what they most desired: a stable, self-regulating system of race relations to replace the conflict and turmoil of the late nineteenth century. Reformers saw in the "Hampton Idea" a powerful means of instilling the habits of rule in those they sought to govern. Industrial education promised to cultivate a new sense of self and social place among African American school children, convincing them to accept their subordination as a normal and inevitable fact of life. At the same time, industrial education also invited black collaboration by leaving ajar "the door of hope and opportunity." Its promoters insisted that with "white aid—through docility, obedience, zeal and fidelity"—African Americans might yet grow into possession of civilization's "highest inheritances." New South whites intended to avoid what they saw as the educational blunders of the past; they would make no attempt to insert "into the mind of the negro, as [if] by a surgical operation, the culture . . . which the

Anglo-Saxon race had [acquired] through long centuries" of development. Instead, blacks would be trained to work out their own salvation through an education adapted to "*their* lives" and "present needs."[13]

Here, it seemed, was a formula for both racial peace and the fulfillment of a divine mission of uplift. "Through sorrow and tears and suffering," George Winston exclaimed, "the South took the savage negro and brought him under the sad tutelage of slavery to the portals of civilization. It will now take him again in the equally sad tutelage of freedom, and lead him up higher and higher, even until he stands side by side with the white man, his equal, if God has so decreed." Winston's northern colleagues responded to those words with enthusiastic applause. His principles were applicable not only to the South but to any situation in which lesser peoples encountered the more "highly developed . . . most masterful . . . all-conquering Anglo-Saxon race." At home, they could be used to guide the assimilation of burgeoning numbers of foreign immigrants; abroad, they might be equally effective in shaping America's new dominion over peoples of color in Cuba, Puerto Rico, Hawaii, and the Philippines. The South, Winston's friends conceded, had much "to teach to the whole world in the way of training for freedom . . . backward, child race[s]."[14]

With the principles of industrial instruction firmly in mind, southern schoolmen and their northern allies set out to remake the educational experiences of African American children, much as they were already doing for whites. In North Carolina, responsibility for implementing the reformers' ideas fell primarily to Nathan Carter Newbold, who in 1913 was named state agent of Negro rural schools. Newbold owed his job to the General Education Board, which agreed to support such workers in twelve southern states. The board paid Newbold's salary and charged him with the responsibilities of an educational diplomat and propagandist. His duty, as he understood it, was "to give special attention and encouragement to the upbuilding of the negro rural schools by helping to introduce into them all kinds of useful and profitable industrial and vocational subjects."[15]

Newbold's background and temperament made him an ideal candidate for the job. He was born in 1871 in rural Pasquotank County, in the northeastern corner of the state, and grew up in the home of his paternal grandfather, William Newbold, who before the Civil War had been a prominent slaveholder and had served for many years as county sheriff. That ancestry guaranteed young Newbold a certain measure of credibility among conservative Democrats and local school officials. On his mother's side, however, he laid claim to a different South. Her parents were Quakers who refused the privilege of slaveholding and bequeathed to their grandson a preference for moral suasion over force or violence as an instrument of social change. Late in his career, Newbold acknowledged that inheritance when he told the state's county superintendents of the two principles that had always guided his work: "time and information." "Reliable factual information properly presented," he contended, "will help to change the attitudes of ignorant, prejudiced and even hostile-minded persons, as quickly and as effectively as a good genuine case of religion."[16]

That preference for the "quiet way" in race relations also had roots in Newbold's experience as a student at Trinity College, where he fell under the influence of historian John Spencer Bassett. Bassett never managed to rid himself of an "inborn Southern feeling that a negro is not to be treated as a white man." Yet as a scholar and teacher he helped to pioneer the study of African American history in North Carolina and used his research to defend principles of moderation in race issues. "I desire to find out what there is in the negro," the professor once explained, "what he has done, and what he can and will do." That curiosity eventually incited a bitter challenge to Bassett's tenure and alienated him from much of the white South. But as is often the case with students, Newbold and his peers were not so easily provoked as their elders. Indeed, many of them admired and took to heart their mentor's devotion to the free and reasoned investigation of southern problems. After graduating from Trinity in 1895, Newbold went to work as a superintendent of graded schools in Asheboro, Roxboro, and "Little" Washington; in his dealings with the towns' residents, he put into practice the lessons of both the classroom and the hearthside. In contrast to the racial exclusionists, he, like so many reform-minded schoolmen, believed that blacks had a role to play in the South's future—albeit a subordinate one—and that if handled properly they would learn to "accept in the white man's country the place assigned [them] by the white man." Sizing up that attitude, a clerk in Superintendent Joyner's office observed that Newbold was "intensely practical." He had, the clerk reported, "as few radical and impractical ideas about him as any man we have among us."[17]

Newbold first approached the cause of black education with "considerable timidity and many misgivings." He felt flattered when invited to interview with Wallace Buttrick, secretary of the GEB, and initially promised to begin work as state agent of Negro rural schools on July 1, 1912. But doubts soon overwhelmed him. Newbold worried about the job's repercussions, fearing most of all that it might "embarrass my family, socially or otherwise." That concern grew even stronger when the Washington school board offered a handsome raise, one that by Newbold's own calculations was much "larger than the school income could bear." The board hoped to retain their popular superintendent and, at the same time, to save him from self-destruction. Surely he was happy with his graded school post, they insisted. Why, then, would he "give it up to enter a new and untried field— one, which to a native Southerner might prove on many occasions to be most embarrassing and difficult?" Not knowing how to answer, Newbold "demurred and hesitated." In June, just weeks before his scheduled move to Raleigh, he wrote to Superintendent Joyner and to Wallace Buttrick asking for more time to consider their offer.[18]

Months later, a dramatic confrontation with a white teacher finally resolved Newbold's doubts. The woman had heard of the new work in Joyner's office. What a "'shame,'" she scolded, that a successful graded school man would think of "'giving all [his] time and talents to Negroes.'" Forced to defend himself, the young superintendent scrambled for a reply. "I am not worried about the matter of talents," he snapped, "but you are mistaken as to giving all my *time* to Negroes. If I do my duty as I conceive it, I shall render [the] greater service to my own people." Newbold explained that improving black education would ultimately "add to the dignity, the self respect and the humanity of the State as a whole," then he challenged the woman to weigh her own Christian and New South principles. Was it not "both good religion and good economics," he asked, "for the strong to help the weak?" Newbold remembered years later that those words seemed to set him free. He realized at once that dedicating his career to black education implied no betrayal of either race or region. Instead, it offered him a place of honor within the New South crusade. Buoyed by that conviction, Newbold arranged to begin work as state agent on June 1, 1913. Trepidation, he confided to Wallace Buttrick, had given way to "broad visions and schemes . . . now 'raging in my brain.'"[19]

Newbold began his efforts at remodeling black education by touring the state to promote the work of the Anna T. Jeanes Fund. The Jeanes Fund was named for a Quaker philanthropist from Philadelphia, who upon her death in 1907 bequeathed $1 million for the "*rudimentary education*" of southern blacks. Under the direction of James Hardy Dillard, a member of the Southern Education Board and dean of the College of Arts and Sciences at Tulane University, most of the income from that endowment was

Nathan Carter Newbold at work in his Raleigh office (Courtesy of the Special
Collections Library, Duke University)

spent helping individual counties pay the salaries of supervising industrial
teachers. Those workers, known more commonly as Jeanes teachers, visited in black schools and neighborhoods to tutor their colleagues, talk with
parents, and offer children demonstration lessons in cooking, sewing, animal husbandry, and other practical skills. A number of North Carolina
counties had already begun to experiment with the Jeanes program by the
time Newbold took office. His aim, however, was to put the work on a permanent footing, particularly in the coastal and Piedmont counties, where
the state's black population was most heavily concentrated. By 1917, he
could claim considerable success in that effort. The number of Jeanes
supervisors had nearly doubled: it had grown from nineteen to thirty-five,
placing North Carolina first among all the southern states. The nearest
rival was Alabama, which had twenty-two supervisors.[20]

Newbold thought of the Jeanes work primarily as a woman's calling. His
reasoning suggested themes familiar from the story of white education,
although considerations of race provided a distinctive twist. A speaker at
the 1903 meeting of the North Carolina Teachers Association, the profes-

sional organization of black educators, noted that men who "try to rear families have had to leave the school room." Among blacks as well as whites, teaching was rapidly becoming feminized. For blacks, however, the cause was rooted less in the economics of school expansion than in the price of white supremacy. After 1900, salaries for black teachers grew slowly and in some cases even declined. In Wake County, for example, both men and women saw their earnings fall by roughly 15 percent between 1899 and 1910. The gap between black and white salaries across the state also widened dramatically. In 1899, blacks had earned on average $68 a year, as compared to $88 for whites; by 1913, the difference had multiplied six-fold. Blacks received $127 a year—about half of the $252 paid to whites. Jeanes teachers fared somewhat better, earning $25 a month for a six- to eight-month term, but even at that rate, black men with family responsibilities could scarcely afford to accept the post. Black women, on the other hand, had few opportunities for more lucrative employment. Newbold and county superintendents therefore viewed them as a bargain. They worked cheaply, and as the state agent observed, they were naturally prepared to teach "the domestic side of the work, such as cooking, sewing and the like," which men would almost certainly neglect.[21]

Newbold and county officials also felt more at ease with black women and viewed them as less of a political liability than black men. Since Reconstruction, champions of white supremacy had caricatured black men as menacing creatures too easily excited by the idea of freedom and too readily inclined toward both criminality and sexual excess. Those images endured well into the twentieth century, clouding the perceptions of even those whites who thought of themselves as racial moderates. In 1916, T. Fletcher Bulla, superintendent of schools in Randolph County, wrote to Newbold of his frustration with the man he had recently hired to conduct the Jeanes work. "I am frank in saying that I am not satisfied with the present Supervisor," Bulla complained. "[The job] has made him feel like he is the biggest man in the county and he makes himself too familiar when he comes into my office. He takes too many liberties." Newbold sympathized, but felt that the superintendent should have known better from the start. The best course of action, he suggested, was to dismiss the Jeanes teacher—gently, if possible—and then replace him with a woman, whom Bulla would no doubt find more pliant and deferential. "A great majority of workers in North Carolina are women," Newbold explained on another occasion, "and, all things considered, we find that they get better results."

James Dillard, director of the Jeanes Fund, concurred. In fact, he had warned Newbold earlier that he would consider cutting off support to any county in which "the employment of a man is insisted upon." "With one or two exceptions," Dillard declared, "we have never had a man on the list that measured up to the work which women accomplish."[22]

The Jeanes program was, from the beginning, tightly hedged in by race and gender. Nevertheless, it won the devotion of both black women and their communities. When county school officials failed to adopt the work on their own initiative, neighborhood leaders often pushed and prodded until they got what they wanted. During the summer of 1916, for example, Bladen County's association of "Colored Teachers" featured the Jeanes program in one of its regular meetings. At the end of the gathering, sixty women signed a petition asking the county to hire an industrial supervisor for their schools. They also "pledged the sum of fifty cents each" toward the Jeanes worker's salary. By early September, the school board, no doubt relieved that its obligations would be partially offset by the teachers' contributions, approved the appeal and wrote to State Agent Newbold to make the appropriate arrangements.[23]

Such grassroots enthusiasm sprang in part from the opportunities that the Jeanes work offered to women who felt a passion for learning and racial self-help. Mamie Turner, a native of Duplin County, came to Jeanes teaching after a long struggle for her own education. She grew up "in dire poverty" and, because she worked as a white child's nurse, received almost no formal instruction before the age of ten. In Sunday school, however, Turner developed a love of reading and a desire to become a teacher. From her teenage years on, she devoured books and magazines of all kinds. Her library contained back issues of *Literary Digest* and of the popular current affairs magazines, *Outlook* and *Atlantic Monthly*; inspirational volumes, such as Booker T. Washington's *Up from Slavery*; up-to-date pedagogical texts; and an assortment of European classics, including *Vanity Fair* and *Adam Bede*. Turner and her mother both sacrificed so that she could attend the public normal school at Elizabeth City and one day lead a classroom of her own. "[My mother] was earning at that time only five dollars a month as a cook," Turner remembered. "She paid $1.50 a month for my lodging and sent me one box of groceries." To help make ends meet, Turner worked in the school's kitchen and lived frugally. She "formed the habit of going to [class] without breakfast" and made do with a single dress.[24]

After graduation, Turner found employment in a country school, where she sought to share with the next generation some measure of her own accomplishment. She began by building a school laundry, which neighborhood women and girls used both to lighten the burden of their own household chores and to earn extra cash by taking in washing from whites. Each spring, Turner drove "a blind horse or a slow gray mule" from one community to the next, organizing plays and other school festivals to raise money for new desks, window shades, and heaters, which county officials refused to buy. Like other Jeanes teachers, she took up those projects with a determination "to be of . . . service to my people." Rather than wait for the white school board to fix things, Turner explained, "we went ahead and got what we needed."[25]

Turner and other black women were also drawn to Jeanes teaching because it offered them access to the public stage at a time when their husbands and brothers had been driven from politics and their communities had been pushed to the margins of civic life. Supervising teachers served as liaisons to white officialdom, often deftly negotiating the needs of their clients. In Anson County, for example, J. R. Faison helped parents in one neighborhood win permission to "move their school to the center of the district, where the pupils may have good water and a larger play ground." Other workers lobbied authorities for small appropriations that made big differences in students' health and comfort. With such assistance, Junia Bennett reported, she was able to have a number of Duplin County schools "remodeled, some painted," and, at others, to have "[sanitary] closets built" so that the children would no longer be forced to relieve themselves in the woods.[26]

In these and other instances, Jeanes teachers went about their work in a quiet, face-to-face manner. But for Annie Welthy Holland, an industrial supervisor in Gates County, the role of intermediary eventually led to the very heart of the state educational bureaucracy. Born in Isle of Wight County, Virginia, in 1871, Annie Holland grew up near the plantation where her ancestors had been slaves. When she was twelve years old, her maternal grandparents packed her off to Hampton Institute for the kind of education that the local common school could never provide. But sickness and money troubles soon got in the way. After only a year and a half of study, Holland was forced to withdraw from Hampton and begin searching for employment in Virginia's country schools.[27]

Holland's work as a teacher ranged far beyond simple classroom lessons. Troubled by scenes of rural poverty and its deprivations, she launched a

Annie Welthy Holland (Courtesy of the North Carolina Division of Archives and History, Raleigh)

variety of schemes designed to create an environment in which her students would find it easier to learn. Her most imaginative venture was a land-buying club through which sharecroppers and renters pooled their savings in order to help one another purchase farms of their own. Holland's appreciation of the connection between schooling and the struggles of everyday life may explain why she crossed the border into North Carolina sometime around 1911 to begin work as a Jeanes teacher in Gates County. Her accomplishments there immediately caught the eye of State Agent Newbold, who frequently highlighted them in 1913 as part of his promotion of the Jeanes program. In fact, Newbold was so impressed that three years later he hired Holland as his assistant, giving her the responsibility of coordinating Jeanes activities throughout the state.[28]

The Jeanes Fund and the North Carolina Teachers Association paid Holland's salary until 1921, when the legislature created within the state Department of Public Instruction a new Division of Negro Education. At that time, Holland became one of only a handful of black professionals to be carried on the public payroll. Hers was a unique position: a black woman in a white bureaucracy, she had the ear of both the state superintendent and his agent for Negro schools. Her travels also brought her an acquaintance "with large numbers of teachers, ministers, housewives, and other leaders of her own race," as well as various county superintendents, who regularly sought "her advice on matters connected with the Negro work." Through those relationships, Holland exercised considerable influence over policymaking for black education statewide.[29]

Newbold wrote glowingly of Jeanes teachers in his reports to both the GEB and state superintendent Joyner. "A good strong, well-qualified Supervising Teacher in every county," he contended, "is perhaps the best single effort that can now be made for the uplifting of our colored schools." But in the same breath Newbold also warned that the long-term success of the Jeanes program was threatened by a desperate shortage of African American teachers. In 1915, at the behest of the GEB, he surveyed county superintendents to determine how many new teachers they needed annually to staff their black schools. Replies pointed toward an alarming figure of five hundred—nearly twice the number of graduates sent into educational work each year by the state's public normals and private black colleges. The lesson of that imbalance was clear: reformers' hopes of turning the schoolhouse into an effective instrument of race-relations management depended on the state's somehow guaranteeing an adequate supply of properly trained teachers. Under existing circumstances, thousands of black children remained untouched by the disciplinary influence of industrial education. Too few teachers were available to acquaint them with the three R's, much less introduce them to the lessons of the Jeanes work.[30]

Efforts to solve the problem of teacher supply tested Newbold's patience and resourcefulness. He hoped at first that most of the deficit could be made up by North Carolina's dozen or so private black colleges. In mid-December 1913, he invited "leading negro educators" to attend a special conference in Raleigh to consider a model curriculum for teacher training. The plan, he explained, would balance "sound academic instruction in the essentials" with a "practical course" in cooking, sewing, farming, and a variety of manual skills. By Newbold's account, his guests all exhibited an encouraging "spirit of frankness and candor." After two days of discussions, "the conference, as a body and without opposition," endorsed his proposal and recommended that it be "used in all the higher educational institutions for negroes in the State." But the inaction that followed suggests that the exchange was somewhat less candid than Newbold had imagined. The college presidents were no doubt sincere when they expressed an interest in expanding their normal departments. Few, however, were likely to have seen industrial training as an essential part of their mission. Shaw University, Biddle Institute, Livingstone College, and Scotia Seminary— indeed, nearly all of the colleges—could trace their origins to the Reconstruction era; they had been founded to prepare "ambitious and competent young Negroes" for positions of leadership as ministers, lawyers, doctors, and educators. Their catalogs listed a variety of industrial offerings—most often as a means of helping students earn their tuition—but their faculties remained loyal to a traditional commitment to liberal studies. A year after the Raleigh gathering, Newbold's exuberance had dimmed. The best he could now say of the conference was that in some ill-defined way, it had "aided the cause." Nearly a decade passed before he bothered with such a venture again.[31]

The state's publicly funded normal schools also gave cause for discouragement. Since their founding in the 1870s and 1880s, they had been hobbled by inadequate financing and the politics of race. Through two acts of consolidation, first in 1903 and again in 1905, the state legislature agreed to merge the six original schools into three "stronger, better equipped, better supervised" institutions located at Elizabeth City, Fayetteville, and Winston. White lawmakers, however, refused to support a single, model school comparable to the white normal at Greensboro. The faculty of such a powerful institution, they feared, would surely manipulate teacher training for unacceptable "political" purposes. Those same misgivings also worked to continue the black normals' starvation for funds, despite the promise that had accompanied consolidation. In 1913, appropriations for the three schools totaled $17,000. By comparison, the white normal college at Greensboro received $95,000, and another $67,500 was budgeted for three one- and two-year schools for whites at Greenville, Cullowhee, and Boone. That inequity was crippling. Because the black schools could offer their students no financial assistance, most young men and women were forced to attend "at irregular intervals." In 1908, for instance, one of the schools reported an initial enrollment of seventy-four students; but within a matter of weeks, nearly half that number had returned home for lack of funds or because they were needed "to assist in gathering and housing the crops." Those who remained received instruction from an overworked faculty who labored in classrooms so poorly equipped that "writing, if done at all, [was] done on the knees."[32]

Those difficulties forced the public normals to deny admission to scores of applicants each year. The schools also lost others who simply turned away from institutions they judged to be substandard. Young folks from Robeson County who hoped to become teachers, for example, seldom attended the state normal at Fayetteville, despite its close proximity. They traveled instead to Lumberton, the county seat, where they enrolled in the privately operated Whitin Normal and Industrial Institute. The reason, explained a local educator, was that graduates of the Fayetteville normal "*generally failed*" their certification exams. Choosing to avoid the state school was therefore "a matter of common sense" and, the teacher added, of "*history also.*" The people of Robeson County, he explained, had for years been acquainted with the sad state of public teacher training.[33]

The Whitin Institute was one of dozens of small, often church-supported normal schools that sprang up all across North Carolina in the years immediately after disfranchisement. As many as sixty such institutions may have been in operation by 1914.[34] Newbold knew little of those schools when he took office, and we know even less today. Most left behind no historical record other than a handful of letters, or perhaps a cache of photographs, that became part of the correspondence files of the state superintendent. But even that fragmentary evidence tells a dramatic story of black communities determined to hold on to the privileges of citizenship. In places like Lumberton, parents, businessmen, and churchgoers answered hostile white officials by establishing normal schools of their own that would provide local children with qualified and devoted teachers.

Such was the work of William Claudius Chance, a native of Martin County. Like so many black educators of the time, Chance belonged to a unique generation, the first to be born and to come of age in the aftermath of emancipation. As a result, he felt a special sense of possibility in life and a binding obligation to uplift his race. Chance was born in 1880 in a tiny lumber town called Parmele. Both his parents and the grandparents who raised him had once been slaves. Chance grew up in poverty, but by laboring on a farm, he managed to earn his tuition at the North Carolina Agricultural and Technical College for Negroes in Greensboro. After receiving a bachelor's degree, he went on for further study at Howard University, including one year of instruction in law. Chance returned home in 1909 and at once began working to improve the plight of Parmele's "poverty stricken and neglected" black children. He considered the local school a disgrace. It had only one teacher to serve sixty students and operated on an annual budget of "scarcely" $160. In an effort to relieve that situation, Chance opened a private alternative, using a church building and his own home for classroom space. His school enrolled thirty boys and girls during its first term, and it continued to grow so rapidly that in 1911 it absorbed both the public school and the county appropriation for black education. Chance called the new consolidated facility the Parmele Industrial Institute. He and his wife and another teacher offered a traditional curriculum combined with studies in agriculture, mechanical arts, and domestic science. Over time, Parmele became the first school in Martin County— white or black—to occupy a brick building, and also the first to lengthen its term from four to eight months. Those achievements bore witness to Chance's perseverance in what he later described as a struggle against "hardship and opposition."[35]

Newbold and his fellow reformers looked upon places like Parmele with ambivalence. The independent schools operated outside the bounds of state supervision, and for that reason they could not be counted on to promote the "harmony" and "kindly feeling" that whites considered so essential "if the best interests of both races [were] to be served." By the same token, however, the schools offered a unique opportunity for teacher training. They were firmly embedded in supportive communities and, with imagination, might be used to tackle the problem of teacher supply at the local level, thereby circumventing both the hostility of white legislators and the suspicions of students who had grown wary of state institutions. By acquiring a controlling interest in the independent schools, reformers could at last begin training a corps of classroom workers loyal to both "southern ideals" and the principles of industrial education.[36]

As it turned out, just such an experiment had already been tried under the auspices of the John F. Slater Fund. The Slater Fund was named for a Connecticut textile manufacturer and financier who in 1882 made a gift of $1 million for use in educating "the lately emancipated population of the Southern States." At first, most of the income from that bequest went to support industrial training at the college level. But when James Dillard took control of the fund in 1910, he quickly began to steer its spending in new directions closely allied to his other work, the Jeanes program. His idea was to convert private black institutes across the South into a network of publicly administered county teacher-training schools. The first such facility was created in Louisiana in 1911, when Dillard brokered a deal between trustees of the Kentwood Agricultural and Industrial Institute and white school officials in Tangipahoa Parish. The trustees agreed to sign the institute over to public control and to change its name to the Tangipahoa Training School for Negro Children. In return, they received a pledge of $500 a year from the Slater Fund to support the new institution and a promise from the parish school board to pay the expense of teachers' salaries and equipment. That arrangement marked a bold departure in black education. "Every county in the South has felt the need for fairly well-trained teachers," Dillard explained, "but so far as we know this is the first time that [local authorities] have deliberately planned to get them by training them at home."[37]

When Dillard offered to fund similar ventures in North Carolina, State Agent Newbold and Superintendent Joyner embraced the proposal "most heartily." So did many principals of the state's independent black institutes. The Slater scheme offered black educators a way to place their work on a more stable footing and ease the fund-raising demands that ordinarily consumed so much of their time and energy. In Martin County, William Chance moved at once to strike a deal with white officials. In the fall of 1913, he invited State Agent Newbold to visit the Parmele Institute and inspect his work there. Newbold, in turn, filed an enthusiastic report. "All

William C. Chance's county training school at Parmele, 1917 (Reprinted from *A Suggested Course of Study for County Training Schools for Negroes in the South*)

the facts in the case bear out the statement that the Principal is a man of sound character and good judgement," he wrote. "If [Chance] can get the help he desires his school will be a genuine benefactor to his race . . . serving a Negro population [of] about 50,000 to 75,000." On the basis of that endorsement, directors of the Anson Phelps-Stokes Fund, another of the many northern charities dedicated to black education, agreed to make a one-time grant of $2,000 to help Chance replace his "very poor and inadequate buildings." Then, in 1914, with the new construction complete, Chance signed over the Parmele property, including his own house and thirty-two acres of land, to the county board of education in return for full training-school status and an annual appropriation of $750 from the Slater Fund. His was one of five such facilities in operation during the 1915–16 term. Three years later, their ranks had grown to fourteen, giving North Carolina the largest network of county training schools in the South.[38]

Newbold and the training-school principals were joined by a calculus of opportunity but not always by a shared sense of purpose. Events at Parmele offered a dramatic illustration of that fact. Within a matter of years, William Chance had used his school's new standing to build something of an educational fiefdom. The institute enrolled students from throughout eastern North Carolina, and each year it sponsored a summer school for teachers who wished to upgrade their certificates. Through the summer program in particular, Chance gained influence over hiring decisions in schools not only in Martin County but in a much larger territory that encompassed neighboring Pitt, Edgecombe, Halifax, Bertie, and Beaufort Counties as well. That growing prestige and power became a source of irritation for Martin County superintendent Asa J. Manning. The two men fought openly in 1920, when Manning tried to clip Chance's wings. Just weeks before the start of the summer session, Manning threatened to move the exercises to Williamston, the county seat, and to place them under the direction of the local Jeanes supervisor, whom he had already tried to establish as Chance's rival. The superintendent was disturbed by Chance's demand for supplemental funds to improve the Parmele campus; his insistence on enrolling the region's most advanced teachers, rather than sending them away to one of the state-run normals; and his plans to employ Parmele's own faculty for the summer term, instead of deferring to choices recommended by the county board of education. In Manning's eyes, each of those acts represented yet another attempt to expand the training school's clout and to challenge his own authority as "the responsible head of the public school system." What happened next remains unclear, although it appears that State Agent Newbold intervened to work out a compromise. Chance conducted his normal school on schedule but without either advanced students or additional funds from state and county coffers. To Newbold's way of thinking, such a resolution seemed ideal: the work for black education in eastern North Carolina went forward without interruption, while Chance's own ambitions were checked "within reasonable bounds."[39]

But the compromise failed to effect a permanent peace. During the summer of 1922, without warning or explanation, Superintendent Manning ordered Parmele closed and relieved Chance of his duties. The principal responded by launching a petition drive among leaders of the black community and a handful of influential white supporters. In an impassioned plea to the county board of education, he reviewed his life's work and insisted on a public airing of the charges against him. "I was born in Martin County," Chance declared. "Every fiber of my being, every pulsation of my heart has been devoted to the . . . improvement of its citizenry. Am I to be penalized for doing this? I ask you, gentlemen of the Anglo Saxon blood, who hold justice the dearest in your possession, to see that I at least be given the protection of the law." Hearing in that appeal an opportunity to be rid of the "Parmele problem" once and for all, Manning and his supporters made arrangements in early November for an emergency meeting of the county board, to which State Agent Newbold—but none of

Chance's defenders—would be invited. In that closed forum, with the benefit of testimony from a "few picked persons," they planned to convict the training-school principal on charges of fraud, moral corruption, and racial insubordination. "By his manner and way of teaching . . . and his influence in the community," exclaimed Manning's bill of indictment, Chance had "sought to encourage and engender strife" between blacks and whites in Martin County and beyond. At the last minute, however, an inside tip revealed the scheme and gave Chance time to employ a white attorney, who managed to stall the proceedings.[40]

Through all of this, State Agent Newbold tried desperately to keep his distance. He was wary of overstepping his authority and becoming entrapped in a conflict that would "finally have to be settled by local officials." But now it seemed that he had no other choice. If Manning were to succeed in his campaign to discredit Parmele's principal, a pall would be cast over the entire training-school program, not to mention the state agent's own office. In mid-January, after several failed attempts to negotiate a settlement, Newbold chose to take a "very firm and decided stand." He wrote to Manning and the county board, warning that their actions had violated the state constitution. Their refusal to open Parmele had deprived local children of a six-months school term and was therefore actionable in a court of law. The school board backed down at once and agreed to Chance's reinstatement, but Manning—who had pledged to leave the state before admitting defeat—had one last card to play. In February, he directed the county treasurer to reduce faculty salaries at Parmele to a level below the minimum required by the Slater Fund, thus jeopardizing the institute's most important source of income. Without support from the county board, however, the order was soon rescinded. At last, Manning gave up the fight. He decided not to resign as county superintendent, but he did agree to excuse himself from the management of Parmele. In the future, that task would belong solely to the board of education.[41]

William Chance had won a crucial victory. For the time being, at least, his work at Parmele was secure. But victory did not necessarily imply vindication. Throughout the long ordeal, State Agent Newbold studiously avoided defending the embattled principal. He even went so far as to deny any "personal knowledge whatever concerning the character or ability of Mr. W. C. Chance." In light of the glowing report on Parmele that he had sent to the Slater Fund nine years earlier, when Chance first sought training-school status, that was a startling declaration. Yet it reflected Newbold's assessment of the Martin County situation: he believed there was plenty of blame to go around. The state agent chastised Manning for allowing personal pique to cloud his professional judgment, and he faulted Chance just as harshly for forgetting that the training school had been "established to benefit the children of Martin County" rather than private ambitions. To Newbold's way of thinking, the conflict at Parmele was no simple struggle to defend black education. He was as eager to discipline Chance's dreams of personal and racial empowerment as he was to limit the damage inflicted by a reckless and vindictive superintendent.[42]

Despite such difficulties, Newbold remained confident that training schools and the Jeanes program, together, were capable of "developing the negro people along the right line." "The whole scheme is intended to do for the negroes what practically every southern white man believes should be done," he explained. "Teach the negroes to observe the ordinary regulations as to sanitation, cleanliness, and health; teach them to be industrious and self-supporting; to be self-respecting and respectful; to be honest and reliable; to give them as much of a general education as they are, at this time, able to use . . . and to enable them to become as intelligent and as useful citizens of the county and State as the conditions under which they labor will permit." But as events at Parmele suggested, that vision alone never defined the whole of African American schooling. Success, after all, depended on the active participation of students, parents, and teachers. As a result, there was always room around the margins for some measure of black autonomy. In the everyday practices of the classroom, training-school instructors and Jeanes teachers managed to read into the lessons of industrial training their own meanings and desires. The outcome was an approach to education shaped no less by African American traditions and aspirations than by the hopes and fears of white reformers.[43]

Consider, for example, the Orange County Training School, located in Chapel Hill within the shadow of the state university. The school traced its origins to the work of L. H. Hackney, who had served for fourteen years as the principal of Chapel Hill's black graded school. Dismayed by the town's meager funding of black education and its refusal to repair the building in which he taught, Hackney resigned his post in 1912 in order to open a school of his own. He called it Hackney's Industrial and Educational Institute. Student tuition and contributions from local churches, however, proved inadequate to pay Hackney's bills and his teachers' salaries. Desperate to keep the school alive, he agreed in 1916 to sign the property over to the county in return for appropriations from both the public coffers and the Slater Fund. Marcus Noble, a professor of education at the university, lobbied tirelessly for county approval of the deal. The new training school, he argued, would stand as a model of its kind and, by virtue of its proximity to the university, would spread its influence far beyond the county's borders. "One thousand young white men are in our university annually from every section of the state," Noble explained, "and a good, practical, successful school right before their eyes from day to day will be a compelling argument for negro education which will bear fruit when these students take their place as men in the public affairs of the state."[44]

The training school's faculty shared that hope for better race relations and an improved white attitude toward black education. But in their daily classroom labors, they also took heed of even broader visions within the black community itself. Like most African American educators, they refused to draw sharp distinctions between industrial and literary studies. Students at the school practiced cooking and carpentry each morning; in the afternoons, they read poetry in their English Club, debated in their Young People's Literary Society, and rehearsed their productions of Shakespeare's plays. Parents and neighbors read of the school's work in a weekly student newspaper called *The Orange Jewel*. The journal's purpose, its editors explained, was "to penetrate the minds and hearts of students and friends of youth throughout our county with the fruits of our intellectual achievements and aspirations, and to give our parents and friends a concrete example of the good things their children are doing as a result of their individual support of our school." The training school would educate body and hand, to be sure, but not at the expense of nurturing the spirit and liberating the mind.[45]

With similar commitment, the faculty also placed their school in service to African American traditions of mutual aid. In their domestic science classes, girls sewed clothes for the poor and sponsored a penny lunch program that fed the sick and indigent throughout the county. During the 1917–18 term alone, they cooked and served nearly seven thousand meals. That kind of work was not unique. At the Pamlico Training School, for example, young boys made rabbit traps in their woodworking class, and the animals they captured put meat on the table for both students and neighbors. "Together with things that the children [bring] from home," the principal bragged, the school could feed itself for up to three days at a time.[46]

Such activities stood in telling counterpoint to the ethic of individualism that resounded so loudly in much of the home and farm demonstration work among white school children. Black educators were as eager as anyone to recognize and reward special talent and accomplishment, but they also sought to remind students of the ties of obligation and responsibility that bound them to their race and to the communities that sustained their learning. Rebecca Lines, a student at the Orange County Training School, captured that sense of duty in an acrostic she wrote for her graduation exercises sometime in the early 1920s. Playing on the meanings of an obvious double entendre, she called her composition "Orange County Commencement":

O, many and bright are the faces we see
Congregated with us here today—
Old Orange hails each in words of the past,
"United we'll stand," through the fray.
Never fear of defeat, for "Union means strength,"
Today see! the victory we claim.
Yet we claim it just now, as an incentive to fan
Courage faint, into bright glowing flame—
Our hopes for our county rise up bright and strong,
Many visions for her we behold,
Many jewels are here for her daughters and sons
Each of which is worth far more than gold.
Now harken! get busy, just "go to the ant,
Consider her ways, and be wise,"
Every one now is needed, each heart and each hand
May help in the struggle to rise—
Each height may be scaled, each victory won,
Not at once, though can prim order grow,
This adage remember, sometimes then my friends,
"The mills of the Gods, grind slow."

For Rebecca Lines and her friends, the triumphs and challenges of race, community, and individual melded almost seamlessly into one.[47]

Jeanes teachers, too, displayed considerable initiative and inventiveness in their rendering of industrial education. For the most part, they labored without the encumbrance of cut-and-dried rules. Dillard and Newbold sent them into the countryside with a broad mandate, encouraging them to pursue virtually "any line of neighborhood improvement which opened up." In turn, many of the teachers made the most of that freedom by fashioning their schools into what historian Glenda Gilmore has aptly described as rural "settlement houses." That was especially true after 1914, when the GEB and the U.S. Department of Agriculture made funds available so that Jeanes supervisors could work during the summer months organizing Homemakers' Clubs among neighborhood women and girls. The teachers began in early spring by calling a meeting of prospective members to discuss the fine points of vegetable gardening: "the matters of selecting a plot[,] . . . preparing the soil, [and] planting the seed." Then, through the heat of July, they offered tips on proper weeding and cultivation and filled idle time with lessons in sewing, cooking, rug-making, and "general cleaning." Young women who came to the clubs without the skill to "run a straight hem in an apron" learned to make their own dresses, while others mastered techniques for remodeling old garments and "mend[ing] old clothes." Finally, by late August, Jeanes teachers arranged canning parties to put away the harvest of tomatoes, onions, beans, and peas. Those gatherings marked the passing of summer and, for most of the participants, the beginning of a new school term.[48]

The young homemakers' accomplishments were inspiring. By 1918, Jeanes teachers had organized 833 clubs, which had a total membership of more than 16,000. "Children and old folks alike," they boasted, took a keen interest in the work. Women in many communities were especially excited to learn to can. The practice was "new to them," the Jeanes teachers discovered, and a most welcome innovation. Canning helped the poorest families to better their living conditions by stretching the bounty of summer into the lean months of winter. For others, it provided a much-needed infusion of cash. Statewide, the Homemakers' Clubs produced goods with a total value of at least $230,000, a significant portion of which was converted into hard currency through local markets. The women used that money to supplement the salaries of neighborhood teachers; to buy the books, desks, and pictures that would make "little homes" of their schools; and, not least, to treat themselves to store-bought luxuries—fine cloth, hats, and home furnishings—that otherwise would have remained far beyond their reach.[49]

The Homemakers' Clubs did not limit themselves to domestic pursuits, however. The women also organized scores of "moonlight schools," in which adults learned to read and write, often with help from their own or their neighbors' children. Club members sponsored "white-wash days" to encourage friends to tidy up their yards and to paint their homes, stores, fences, and barns. And, most notable of all, the clubs joined forces with the state Board of Health to fight the spread of tuberculosis, one of poverty's cruelest afflictions and a leading cause of death among African Americans.[50]

Like other Jeanes teachers across the state, Carrie Battle organized Edgecombe County students into brigades of "modern health crusaders." Battle's pupils stood for daily inspections of personal hygiene, made a study of home sanitation, and exhorted their parents on the benefits of fresh air and individual drinking cups. Before long, they had their mothers collecting "baking-powder cans [and] jelly glasses" for family use at the water bucket, and even reluctant fathers were agreeing to sleep with the windows open. The young crusaders also acted as junior health officers; they fashioned homemade "sputum cups" for tubercular patients in their neighborhoods and took up classroom collections to assist those of the most humble means. In places where the health work caught on, whole communities seemed to be transformed. Homes and schools were "clean and airy," Battle reported, and people wore their tidiness as a badge of honor. With banners and slogans, children competed to advertise the new-found spirit. " 'We own a clean body, clean home and a clean school,' " boasted one; " 'Nobody but a crusader can enroll [here],' " proclaimed another.[51]

The Homemakers' Clubs bore an obvious resemblance to the health and home demonstration work that became such an integral part of white schooling during the same years. Jeanes teachers spoke a language of thrift, self-help, and community development that white reformers found familiar and easily understood. In fact, many on both sides of the color bar hoped that shared interests would lay the foundation for improved race relations. Newbold, for example, noted with enthusiasm that "white people, as a rule, are more interested in the colored schools in counties that have had Supervisors than in those that have not." But the vocabulary of reform also shifted meaning as it passed through the filters of race. Jeanes teachers and their clients viewed the classroom less as an instrument of rural redemption and racial management than as a means of laying claim to New South "progress." Through the Homemakers' Clubs, parents and children learned "the value of united effort" and struggled to obtain the "better things in life—better schools, better homes, [and] better living conditions"—that whites so often reserved for themselves. In a society founded

Commencement parade in Gaston County, April 1916. The man carrying the Neely's Grove sign was seventy-three years old. He was actively involved in improving his neighborhood school and had just learned to read in "moonlight" classes arranged by the county Jeanes teacher. (Courtesy of the Rockefeller Archive Center)

on the assumption of black subordination and dependency, those were powerful accomplishments; they affirmed the ability of ordinary black men and women in some small measure to shape and direct their own destinies. Little wonder, then, that Jeanes teachers viewed the club work as "*the best*," most gratifying aspect of their labor. It was, a teacher explained, one means of ensuring that "might will not [always] prevail over right."[52]

Such sentiments also found expression in the commencement festivals that marked the end of the school year in black communities all across North Carolina. The first celebrations were organized in 1914, probably by Jeanes teachers eager to promote their work among parents and local school officials; by 1917, they had become a regular spring event in at least thirty counties. Commencement-day exercises usually began with "a grand parade" of "school children, teachers and patrons in buggies, wagons, floats, carts, and on foot"—all of them led by "a chief marshall" mounted on horseback and proudly regaled "in silk hat and sash." Often the columns of students alone stretched on for more than a mile. The parades ended at the county courthouse or some other suitable hall—perhaps a cotton or tobacco warehouse—where celebrants listened to speeches by local dignitaries and enjoyed "declamations and readings by the children, songs[,] . . . spelling contests and the like." Then, with the official ceremonies completed, teachers and women volunteers laid out a lavish dinner on the courthouse grounds or in the yard of a nearby church. "Everybody," State Agent

The Perquimans County Jeanes teacher standing before an exhibit of her students' wares (Courtesy of the Rockefeller Archive Center)

Newbold observed, was "expected to partake"—even curious whites, who supped at segregated tables set aside by their black hosts.[53]

During the afternoon and early evening, parents and neighbors could also view exhibits of the children's "industrial" handicrafts. Girls sat proudly behind displays of "handsome . . . embroidery and drawn work," lace, and "plain gingham aprons," while boys showed off their skills in carpentry, blacksmithing, and leather work with scale models of country homes and walls of tools, bridles, and harness leather. Like the rest of the day's activities, those exhibits offered celebrants a chance to take the measure of their community, to affirm common aspirations, and to spell out a distinctively African American understanding of industrial education.[54]

Black commentary on commencement exercises is difficult to come by, but the writings of black teachers printed in the *Star of Zion* shortly before the turn of the century suggest how visitors most likely "read" the industrial fairs. In the boys' shopwork, for instance, many undoubtedly saw a strategy for holding on to craft skills otherwise wrenched away by segregation. "Skilled labor," the *Star* had explained, was "steadily drifting into the hands of white workmen," who, by refusing to accept black apprentices, secured a "monopoly both of the labor market and the science of [their] craft." It was therefore essential that one generation of black artisans pass its skills on to the next, lest the trades "fall among the lost arts" and poverty completely overwhelm the "Negro . . . rank and file." Girls' domestic wares spoke in similar fashion to a claim on the spiritual and material fullness of American citizenship. A history of great "sufferings," the *Star* observed, had burdened many African Americans with "a settled hopelessness of things temporal." Schooling offered the only effective antidote. "Let the laboring classes of the coming generation be swelled by men [and women] who have at least a plain English and industrial education," the paper exclaimed. "It will prepare the way for a piano or organ to go into the farm house, and that will call for paint on the outside, and a few vines on the porch, and of course the village daily." State Agent Newbold once noted that parents and visitors approached the children's exhibits as "a revelation [and] a wonder"; it seems now that he was on to even more than he realized—or perhaps admitted. Through the commencement exercises, and the industrial fairs in particular, black celebrants found a public voice for making moral and political claims on the rest of society. "This," they seemed to exclaim, "is how the world should be."[55]

Newbold gave little attention to the potentially subversive meanings of the commencement exercises. His own assumptions about African American life may have filtered out the message of the celebrations, or perhaps an overwhelming desire to win converts to the gospel of industrial education simply led him to discount any evidence of apostasy. Whatever the case, he emphasized to white audiences the order and decorum of African American parents and children. "Ten years ago," the state agent wrote, "it would have been impossible to bring together [a great crowd of] colored people without many arrests and much disorder." But now, gatherings of up to 25,000 or 30,000 regularly assembled for the county commencements without a single disturbance of any kind. Indeed, "the best white people" often commented on the good behavior that prevailed "and also upon the fact that the Negroes were well dressed and seemed contented and happy." "From this standpoint alone," Newbold concluded, "commencements are very much worth-while." They seemed to offer proof that industrial instruction had worked its magic, inculcating in black men and women the habits of responsible living.[56]

Other white observers, particularly those situated in North Carolina's heavily black eastern counties, were not so sanguine. They understood, quite correctly, that what began as a demonstration of responsibility could easily turn into an assertion of rights. Commissioners in Nash County voiced a common concern: Newbold's program, they worried, came perilously close to "putting the negro [back] in politics." The board of education in Pasquotank County agreed. After two years of experimenting with the Jeanes work, they announced "plainly that they did not care to try it any longer." In other eastern counties, where politicians were less decisive, white citizens sometimes took matters into their own hands. At the Columbus County Training School in Whiteville, for instance, principal James P. Spencer found himself besieged by night riders. During the spring of 1923, he laid plans to expand the campus and to bring his institution up to the standards of a high school, complete with boarding facilities for students who lived "some little distance" away. A "new building," he reported, was soon to be erected on "ground that I have had a great love for, over which I have cried in [hope] that I might . . . bring about . . . a new order of things [and] a brighter day for the Negro boys and girls in this County." But just as construction began, white vigilantes—abetted by a black rival who played the role of Judas—began to terrorize Spencer's family and students. They came "to do acts of vandalism to school property; tear down screens at night; pull up school pumps, and the like." Before long, Spencer was ready to leave. "Sir," he wrote to State Agent Newbold, "I feel that I owe it . . . to my dear wife, who has toiled in fear [and] wept as a child . . . to make a change of school, where we shall at least rest at night." Dreams and high hopes, he conceded, had—at least for the moment—been "blasted to powder."[57]

Not far away, in Greene County, the tribulations of Mary Battle offered a similar illustration of the great divide that could separate black educators even from the moderate whites who claimed to be their friends. Battle began work as Greene County's Jeanes teacher in 1914, and by every indication she was "untiring" in her efforts. During one summer season alone, she oversaw the planting of 115 gardens and guided the women and girls in her Homemakers' Clubs through the canning of 20,000 quarts of vegetables. A year later, she "put in an order for an automobile, a Ford roadster," which she hoped "would enable her to do [even] more work in the same time." Battle also seems to have been one of State Agent Newbold's favorites and to have gotten along well with her county superintendent, J. E. Debnam. At the end of her first term, Debnam reported to the county board of education that she was "doing some much needed work and doing it well." But in 1916, when Battle organized a campaign among black parents and teachers for a county training school, those relations were strained nearly to the breaking point.[58]

Battle first got the idea of establishing a training school from a pamphlet Newbold had distributed in the spring of 1915. "Your 'Biennial Report' came to me today," she wrote the state agent, and "I have read it from cover to cover. Everything I read was encouraging but [the section on the Slater Fund] appealed to me most because I think of the great need of a 'County Training School' . . . daily (yes sir, daily)." Greene County, she explained, was terribly far behind in its provisions for black education. Statistics gathered by the state superintendent's office bore out that claim. Black teachers in Greene County earned roughly 15 percent less than their counterparts in other rural areas; only one in five held a first-grade certificate, compared to one in three for the state as a whole; and only 64 percent of black school-aged children were actually enrolled in classes, compared to 76 percent for rural districts statewide. Battle was convinced that a training school would help to right those conditions. Within a matter of months, she and black parents had raised over $1,400 in private donations and had made all of the arrangements necessary to turn a local academy and ten acres of land over to the county.[59]

But when Battle and her supporters took their plan to the board of education, they were sorely disappointed. Some board members seem to have opposed on principle any increase in public spending for black education. Others worried about heightened racial tensions in the aftermath of a recent lynching and the consequences of appearing soft on matters of race. As a result, the board, led by Superintendent Debnam, refused to make the special appropriation of $750 needed to obtain a matching grant from the Slater Fund. That decision prompted an angry confrontation. When challenged by Battle and her supporters, the school board dug in their heels. Whites, they scolded, "*paid [the bulk of the] School taxes*" and therefore had no obligation to make special provisions for black education. In point of fact, Battle replied, black citizens paid into the school fund far "more than they [got] out." Superintendent Debnam could hardly believe his ears. He complained to State Agent Newbold that Battle was creating a most "embarrassing" situation. He had tried to show her in private that "the negro schools in this county cost in round numbers $1000 more than the negroes contribute," but she would not believe him. What, then, was he to do? To make his case publicly would only heighten the risk of a white backlash. "The best thing for the negroes themselves," the superintendent concluded, "is to let the matter severely alone."[60]

Debnam was surely caught in a predicament, but it was of his own making. His effort to exonerate the Greene County board rested on indefensible assumptions. No matter how common the practice, the state's courts had opposed the racial division of school funds for more than three decades. Newbold, Debnam, and Battle all understood that fundamental point of law. Nevertheless, it was Battle who caught the full brunt of State Agent Newbold's anger and frustration. Shortly after receiving Debnam's complaint, he wrote to reprimand her for overstepping the bounds of racial propriety. It was not her place to make demands of white officials, nor to raise the delicate issue of financial equity. She should instead defer to the judgment of the "school authorities," who, after all, were her "friends, and the friends of [her] race." They were "better informed as to the financial conditions [of the county school system] than any one else," Newbold scolded, and could be trusted to act when the timing and the circumstances were right.[61]

Newbold's letter forced Mary Battle to make a painful choice. To back down was to violate both her own principles and the interests of the community she served, yet to stand firm was to risk alienating the only white patrons who could be counted on for some measure of sympathy and support. In the end, Battle swallowed her pride and penned a reply that remains as difficult to read as it must have been to write. "What I did was not [meant] to do . . . harm," she explained. Her "steps taken for good" had been "mistaken" and misconstrued by the board. Yet, all of that aside, Battle agreed to accept the burden of blame as hers alone. She promised "not to press the Training School issue" again and to do her best to "*live down*" the affront that she had given her white benefactors.[62]

The struggle over the training school was a trying experience for Mary Battle; in fact, it may have contributed to her untimely death. In January 1918, a year and a half after the training-school dispute, she died of tuberculosis. Battle fell victim to the very circumstances of poverty and ill health that she had "toiled so zealously" to improve. Stunned by the loss, black parents launched a fund-raising drive to build a monument to her memory. Even Superintendent Debnam, who had taken such strong exception to Battle's assertiveness, joined in. He helped to start the "subscriptions with a personal gift of $5.00." One year later, in April 1919, teachers, students, and school patrons gathered in Snow Hill, the county seat, for a special commencement exercise. The customary parade wound its way not to the courthouse but to the local black school, where the chief marshal led a crowd of several hundred in dedicating an obelisk of white marble. "It is a

Monument erected in honor of Mary Battle. Today the obelisk stands in front of a
Rosenwald school that is used as part of the Greene County campus of Lenoir
Community College. (Courtesy of the Rockefeller Archive Center)

very creditable piece of work," State Agent Newbold reported, "an evidence of genuine appreciation by a grateful people."[63]

Greene County never built a training school, but in the years after Battle's death, local children did begin to benefit from new schoolhouses constructed with assistance from the Julius Rosenwald Fund of Chicago. Those facilities were sorely needed, for in Greene County, as in the rest of the state, the value of school buildings for blacks lagged far behind that for whites—$1,643 for whites statewide, compared to $483 for blacks. What those numbers meant in practical terms was that African American children often labored over their lessons in overcrowded, ramshackle classrooms. The black school in Greene County's Ormonds township, for instance, was little more than "an old hull of a house" measuring 18 by 26 feet, "unceiled and in bad condition." The school had an average daily attendance of eighty-eight students, and the teacher frequently had no choice but to send many of her pupils outdoors, even in the dead of winter. "To try to teach children in such shacks," one observer concluded, was a pitiable "waste of time." The school in Snow Hill was hardly better. In 1921, local officials had it torn down and replaced with a three-room brick Rosenwald building that still stands as a backdrop to Battle's monument.[64]

That school and at least half a dozen others in Greene County were built as part of a regionwide campaign prompted in large measure by World War I and the challenge it posed to southern race relations. When fighting in Europe choked off the supply of immigrant labor, many American industrialists turned to the South for its ready reserve of African American workers. Labor agents scoured the region enticing black men and women with often fantastic promises of high wages and a new life free from the rule of Judge Lynch and mob violence. Some recruits viewed the North as a "promised land"; others understood the harsher realities. But few failed to recognize in the exigencies of wartime a chance to seize control of their own fortunes and to secure new opportunities for their children. A steady stream of black migrants had been flowing out of the South since the end of Reconstruction. That trickle of people now swelled into a flood tide. Between 1914 and 1920, roughly half a million black southerners relocated to the North, and during the next decade, nearly twice that number followed in their footsteps.[65]

The Great Migration, as it came to be called, rekindled old fears of black mobility. Although North Carolina lost a smaller portion of its African American population than Deep South states, the consequences were nonetheless profound. Eighty-seven of the state's one hundred counties reported severe labor shortages by 1916, and in heavily black cotton- and tobacco-growing sections, exasperated white landowners turned to "sewing grasses and raising stock" rather than pay the "outrageous wages" of up to $1.25 a day necessary to attract and hold on to reliable field hands. The loss of cheap labor, however, was only part of the problem. The exodus also signaled the unwillingness of black North Carolinians to live according to the racial mores that whites had defined. "We want to stay here, be good and law abiding citizens, and assist in developing this the garden spot of creation, enriched by [the] tears, blood, sweat, labor and precious bones of our fathers and mothers," a contributor to the *Star of Zion* exclaimed, "but we must first have right treatment. . . . Jim Crowism . . . MUST GO."[66]

Fearful that the South would soon be drained of its labor supply—and that its racial troubles might spread just as quickly throughout the nation—both federal officials and regional reformers began to search for a means of curing what they called "migration fever." Most white southerners were inclined to turn first to repression, but that strategy often proved to be self-defeating. "The white man may know something of the 'Old Black Tom' and the 'Old Black Mammy,'" explained the *Star of Zion*, "but he is absolutely ignorant—despite his boast to the contrary—of the thought that is in the mind of [the] new and younger Negro. It will require the new and younger brain of the white race to meet the new and young brain of the Negro. Old methods will not apply, [not] 'by a long shot.'"[67]

Many reform-minded whites agreed. In their view, the only hope of slowing the "exodus movement" lay in putting "some check . . . upon rampant 'Jim Crow' legislation and restrictions." The reformers never called for an end to segregation, but they did insist that, for its own sake, the white South had to afford African Americans wider opportunities to "better themselves." That meant, among other things, providing more equitable school facilities for black children. When federal officials set out to document the causes of the Great Migration, they found that, among other concerns, "the inadequacy of school facilities" was a reason "universally given for leaving the South." Such testimony made a profound impression. During the late summer and early fall of 1917, the Southern University Commission on Race Relations, which had been established five years earlier by James Dillard and other advocates of educational reform, held a series of meetings in Raleigh to consider possible cures for the mounting labor shortage that was causing "so much concern to planters and farmers." The participants worked from the assumption that most black southerners "would prefer to remain in the land of their birth if guaranteed a living wage . . . and proper instruction for their children." To that end, the commission issued an open letter highlighting education as the most effective defense "against all allurements." Better schools, they and others insisted, would enable the white South to "keep the Negro and have him satisfied."[68]

That argument caught the ear of Julius Rosenwald, president of Sears Roebuck and Company, who by the time of World War I had already established himself as an influential player in black education. He first became interested in the subject after reading a biography of William Baldwin, the railroad magnate who had helped shape the Capon Springs conferences on southern education and had served as a founding member of both the SEB and the GEB. Rosenwald was taken by Baldwin's quest for an orderly, consensual system of race relations and by his desire to remove questions of racial justice from the realm of politics to that of individual initiative, merit, and ambition. The Chicago philanthropist took as his motto a line from Booker T. Washington's autobiography, *Up from Slavery*: "The individual who can do something that the world wants done will, in the end, make his way regardless of race." Those words summed up Rosenwald's vision of America's racial future as well as an understanding of his own life's story. Though he was now a prosperous merchant, he had been born to Jewish-émigré parents who, nearly half a century before, had struggled to escape the evils of militarism and ethnic persecution in their native Germany. Rosenwald intimated that there was a certain parallel between his own family's struggles and those of southern blacks.[69]

As a resident of Chicago, Rosenwald was well situated to observe the magnitude of the Great Migration and to ponder its implications for the country's economic and social life. The majority of southern emigrants either passed through the city or made it their final destination; between 1910 and 1920, Chicago's black population nearly tripled, from 44,000 to more than 109,000. Concerned by those numbers, Rosenwald began to commit his private fortune to the pursuit of Baldwin's principles. Close to home, he donated more than $700,000 to fund the construction of African American YWCA's and YMCA's, most of which were scattered across the nation's industrial heartland. Their purpose was to give refugees from the South temporary shelter, to help them find employment, and—through sports programs, cultural and vocational classes, and home visits—to train them in the virtues of thrift, sobriety, hard work, and respectable behavior. In 1925, Rosenwald explained his motives to the readers of *Collier's National Weekly*. "Because I am interested chiefly in white people," he wrote, "I take an interest in the Negro. . . . It's a question of whether we want them to be vicious or decent. I prefer to have my children and grandchildren live where there is no ignorant, uncouth and vicious underprivileged class." In the South, Rosenwald hoped that his spending on rural schoolhouses might accomplish the same ends. Through proper instruction in uplifting surroundings, African American children would learn to be productive citizens, to take pride in rural life, and—most important—to avoid the temptations of political agitation and public strife.[70]

Rosenwald built his first schoolhouses under the influence of Booker T. Washington. The two men met in Chicago in 1911, and a year later Rosenwald agreed to serve as a trustee for Washington's Tuskegee Institute. To mark both that appointment and the occasion of his own fiftieth birthday, Rosenwald gave Washington $25,000 to divide among black colleges and industrial schools dedicated to the Tuskegee idea. The black educator disbursed most of the money as instructed, but he asked to use a small portion of it—$2,800—for the construction of six model schoolhouses in rural Alabama. Rosenwald was so pleased with the results that in 1914 he made another donation of $30,000 to be used in building one hundred additional schools. Grants of up to $300 were given to black communities in Alabama and six other southern states—including North Carolina—on the condition that both parents and local school officials match the gifts with private donations and public funds. Three years later, that work was the main topic of discussion among southern educators meeting in Washington, D.C. State Agent Newbold and others encouraged Rosenwald to make his school-building program a regional enterprise and to give it solid financial backing. Such a venture, they argued, offered the best means of securing the South's supply of agricultural labor and of shoring up its system of race relations. Rosenwald agreed. On October 30, 1917, he chartered the Julius Rosenwald Fund, which over the next decade spent all but $600,000 of its $4 million budget on the construction of schoolhouses for African American children.[71]

Black communities in North Carolina greeted news of the fund with jubilation. State Agent Newbold reported that "School Superintendents, Jeanes teachers, County Training School principals," and parents "all seized upon the Rosenwald [plan] as . . . the 'missing link' . . . needed to round out a complete program for Negro [education]." His office was inundated with requests to share in the Chicago philanthropist's largesse. In Aberdeen, a small farming community in Moore County, for example, parents collected $425 among themselves in hopes of moving their plans for a new school to the top of Newbold's list. When the county superintendent wrote to plead their case, he emphasized what an extraordinary undertaking their fund-raising efforts had been. The parents had made a kind of "sacrifice," he advised Newbold, "of which you and I know but little." All of them were day laborers; none possessed more than $500 worth of property; and most did not own their own homes.[72]

In other, still poorer communities, where families simply had no cash to spare, people turned to familiar customs of mutual aid and offered their contributions in kind. That was the case in Mecklenburg County's Lemley School District No. 2, where the local Jeanes teacher, Elizabeth Harris, tallied an account of nearly $200 worth of labor and materials. A number of households supplied wagons and teams to haul bricks and timber; others helped to clear a construction site; and still others offered their skills in carpentry, bricklaying, shingling, and painting. State Agent Newbold described such efforts as both "pathetic" and inspiring. They confirmed that in the eyes of black patrons, a Rosenwald school promised the "dawn[ing] of a new day."[73]

African American leaders across the state shared that perception. In fact, when the first Rosenwald money came to North Carolina, the black teachers association quickly made arrangements to provide Newbold with an assistant to help in promoting the work. The organization chose Charles Henry Moore to fill the post and paid his salary with funds drawn from their own coffers, along with donations from black businessmen. Moore came to the job with illustrious credentials. He was born a slave in Wilmington in 1853, and while little is known of his early life, it seems that he spent several years in Chapel Hill, where his mother labored as a domestic servant for students at the university. When Moore was old enough to attend college, he studied first at Howard University from 1871 to 1873, and then went on to earn a bachelor's degree from Amherst in 1878. Again,

The Rosenwald Fund gave black communities the leverage they needed to replace dilapidated schoolhouses, like the one at Sneads Grove in Scotland County (above), with new structures similar to Anson County's Salem school (below). The Salem school was built from standardized blueprints and had two classrooms separated in the middle by an "industrial" room for vocational training. In most communities, black teachers treated the industrial room's special purpose as a polite fiction. They often used the room not to provide manual training but to offer traditional instruction to additional numbers of children. (Courtesy of the Rockefeller Archive Center and Fisk University Special Collections)

details are sketchy, but it appears that both ventures were sponsored by George W. Kidder, a lumber merchant and the son of one of Wilmington's most prominent white Republicans.[74]

After graduation, Moore returned to Wilmington, where he dabbled briefly in journalism; then he moved to Greensboro, where he worked as principal of the city's black graded school and as professor of ancient languages at Bennett Seminary, a private black college founded by the Freedmen's Aid Society of the Methodist Episcopal Church. Moore used both positions to distinguish himself as a man of vision and influence among African American educators. He helped to organize the North Carolina Teachers Association in 1880, and ten years later he spearheaded the drive to bring to Greensboro a new state-supported Agricultural and Mechanical College for Negroes. Moore served briefly as the college's vice president and then as chairman of its Department of English. There he remained until 1915, when he resigned to join State Agent Newbold in the Rosenwald work.[75]

Moore labored tirelessly to "sound the tocsin of better schools" in African American communities throughout the state. During his first year in Newbold's office, he logged more than 12,000 miles in visits to thirty-five counties and spoke to at least 100,000 citizens. "Wherever I have gone," Moore reported, "I have endeavored to commit our people to the policy of self-help, and be it said to their credit, they have become aroused and enthusiastic." That excitement grew at least in part from awareness that the Rosenwald program could be used to temper the balance of power between black parents and white school officials. Local school boards routinely offered poverty as an excuse for turning away appeals for new buildings. But that tactic lost much of its credibility when set against grassroots fundraising efforts and the prospect of a matching Rosenwald grant. As a result, State Agent Newbold explained, advocates of black education found it easier to press their cause and to "get a hearing" from even the most recalcitrant white officials. It was no surprise, then, that the Rosenwald work became "almost a crusade [among] the Negro people." Each spring, the flood of applications grew larger. In June 1919, for instance, Newbold reported that forty-nine appeals had already been funded for the summer building season, another forty-six were pending, and still others continued to pour in. "It is not unusual," the state agent boasted, "to get ten to fifteen applications in one day's mail." By any measure, such numbers were a sign of "gratifying success."[76]

But even as Newbold gloried in the Rosenwald work, he continued to confront what he once described as a "wilderness of . . . difficulties." Although the school-building program helped some county boards find new enthusiasm for black education, others attempted to turn it to their own advantage. Newbold complained bitterly of county officials who submitted construction plans for his approval and then, with Rosenwald money and the contributions of black parents in hand, erected buildings of inferior quality or diminished proportions. Sometimes the trouble resulted from poor supervision of incompetent contractors. Most often, though, the cause was calculated fraud. Dishonest school boards handled the money saved by such trickery in much the same way that they dealt with tax revenues: they used it to upgrade white schoolhouses, while leaving black classrooms overcrowded and inadequately furnished. Under those circumstances, African American parents had every reason to believe that Newbold had betrayed "their confidence . . . and sold them out to the whites." "I hope you ask your own self a question," one father wrote, "that if your Race was treated that way by my race would that be right?" Newbold shared the man's anger, for he too had been "stung." Nevertheless, there was little that he could do to set matters straight. Refusing to certify a second-rate building might offer some sense of personal satisfaction, but by denying black children a place to study, such a policy would only compound the injustice already done. To Newbold's consternation, "slick" county officials understood his predicament all too well.[77]

There were also problems within the state agent's own office, where Charles Moore sought to capitalize on his independent status and easy access to the public stage. Moore was a man of independent opinions who openly defied white standards of racial propriety. In his first annual report to the North Carolina Teachers Association, published privately in 1916, he wasted no time in raising the delicate issue of "irregularities" in the appropriation of school funds. He charged that in the thirty-five counties he had visited during the preceding year, "thousands of dollars were being diverted from their proper channel" through the corrupt practice of financing white education at black expense. Statistics drawn from the reports of the state's Tax Commission and Newbold's own boss, state superintendent James Joyner, seemed to verify the claim. During the 1912–13 fiscal year, those thirty-five counties collected taxes from black families on more than $20 million worth of real and personal property. They were also home to over 100,000 "colored school children," or about one-half of the state's black school population. The same counties, however, built only forty-three new schoolhouses in African American communities. "I make no comment on the obvious and striking contrast," Moore quipped. "These figures convey their own silent testimony."[78]

That biting tone was characteristic of Moore's public style. He pursued the argument over funding with relentless zeal. At a commencement exercise in Louisburg, for example, he "called attention to the fact that some of the [local] colored schools did not receive justice," and he boasted loudly of his efforts statewide to save "negroes over $75,000 by requiring the white authorities to do their duty." The speech enraged county superintendent E. L. Best, whom Moore had not even paid the courtesy of a visit upon his arrival in town. "If he had come to see me . . . and had shown the proper spirit and attitude towards the work," Best protested, "I would have taken great pleasure in cooperating & helping him in every way possible." But Moore seemed to have other ideas. His words, the superintendent scowled, were "calculated [to] arouse a bad feeling between the negroes and the whites" and thus "to do . . . a great deal of harm." When news of the incident reached Raleigh, State Agent Newbold offered to "come at once" to smooth Best's ruffled feathers. Moore's behavior, however, did not surprise him. Other superintendents had made similar complaints, and some had even barred the black agent from their schools. Newbold agreed that Moore needed to be "taught a lesson" in "tact and good judgment." His independence bordered on arrogance and was, in Newbold's view, inappropriate for a black man of his station.[79]

Other state agents across the South faced similar troubles. They despaired over the obstructionist behavior of local school boards and worried openly about the political leverage that the Rosenwald work seemed to offer black critics of segregation. The problem, they argued, was that the school-building program had been entirely too successful in inspiring "negroes to take courage and become conscious of their own resources." As a result, black school advocates tended to overestimate the extent to which the Rosenwald campaign was "the work of the colored people themselves," and local whites remained deeply suspicious of the entire enterprise. Louisiana's state superintendent, T. H. Harris, traced those difficulties to a fault at the very core of the Rosenwald Fund's organization. While state agents were responsible for managing individual grant applications, final decision-making authority rested in the hands of an all-black committee made up of faculty and administrators at Tuskegee Institute. That arrangement, Harris argued, was "very unwise": "Mr. Rosenwald has accomplished a wonderful amount of good in stimulating the erection of negro schoolhouses, but I shall expect to see his efforts collapse wholly within the next few years unless he shall adopt a different organization for the handling of his aid. If the negro committee shall continue to administer the funds, I predict that the Southern States will soon begin to withdraw, one by one, from participation." The reason seemed obvious. "Negroes," Harris continued, had not yet "reached that degree of development" necessary for handling such "important matters."[80]

For Newbold and other state agents, that critique defined a clear path into the future: the key to saving the Rosenwald work was to consolidate their own authority. During the spring of 1919, the state agents convinced Rosenwald and his advisers to cut the fund's ties to Tuskegee and open a new regional office headed by a "thoroughly competent white Southern man." News of the decision left Booker T. Washington's widow, Margaret, and his successor, Robert R. Moton, angry and distraught. Rosenwald, they charged, had capitulated to the prejudices and "whims" of southern whites. But in the end there was little that either Washington or Moton could do except "yield their own judgment" and submit to their benefactor's "verdict." "One cannot easily argue with a man about what is his own," they conceded, "even though you may differ absolutely with him." In June 1920, the Rosenwald committee at Tuskegee packed its files and shipped them off to Nashville, Tennessee, where Samuel Leonard Smith, a former state agent, was preparing to take control of the fund's operations. The job had almost gone to Newbold, but Smith's advantage was his thorough knowledge of schoolhouse planning. As a student at Nashville's George Peabody College for Teachers, he had worked closely with Fletcher B. Dresslar, one of the nation's leading authorities on school design and architecture.[81]

Once in office, Smith drew on that background to bring new discipline to the Rosenwald program. He published in pamphlet form a series of stock blueprints to be distributed among county school boards, and in 1924 he brought all of his designs together in a single booklet called *Community School Plans*. That publication included not only architectural drawings but also detailed instructions for the selection of quality materials, the management of building contracts, the layout and planting of school grounds, and the construction of sanitary privies. With the help of those guidelines, Smith hoped to tame local officials, who too often went about school building "according to their own notion[s]." He advised county superintendents that all Rosenwald schools were to be built to his specifications and that before making final payment on any project, his office would insist on receiving both written and photographic evidence of compliance.[82]

In North Carolina, State Agent Newbold undertook similar measures. He convinced the legislature, as part of a general overhaul of the public school laws in 1921, to create within the state superintendent's office a separate Division of Negro Education. That act transformed Newbold's status. As chief of the new division, he was no longer a mere adviser supported by outside agencies but rather a true deputy superintendent with authority to enforce school policy. The change made little difference in the way that Newbold dealt with most county school officials; under normal circumstances, he still preferred to press his views through diplomacy and gentle persuasion. But when that approach failed, he now possessed the option of speaking with an uncompromised official voice.[83]

After 1921, Newbold's letters acquired a new tone. He wrote candidly to troublesome superintendents, reminding them that efforts to obstruct or subvert the Rosenwald campaign not only violated basic standards of "justice and fairness" but were also potentially actionable in a court of law. There is no evidence that Newbold ever followed through on the threat that such letters implied; he was too mindful of "public sentiment" to consider "making any show." Nevertheless, in negotiating the fine points of race relations, the weight of office made a subtle but important difference in the state agent's ability to command adherence to his own standards of thought and behavior. Take, for example, the case of L. Berge Beam, superintendent of Lincoln County. Lincoln had one of the state's poorest records on black education, and Beam himself was known for being openly hostile and unsympathetic "in dealing with his Negro [patrons]." One observer exclaimed that the superintendent "would let the millennium swoop down" before ever "building a colored school." But after a month of pointed correspondence with Newbold and his assistants in November 1925, Beam finally capitulated. In a long letter of contrition, he declared a new allegiance to the "educational interests of the negroes" and agreed at last to launch a construction program with a combination of Rosenwald funds, local appropriations, and state loans.[84]

In the process of reorganizing his office, Newbold also pursued the resignation of Charles Moore, whose outspoken criticisms of school funding had proved so difficult to restrain. Moore left the Rosenwald work in

July 1920 and returned to private life in Greensboro, where he continued his crusade against the injuries of segregation. In 1927, he became one of the founders of the city's first black hospital. Later Moore moved to New York City, where he died in 1952 at the age of ninety-nine. His was an extraordinary century. Born a slave, he lived to see emancipation's promise of citizenship crushed by the weight of segregation and disfranchisement; a determined soldier for racial justice, he died on the eve of the Second Reconstruction, to which his life's work had been committed.[85]

Newbold replaced Moore with two new assistants. One of them, William Frontis Credle, had joined the office in 1919 and was now named "supervisor of the Rosenwald Fund." Credle was a graduate of the university at Chapel Hill and a former superintendent from Hyde County. The other assistant was George Edward Davis, the first black member of the faculty at Biddle Institute, a freedmen's college on the outskirts of Charlotte, founded in 1867 by white Presbyterian missionaries. Davis was born in Wilmington in 1863 and completed graduate work at Howard University during the early 1880s; at Biddle he served as a professor of natural science and sociology. He was, one recent observer has written, a "study in contradictions": a lifelong Presbyterian who was buried a Catholic; a man committed to overcoming white racism who, on one occasion, asked for time off from the Rosenwald work to participate in a memorial service for the Confederacy.[86]

It was no surprise, then, that Davis's approach to "handling white people" contrasted sharply with that of his predecessor, Charles Moore. "My attitude in all my work," he confided to Credle, "has been conciliatory—*not* truckling, if you please—but an attitude of patient waiting and persistent working." In a county commencement address, Davis pressed the point even further; he claimed high moral ground beyond the fetish of color, and at the same time, he conceded to whites the initiative in matters of racial equality. "I deplore the habit of some of our own people who make the mistake of saying so much of race and color as a basis of justice," he explained to a crowd of black parents, students, and teachers. "We hear too much today from would-be race leaders, about race pride [and] race love. . . . The evils that are now crushing us have root and sap in the narrow spirit of race and color, and Negroes have no more right to foster them than any other race. Such feeling is too narrow for a basis of motive and action." That outlook, Davis insisted, had enabled him to enjoy "many tender friendships . . . with the white race"—friendships, he said, "that have taught me the lessons of forgiveness and have awakened in me a patient, tolerant waiting for better days to come." Those words so impressed State Agent Newbold that he prepared a transcript for distribution among his co-workers and other white friends of black education.[87]

Davis and Credle pursued the Rosenwald work along strict racial lines. That arrangement "seemed wise," State Agent Newbold explained, because "the white supervisor of the Rosenwald Fund can speak with more force and authority to white school boards and white superintendents and the Negro supervisor . . . can speak with more force and effectiveness to the Negro people." Credle served as Newbold's second-in-command, and in that capacity he had only limited contact with black school patrons. He divided his time between office work in Raleigh, where he administered the state's Rosenwald budget, and field visits to individual counties, where he met with white officials to negotiate construction plans and inspect finished projects. Davis, on the other hand, answered to Credle as his immediate superior and spent most of his time on the road. His report for March 1929 summed up a typical month's work: "Traveled approximately 1100 miles. . . . Helped in raising $600.00 for Rosenwald buildings. Addressed 2000 people."[88]

The new racial division of labor laid bare the tensions and contradictions at the heart of the Rosenwald campaign. In obvious ways, it sharply curtailed the work's capacity to provoke and sustain an open debate on race and schooling; in deference to white supremacy, black educators had once again been pushed to the margins of public life, a safe distance from the cords of power. By affirming segregation's logic, however, the reforms in Newbold's office also made the task of promoting the school-building enterprise considerably less challenging. The openly hierarchical relationship between Credle and Davis comforted county officials, many of whom saw in it welcome evidence that whites, rather than their black clients, would retain ultimate control over the course and direction of African American schooling. In turn, that assurance helped to cultivate what Newbold and his lieutenants viewed as a quickening spirit of interracial cooperation. Davis, for example, took special pleasure in the dedication of a Rosenwald school in the Pender County community of Long Creek:

The chairman of the County Board of Education . . . and the principal and the faculty of the white school of the community came out and joined with the colored people in expressions of appreciation. The building was filled to capacity and perhaps as large a number were at the windows and around the doors and grounds. . . . I think as much satisfaction over the building was shown by the large number of white people present, most of whom were served dinner in the building, as by the Negroes themselves. I was born within thirty miles of this place and I have known the time that white people would have lost their social prestige among their fellows had they been courageous enough to come out and dine "with publicans and sinners."

Such enthusiasm continued to be cast in the mold of racial paternalism; nevertheless, it helped to fuel a new surge in school construction. By 1928, when the Rosenwald Fund began to phase out its school-building efforts, North Carolina claimed a place of regional leadership. Although the state ranked only fourth in black school-aged population, it led the South in Rosenwald facilities, with a total of 675. Mississippi ranked a distant second with 493, and only four other states—South Carolina, Texas, Alabama, and Louisiana—boasted more than 300.[89]

That achievement gave cause for celebration. On April 4, 1928, Julius Rosenwald and dignitaries from across the South traveled to Method, North Carolina, a small settlement on the outskirts of Raleigh, to join with state school officials and members of the local black community for the dedication of the four-thousandth Rosenwald building, an eleven-room structure on the campus of Wake County's Berry O'Kelly Training School. The crowd packed the school's auditorium for nearly a full day of speech-making. William Credle led off with an account of how the Rosenwald program had transformed the material conditions of black education in North Carolina. When the school-building campaign began, most African American children studied their lessons in hovels that State Agent Newbold had once described as "a disgrace to an independent, civilized people." But now, more than a decade later, at least half of those young people attended well-built, "modern schools distributed over 86 of the 100 counties in the state." Credle had no doubt but that those children shared the sentiments of members of the Edgecombe County choir, who had composed a special school song. Their refrain was simple and direct: " 'Mr. Rosenwald has blessed us.' "[90]

Other speakers championed the moral triumphs of the Rosenwald work, noting that it had " 'brought order, peace, [and] docility' " out of the " 'more or less chaotic disorderliness' " of southern race relations. On one side of the equation, State Agent Newbold observed, the school-building campaign had helped to "cement the love and devotion of the Negro people for their State" by demonstrating that North Carolina's political leaders "really wanted to give them educational advantages." On the other side, the program had served as a "staff and a support" for whites who were concerned about promoting "interracial goodwill." The fact that "colored and white people [could] get together in the construction of good schoolhouses," supporters had declared on an earlier occasion, was "proof of a relation growing in the right direction." Indeed, Newbold saw the Rosenwald work as the culmination of a long program of tutelage—for whites and blacks alike—aimed at updating paternalism, moderating conflict, and promoting civility as the "guiding star" in all race matters. It promised a new social order characterized by *"discussion"* rather than *"argument,"* one in which African Americans could aspire to "better things" in life within the safe confines of a patron-client relationship. On those terms, Newbold exclaimed, blacks and whites could at last work together to guarantee "that the Negro people of North Carolina shall not be a liability, but a powerful asset in the unfolding between Cape Hatteras and Mount Mitchell of the most glorious civilization that the New World has yet seen."[91]

That assessment won endorsements from well beyond North Carolina's borders. By the time of the 1928 celebration, the state had already played host to a parade of visitors from the British Colonial Office, who were scouting programs of black education that might be adapted to the empire's African outposts. One of those visitors was Basil Mathews, head of the Press Bureau of the Conference of British Missionary Societies, whose influential book *The Clash of Color* described the challenge at hand. Mathews observed that World War I had raised among peoples of color throughout the colonial world a dangerous and frightening *"cry for self-determination"*; they could no longer be ruled by old, familiar methods of direct exploitation. But given that reality, what was the alternative? "To resist the claim of the other races for new power," Mathews insisted, would lead to yet another, even more bitter war. "To accept it swiftly without qualification" would just as surely "lead to chaos" and jeopardize the "rich heritage" of Western civilization.

The only path to safety, Mathews contended, was along a third course— that of industrial education, which had been pioneered in the American South. By applying that model to "subject races" around the globe, whites might yet push back the " 'rising tide of color' " and at the same time redeem lesser peoples through the counsel of "infinite patience." Mathews envisioned a world of interracial cooperation best described by biological metaphors that emphasized interdependence as well as hierarchy. "A perfect picture of this tremendous [ideal]," he explained, "is that of the arms and feet, ears and eyes, and all the members of the body, each different from the other; all of varying powers; not all equal in the sense identical; yet all alike essential to the full body; each contributing to the body; and in return the body as a whole giving life and meaning to each member." State Agent Newbold delighted in his visitor's observations. They seemed to confirm what southern schoolmen had predicted nearly a quarter century before. " 'North Carolina's Program for Negro Education,' " Newbold crowed to associates, was "in a position to render [its] service as an aid in interracial matters everywhere."[92]

For a white society still struggling with the "race question," those were reassuring words. But they were also flawed by a failure to acknowledge the depth of bitterness and indignation that lay behind the African American posture of accommodation. Blacks surely welcomed the new schools, better-trained teachers, and improved race relations to which the state agent and his co-workers devoted their labor. But they also recognized that those efforts fell far short of redressing the injuries of Jim Crow. In 1927, an article published in *The Crisis* and widely circulated among black parents and teachers exposed the persistent inequities in North Carolina's school budget. The daily expenditure for white students throughout the state was nineteen cents, nearly double the eleven cents a day spent on black children; white teachers earned on average $800 a year, while their black counterparts received only $436; and, most telling of all, the average value of white schoolhouses per child enrolled was $155 for whites, as compared to $39 for blacks. "We have come a long distance to be able openly in this State to discuss [those] facts," one anonymous informant conceded, but it was still necessary to "do so 'appealingly.' "[93]

African Americans were also quick to point out that the advances that had been made were "not simply [attributable] to the good will of the whites." North Carolina's Rosenwald schools were built by a system of double taxation in which black parents first paid their regular school levies and then dug into their pockets once more to raise the matching funds that the Rosenwald program demanded. By 1928, the cost of all Rosenwald schools in the state totaled $3,606,386. Of that figure, public funds accounted for just under $2.4 million; Rosenwald donations provided roughly $550,000;

and contributions from black communities added up to nearly $600,000 in cash and kind. As one school official noted at the time, the money and labor given by black school builders appears all the "more remarkable . . . when we consider the [conditions of] poverty" in which those people lived. In order to secure their contributions, old folks scraped together "pennies, nickels and dimes," while school children sacrificed their "lunches and other things children love."[94]

State Agent Newbold thought such double taxation was "only fair to the white people of the state." In the past, he explained, blacks had "expected the white people to furnish them schools without any aid or sacrifice on their part"; now "that condition" was "happily change[d]." But black parents and teachers saw things differently. In a rare moment of candor, Margaret Washington, Booker T.'s widow, made their point directly to one of Julius Rosenwald's closest advisers. She penned a *"personal and confidential"* note to Wallace Buttrick in May 1920 to protest the decision to take the administration of the Rosenwald Fund away from Tuskegee. "There are two things in connection with this Fund of which I am sure," she declared. First, it had been "handled with effectiveness" and honesty. Second, "it was not Mr. Rosenwald's money" alone that put up schoolhouses all across the South. "You can tell this by the report of what he gave, and by what the colored people contributed." For Washington and many others, the Rosenwald work said less about white generosity than about black "confidence" and a determination to prevail in the face of oppressive circumstances. Several years later, journalist Joseph K. Hart captured something of that same spirit in a piece that he prepared for *The Survey*, a national journal of liberal reform. Although Hart emphasized the role of white noblesse oblige in uplifting a less fortunate race, his title spoke a more poignant truth: it proclaimed, "The Negro Builds for Himself."[95]

In their eagerness to secure black deference, Newbold and his co-workers often misread their clients' motives and innermost convictions. Throughout the school campaign of the 1910s and 1920s, black parents and teachers sacrificed to provide their children with the rudiments of education. They did so, one Jeanes supervisor explained, with a determination that external constraints should never be allowed to "segregate mind or soul." In the aftermath of the triumph of white supremacy in 1900, African Americans had little choice but to accept their banishment from politics and acknowledge their subordinate status. They retreated from the electoral stage and concentrated on educating their children—instilling in them a sense of pride, independence, and self-respect—and preparing them for the struggles that lay ahead.[96]

Decades later, after a second world war had once again shifted the terrain on which racial matters were negotiated, those classroom lessons boiled to the surface. During the late 1940s, the North Carolina Teachers Association, with which State Agent Newbold had maintained a long and close working relationship, began giving moral and financial support to "law suits designed to seek equal educational opportunities for Negro boys and girls"; and in 1951, shortly after Newbold's retirement, the organization took its militancy one step further by demanding in a formal resolution that the Division of Negro Education be dismantled and its work integrated into the other divisions of the State Department of Public Instruction. Three years later, the former state agent watched from the sidelines as the Supreme Court and an ascendant civil rights movement struck a felling blow to all that he had worked to build.[97]

For nearly half a century, the schools to which Newbold committed his life and career helped to enforce a segregated peace that tightly constrained black lives and meted out opportunity according to white renderings of black aspirations and needs. But in equally important ways, those schools also served as vital bridges between the freedom struggles of the late nineteenth century and those of the mid-twentieth. In a world deprived of politics, black North Carolinians found in the classroom both a refuge and a place to test and renegotiate the limits of white supremacy. That was the legacy inherited by Joseph McNeil, one of the four young men who sat down at a Greensboro lunch counter in February 1960 and helped to inaugurate the sit-in phase of the modern civil rights struggle. When asked to account for his courage, McNeil pointed to his public school and the black women who had been his teachers. From an early age, he recalled, those women had led him to understand by both precept and example "what your rights were as citizens, what you should have, what you don't have," and how the South might yet again be made anew.[98]

Afterword

These little human plants that men call children . . . grow to
their fullest development and bear their richest fruit . . . only
in that mysterious process that men call education.

—*Biennial Report of the Superintendent of Public Instruction,*
1900-1901 and 1901-1902

Looking back on their labors, North Carolina's school
reformers could boast of considerable accomplish-
ment. Within a single generation, they had succeeded in placing a new
institution and a new social grammar at the center of everyday life. By
1925, the one-room common school, with its potbellied stove and homemade benches, had lost its place in all but the most isolated communities.
Such facilities—once a defining feature of the rural landscape—accounted
for less than a third of all the schoolhouses in the state and enrolled an even
smaller fraction of the school-aged population. In their place stood impos-
ing city schools built of brick and stone, or, in the countryside, three- and
four-room consolidated schools staffed by teams of teachers. That architectural revolution bore material witness to public education's vital role in
the creation of a New South. The graded school campaign had helped to
rearrange the boundaries of self and society, elevating the individual above
the claims of family and community. It had shaped new notions of manhood and womanhood, notions that were still anchored in ancient sexual
hierarchies yet were more attuned to the sovereignty of the self. And above
all, school reform had made the classroom into a focal point for continuing
debates over race, class, and gender. In the late nineteenth century, few
North Carolinians—indeed, few Americans—would have considered turning to public education to resolve such issues. Today, as heirs of the new

education, we do so almost instinctively because schooling has become central to how we define ourselves and distribute life's economic rewards.[1]

By the late 1920s the graded school revolution was so complete that its history was already fading from public memory. The journals that had once served as forums for competing pedagogical ideas now spoke in more empirical and seemingly neutral terms; their contributors wrote to refine the techniques of a triumphant system of instruction rather than to champion and make plain its social purposes. History writing had the same instrumentalist aim. When authors like Edgar Wallace Knight and Charles William Dabney set out tell the story of the new education, they were more concerned about presenting a narrative of ascendancy than about describing the competing social visions that had once turned classrooms into ideological battlegrounds. In 1936, Dabney, a founding member of the Southern Education Board, published a two-volume history titled *Universal Education in the South*, made possible in large part by funding from the Rockefeller family philanthropies. He filled more than a thousand pages with what he described as "a series of biographical sketches—a story of the struggles of the men and women who fought the battles of public schools" from colonial times to his own day. Edgar Knight, a professor of education at the University of North Carolina, recounted a similar tale, although he was too young to share Dabney's sense of personal investment in the events he narrated. In back-to-back volumes—the first, on North Carolina, published in 1916 and its sequel, treating the South as a whole, in 1922—Knight offered accounts of the "educational conditions of the past" designed to "assist in breaking up a complacent acceptance of those practices which are more traditional than rational." That concern stayed with him throughout his career. Indeed, the crowning achievement of more than forty years of academic labor was his five-volume *Documentary History of Education in the South before 1860*. In that work, Knight traced back in time the antecedents of modern pedagogy and cataloged the unenlightened practices of the past that for so long "retarded . . . the wholesome growth of public schools."[2]

That approach to history writing also informed the scores of master's theses produced under Knight's direction during the late 1920s and 1930s. His students prepared themselves for careers as school administrators by conducting county-level studies that were strikingly formulaic in their conception and execution. Each opened with a historical chapter that looked back on the nineteenth century to identify noble attempts at establishing support for modern methods of public education. A second chapter inventoried the remaining obstacles to reform, and a third wrapped up with a progressive plan of action. Like their mentor, the young authors of these studies viewed their work as contributions to the final skirmish in a long and "heroic struggle" against the "hindering hand of [tradition] . . . reaching out from a revered but dead past." They sought historical legitimacy for the schools they now commanded, but in doing so they approached the new education as a self-evident ideal rather than as the product and progenitor of a particular moment in time. Ultimately, Knight's protégés placed the schoolhouse outside the very historical forces that they labored to document.[3]

In all of these ways, chroniclers of the new education quickly forgot that turn-of-the-century school reform had enshrined one set of values at the expense of another. Questions of pedagogy that had once been hotly contested vanished from public discourse, and their relationship to basic issues of social and economic organization was lost to the vagaries of time. New institutions, barely half a century old, came to have no past, and because they were beyond history, they seemed immutable and closed to debate. The new education constituted the natural order of things and, in that sense, was no longer new at all.

Today, as we wrestle with the legacies of the late nineteenth century's classroom revolution, the loss of historical memory continues to impoverish our imaginations. At its best, the new education sought to cultivate children's unique, individual qualities and to loosen the constraints of inward-looking communities so that students might imagine novel possibilities for themselves and their society. There was much in that effort to celebrate and cherish. But by the same logic, reform efforts also enshrined an output model of instruction that at its worst reduced the labor of teachers and students to a lifeless matter of numbers and scores, percentages and efficiencies. A report on the Orange County public schools prepared in 1919 by the University of North Carolina's professor of school supervision offered dramatic evidence of that model's growing appeal. The report compared the schools to a manufacturing firm. Taxpayers, it explained, stood in the place of stockholders; members of the county board of education acted as executive directors; the superintendent filled the role of general manager; principals functioned as foremen; teachers played the part of operatives; and at the heart of the enterprise, students comprised the "raw material" waiting to be molded into "a finished product" capable of serving the best "industrial, social, [and] commercial . . . interests of the State." In such an undertaking, there was little room for creativity and individual differences or for what the report called "easy-going, happy-go-lucky, lackadaisical workmanship" on the shop floor. Schools aimed instead to enforce a standardized process of instruction that would move students along "without loss of time" and that would monitor their progress by compiling "careful, systematic, accurate, uniform records." Only in that way, the report insisted, could schools provide an adequate return on their investors' capital and ensure "more nearly universal, more general and uniform results."[4]

Seventy-five years later, that conception of the school as a learning factory persists. As dissenters within the graded school movement pointed out nearly a century ago, it is an approach to instruction that is preoccupied with "details and mechanism" as opposed to "genuine knowledge." Such a pedagogy confines teachers within prescribed curricula and drains much of the wonder from learning. In the end, it also contributes to the alienation that steers roughly thirty percent of new teachers away from the profession within three years and leads fully a third of all students to drop out before finishing high school. Even those who want to fix the shortcomings of today's schools find it difficult to escape the grip of this ledger mentality. In North Carolina, as elsewhere in the nation, they have placed their faith in a new battery of standardized tests and have gone so far as to propose a money-back guarantee for businesses whose employees come to work without basic intellectual skills. The results are that tests too often define knowledge rather than measure it and that classrooms grow ever more lifeless as teachers are encouraged to teach to the tests rather than kindle their students' imaginations.

Such solutions, as well-intentioned as they may be, are bad history and even worse public policy. The contemporary rage for testing comes perilously close to reviving a straightjacketed definition of knowledge as the "furniture of the mind" and, with it, an approach to learning that fills students' heads with information but teaches them little or nothing about adapting what they know to the challenges of a dynamic world. That is a formula for failure. It ignores the most basic principles of child development; it fails to serve the needs of a postindustrial society; and it threatens to widen rather than narrow the gap between the haves and the have-nots. In an emerging global economy, the wealth of nations is coming to depend less on trade in finished goods and more on the exchange of the high-value, problem-solving services of people whom economist Robert Reich has described as "symbolic analysts." The nations that prosper in this new economic order—and, within nations, the citizens who escape the ravages of global competition for cheap labor—will be those who possess the skills of abstraction and relational thinking required to manipulate ideas and information in ways that generate new knowledge, goods, and markets. That is as true for production workers as for researchers and engineers, yet an educational system driven by a desire to get "back to the basics" teaches just the opposite kind of lessons. It aims for a curriculum that is more, not less, uniform and compartmentalized; it feeds students solutions, not problems; and it encourages its graduates to believe that someone else has responsibility for ordering and giving meaning to the world that they inhabit. Such instruction also threatens political peril as well as economic decline, for it produces subjects more readily than citizens. It is, in the final analysis, a pedagogy of limits rather than possibilities.[5]

In that light, the messiness of history seems to provide a better guide for the future than the comforts of an imagined golden age of teaching and learning. We might do well to take a lesson from both the ideals of turn-of-the-century reformers and the anxieties of their opponents. Our children must learn to master letters and numbers, and we have every right to hold schools accountable for that work. But we must also remember that such skills are acquired through the irreducibly human interactions that join teachers and students in common labor; they can neither be taught nor adequately assessed by means of test scores and percentile rankings alone. Meaningful reform requires that we act more boldly, that we give teachers a larger voice in efforts to rehabilitate American education and allow them broader discretion in shaping children's learning opportunities. The most successful schools will always be those in which teachers are free to challenge, inspire, and encourage their students—free not only from the fetters of parochialism but from the fetish of efficiency and routinization as well. As the author of a popular turn-of-the-century handbook on teaching reminded his readers, education entails more than simply equipping students with a store of "positive knowledge." It demands in addition that we introduce children to the delights of inquiry; that we train them in the habits of critical thought; and that we offer them learning that is alive with power, passion, and purpose.[6]

A forthright confrontation with the past might also help us to deal more constructively with the mounting ideological and financial crises of public education. Over the last thirty years, white middle-class Americans have abandoned the schools in growing numbers, taking with them both their money and their political clout. The flight to private academies began in response to the civil rights movement of the 1960s and has continued with a broadening perception that public education has fallen prey to "special interests" intent on promoting what critics describe as a corrosive agenda of secularism, political correctness, and multiculturalism. As faith in the public schools has grown less certain, so too has the willingness to pay for them. In a distressing number of districts both in North Carolina and across the nation, students learn their lessons from textbooks that are woefully out of date and in classrooms and laboratories that were built for another era, all because elected officials cannot—or often will not—provide better. And so the cycle of erosion continues, with disillusionment feeding upon itself and no escape in sight.

From Washington think tanks to local polling booths, critics of public education respond to that downward spiral by insisting that schools are ill-suited to the work of social reconstruction and should be left alone to pursue the self-evident business of reading, writing, and arithmetic. That argument has an obvious appeal; it offers a simple, direct solution for difficult and seemingly intractable problems. But contemporary critiques of public education miss the fact that the three R's have a history and that for the last century or more, schools have provided Americans with a common arena in which to debate the meanings of citizenship and civic obligation. That history speaks of hope and failure alike. It cannot provide answers for the future, but it can help us to understand how ordinary classroom experiences reflect priorities and influence outcomes.

Schools are key institutions for framing and passing along from one generation to the next the values and ethical principles that shape our lives together. That fact leaves us no escape from the question that weighed so heavily on African American teachers like Mary Battle and Charles Moore. If our society cannot be held to its promise of justice and opportunity in the lessons of the classroom, then where can such work be done? If not in the schools, then our only alternative may be to settle for what the critics of public education fear most—a balkanized society divided by race, class, and culture, its constituent elements walled off from one another by vouchers, privatization schemes, security guards, and prisons. Public schools matter if our sense of ourselves as a society is not to wither at the root and if we are to have any hope of preserving and cultivating in our own time a shared and inclusive democratic culture. That task cannot be accomplished by defending inherited wisdom or by turning to stock solutions from nostalgic and self-affirming readings of the past. We must tackle instead the difficult and contentious issues of what counts for knowledge and what our answer to that question says about who we believe ourselves to be. That challenge is perhaps the most important legacy left to us by the teachers, students, and school enthusiasts of the New South.

Notes

Abbreviations

Annual Report	*Annual Report of the State Superintendent of Public Instruction*
Biennial Report	*Biennial Report of the State Superintendent of Public Instruction*
DNE	Department of Public Instruction, Division of Negro Education
GEB	General Education Board
RSC	Rockefeller Sanitary Commission for the Eradication of Hook-worm
SEB	Southern Education Board
SPI	Superintendent of Public Instruction

Preface

1. Most of the standard accounts of southern school reform were written more than fifty years ago by either the reformers themselves or the heirs to their legacy. See, for example, Dabney, *Universal Education*; Noble, *History of the Public Schools of North Carolina*; and Knight, *Public School Education in North Carolina*. Those books offered legitimacy to the schoolmen's rejection of old ways by casting their story in terms of an ancient and steadily unfolding democratic ideal. Louis R. Harlan challenged that account in 1958 in his now classic work *Separate and Unequal*. Ten years later, Michael B. Katz launched a similar reevaluation of American educational history in general with *The Irony of Early School Reform*. His writings since that time are neatly synopsized in *Reconstructing American Education*. The themes of social control and social reproduction set forth in those works continued to steer the scholarship on southern education along productive and revealing paths well into the 1980s. See, for example, Link, *Hard Country*, and James D. Anderson, *Education of Blacks*.

2. My effort to peer into the classrooms of the past draws on the models and insights of anthropologists and sociologists who have sought to decipher the inner workings of contemporary schools. See especially Gary L. Anderson, "Critical Ethnography in Education"; Apple, *Ideology and Curriculum*; Norris Brock Johnson, *West Haven*; and Woods, *Inside Schools*. An exciting and promising development at the 1994 meeting of the American Educational Research Association was the creation of a new working group that will formally bring together ethnographers

and historians interested in collaborative efforts to study the social grammar of classrooms, past and present.

3. *Biennial Report, 1891–1892*, p. 16, and *Biennial Report, 1918–19/1919–20*, p. 109.

4. Especially helpful in constructing a comparative perspective on southern school reform are Curtis, *Building the Educational State*; Hogan, "Market Revolution and Disciplinary Power"; and Eklof, *Russian Peasant Schools*.

Chapter One

1. "The Normal School," *Wilson Advance*, July 1, 1881; "Professor Hassell's Lecture on Astronomy," *Wilson Advance*, June 24, 1881; Noble, *History of the Public Schools of North Carolina*, p. 418; and Shreve, "Development of Education to 1900 in Wilson," pp. 64–69. In 1877, lawmakers established a summer normal school for whites at the University of North Carolina in Chapel Hill and one for blacks in Fayetteville. Four years later, funds were allocated for four additional normals for each race. The black normals met in Franklinton, New Bern, Plymouth, and Salisbury, and the white normals in Elizabeth City, Franklin, Newton, and Wilson. For more on these early efforts at teacher training, see Noble, *History of the Public Schools of North Carolina*, pp. 410–27.

2. "Graded Schools," *Wilson Advance*, July 1, 1881; "The Graded School Question," and "A Graded School," *Wilson Advance*, July 8, 1881. Alexander Graham was superintendent of the Fayetteville graded school, established in 1878. He was born in 1844 near Fayetteville. As a young man he served as headmaster of the Richland Academy near Spring Hill until 1865, when he closed the school to join the Confederate army. Graham graduated from the University of North Carolina in 1869 and taught briefly in New York City, which was probably the first place he encountered graded education. After returning to North Carolina in 1873, he became a leading advocate of graded schools. He spent the next fifty years traveling throughout the state extolling their merits. See Powell, *Dictionary of North Carolina Biography*, 2:328–29.

3. "The Graded School Meeting" and "Our Graded School," *Wilson Advance*, July 22, 1881; "The Graded School," *Wilson Advance*, July 29, 1881; "Commissioners Meeting," *Wilson Advance*, August 12, 1881; "The Graded School," *Wilson Advance*, August 26, 1881; "Wilson Graded School," *Wilson Advance*, September 2, 1881; "Graded School," *Wilson Advance*, September 23, 1881; and Boykin, *Wilson County, North Carolina, 1880 Census*.

4. "A Graded School," *Wilson Advance*, July 8, 1881; "A Merited Compliment," *Wilson Advance*, March 17, 1882; "The Graded School," *Wilson Advance*, June 23, 1882; and "What the Leading Educational Journal Says of the Graded Schools," *Wilson Advance*, April 21, 1882. Several hundred visitors a month continued to come to the school during its second term. See, for example, "Graded School Report," *Wilson Advance*, December 15, 1882.

5. Lefler and Newsome, *North Carolina*, pp. 314–26, 362–66; Guion Griffis

Johnson, *Ante-Bellum North Carolina*, pp. 20–73; and Cecil Kenneth Brown, *State Movement in Railroad Development*, pp. 1–147. This discussion of slavery's effects on economic development is drawn primarily from Wright, *Old South, New South*, pp. 17–33. See also Genovese, *Political Economy of Slavery*; and Bateman and Weiss, *Deplorable Scarcity*.

6. Escott, *Many Excellent People*, pp. 3–31; Kenzer, *Kinship and Neighborhood*; *Biennial Report, 1896–97/1897–98*, pp. 449–50; *Special Report of the General Superintendent of Common Schools, 1854*, p. 30; and "Among the Pines," *State Chronicle*, September 22, 1883.

7. On the early history of public education in North Carolina, see Mayo, "Final Establishment of the American Common School System in North Carolina"; Weeks, "Beginnings of the Common School System in the South"; Pippin, "Common School Movement in the South"; Noble, *History of the Public Schools of North Carolina*, pp. 45–48, 56–63, 285–98; Lefler and Newsome, *North Carolina*, pp. 332–33, 368–69, 531–32; Samuel Thompson, "Legislative Development of Public School Support," pp. 46–373; and King, "Era of Progressive Reform," pp. 2–22. The statistics on school districts and enrollment are from the *Report of the Superintendent of Common Schools of North Carolina, for the Year 1860*, part 1, p. 18.

8. Noble, *History of the Public Schools of North Carolina*, pp. 285–98; Butchart, "Educating for Freedom," pp. 430–31; James D. Anderson, *Education of Blacks*, pp. 4–32; and *Biennial Report, 1898–99/1899–1900*, p. 234. Many communities found it difficult to achieve a four-month term, because the same constitution that mandated the longer session also limited poll taxes to $2 and property taxes to 66⅔ cents per $100 valuation, ceilings that were often too low to provide the necessary revenues. A four-month term did not become commonplace until after the turn of the century, when most counties adopted special local-option school taxes. See Noble, *History of the Public Schools of North Carolina*, p. 391.

9. Peter Wilson, *Southern Exposure*, p. 102; *Public Laws and Resolutions of the State of North Carolina, 1899*, chap. 732; *Public School Law of North Carolina, 1885*, pp. 16–17, 22–33, 38; and *Biennial Report, 1889–90*, p. 29. The commissioners in each county appointed three men "of good moral character" to serve as a board of education, which was only required to meet four times a year. County superintendents received no more than $3 and no less than $2 for each day they devoted to school business. Until 1881, the county superintendent was known as the county examiner. See *Public School Law of North Carolina, 1885*, pp. 11–13, 27–28, and *Public School Law of North Carolina, 1881*, p. 8. Before 1868, each county court of pleas and quarter sessions appointed five to ten men to act as a county board of common school superintendents. The law allowed the chairman of the board to retain up to 2½ percent of the local school fund as compensation for his services. District committeemen were elected each year by the male residents of each school district. Neither board members nor district committeemen received any remuneration for their services. See *Acts of Assembly, Establishing and Regulating Common Schools in North Carolina, 1853*. Between 1872 and 1885, the county commissioners themselves constituted the boards of education. See *Public Laws and Resolu-*

tions of the State of North Carolina, 1871–72, chap. 189, and *Public School Law of North Carolina, 1885*, pp. 11–12.

10. Kenzer, *Kinship and Neighborhood*, p. 145, and S. M. Hill to Charles H. Mebane, May 17, 1897, box 189, SPI Correspondence.

11. Harris, "Development of the Rural Public Schools in Cabarrus County," p. 35.

12. *North Carolina Teacher* 12 (February 1895): 228, and Raymond, *Then and Now*, pp. 34–35, 184.

13. *Biennial Report, 1898–99/1899–1900*, p. 229, and Tyack, *One Best System*, p. 17.

14. *Biennial Report, 1898–99/1899–1900*, p. 229, and W. D. Glenn to Sidney M. Finger, January 31, 1888, box 154, SPI Correspondence.

15. *Public School Law of North Carolina, 1889*, p. 13; M. McG. Shields to Sidney M. Finger, September 13, 1887, box 153, and J. A. Cameron to Sidney M. Finger, January 19, 1886, box 149, SPI Correspondence. A case of schoolhouse arson is described in I. W. Thomas to Sidney M. Finger, January 11, 1887, box 151, SPI Correspondence. For an example of how personal "hatred" among parents could spill over into the classroom, see M. McG. Shields to Sidney M. Finger, August 14, 1886, box 150, SPI Correspondence.

16. Coon, *Statistical Record*, p. 16, and *Raleigh News and Observer*, February 25, 1885.

17. King, "Era of Progressive Reform," pp. 9–10, and "A Teacher's Commendation," *Wilson Advance*, August 25, 1882.

18. *Fifth Annual Report of the General Superintendent of Common Schools*, p. 52; *Biennial Report, 1885–86*, pp. 17–18; S. W. Reid to Sidney M. Finger, August 24, 1887, box 152, SPI Correspondence; and *Public School Law of North Carolina, 1889*, p. 22. For an example of another teacher who came under fire because of "charges of disbelief in the divinity of Christ, the inspiration of scriptures &c. &c.," see James Kelly to Sidney M. Finger, November 30, 1886, box 150, SPI Correspondence.

19. *Biennial Report, 1889–90*, p. xxix; *Biennial Report, 1898–99/1899–1900*, p. 234; and Mrs. John E. Osborne to Sidney M. Finger, March 16, 1887, box 151, SPI Correspondence.

20. Myrther Tull Wilson to Charles D. McIver, November 1899, box 4, Charles McIver Papers. For two examples of self-serving committeemen, see S. W. Reid to Sidney M. Finger, May 20, 1886, box 149, and T. H. Edwards to Sidney M. Finger, June 20, 1887, box 152, SPI Correspondence.

21. *Biennial Report, 1889–90*, pp. 5, 9, 17, 27; Nannie Seawell to Charles D. McIver, May 2, 1890, box 1, Charles McIver Papers; *Biennial Report, 1896–97/1897–98*, p. 520; and Raymond, *Then and Now*, p. 225.

22. Raymond, *Then and Now*, pp. 36–37, 136–37.

23. Ibid., p. 38, and J. T. Alderman to Sidney M. Finger, December 14, 1887, box 153, SPI Correspondence. For examples of teachers who lost their jobs because of

low attendance, see A. A. Parker to Sidney M. Finger, July 16, 1886, box 150, and J. P. Judkins to Sidney M. Finger, September 24, 1887, box 153, SPI Correspondence. Also compare Tyack, *One Best System*, p. 19, and Link, *Hard Country*, p. 62.

24. *Biennial Report, 1881–82*, p. 27; *Biennial Report, 1896–97/1897–98*, p. 11; *Biennial Report, 1898–99/1899–1900*, pp. 110, 113; John R. Hyde to Sidney M. Finger, January 3, 1888, box 154, SPI Correspondence; King, "Era of Progressive Reform," p. 22; *Proceedings of the North Carolina Teachers Assembly, 1884*, p. 42; Raymond, *Then and Now*, p. 137; and *North Carolina Teacher* 8 (May 1891): 429. In some communities, imaginative district committeemen met the four-months requirement by running two schools, each for two months apiece. See, for example, J. C. Getsinger to Sidney M. Finger, October 27, 1887, box 153, SPI Correspondence. In 1890, the average school term for black and white common schools alike was only fifty-seven days. See Coon, *Statistical Record*, p. 16.

25. *Biennial Report, 1887–88*, p. xxxi.

26. Compare Tyack, "The Tribe and the Common School," p. 4.

27. Raymond, *Then and Now*, pp. 37, 40, and Francis Lieber to "a committee of the Euphradian Society," November 22, 1848, Francis Lieber Papers, South Caroliniana Library, University of South Carolina at Columbia, quoted in Steven M. Stowe, *Intimacy and Power*, p. 130. Compare Tyack, *One Best System*, pp. 19–20, and Link, *Hard Country*, pp. 64–68. On the great variety of books in use, see also *First Annual Report of the General Superintendent of Common Schools*, p. 10. Superintendent Calvin Wiley complained of the "multiplicity" of textbooks, which left "teachers greatly embarrassed by having large schools with nearly every child in a class by itself."

28. Parker, *Talks on Pedagogics*, p. 408; Warren Colburn, *Intellectual Arithmetic*, quoted in Smith, Eaton, and Dugdale, "One Hundred Fifty Years of Arithmetic Textbooks," p. 57; Calhoun, *Intelligence of a People*, pp. 102–7; Cohen, *Calculating People*, pp. 120–22; and Swett, *Methods of Teaching*, p. 143. Edwin Alderman found that in most rural schools, teachers had "the idea that knowing facts constitutes education." See Henderson County remarks, Institute Notebooks, Edwin Alderman Papers.

29. Cohen, *Calculating People*, p. 122; Smith, Eaton, and Dugdale, "One Hundred Fifty Years of Arithmetic Textbooks," p. 87; and Knight, *Documentary History*, 5:235. On the merchant princes of Renaissance Italy and their role in transforming arithmetic from a branch of philosophy into practical rules of reckoning, see Swetz, *Capitalism and Arithmetic*.

30. This example is adapted from Cohen, *Calculating People*, p. 122.

31. Calhoun, *Intelligence of a People*, pp. 106, 230–56.

32. Raymond, *Then and Now*, pp. 45, 87–89; Link, *Hard Country*, p. 65; Knight, *Documentary History*, 5:234; "Howling Schools," *North Carolina Teacher* 4 (March 1887): 356–58; and "Schooldays," box 9, Charles McIver Papers.

33. *Biennial Report, 1881–82*, p. 25, and *Proceedings of the North Carolina Teachers Assembly, 1884*, p. 42.

34. Grumet, *Bitter Milk*, pp. 140–41; Graff, *Legacies of Literacy*, pp. 2–14; *Raleigh News and Observer*, September 22, 1886; "Plutarch on the Training of Children," *Schoolteacher* 2 (January 1888): 8; Raymond, *Then and Now*, pp. 158–62; and "The Spelling Book vs. Spelling," *North Carolina Journal of Education* 1 (December 1906): 12. For comparative purposes, see Tyack, *One Best System*, pp. 19–20; Link, *Hard Country*, pp. 68–70; Eklof, *Russian Peasant Schools*, pp. 251–82; and Eggleston, *Hoosier School-Master*, p. 34.

35. Knight, *Documentary History*, 5:235, and Battle, "Old or Extinct Schools of North Carolina, Supplemental," pp. 430–32.

36. Knight, *Documentary History*, 5:211–18, 236. One reform-minded schoolman declared, "The practice of 'turning out teachers' is full of mischief, and should be 'hooted' from civilized society." See Highsmith, "State Normal School Idea," p. 11.

37. Eklof, *Russian Peasant Schools*, pp. 251–82, 389–418. See also Steven M. Stowe, *Intimacy and Power*, pp. 130–31.

38. Foushee, *Reminiscences*, pp. 14–15.

39. Rose, "Educational Movement in the South," p. 361; *Inauguration of Edwin Anderson Alderman*, pp. 23–24; Eller, "New University," p. 2; and Foushee, *Reminiscences*, pp. 14–15.

40. On the need to take the New South ideologists more seriously, see Wright, *Old South, New South*, pp. 18–19, and Ayers, "Toward a New Synthesis of the New South." Both argue that the New South was considerably "newer" than many scholars have recognized. For arguments stressing New South mythmaking and the limits of change, see Gaston, *New South Creed*; Billings, *Planters and the Making of a "New South"*; and Wiener, *Social Origins of the New South*.

41. Rose, "Educational Movement in the South," p. 361, and Wright, *Old South, New South*, pp. 17–50. For an overview of the process of economic change, see Hall et al., *Like a Family*, pp. 3–43.

42. Lefler and Newsome, *North Carolina*, pp. 517–18; "What Railroads Do," *State Chronicle*, December 1, 1883; "Cash," *State Chronicle*, March 22, 1884; and *Proceedings of the North Carolina Teachers Assembly, 1884*, p. 26. See also "Made Accessible," *State Chronicle*, June 28, 1884, and "Thomas's Humbug," *State Chronicle*, August 25, 1887.

43. Lefler and Newsome, *North Carolina*, pp. 508, 512–13. See also "Cash," *State Chronicle*, March 22, 1884. On town building and mill building, see Hall et al., *Like a Family*, pp. 24–31.

44. "A Good Social Result," *State Chronicle*, March 22, 1884; Alderman, "University of To-day," p. 296; "Goldsboro," *State Chronicle*, February 9, 1884; "A Pen Picture of Winston's Thrift," *State Chronicle*, October 20, 1883; and "A New Social Force," *State Chronicle*, September 29, 1883.

45. "A Generalization or Two," *State Chronicle*, December 15, 1883; "You Don't 'Understand the Above,' " *State Chronicle*, February 16, 1884; Holland Thompson, *New South*, p. 204; and "Take Heed," *Carolina Messenger*, January 8, 1874. See also Page, "Study of an Old Southern Borough."

46. Rose, "Educational Movement in the South," pp. 361–62, and *Proceedings of the North Carolina Teachers Assembly, 1884,* p. 46.

47. On the development of graded education, see Cubberly, *Public Education in the United States,* pp. 304–12, and Barney, *Report on the American System of Graded Free Schools.*

48. Illinois Superintendent of Public Instruction, *Annual Report* (Springfield, 1862), p. 120, quoted in Kaestle, *Pillars of the Republic,* p. 98. Kaestle's book offers the best survey of the antebellum common school movement throughout the United States. See especially chapter 5, "Ideology."

49. *Special Report of the General Superintendent of Common Schools of North Carolina, 1854,* p. 30; *Report of the Superintendent of Common Schools of North Carolina, for the Year 1859,* pp. 36–37; *Report of the Superintendent of Common Schools of North Carolina, for the Year 1860,* part 2, pp. 12–15; and Calvin Wiley, undated, untitled manuscript, cited in Ford, "Calvin H. Wiley and the Common Schools of North Carolina," p. 285.

50. The quotation is from *Report of the Superintendent of Common Schools of North Carolina, for the Year 1859,* pp. 35–37. For comparative purposes, see Labaree, *Making of an American High School.* The language of morals and politics seems to have persisted more strongly in the Northeast, in part because of reformers' confrontation with a growing population of non-Protestant Eastern and Southern European immigrants. See Kemal, "Moral Education in America."

51. The quotation is from Noble, *History of the Public Schools of North Carolina,* pp. 405–6. It is virtually impossible to tally the exact number of graded schools in operation by the end of the century, because the city systems were not required to make special reports to the state superintendent. For the general outlines of the graded school movement, see "Capt. John E. Dugger," *North Carolina Teacher* 2 (July 1884): 6–7; Eugene Clyde Brooks, "Some Forgotten Educational History"; Coon, "Beginnings of the North Carolina City Schools"; *Biennial Report, 1887–88,* p. 105; Noble, *History of the Public Schools of North Carolina,* pp. 398–409; Coon, *Statistical Record,* p. 18; and King, "Era of Progressive Reform," pp. 47–66.

52. Broadside, "Normal and Classical Institute, Goldsboro, N.C.," box 474, SPI Papers; King, "Era of Progressive Reform," pp. 53–54, 60–62; and "Fayetteville," *State Chronicle,* November 17, 1883. See also *Biennial Report, 1887–88,* pp. 91–92, 104, and "Charlotte Training School," *State Chronicle,* September 25, 1881.

53. Lasch, "Origins of the Asylum," p. 17; George W. Dale, "About Normal Colleges," *North Carolina Teacher* 5 (February 1888): 242; and "School Government," *North Carolina Teacher* 3 (November 1885): 107. The editor of the *Wilson Advance* described the town's graded school as the source of "formative influences which are to mould and shape society." See "Our Public Schools," December 1, 1883. For further discussion of the creative and formative aspects of such institutional remodeling, see Katz, *Reconstructing American Education;* Apple, *Ideology and Curriculum;* and Agnew, *Worlds Apart.* Pavla Miller, *Long Division,* and Curtis, *Building the Educational State,* offer revealing international perspectives.

54. "To the Patrons of the Wilson Graded School," *Wilson Advance,* September

2, 1881; "The Graded School," *Wilson Advance*, September 9, 1881; and undated manuscript, box 9, Charles McIver Papers.

55. Coon, *Statistical Record*, p. 16; "The Wilson Graded School," *Wilson Advance*, April 21, 1882; "The Graded School," *Wilson Advance*, April 6, 1883; and "Universal Education," box 9, Charles McIver Papers. For an example of the "roll of honor" in Wilson, see "The Wilson Graded School," *Wilson Advance*, January 6, 1882. See also *Report of the Winston Graded Schools, 1888*, pp. 14–16. One of the graded school's highest aims, explained Winston's superintendent, was "to teach the young habits of order, punctuality, regularity, and *strict attention to business*— habits which will last them through life and have an important bearing upon their usefulness and happiness."

56. "The Wilson Graded School," *Wilson Advance*, January 6, 1882, and untitled manuscript, box 9, Charles McIver Papers.

57. *Proceedings of the North Carolina Teachers Assembly, 1887*, p. 19, and *North Carolina Teacher* 5 (January 1888): 208. I am indebted here to insights drawn from Foucault, *Discipline and Punish*, pp. 177–94, and Hoskin and Macve, "Accounting and the Examination."

58. "The Graded School," *Wilson Advance*, September 30, 1881, and "The Wilson Graded School," *Wilson Advance*, January 6, 1882.

59. "The Graded School," *Wilson Advance*, September 15, 1882; Eugene Clyde Brooks, "Status of the Graded School," p. 7; untitled manuscript, box 9, Charles McIver Papers; and Kramnick, *Republicanism and Bourgeois Radicalism*, pp. 14–15. For more on record-keeping and promotion, see *Annual Report of the Board of School Commissioners of the City of Winston, 1895*, pp. 6–7, and 34–35.

60. *Biennial Report, 1887–88*, p. 103.

61. *Biennial Report, 1891–92*, p. lxiv; Dickinson, "Results of Methods Teaching"; *Biennial Report, 1889–90*, p. lii; and *Biennial Report, 1887–88*, pp. 89–90.

62. Mayo, "New Education and Col. Parker." On Parker's early life and European travels, see Campbell, *Colonel Francis W. Parker*, pp. 1–74. The label "new education," used to describe reformed methods of reading and arithmetic instruction, seems to have entered the popular vocabulary with the publication of J. R. Buchanan's *New Education*. Buchanan was a Boston physician, lecturer, and educator. See Hogan, *Class and Reform*, p. 279, n. 125. For more on Pestalozzi, Froebel, and Herbart, see Silber, *Pestalozzi*; Downs, *Heinrich Pestalozzi*; Downs, *Friedrich Froebel*; Dunkel, *Herbart and Education*; Hughes, *Froebel's Educational Laws*; and DeGarmo, *Herbart and the Herbartians*.

63. The quotations are from "Our Schools: From the *New York Tribune*," *Quincy Patriot*, January 24, 1880, quoted in Campbell, *Colonel Francis W. Parker*, p. 87. On Parker's work in Quincy and Chicago, as well as his influence on other reformers, see Campbell, *Colonel Francis W. Parker*, pp. 75–230; U.S. Commissioner of Education, "Francis Wayland Parker"; Cremin, *Transformation of the School*, pp. 128–35; Katz, " 'New Departure' in Quincy"; and Hogan, *Class and Reform*, pp. 82–85. A revealing account of his teaching methods is offered in Patridge, *"Quincy Methods"*

Illustrated. For more on Henry Barnard and early American champions of Pestalozzi, see Monroe, *History of the Pestalozzian Movement in the United States.* The characterization of Barnard as a Pestalozzian propagandist is from p. 164.

64. *North Carolina Teacher* 2 (December 1884): p. 256, and 3 (September 1885): 28; *Biennial Report, 1887–88,* pp. xl–xli.

65. Cohen, *Calculating People,* pp. 134–38; *Biennial Report, 1887–88,* pp. 91, 103; and *Biennial Report, 1883–84,* p. 51.

66. "Multiplication and Division," *North Carolina Teacher* 1 (July 1883): 64–65. In all likelihood, "C. L. Dowell" was a misprint for C. J. Duell, a Raleigh teacher. See *Branson's North Carolina Business Directory for 1884,* p. 655.

67. U.S. Commissioner of Education, "Francis Wayland Parker," p. 246; *Biennial Report, 1887–88,* p. 103; and *Biennial Report, 1889–90,* p. liii.

68. U.S. Commissioner of Education, "Francis Wayland Parker," pp. 245–46; *Proceedings of the North Carolina Teachers Assembly, 1884,* p. 47; *Biennial Report, 1887–88,* p. 103; and *Biennial Report, 1889–90,* p. lii.

69. Grumet, *Bitter Milk,* p. 140, and *Biennial Report, 1889–90,* pp. liv–lv. A number of historians have begun to suggest that the context in which literacy is acquired is at least as important as literacy itself in restructuring personality. See, for example, Eklof, *Russian Peasant Schools*; Natalie Zemon Davis, *Society and Culture in Early Modern France*; and Graff, *Legacies of Literacy.* For more on the development of reading instruction, see Lamport, "History of the Teaching of Beginning Reading," pp. 208–516; Mitford M. Mathews, *Teaching to Read,* pp. 53–74, 97–108, 122–39; Kellogg, *Teaching Reading in Ten Cities*; and William J. Gilmore, *Reading Becomes a Necessity of Life.* For silent reading's transformative effects in a very different setting, see Saenger, "Silent Reading."

70. U.S. Commissioner of Education, "Francis Wayland Parker," p. 245, and C. Falk to Charles D. McIver, January 5 and February 5, 1899, box 3, Charles McIver Papers.

71. Lewis, *Philander Priestley Claxton,* pp. 63–64.

72. Mayo, "New Education and Col. Parker," p. 85, and U.S. Commissioner of Education, "Francis Wayland Parker," p. 246.

73. *Biennial Report, 1896–97/1897–98,* pp. 217–23; U.S. Commissioner of Education, "Francis Wayland Parker," p. 247; untitled manuscript, box 9, Charles D. McIver Papers; and *Biennial Report, 1898–99/1899–1900,* p. 240.

74. Storm, "Discipline as the Result of Self-Government"; *Biennial Report, 1889–90,* p. li; and *Proceedings of the North Carolina Teachers Assembly, 1887,* p. 17. See also *Biennial Report, 1889–90,* p. 6; *Biennial Report, 1896–97/1897–98,* pp. 104, 229–30; and *Proceedings of the North Carolina Teachers Assembly, 1887,* p. 37. See also *Annual Reports of the Public Schools of Raleigh Township, 1885–86,* pp. 16–17.

75. Lucy Brooks, "Day in My School Room," p. 11.

76. "Recollections of My School Days," *North Carolina Education* 5 (September 1910): 4–5, and "The Autobiography of a School Boy—A Story of Human Interest," *North Carolina Education* 5 (October 1910): 3, 5.

Chapter Two

1. "The Prophet in Education," March 8, 1906, clipping in series 1.5, box 718, folder 7402, GEB Papers; and Alderman, *Woodrow Wilson*, p. 16. Joyner and Alderman were roommates at Chapel Hill. See Malone, *Edwin A. Alderman*, p. 14. For more on this generational experience, see Cooper, *Walter Hines Page*, pp. 3–30, 69–70; Josephus Daniels, *Tar Heel Editor*, pp. 3–17; and Burton, "Effects of the Civil War." The chapter title is from Wallace Buttrick to Rev. W. S. Richardson, February 5, 1914, series 1.1, box 105, folder 953, GEB Papers.

2. Smith, Boddie, and Sharpe, *Charles Duncan McIver*, pp. 134, 146; Holder, *McIver*, p. 53; "A Partial List of Superintendents and Principals of Schools Sent Out by the University," *University Record* 1 (February 1897): 22–23; "Present Occupations of the Graduating Class of 1897," *University Record* 2 (October 1897): 8–9; and "Report of the President of the University to the Board of Trustees," *University Record* 6 (January 1901): 23. See also "Current Comment," *University Magazine*, n.s. 14 (March 1895): 329.

3. Alderman, "Life and Work of Dr. Charles D. McIver," p. 4. For similar sentiments among Alderman's classmates, see inaugural address of R. L. Payne Jr., February 4, 1876, folder 23, and inaugural address of W. P. Cline, March 15, 1878, folder 3, Student Organizations and Activities, Dialectic Society Records, Series 2, Subseries 1, Addresses/Debates, University of North Carolina Archives (hereafter cited as Dialectic Society Records). Approximate dates for undated speeches and compositions in the Dialectic Society Records are based on information in *Alumni History of the University of North Carolina*.

4. *University Record* 2 (January 1898): 21; Brabham, "Defining the American University," p. 429; and Waddell, "Ante-Bellum University," p. 11. On the world view of the South's slaveholding elite, see Genovese, *Slaveholders' Dilemma*; Kolchin, *Unfree Labor*, pp. 157–77; Steven M. Stowe, *Intimacy and Power*, pp. 128–59; and Wyatt-Brown, *Southern Honor*, pp. 149–74.

5. Battle, *History of the University of North Carolina*, 1:98, 255–57, 462–64, 552–54; Brabham, "Defining the American University," p. 431; and address of Thomas J. Robinson, July 21, 1848, folder 24, Dialectic Society Records. For a comparison to the classical curriculum at other American universities before 1870, see Veysey, *Emergence of the American University*, pp. 21–56. For more on science teaching in Chapel Hill and elsewhere in the South, see Peter Wilson, *Southern Exposure*, p. 35; Mauskopf, "Elisha Mitchell and European Science"; and Bruce, *Launching of Modern American Science*, pp. 57–63. Kemp Battle's *History of the University of North Carolina* deserves a brief comment. It is a remarkable work based on the author's nearly seventy-five years of association with the university, first as the son of a faculty member, then as a student and trustee, and finally as the institution's president and distinguished professor of history. Much of the information contained in the history is drawn from Battle's own memories and those of his acquaintances and is otherwise unavailable in the University Archives and other manuscript sources.

6. On the early history of the university and its curriculum, see Drake, *Higher Education in North Carolina before 1860*, pp. 35–71; Connor, *Documentary History of the University of North Carolina*, 1:375–79; Novak, *Rights of Youth*, pp. 106–15; and Blackwell P. Robinson, *William R. Davie*, Appendix C, pp. 406–10. The quotation is from John H. Hobart to Joseph Caldwell, November 30, 1796, in Connor, *Documentary History of the University of North Carolina*, 2:79. For a long view of the place of the classics in European and American higher education, see Kimball, *Orators and Philosophers*, pp. 43–113.

7. For accounts of the riot and its aftermath, see Battle, *History of the University of North Carolina*, 1:155–80; Battle, *Sketches of the History of the University of North Carolina*, pp. 42–43; and Novak, *Rights of Youth*, pp. 18, 110–13. The university's most outspoken critic was Samuel Eusibius McCorkle, a Presbyterian minister and leading figure in the institution's founding. For his views on "the modern French Jacobine system of education," see Samuel E. McCorkle to John Haywood, December 20, 1799, series 1, folder 27, Ernest Haywood Collection, and McCorkle, *Work of God for the French Republic*.

8. Novak, *Rights of Youth*; address of James K. Polk, n.d. (ca. 18), folder 24; address of M. F. Taylor, March 9, 1861, folder 28; inaugural address of Thomas B. Slade, September 10, 1819, folder 25; and junior speech of E. B. Withers, 1858, folder 30, Dialectic Society Records. For other student defenses of the classical curriculum, see address of [William Bingham] Lynch, n.d. (ca. 1858), folder 15; address of Ivesan L. Brooks, September 1818, folder 2; address of Angus C. McNeill, April 17, 1839, folder 20; and unsigned address, July 17, 1852, folder 27, Dialectic Society Records.

9. Address of Robert H. Cowan, May 19, 1843, folder 4, Dialectic Society Records. Novak, *Rights of Youth*; and Howard Miller, *Revolutionary College*, pp. 259–93, place events in Chapel Hill in a larger national and international context.

10. Senior oration of Edward T. Sykes, [1858], folder 27; "Progress of Humbuggery," address by David G. Worth, April 9, 1853, folder 28; "Progress: Moral & Material," Senior Oration of Thomas Conway, August 20, 1857, folder 4; "The American Union a Failure," senior speech of E. B. Withers, November 7, 1858, folder 30; address of A. C. McNeill, July 28, 1838, folder 20; address of W. W. Avery, n.d. (ca. 1837), folder 1; and senior oration of James A. Wright, October 29, 1853, folder 30; valedictory address of Peter King Roundsville, June 5, 1844, folder 24; valedictory address of Belfield W. Cave, May 1848, folder 3; and address of R. M. Roseborough, February 1832, folder 24, Dialectic Society Records. For a faculty perspective, see Elisha Mitchell, *Other Leaf of the Book of Nature*.

11. Battle, *History of the University of North Carolina*, 1:291–94, 334–36, 444, 780. See also Henderson, *Campus of the First State University*, pp. 97–108.

12. Battle, "Recollections," p. 296; and senior oration of James Kelly, March 10, 1860, folder 14, Dialectic Society Records.

13. Address of Marshall Polk, 1824, folder 24, Dialectic Society Records; Battle, *History of the University of North Carolina*, 1:554–55, 661, 782; Battle, "Recollections," pp. 296, 308–9; and Bagg, *Four Years at Yale*, pp. 552–53, quoted in Veysey,

Emergence of the American University, pp. 37–38. For more on the use of the recitation in Chapel Hill, see George P. Bryan to John H. Bryan, October 7, 1856, box 13, John Heritage Bryan Papers, and Thomas William Mason, "Journal of a Day," folder 10, Sally Long Jarman Papers.

14. Battle, *History of the University of North Carolina*, 1:408, and Winston, "First Faculty," p. 23. For an overview of the library's early history, see Brewer, *Library of the University of North Carolina*. The failure to consolidate the university's books in a single collection became a source of great confusion. Elisha Mitchell, professor of chemistry, mineralogy, and geology, died from a fall in 1857 while confirming the height of the North Carolina mountain that now bears his name. When his personal library was offered for public sale the next year, the university purchased more than 1,800 volumes, only to discover that it was paying for many of them a second time. A survey of Mitchell's catalog indicated that most of the books had been purchased with student fees during the 1820s but had never been marked as university property. See McVaugh, "Elisha Mitchell's Books and the University of North Carolina Library."

15. Winston, "First Faculty," pp. 25–26; Battle, *History of the University of North Carolina*, 1:222, 781; and Battle, "Lives of the University Presidents." Compare Veysey, *Emergence of the American University*, p. 45. For a helpful discussion of the relationship between institutional settings and faculty self-perceptions in German universities, see Turner, "University Reformers and Professional Scholarship in Germany."

16. Battle, "Recollections," pp. 308–11, and Battle, *History of the University of North Carolina*, 1:190–93, 304–9. On Sunday afternoons, students also stood for an examination "on the general principles of religion and morality." To help the junior class through that exercise, Professor Elisha Mitchell, an ordained Presbyterian minister, prepared a pamphlet that outlined the geography, history, and economy of Palestine together with key dates in the development of Christianity, from God's call to Abraham in 1921 B.C. to the beginning of the Reformation nearly 3,500 years later. See Connor, *Documentary History of the University of North Carolina*, 1:376; Battle, *History of the University of North Carolina*, 1:462; and Elisha Mitchell, *Statistics, Facts, and Dates*.

17. Battle, *History of the University of North Carolina*, 1:563–64. Compare Horowitz, *Campus Life*, pp. 32–34, and Veysey, *Emergence of the American University*, pp. 299–300.

18. Presidential address of William Lafayette Scott, July 22, 1853, folder 25; address of William Hill, October 25, 1843, folder 10; speech of W. F. Foster (Junior Debate, 1858), "Are the Ancient Languages worthy of the place which they now hold in the course of education?," folder 7; presidential address of W. F. Foster, n.d. (ca. 1859), folder 7; address of Ivesan L. Brooks, September 1818, folder 2; and address of Samuel F. Phillips, January 1841, folder 23, Dialectic Society Records. See also presidential address of John I. Morehead, December 1852, folder 19, and debater's speech of Lee M. McAfee, June 2, 1857, folder 20, Dialectic Society Records.

19. Battle, *History of the University of North Carolina*, 1:72–85, 565–69, and Waddell, "Ante-Bellum University," p. 13. For the societies' efforts to police their members' behavior, see Student Organizations and Activities, Dialectic Society Records, Series 1, Minutes, and Philanthropic Society Records, Series 1, Minutes, University of North Carolina Archives. Other than the minute books, few Philanthropic Society materials from the antebellum era have survived. The Dialectic Society Records are more complete. For general histories of the societies, see "The Dialectic Literary Society" and "The Philanthropic Literary Society," *University Magazine*, n.s. 16 (December 1898): 85–89, 100–103.

20. Address of William Hooper, June 20, 1835, folder 7; inaugural address of A. Haywood Merritt, October 18, 1855, folder 17; valedictory address of Jno. W. Cameron, n.d. (ca. 1848), folder 3; presidential address of Sion Rogers, Wake Co., n.d. (ca. 1846), folder 24; address of William W. Avery, n.d. (ca. 1837), folder 1; valedictory address of A. C. McNeill, June 26, 1839, folder 21 (misfiled as Neill); and address of A. C. McNeill, September 20, 1838, folder 20, Dialectic Society Records. For a comparison with similar societies at other antebellum colleges, see McLachlan, "*Choice of Hercules*," and Wakelyn, "Antebellum College Life," pp. 120–21.

21. Battle, *History of the University of North Carolina*, 1:566; address of Augustus Foster, October 1834, folder 7; address of Owen H. Whitfield, n.d. (ca. 1846), folder 30; and address of Alfred G. Foster, January 1844, folder 7, Dialectic Society Records. Although I do not share his perspective on the decline of nineteenth-century oratory, I am nevertheless indebted to Richard Weaver's insightful essay "The Spaciousness of the Old Rhetoric," in Weaver, *Ethics of Rhetoric*, pp. 164–85. On student concern for debating style and proper decorum, see Student Organizations and Activities, Dialectic Society Records, Series 1, Minutes; Series 3, Subseries 7, Correctors' Records; and Philanthropic Society Records, Series 1, Minutes, University of North Carolina Archives. For other comparisons of the relative value of the college course and the society exercises, see address of W. C. Hooper, September 26, 1811, folder 11; address of D. M. Barrenger, November 1825, folder 2; composition of J. G. Shepherd, n.d. (ca. 1841), folder 25; inaugural address of Washington C. Kerr, July 1849, folder 14; inaugural address of A. A. Lawrence, 1851, folder 15; and inaugural address of Coleman Sessions, September 20, 1855, folder 25, Dialectic Society Records.

22. Battle, *History of the University of North Carolina*, 1:275, 267, 453, 576, and Battle, "Recollections," pp. 308–9. Compare Horowitz, *Campus Life*, p. 42.

23. Battle, *History of the University of North Carolina*, 1:262, 275, 278, 290, 305, 307, 465, 532, 545, 577–78. For other examples of "faculty baiting," see Coates and Coates, *Story of Student Government*, pp. 10–31. For a revealing account of student life outside the classroom, see the Lawrence Dusenberry Diary.

24. Battle, *History of the University of North Carolina*, 1:305; Battle, "Recollections," p. 309; and Waddell, "Ante-Bellum University," p. 12.

25. Battle, "Recollections," p. 305, and Battle, *History of the University of North Carolina*, 1:630–31.

26. Waddell, "Ante-Bellum University," pp. 13–14; Battle, "Recollections," p. 297; and Battle, *History of the University of North Carolina*, 1:781–82.

27. Battle, *History of the University of North Carolina*, 1:783, 832–36. For a student critique of the classical curriculum and call for change, see speech of W. F. Foster (Junior Debate, 1858), "Are the Ancient Languages worthy of the place which they now hold in the course of education?," folder 7, Dialectic Society Records.

28. Battle, *History of the University of North Carolina*, 1:642–44; Brabham, "Defining the American University," 431; Cherry, "Bringing Science to the South."

29. "Our Union, Will it be Preserved?" (senior oration of James McNabb), March 1857, folder 20; "Progress: Moral & Material" (senior oration of Thomas Cowan), August 20, 1857, folder 4; "Progress of Humbuggery" (address of David G. Worth), April 9, 1853, folder 30, Dialectic Society Records; Cox, "Freedom during the Fremont Campaign"; and Battle, *History of the University of North Carolina*, 1:780. On the state and regional effort at agricultural reform, see Lefler, *History of North Carolina*, 1:393–400; *North-Carolina Planter*, 1858–60; and Genovese, *Political Economy of Slavery*, pp. 124–53. John Ericsson surely vindicated student fears when he later placed his considerable engineering skills in service to the Northern war effort. He was the chief designer of the Union ironclad, the USS *Monitor*. See *Dictionary of American Biography*, 3:171–76. For more on student concerns over the dangers of imagination and speculation, see "Have Men of Action been more beneficial to the world than men of Thought?" (speech by Hugh T. Brown), June 2, 1857, folder 2, and debater's speech of Lee M. McAfee, June 2, 1857, folder 20, Dialectic Society Records.

30. Veysey, *Emergence of the American University*, p. 9. On the faculty and their length of service, see "North and South Carolina Colleges," *Southern Literary Messenger* 22 (January 1856): 69.

31. Daniel Harvey Hill, "Education," pp. 5, 9, 11, 87–88, and Battle, *History of the University of North Carolina*, 1:724–54.

32. Daniel Harvey Hill, "Education," pp. 3, 11, 10; Andrew Dousa Hepburn to David Lowry Swain, June 23, 1866, folder 54, David Swain Papers; and William Horn Battle to Kemp Plummer Battle, August 1, 1867, series A, folder 62, Battle Family Papers.

33. Brabham, "Defining the American University," pp. 438–40, and Battle, *History of the University of North Carolina*, 1:764.

34. Battle, *History of the University of North Carolina*, 1:764, and Daniel Harvey Hill, "Education," p. 4. For the national movement toward curriculum reform, see Veysey, *Emergence of the American University*, pp. 57–262; Diehl, *Americans and German Scholarship*; Bledstein, *Culture of Professionalism*, especially chap. 8; and Horowitz, *Campus Life*, pp. 69–70.

35. Battle, *History of the University of North Carolina*, 1:764, 767, 774–78, 784–85.

36. Battle, *History of the University of North Carolina*, 1:2–12, 28–33, and Louis Round Wilson, *Selected Papers of Cornelia Phillips Spencer*, p. 616.

37. Battle, *History of the University of North Carolina*, 2:27, 41; Brabham, "Defining the American University," pp. 446–48; and Peele, "Pen-Pictures," p. 33.

38. Escott, *Many Excellent People*, pp. 136–70; Battle, *History of the University of North Carolina*, 2:50–51; Brabham, "Defining the American University," pp. 450–52; and Battle, "Struggle and Story of the Re-Birth."

39. Battle, *History of the University of North Carolina*, 2:71–72; Brabham, "Defining the American University," p. 454; and *Catalogue of the Trustees, Faculty, and Students of the University of North Carolina, 1875–76*.

40. Winston, "First Faculty," pp. 18, 21; Winston, "University of To-Day," p. 327; *University Record* 2 (January 1898): 19; and Battle, *History of the University of North Carolina*, 2:1, 114–16.

41. Winston, "First Faculty," p. 26, and Battle, *History of the University of North Carolina*, 2:139, 238–39, 334, 475, 499, 525–26, 540–42, 558, 571, 608. For a comparative perspective on the effects of curriculum reform at other American universities, see Veysey, *Emergence of the American University*, pp. 121–79, and Horowitz, *Campus Life*, pp. 70–73.

42. Battle, *History of the University of North Carolina*, 2:79–82, 509; Winston, "First Faculty," p. 21; Winston, "University of To-Day," p. 326; and *University of North Carolina Catalogue, 1894–95*, pp. 20–21. Development of elective system can be traced in the university catalogues, 1875–1900.

43. Battle, *History of the University of North Carolina*, 2:93; Alderman, "The University," p. 51; Battle, "Recollections," p. 296; "University and the State," *University Record* 6 (November 1900): 14; and Winston, "University of To-Day," p. 325. For an example of the new grading system, see Charles D. McIver's report card, December 23, 1879, box 1, Charles McIver Papers. The *University of North Carolina Catalogue, 1896–97*, contains an example of the new class schedule (see pp. 44–45).

44. Winston, "First Faculty," p. 25, and Battle, *History of the University of North Carolina*, 2:273. The university began publishing reports on faculty research in the late 1890s. See, for example, "Literary Activity of the Alumni, Faculty, and Students during 1896," *University Record* 1 (December 1896): 7–8.

45. Battle, *History of the University of North Carolina*, 2:333, 475; Battle, *Sketches of the History of the University of North Carolina*, p. 59; Harrington, *Shall the Classics Have a Fair Chance?*, p. 231; and Dey, "Beginnings of the Philological Club." Particularly helpful in understanding these changes is Diehl, *Americans and German Scholarship*, pp. 15–27. For an example of the new scholarship as pursued by students, see Towers, "Ancient Greek and Modern Elizabethan Drama Compared." Professors Alexander and Harrington organized the Philological Club with help from colleagues in English and the Modern Languages. The club's journal is still associated with the university today.

46. Battle, *History of the University of North Carolina*, 1:643, 2:273; *Biennial Report 1898–99/1899–1900*, p. 421; and Malone, *Edwin A. Alderman*, p. 89. Battle's 1867 plan for curriculum reform had included a call for more extensive classroom lecturing. See Brabham, "Defining the American University," p. 444. For Charles Phillips's thoughts on the connection between lecturing and the creation and dis-

semination of new knowledge, see Phillips to Kemp Plummer Battle, n.d. (September 1867), box 5, University Papers, University of North Carolina Archives.

47. Winston, "First Faculty," pp. 23–24, and Battle, *History of the University of North Carolina*, 2:356–58.

48. *Biennial Report 1887–88*, pp. 114–15; *Catalogue of the University of North Carolina, 1885–86*, p. 22; Battle, *History of the University of North Carolina*, 2:77–78, 203–4; and Winston, "University of To-Day," p. 325. See also *Catalogue of the Trustees, Faculty, and Students of the University of North Carolina, 1875–76*, p. 11.

49. Winston, "University of To-Day," pp. 325–27; Battle, *History of the University of North Carolina*, 2:289; and William Bingham to Charles Phillips, September 20, 1866, folder 224, University Papers. Bingham advised Phillips that the new university should "give the ascendancy to diligence and scholarly attainment, instead of idleness and rowdyism."

50. *Inauguration of Edwin Anderson Alderman*, p. 27; *University Record* 1 (February 1897): 18–19; *University Record* 2 (January 1898): 19–21, and (April 1898): 34–35; and Battle, *History of the University of North Carolina*, 2:587. The university enrolled 542 students in 1897. See Horowitz, *Campus Life*, pp. 56–81, for related changes at other American colleges. For a comparative perspective on a similar generation of reform-minded university students in Russia, see Gleason, *Young Russia*, and Lincoln, *In the Vanguard of Reform*.

51. Smith, Boddie, and Sharpe, *Charles Duncan McIver*, p. 134, and *University Record* 1 (February 1897): 19.

52. Malone, *Edwin A. Alderman*, pp. 3–6; Powell, *Dictionary of North Carolina Biography*, 1:11–12; manuscript census, population schedule, New Hanover County, North Carolina, 1870; Lefler and Newsome, *North Carolina*, p. 398; Kyriakoudes, "Southern City," pp. 27–34; Perry, "Naval Stores Industry"; and Olmsted, *Journey*, pp. 339–40, 344.

53. James, "Historical and Commercial Sketch," pp. 26–39, 46.

54. *Inauguration of Edwin Anderson Alderman*, p. 23, and Frank A. Daniels, "New South," pp. 102, 106.

55. Holder, *McIver*, pp. 3–19, and autobiographical notes, box 9, Charles McIver Papers.

56. Holder, *McIver*, pp. 22–35, and Branson, *North Carolina Business Directory, 1877 and 1878*, p. 207.

57. "Industry," January 2, 1874, and "Time," February 26, 1874, composition book, box 10, Charles McIver Papers; and Holder, *McIver*, p. 35.

58. Sarah McIver to Charles D. McIver, March 21, 1878, box 1, Charles McIver Papers.

59. Elmer Johnson, "James Yadkin Joyner," pp. 359–61; Ashe et al., *Biographical History of North Carolina*, 6:335–37; manuscript census, population and agricultural schedules, Lenoir County, North Carolina, 1860; and manuscript census, population and agricultural schedules, Lenoir County, North Carolina, 1870.

60. "A Student's Life as Controlling Professional Life," *University Magazine* 1 (April 1878): 43, and "A Definite Plan of Action Necessary," *University Monthly* 1

(September 1882): 24. See also senior oration of E. M. Foust, [1885], folder 7; and inaugural address of John Cicero Angier, n.d. (ca. 1979), folder 1, Dialectic Society Records.

61. "A Student's Life as Controlling Professional Life," *University Magazine* 1 (April 1878): 43, and "Wholesome Hints to College Students," *University Monthly* 1 (September 1882): 22. See also "Our Boys, and How They Differ," *University Magazine*, n.s. 4 (December 1884): 120.

62. "The Lecture System," *University Magazine*, n.s. 4 (March 1885): 241–45.

63. "Society Politics," *University Monthly* 3 (September 1883): 18–19; Battle, *History of the University of North Carolina*, 2:270–71; Holder, *McIver*, pp. 49–50; "The Literary Societies from a Student's Point of View," *University Record* 1 (June 1897): 38; and "The Dialectic and Philanthropic Societies," *University Record* 3 (October 1898): 4. For more on the decline of the societies and the proliferation of specialized student clubs, see "The Age of Societies," *University Magazine*, n.s. 8, no. 1 (1888): 30–31; inaugural address of J. F. Schenck, spring term 1886, folder 25; inaugural address of [Henry Fries?] Shaffner, May 1887, folder 25; and address of Julius I. Foust, October 11, 1889, folder 7, Dialectic Society Records.

64. Inaugural address of W. P. Cline, March 15, 1878, folder 3, and inaugural address of J. F. Schenck, spring term, 1886, folder 25, Dialectic Society Records.

65. Inaugural address of W. P. Cline, March 15, 1878, folder 3, Dialectic Society Records; and Francis P. Venable, "The Educational Value of College Athletics," folder 129, and "To What Extent Should Non-Athletic Events Be Encouraged?" folder 132, series 4:2, Venable Papers. On the development of intercollegiate sports at UNC and other American colleges, see Sumner, "North Carolina Inter-Collegiate Foot-Ball Association," and Ronald A. Smith, *Sports and Freedom*. For a helpful discussion of changing notions of masculinity during the late nineteenth century, see Griffen, "Reconstructing Masculinity."

66. Alderman, "Life and Work of Dr. Charles D. McIver," p. 5, and Smith, Boddie, and Sharpe, *Charles Duncan McIver*, pp. 146–47. Years later, Alderman wrote to McIver, "I am one of the few, I fancy, who can more nearly enter your mind." See Alderman to Charles D. McIver, December 24, 1899, box 4, Charles McIver Papers. Also see Malone, *Edwin A. Alderman*, pp. 251–52.

67. Battle, *History of the University of North Carolina*, 1:620–21, 2:136, 343, and Peele, "Pen-Pictures," p. 41. The first fraternities seem to have emerged as a by-product of the university's growth during the 1850s. As the student population approached five hundred, the Dialectic and Philanthropic Societies became too large and factionalized to serve college men's social needs or to provide adequate opportunities for leadership. See inaugural address of James F. Bell, November 14, 1851, folder 2; inaugural address of James H. Colton, August 18, 1854, folder 4; and inaugural address of William Lafayette Scott, May 26, 1854, folder 25, Dialectic Society Records.

68. Peele, "Pen-Pictures," pp. 41–42.

69. "Our Boys, and How They Differ," *University Magazine*, n.s. 4 (December 1884): 120–21.

70. Eller, "New University," p. 10; Waddell, "Address," pp. 6, 9, 19, 21; and Engelhard, "Address," pp. 6, 22.

71. Piaget, *Six Psychological Studies*, pp. 67–68; Frank A. Daniels, "New South," pp. 102, 110; undated manuscript, box 8, Charles McIver Papers; and Charles W. Dabney to Walter Hines Page, May 20, 1885, American Period file 293, Walter Hines Page Papers. Compare Gleason, *Young Russia*, p. 119.

72. Frank A. Daniels, "New South," p. 100; Waddell, "Address," p. 9; Alderman, "Obligations and Opportunities of Scholarship," pp. 88–91; Alderman, "Higher Education in the South," pp. 981–82; and undated manuscript, box 8, Charles McIver Papers. Compare Josephus Daniels, *Tar Heel Editor*, pp. 113–14.

73. Noble, *History of the Public Schools of North Carolina*, p. 416; *Annual Report, 1868*, p. 9; *Proceedings of the North Carolina Teachers Assembly, 1884*, pp. 12–13; Battle, *History of the University of North Carolina*, 2:142–50, 157–65, 186–90, 198–200, 240–42; *Annual Report, 1878*, p. 10; *Annual Report, 1879*, pp. 11–12, 14–15; *Annual Report, 1880*, pp. 18, 20; *Biennial Report, 1881–82*, pp. 68–69, 115, 118–20; and *Biennial Report, 1883–84*, pp. 50–51. For student interest in the Summer Normal, see "The University Normal School," *University Magazine* 1 (May 1878): 93–95. The university's Summer Normal also received financial assistance from the George Peabody Fund, which helped to establish the first graded schools. Peabody, a London merchant banker and Massachusetts native, created the fund in 1867 to aid the southern states in overcoming the "destructive ravages, and the not less disastrous consequences, of civil war." For more on Peabody and the fund, see Curry, *Brief Sketch of George Peabody*.

74. Powell, *Dictionary of North Carolina Biography*, 1:11–12; Holder, *McIver*, pp. 55–61; Ashe et al., *Biographical History of North Carolina*, 6:337; Strayhorn, "Southern Development," p. 21; and *University Record* 3 (January 1899): 26.

75. Smith, Boddie, and Sharpe, *Charles Duncan McIver*, p. 145.

76. Orr, *Charles Brantley Aycock*, pp. 64–65; undated manuscript, box 9, Charles McIver Papers; Holder, *McIver*, pp. 60–61, 82; Malone, *Edwin A. Alderman*, p. 24; Lewis, *Philander Priestley Claxton*, p. 35; Ashe et al., *Biographical History of North Carolina*, 6:337; and Elmer Johnson, "James Yadkin Joyner," pp. 361–63.

77. Dabney, *Universal Education*, 1:196; Holder, *McIver*, p. 69; Malone, *Edwin A. Alderman*, p. 32; W. A. Blair to Charles D. McIver, February 14, 1886, box 1, Charles McIver Papers; Alderman, *J. L. M. Curry*, pp. 18–19; and "Carolinians Honor President Alderman," *Alumni Bulletin of the University of Virginia* 8 (3d series, April 1915): 174. For a description of one of the reformers' Raleigh meetings, see the *Raleigh News and Observer*, December 28, 1889. When McIver resigned his Durham post to move to Winston, a local paper described him as one of the "first educators of the state." See Holder, *McIver*, p. 60.

Chapter Three

1. *Biennial Report, 1891–92*, p. liv; *Biennial Report, 1885–86*, pp. 12–13; *Biennial Report, 1896–97/1897–98*, p. 520; and *Biennial Report, 1889–90*, p. 8. The re-

formers echoed antebellum superintendent Calvin Wiley on the need to train a new teaching corps. Wiley, however, had been less concerned with professionalization than with establishing minimal state supervision of the common schools.

2. *Annual Report, 1878*, p. 77, and *Biennial Report, 1898–99/1899–1900*, pp. 296–97.

3. *Annual Report, 1879*, pp. 36–37.

4. *Annual Report, 1878*, pp. 7–38; *Annual Report, 1880*, p. 53; *Laws and Resolutions of the State of North Carolina, 1881*, chap. 141; *Laws and Resolutions of the State of North Carolina, 1885*, chaps. 143, 229, 241; and *Laws and Resolutions of the State of North Carolina, 1887*, chap. 400. In 1887, the legislature also moved the black normal in New Bern to Goldsboro and relocated the white normal in Boone to Sparta. See *Biennial Report, 1887–88*, p. 67.

5. *Biennial Report, 1887–88*, p. 15; "Newton Normal School," *State Chronicle*, July 19, 1884; King, "Era of Progressive Reform," pp. 81–87; *Biennial Report, 1885–86*, p. 4; Charles D. McIver to Lula M. McIver, July 5, 1888, box 6, Charles McIver Papers; *Biennial Report, 1887–88*, p. 40; *Biennial Report, 1881–82*, p. 19; and "Normal Schools," *State Chronicle*, August 11, 1887. Beginning in 1878, the state superintendent's reports include detailed accounts of each normal school's operation.

6. "Normal Schools," *State Chronicle*, August 11, 1887; *Biennial Report, 1885–86*, p. 24; Battle, *History of the University of North Carolina*, 2:341; Nelson B. Massey to Sidney M. Finger, November 28, 1886, box 150, SPI Correspondence; Holder, *McIver*, pp. 73–74; and Alderman, "Life and Work of Dr. Charles D. McIver," p. 4. The idea of a state-supported normal college was not original to McIver. Efforts to establish such an institution were first made in the 1850s but met with hostility from university officials. See Highsmith, "State Normal School Idea," pp. 8–18.

7. *North Carolina Teacher* 5 (May 1888): 394; Booth, "Teaching as a Profession," p. 109; *North Carolina Teacher* 4 (June 1887): 463–64; summary remarks, Institute Notebooks, Edwin Alderman Papers; *North Carolina Teacher* 6 (March 1889): 345; *Proceedings of the North Carolina Teachers Assembly, 1887*, p. 44; and *Memorial to the General Assembly of North Carolina, from the State Teachers Assembly*. For more on the comparison of teaching to law and medicine, see untitled address to the National Educational Association, Peoria, Ill., 1905, box 9, Charles McIver Papers. The history of the Teachers Assembly is recounted in the *North Carolina Teacher* 8 (June 1891): 471–78; and Gilbert and Warren, "Teachers Association Reorganized," "Wanted—A Normal School," and "Assembly Moves to the Beach."

8. *Biennial Report, 1889–90*, p. 11.

9. Desmond, "Evolution of the Educator," p. 247; Page, "School That Built a Town," p. 77; and Strober and Tyack, "Why Do Women Teach and Men Manage?," p. 500. A newspaperman explained the "naturalness" of the division of labor that emerged in the graded schools between teachers and administrators. "As in an advanced state of civilization men come to a division of labor system in mechanics and manufacturing," he observed, "so the same rule applies to educational mat-

ters." See the *Wilson Advance*, July 29, 1881. For comparative perspectives on the feminization of teaching and the development of bureaucratic hierarchies in Canada, Great Britain, and the northeastern United States, see Apple, *Teachers and Texts*, pp. 54–78; Apple, "Teaching and 'Women's Work' "; Apple, "Work, Class, and Teaching"; Bergen, "Only a Schoolmaster"; Copelman, "Women in the Classroom Struggle"; Danylewycz, Light, and Prentice, "Evolution of the Sexual Division of Labour in Teaching"; Danylewycz and Prentice, "Teachers, Gender, and Bureaucratizing School Systems"; Danylewycz and Prentice, "Teachers' Work"; Prentice, "Feminization of Teaching in British North America and Canada"; Purvis, "Women and Teaching in the Nineteenth Century"; and Prentice and Theobold, *Women Who Taught*.

10. In 1886, men constituted 61 percent of the teaching force, women 39 percent. See *Biennial Report, 1885–86*, pp. 141, 145. The effects of the graded schools on teacher pay differentials can be seen in the statistical tables appended to each of the state superintendent's reports between 1891 and 1900.

11. *Proceedings of the North Carolina Teachers Assembly, 1887*, p. 61. On the battle against false notions of economy, see *Biennial Report, 1889–90*, p. 27; *Biennial Report, 1896–97/1897–98*, p. 72; and *Biennial Report, 1898–99/1899–1900*, p. 104. For discussion of a similar revolt of women teachers in Memphis, Tenn., see Berkeley, " 'Ladies Want to Bring About Reform.' "

12. Transylvania County remarks, Institute Notebooks, Edwin Alderman Papers; Hurt, "Educational Development of Ashe County," p. 54; Strober and Tyack, "Why Do Women Teach and Men Manage?," pp. 497–98; and *North Carolina Teacher* 8 (June 1891): 504.

13. *Biennial Report, 1891–92*, p. liv; Page, "Study of an Old Southern Borough," pp. 653–54; and Charles McIver, untitled address, n.d., box 9, Charles McIver Papers. On women's greater openness to innovation, see Natalie Zemon Davis, *Society and Culture in Early Modern France*, pp. 124–51; Ulrich, *Good Wives*, pp. 191–97; and Hall, "Disorderly Women," pp. 372–77. School reformers commented endlessly on the conservative nature of male teachers. See especially Institute Notebooks, Edwin Alderman Papers, and *Biennial Report, 1889–90*, p. 6.

14. Smith, Boddie, and Sharpe, *Charles Duncan McIver*, p. 5; *Journal of the House of Representatives of the General Assembly, 1887*, p. 167; *Journal of the Senate of the General Assembly, 1887*, pp. 443, 459, 492; Holder, *McIver*, pp. 88–90; *Journal of the House of Representatives of the General Assembly, 1889*, pp. 637–38; and *Journal of the Senate of the General Assembly, 1889*, p. 409.

15. *Biennial Report, 1889–90*, pp. xlix–lviii; Sidney M. Finger to J. L. M. Curry, September 19, 1889, SPI Letterbook 88; and *Laws and Resolutions of the State of North Carolina, 1889*, chap. 200. Finger first broached the idea of creating an institute program before the legislature convened. See *Biennial Report, 1887–88*, pp. xxxvi–xxxvii.

16. Sidney M. Finger to Charles D. McIver, March 22, 1889, box 1, Charles McIver Papers; Sidney M. Finger to J. L. M. Curry, September 19, 1889, SPI Letterbook 88; Edwin A. Alderman to Sidney M. Finger, March 1889, box 156,

SPI Correspondence; and Edwin A. Alderman to Charles D. McIver, April 3, 1889, box 1, Charles McIver Papers. Alderman wedded Emma Graves, sister of Ralph Henry Graves of the university faculty, in 1885 and celebrated the birth of his first child in 1886. McIver also married in 1885. His wife was Lula Martin, a teacher whom he had met while working at the Winston graded school. They, too, had their first child in 1886. See Malone, *Edwin A. Alderman*, pp. 33–34, and Holder, *McIver*, pp. 66, 74.

17. Institute Notebooks, Edwin Alderman Papers; *Biennial Report, 1889–90*, pp. xlix–lviii, 15; *Biennial Report, 1891–92*, pp. l–lxiv; and Sidney M. Finger to J. L. M. Curry, December 7, 1889, SPI Letterbook 88.

18. Charles D. McIver to Sidney M. Finger, July 16, 1889, box 158, SPI Correspondence; Holder, *McIver*, p. 95; Edwin A. Alderman to Charles D. McIver, September 5, 1891, box 1, Charles McIver Papers; and Edwin A. Alderman to Sidney M. Finger, July 6, 1889, box 158, SPI Correspondence.

19. Charles D. McIver to Lula M. McIver, September 15, 1890, box 6, Charles McIver Papers.

20. Ibid., September 21, 1890, box 6, Charles McIver Papers.

21. Ibid., June 11, 1890, and February 3, 1890, box 6, Charles McIver Papers.

22. Ibid., March 13, 1890; December 8, 1890; September 30, 1890; March 15, 1890; and December 7, 1890, box 6, Charles McIver Papers; and Holder, *McIver*, pp. 100, 111.

23. Lula M. McIver to Charles D. McIver, December 9, 1890, box 6; June 21, 1898, box 7; and March 19, 1890, box 6, Charles McIver Papers.

24. Malone, *Edwin A. Alderman*, pp. 34–35; Charles D. McIver to Lula M. McIver, November 30, 1890, box 6, Charles McIver Papers; Charles D. McIver to Sidney M. Finger, August 7, 1889, box 159, SPI Correspondence; and Charles D. McIver, memorial address for Sidney M. Finger, box 9, Charles McIver Papers.

25. Smith, Boddie, and Sharpe, *Charles Duncan McIver*, p. 138; *Biennial Report, 1889–90*, pp. 1–37; and *Biennial Report, 1891–92*, pp. liii, lxii.

26. *Biennial Report, 1889–90*, pp. 4, 15; *Biennial Report, 1891–92*, p. liii; Dale, "About Normal Colleges," p. 243; and Mecklenburg County remarks, Institute Notebooks, Edwin Alderman Papers. On the growth of schools of law, medicine, and theology in the late nineteenth century and the emergence of a new professional ethos, see Bledstein, *Culture of Professionalism*.

27. Charles D. McIver to Lula M. McIver, July 5, 1890, and June 9, 1890, box 6, Charles McIver Papers; Ashe, Polk, and Transylvania County remarks, Institute Notebooks, Edwin Alderman Papers; and *Biennial Report, 1889–90*, pp. 22–23. See also Wilkes County and Williamston remarks, Institute Notebooks, Edwin Alderman Papers; Edwin A. Alderman to Charles D. McIver, September 26, 1889, box 1, and Charles D. McIver to Lula M. McIver, March 14, 1890, box 6, Charles McIver Papers.

28. Summary remarks, Institute Notebooks, Edwin Alderman Papers. See also Cabarrus, Montgomery, and Stanly County remarks.

29. Gaston County remarks, Institute Notebooks, Edwin Alderman Papers;

Biennial Report, 1889–90, pp. 6, 8; and Edwin A. Alderman to Sidney M. Finger, July 6, 1889, box 158, SPI Correspondence. See also Alleghany, Anson, Ashe, Cabarrus, and Union County remarks, Institute Notebooks, Edwin Alderman Papers.

30. Pamlico County remarks, Institute Notebooks, Edwin Alderman Papers, and *Biennial Report, 1889–90*, pp. 5–6, 8.

31. Edwin A. Alderman to Charles D. McIver, April 3, 1889, box 1; Charles D. McIver to Lula M. McIver, June 10, 1890, box 6; and G. W. Byrd to Charles D. McIver, June 27, 1889, box 1, Charles McIver Papers; and Cumberland County remarks, Institute Notebooks, Edwin Alderman Papers. See also Edwin A. Alderman to Sidney M. Finger, November 12, 1889, box 164, SPI Correspondence.

32. Charles D. McIver to Lula M. McIver, January 27, 1890, box 6, Charles McIver Papers; Edwin A. Alderman to Sidney M. Finger, August 16, 1889, box 159, SPI Correspondence; and Ashe County remarks, Institute Notebooks, Edwin Alderman Papers.

33. Malone, *Edwin A. Alderman*, p. 18, and Dabney, *Universal Education*, 1:198. Josephus Daniels explained the difference between the two crusaders this way: "McIver hit with a sledge hammer; when people heard him they left the meeting place saying, 'We've got to do something about this,' and went out the door rolling up their sleeves. Alderman, a natural born orator, left his audience spell bound and thinking how wonderfully he commanded the English language, but very often the average citizen did not get the message" (see Satterfield, *Charles Duncan McIver*, p. 31).

34. Ashe County and Pamlico County remarks, Institute Notebooks, Edwin Alderman Papers, and Edwin A. Alderman to Charles D. McIver, September 26, 1889, box 1, Charles McIver Papers.

35. Dabney, *Universal Education*, 1:198, and Charles D. McIver to Lula M. McIver, May 13, 1890, box 6, Charles McIver Papers. For more on McIver's struggles to compete with circuses and church meetings, see Charles D. McIver to Lula M. McIver, December 9, 1889; September 30, 1890; October 8, 1890; and November 10, 1890, box 6, Charles McIver Papers.

36. Alderman, "Life and Work of Dr. Charles D. McIver," p. 5; untitled address, n.d., box 9, Charles McIver Papers; and Holder, *McIver*, pp. 94, 96–97, 107.

37. Charles D. McIver to Lula M. McIver, April 10, 1891, and March 12, 1890, box 6, Charles McIver Papers.

38. Ibid., March 20, 1890, and November 10, 1890, box 6, and Henry Blount to Charles D. McIver, February 6, 1899, box 3, Charles McIver Papers. See also Charles D. McIver to Lula M. McIver, September 19, 1890, box 6, Charles McIver Papers.

39. Josephus Daniels, *Editor in Politics*, pp. 376–77; "Largest State Membership in the Union," *North Carolina Teacher* 8 (January 1891): 252; *North Carolina Teacher* 8 (June 1891): 471–78; Gilbert and Warren, "Assembly Moves to the Beach"; and David F. St. Clair to Charles D. McIver, December 11, 1889, box 1, Charles McIver Papers.

40. Charles D. McIver to Sidney M. Finger, August 25, 1890, box 163, SPI Correspondence; *Biennial Report, 1891–92*, p. xvii; Charles D. McIver to Josephus Daniels, August 8, 1899, box 3, and Charles D. McIver to Lula M. McIver, January 24, 1891, box 6, Charles McIver Papers; King, "Era of Progressive Reform," pp. 125–30; *Raleigh News and Observer*, January 22, 23, 27, 28, 1891; *Journal of the Senate of the General Assembly, 1891*, p. 166; *Journal of the House of Representatives of the General Assembly, 1891*, p. 372; and *Laws and Resolutions of the State of North Carolina, 1891*, chap. 139. The institution's name was changed from "school" to "college" in 1897. See *Public Laws and Resolutions of the State of North Carolina, 1897*, chap. 230.

41. *Laws and Resolutions of the State of North Carolina, 1891*, chap. 139, and *Alamance Gleaner*, June 18, 1891. See also Bowles, *Good Beginning*, pp. 7–8; George Allen Mebane to Charles D. McIver, April 28, 1891; and W. S. Halliburton to Charles D. McIver, May 22, 1891, box 1, Charles McIver Papers.

42. Bowles, *Good Beginning*, pp. 7–9; *Alamance Gleaner*, June 18, 1891; *Salisbury Carolina Watchman*, July 9, 1891; *Greensboro Patriot*, June 11, 1891; *Raleigh News and Observer*, June 13, 1891; and *Durham Weekly Globe*, June 12, 1891, quoted in Bowles, *Good Beginning*, p. 8.

43. George T. Winston to Charles D. McIver, February 28, 1891, box 1, Charles McIver Papers, and Holder, *McIver*, p. 116.

44. Edwin A. Alderman to Charles D. McIver, June 13, 1891, box 1, Charles McIver Papers; Holder, *McIver*, p. 116; King, "Era of Progressive Reform," pp. 131–33; and Malone, *Edwin A. Alderman*, pp. 52–53, 71–74. See also Edwin A. Alderman to Charles D. McIver, June 11, 1891, box 1, Charles McIver Papers, and Charles D. McIver to Sidney M. Finger, June 6, 1891, box 166, SPI Correspondence.

45. Holder, *McIver*, pp. 119–26; J. L. M. Curry to Charles D. McIver, July 6, 1891; and George T. Winston to Charles D. McIver, June 22, 1891, box 1, Charles McIver Papers.

46. *Raleigh News and Observer*, May 24, 1892; Bowles, *Good Beginning*, pp. 9–10, 23, 29–38; King, "Era of Progressive Reform," pp. 135–36; T. M. Robinson, "What Can a Woman Do to Earn a Living?," pp. 393–93; and Sallie S. Cotten to Charles D. McIver, April 24, 1893, box 2, Charles McIver Papers. For later additions to the faculty, see Bowles, *Good Beginning*, pp. 38–67. North Carolina licensed its first two female physicians in 1894. A lady doctor was such a rarity that male physicians traveled to Greensboro to meet their unusual colleague. See Bowles, *Good Beginning*, p. 39, and Lathrop, *Educate a Woman*, p. 14.

47. Holder, *McIver*, pp. 123–26; *Laws and Resolutions of the State of North Carolina, 1891*, chap. 139; John Thompson to Charles D. McIver, August 31, 1893, box 2, Charles McIver Papers; and *First Annual Catalogue of the State Normal and Industrial School*, p. 47.

48. Holder, *McIver*, pp. 124–29; Forney, Buie, and Austin, *Leaves from the Stenographers' Notebooks*, p. 15; and Mary Wiley Diary, July 14, 1894, Calvin Wiley Papers.

49. *First Annual Catalogue of the State Normal and Industrial School*, pp. 36–37, 47–48; *Second Annual Catalogue of the State Normal and Industrial School*, pp. 51–52; *Third Annual Catalogue of the State Normal and Industrial School*, p. 42; *Fourth Annual Catalogue of the State Normal and Industrial School*, pp. 48–49; *Fifth Annual Catalogue of the State Normal and Industrial College*, p. 50; *Sixth Annual Catalogue of the State Normal and Industrial College*, pp. 53–54; *Seventh Annual Catalogue of the North Carolina State Normal and Industrial College*, p. 53; *Eighth Annual Catalogue of the North Carolina State Normal and Industrial College*, pp. 54–55; and *Ninth Annual Catalogue of the North Carolina State Normal and Industrial College*, pp. 54–55.

50. Raymond, *Then and Now*, pp. 1–26.

51. *First Annual Catalogue of the State Normal and Industrial School*, pp. 47–48; *Second Annual Catalogue of the State Normal and Industrial School*, pp. 51–52; *Third Annual Catalogue of the State Normal and Industrial School*, p. 42; *Fourth Annual Catalogue of the State Normal and Industrial School*, pp. 48–49; *Fifth Annual Catalogue of the State Normal and Industrial College*, p. 50; *Sixth Annual Catalogue of the State Normal and Industrial College*, pp. 53–54; *Seventh Annual Catalogue of the North Carolina State Normal and Industrial College*, p. 53; *Eighth Annual Catalogue of the North Carolina State Normal and Industrial College*, pp. 54–55; *Ninth Annual Catalogue of the North Carolina State Normal and Industrial College*, pp. 54–55; Mrs. J. C. Powell to Charles D. McIver, July 15, 1892, and Mary Bayard Morgan to Charles D. McIver, July 13, 1892, box 29, Charles McIver Papers. See also Ethel Finlator to Charles D. McIver, June 28, 1882; Carrie Mullins to Charles D. McIver, July 2, 1892; Virginia Patrick to Charles D. McIver, July 15, 1892; Mrs. G. B. Ayers to Charles D. McIver, August 1892, box 29; and Mrs. S. T. Brice to Charles D. McIver, July 6, 1895, box 38, Charles McIver Papers.

52. Mattie D. Gay to Charles D. McIver, August 22, 1892, and M. L. Albritton to Charles D. McIver, July 6, 1892, box 29, Charles McIver Papers; and *First Annual Catalogue of the State Normal and Industrial School*, p. 8. Kate Davis and her mother also wanted to move to Greensboro and open a boardinghouse. See Kate Davis to Charles D. McIver, August 16, 1895, box 38, Charles McIver Papers.

53. *First Annual Catalogue of the State Normal and Industrial School*, pp. 47–48; *Second Annual Catalogue of the State Normal and Industrial School*, pp. 51–52; and Mrs. C. A. Sater to Charles D. McIver, July 29, 1892, box 29, Charles McIver Papers. For other examples of parents interested in sending a daughter to the normal so that she could help educate her siblings, see J. L. Bell to Charles D. McIver, July 28, 1892, box 29, and Hattie Everett to Charles D. McIver, July 29, 1895, box 38, Charles McIver Papers.

54. Pauline Harris to Charles D. McIver, July 19, 1892; Ellen Small to Charles D. McIver, July 13, 1892, box 29; and Katie Moore to Charles D. McIver, October 27, 1895, box 38, Charles McIver Papers.

55. Ethel A. Wicker to Charles D. McIver, July 4, 1892; Lottie Watkins to Charles D. McIver, September 14, 1892; Mary P. Bell to Charles D. McIver, July 25, 1892; Ada and Rebecca Vance to Charles D. McIver, July 13, 1892, box 29; Eulalie Elliott

to Charles D. McIver, September 19, 1892, box 1; Mabelle Pearce to Charles D. McIver, July 22, 1895; Katie Moore to Charles D. McIver, October 27, 1895, box 38; and Julia Pasmore to Charles D. McIver, December 8, 1899, box 4, Charles McIver Papers; and *First Annual Catalogue of the State Normal and Industrial School*, pp. 40–41.

56. Charles D. McIver, undated commencement address, box 9, Charles McIver Papers.

57. Lu Ann Jones, " 'Task That Is Ours,' " pp. 48–65; Nathans, *Quest for Progress*, pp. 52–62; Bordin, *Woman and Temperance*; and *Biennial Report, 1889–90*, p. 11.

58. Holder, *McIver*, pp. 63–68, 111; Bowles, *Good Beginning*, p. 33; Charles D. McIver to Lula M. McIver, March 3, 1890, box 6, Charles McIver Papers; and *Biennial Report, 1889–90*, p. 21. Harriet Beecher Stowe first published *My Wife and I* in 1871. The McIvers were probably reading the 1888 reprint. Like Stowe, their belief in sexual equality and expanded opportunities for women was grounded in the ideology of separate spheres. For more on Stowe, see Boydston, Kelley, and Margolis, *Limits of Sisterhood*, especially pp. 262–63, 295.

59. Lizzie (Elizabeth) P. McIver to Charles D. McIver, June 8, 1892, box 1; Maggie Harrison to Charles D. McIver, July 30, 1892; and Lizzie McDuffie to Charles D. McIver, box 29, Charles McIver Papers; and Holder, *McIver*, p. 130. See also Charles McIver, untitled autobiographical writing, box 9; Gertrude M. Bagby to Charles D. McIver, July 6, 1892; and Annie Parker to Charles D. McIver, July 8, 1892, box 29, Charles McIver Papers.

60. Raymond, *Then and Now*, p. 15; Josephus Daniels to Carroll Wright, March 15, 1895, box 2, Charles McIver Papers; *Laws and Resolutions of the State of North Carolina, 1891*, chap. 139; Charles D. McIver to S. P. Alexander, September 7, 1891, box 1; and Charles D. McIver to Howard Russell Butler, November 16, 1901, box 4, Charles McIver Papers. On McIver's interest in modeling his school after the Seven Sisters, see also Charles D. McIver to Lula M. McIver, September 2, 1886, box 6, Charles McIver Papers.

61. Bowles, *Good Beginning*, pp. 20–25; *First Annual Catalogue of the State Normal and Industrial School*, pp. 20–36; "The Lady Teacher," *North Carolina Teacher* 7 (January 1890): 263; and Mary Dail to Charles D. McIver, June 12, 1895, box 2, Charles McIver Papers. McIver had a profound interest in dress reform. See Charles D. McIver to Lula M. McIver, April 10, 1891, box 6, Charles McIver Papers. For examples of the students' literary and historical writings, see the *State Normal Magazine*.

62. D. Matt Thompson to Charles D. McIver, November 10, 1892, box 1, and Sallie Wellford Scott to Charles D. McIver, July 6, 1893, box 2, Charles McIver Papers; and Mary Wiley Diary, April 28, 1893, Calvin Wiley Papers. Mary Wiley was the daughter of Calvin Henderson Wiley, the state's first superintendent of public instruction, who served from 1853 to 1865.

63. Mary Dail to Charles D. McIver, June 12, 1895; M. Caldwell to Charles D. McIver, October 9, 1895, box 2; and Nannie Seawell to Charles D. McIver, May 2,

1890, box 1, Charles McIver Papers; Holder, *McIver*, pp. 256–57; and Smith, Boddie, and Sharpe, *Charles Duncan McIver.*

64. Mrs. R. M. Middleton to Charles D. McIver, November 25, 1892, box 1; Mrs. N. W. Steinhilper to Charles D. McIver, September 14, 1892; J. D. Currie to Charles D. McIver, September 12, 1892; J. S. Grant to Charles D. McIver, September 21, 1892, box 29; and John A. Coke to Charles D. McIver, September 14, 1892, box 1, Charles McIver Papers.

65. Bowles, *Good Beginning*, pp. 17–20; *First Annual Catalogue of the State Normal and Industrial School*, p. 44; and Charles D. McIver to John O'Hagan, May 20, 1894, box 2, Charles McIver Papers. On April Fool's Day, 1897, the young women organized a smoking party in defiance of college rules. When McIver learned of the offense, he confined them to their rooms and suspended their visiting privileges with anyone other than family members. For the ensuing controversy over the punishment, see the exchanges between McIver and Logan D. Howell, box 3, Charles McIver Papers. The students' formal confessions and petitions of apology are in boxes 3 and 52.

66. Charles D. McIver to John O'Hagan, May 20, 1894, box 2, Charles McIver Papers, and Mary Wiley Diary, October 30, 1892, and March 14, 1893, Calvin Wiley Papers.

67. Mary Wiley Diary, January 17, 1894; August 26, 1894; November 13, 1892; January 15, 1893; March 14, 1893; March 25, 1893; March 1, 1893; May 28, 1893; and January 8, 1894, Calvin Wiley Papers. For a comparative perspective on female friendships in English boarding schools, see Vicinus, *Independent Women*, pp. 187–99.

68. Mary Wiley Diary, January 17, 1894, Calvin Wiley Papers; Della E. Stikelether to Charles D. McIver, September 2, 1893; and Charles D. McIver to John O'Hagan, May 20, 1894, box 2, Charles McIver Papers.

69. J. Carson Watson to Charles D. McIver, July 6, 1894, box 2, and J. A. McAllister to Charles D. McIver, July 27, 1892, box 29, Charles McIver Papers.

70. P. L. Murphy to Charles D. McIver, December 25, 1899, box 4, Charles McIver Papers, and Holder, *McIver*, p. 121.

71. Charles D. McIver to J. A. Holmes, November 25, 1898, box 106, Charles McIver Papers; Smith, Boddie, and Sharpe, *Charles Duncan McIver*, p. 223; Holder, *McIver*, pp. 134–35; untitled address to the National Educational Association, Peoria, Ill., 1905, box 9, Charles McIver Papers; and Sims, "Feminism and Femininity," pp. 216–22. For more on campus culture at the Normal, see Dean, "Learning to Be New Women," and Dean, "Covert Curriculum."

72. Raymond, *Then and Now*, pp. 224–25, 230, and Smith, Boddie, and Sharpe, *Charles Duncan McIver*, pp. 154–55.

73. Holder, *McIver*, p. 173. "Shadowed" is Nancy Hoffman's word for the ambiguous status that has characterized teaching since the late nineteenth century. See Hoffman, *Woman's "True" Profession*, pp. 15–17, and Lortie, *Schoolteacher*, pp. 10–12.

Chapter Four

1. George T. Winston to Charles D. McIver, March 19, 1891, and Edwin A. Alderman to Charles D. McIver, September 5, 1891, box 1, Charles McIver Papers.

2. Escott, *Many Excellent People*, p. 176, and Williams and Wakefield, "Farm Tenancy in North Carolina," pp. 22–23. The production declines for some foodstuffs were particularly dramatic. Corn harvests, for example, fell 14.28 percent from 1860 to 1890, while the number of swine dropped 33.52 percent.

3. Lefler and Newsome, *North Carolina*, pp. 524–26, and Goodwyn, *Democratic Promise*, pp. 116–17.

4. For an overview of the alliance, see Goodwyn, *Democratic Promise*, pp. 3–274, and McMath, *Populist Vanguard*.

5. *Public Documents of the State of North Carolina, 1893*, document 30, pp. 5–7, and Escott, *Many Excellent People*, pp. 244–49.

6. Kousser, *Shaping of Southern Politics*, p. 183; Democratic voter quoted in Durden, *Climax of Populism*, pp. 16–17; Crow and Durden, *Maverick Republican*, pp. 49–50; and Edmonds, *Negro and Fusion Politics*, pp. 3–66.

7. *Raleigh News and Observer*, October 31, 1894, and March 18, 1895; *Charlotte Observer*, September 18, 1894; W. D. McIver to Charles D. McIver, January 11, 1895, box 2, Charles McIver Papers; and Bode, *Protestantism and the New South*, p. 55.

8. *Raleigh News and Observer*, March 6, 1895; Gobbel, *Church-State Relationships*, p. 143; Holder, *McIver*, pp. 153–55; Bode, *Protestantism and the New South*, p. 31; Edmonds, *Negro and Fusion Politics*, p. 37; *Biblical Recorder*, January 16, 1895; and Edwin Alderman to Cornelia Phillips Spencer, January 17, 1895, box 2, Cornelia Phillips Spencer Papers (Raleigh). See also E. C. Beddingfield to Charles D. McIver, July 26, 1894, and Josephus Daniels to Charles D. McIver, November 9, 1894, box 2, Charles McIver Papers.

9. Sidney M. Finger to Charles D. McIver, December 11, 1891, box 1, Charles McIver Papers; Gobbel, *Church-State Relationships*, pp. 121, 132–33; Paschal, *History of Wake Forest College*, 2:293–94; Charles Williams, *History of the Baptists*, p. 175; Battle, *History of the University of North Carolina*, 2:304–8; and Bode, *Protestantism and the New South*, pp. 21–22.

10. Holder, *McIver*, pp. 152–53; *Biblical Recorder*, September 5, 1894; and W. D. McIver to Charles D. McIver, January 11, 1895, box 2, Charles McIver Papers.

11. Charles D. McIver to the editor of the Jonesboro *Leader*, May 18, 1893, box 2, Charles McIver Papers; Groom, "North Carolina Journals of Education—A History," p. 9; Eugene G. Harrell to Charles D. McIver, November 10, 1892, box 1, Charles McIver Papers; *North Carolina Teacher* 10 (April 1893): 301–10, 312–13, and (May 1893): 391–94; Holder, *McIver*, pp. 136–40; and King, "Era of Progressive Reform," pp. 153–55. See also W. F. St. Clair to Charles D. McIver, March 23, 1893, and R. H. Stancell to Charles D. McIver, May 5, 1893, box 2, Charles McIver Papers.

12. D. E. McIver to Charles D. McIver, May 22, 1893, box 2, Charles McIver Papers; Holder, *McIver*, p. 139; minutes of student meeting, spring 1893, and incomplete copy of student letter to Eugene G. Harrell, March 2, 1893, box 2, Charles McIver Papers; and *North Carolina Teacher* 10 (June 1893): 456–61.

13. King, "Era of Progressive Reform," pp. 55–57; J. I. Foust to Edward P. Moses, September 8, 1941, Edward Moses Papers; and E. McK. Goodwin to Charles D. McIver, December 28, 1894, B. F. Aycock to Charles D. McIver, March 1, 1895, and J. A. Holmes to Charles D. McIver, May 26, 1895, box 2, Charles McIver Papers. See also Sidney M. Finger to Charles D. McIver, [spring 1893], and George T. Winston to Charles D. McIver, April 11, 1895, box 2, Charles McIver Papers. Finger wrote: "I am glad Moses feels hurt. . . . He & H[arrell] are a pretty pair. Poor little envious disappointed fellows. I pity them both . . . but I do want the state to understand their motives. One activated by envy and jealousy & the other by a *commercial* view."

14. *Biennial Report, 1896–97/1897–98*, part 2, p. 18; Alderman, "The University," p. 50; *Biennial Report, 1889–90*, p. 1; Smith, Boddie, and Sharpe, *Charles Duncan McIver*, p. 145; *Christian Educator*, August 1897; and Gobbel, *Church-State Relationships*, p. 168. See also *Proceedings of the North Carolina Teachers Assembly, 1884*, p. 13.

15. Bode, *Protestantism and the New South*, pp. 25–26, and Taylor, *How Far Should a State Undertake to Educate?*, p. 3.

16. Taylor, *How Far Should a State Undertake to Educate?*, pp. 5, 11.

17. *Journal of the House of Representatives of the General Assembly, 1891*, pp. 135, 159, 167, 802; *Journal of the Senate of the General Assembly, 1891*, pp. 133, 156, 353, 413; and *Biennial Report, 1896–97/1897–98*, pp. 269–72. The official editor of the *Biblical Recorder*, the Reverend Christopher Thomas Bailey, fell ill in 1894. His son, Josiah, a young man only in his twenties, stepped in to make the paper a political force. Josiah Bailey remained at the helm of the *Biblical Recorder* until 1907, when he resigned and devoted himself full-time to a political career. He eventually found his way to the U.S. Senate, where he served from 1931 until his death in 1946. Bailey distinguished himself as a sharp critic of Franklin Roosevelt's New Deal and as a champion of localism in the face of an expansive federal government. For a more detailed account of his life, see John Robert Moore, *Senator Josiah William Bailey*.

18. For the comparison to other turn-of-the-century dissenters, see Thelen, *Paths of Resistance*; Waller, *Feud*; and Fink, *Workingmen's Democracy*.

19. *Biennial Report, 1896–97/1897–98*, pp. 269–72.

20. Sidney M. Finger to Charles D. McIver, March 26, 1894, box 2, Charles McIver Papers; Taylor, *How Far Should a State Undertake to Educate?*; and *Biblical Recorder*, February 24, 1897.

21. "The Battle Royal," *Raleigh News and Observer*, March 6, 1895; Paschal, *History of Wake Forest College*, 2:294; Bode, *Protestantism and the New South*, pp. 27–35; Josephus Daniels, *Editor in Politics*, pp. 102–3; Josiah Bailey to John C. Kilgo, July 14, 1897, John Kilgo Papers; and Cornelia Phillips Spencer to George T. Winston, March 26, 1895, folder 657, University Papers.

22. George T. Winston to Charles D. McIver, May 4, 1891, box 1, Charles McIver Papers; *University Magazine*, n.s. 14 (January 1895): 232–33; Edwin A. Alderman to Cornelia Phillips Spencer, January 17, 1895, box 2, Cornelia Phillips Spencer Papers (Raleigh); Josephus Daniels to Charles McIver, November 9, 1894, box 2, Charles McIver Papers; and *Raleigh News and Observer*, February 10, 1895. See also Charles D. McIver to Board of Directors, State Normal and Industrial School, February 16, 1895, box 170, SPI Correspondence.

23. "The Battle Royal," *Raleigh News and Observer*, March 6, 1895; "Politics in North Carolina," *Star of Zion*, July 26, 1894; Marion Butler, "Resolved that North Carolina should tax her two races separately to support their respective school systems," June 4, 1883, folder 2, Student Organizations and Activities, Dialectic Society Records, Series 2, Subseries 1, Addresses/Debates, University of North Carolina Archives; and *The Caucasian*, September 26, 1889, and September 10, 1891.

24. "The Battle Royal," *Raleigh News and Observer*, March 6, 1895, and *Raleigh News and Observer*, March 8, 1895.

25. George T. Winston to Cornelia Phillips Spencer, April 9, 1895, box 2, Cornelia Phillips Spencer Papers (Raleigh).

26. Lula McIver to Charles D. McIver, March 9, 1895, box 7, Charles McIver Papers.

27. *Biennial Report, 1892–93/1893–94*, pp. 11–13; *Public Laws and Resolutions of the State of North Carolina, 1895*, chap. 297; T. D. McCauley to John C. Scarborough, April 19, 1895, box 180, and W. D. Feimster to John C. Scarborough, March 19, 1895, box 179, SPI Correspondence; John C. Scarborough to T. D. McCauley, March 18, and April 22, 1895, SPI Letterbook 101; and John C. Scarborough to J. L. M. Curry, July 8, 1895, SPI Letterbook 102.

28. Kousser, *Shaping of Southern Politics*, pp. 184–87; Escott, *Many Excellent People*, pp. 164–70, 248; and King, "Era of Progressive Reform," p. 163.

29. Escott, *Many Excellent People*, p. 184; Logan, "Legal Status of Public School Education for Negroes," pp. 346–48; *Biennial Report, 1887–88*, p. xlii; and Noble, *History of the Public Schools of North Carolina*, pp. 406–8.

30. Logan, "Legal Status of Public School Education for Negroes," pp. 348–51, and *Tarboro Southerner*, May 10, 1883. Business leaders in Smithfield also feared that "an almost solid negro vote" would defeat their graded school proposition. See N. R. Richardson to Sidney M. Finger, April 22, 1885, box 147, SPI Correspondence.

31. Logan, "Legal Status of Public School Education for Negroes," pp. 352–56; Noble, *History of the Public Schools of North Carolina*, pp. 408–9; King, "Era of Progressive Reform," pp. 63–64; Branson, *Branson's North Carolina Business Directory for 1884*, p. 319; manuscript census, population schedule, Gaston County, North Carolina, 1880; *North Carolina Reports*, vol. 94, February Term, 1886, p. 519; and C. Jeffers to Sidney M. Finger, March 10, 1887, box 151, SPI Correspondence. The supreme court affirmed its decision against the Dortch law later in the same term in the case of *A. M. Riggsbee v. The Town of Durham*. Riggsbee, too, was a

white merchant. See *North Carolina Reports*, vol. 94, February Term, 1886, pp. 577–82, and Branson, *Branson's North Carolina Business Directory for 1884*, p. 287.

32. King, "Era of Progressive Reform," pp. 10–11; *Raleigh News and Observer*, February 7, 1885; Escott, *Many Excellent People*, pp. 184–85; Logan, "Legal Status of Public School Education for Negroes," pp. 348–53; and *Public School Law of North Carolina, 1885*, pp. 15–16.

33. B. F. Grady to Sidney M. Finger, August 9, 1887, box 152, SPI Correspondence.

34. *Biennial Report, 1891–92*, p. xii; *Proceedings of the North Carolina Teachers Assembly, 1884*, p. 27; and R. R. King to Sidney M. Finger, October 14, 1885, box 148, SPI Correspondence. See also George N. Thompson to Sidney M. Finger, April 7, 1885, box 147; S. Watson Reid to Sidney M. Finger, December 28, 1885, box 148; Rev. T. B. Haughton to Sidney M. Finger, July 24, 1886, box 150; Harmon Corey, C. C. Coltrain, and Noah Robertson to Sidney M. Finger, November 26, 1886, box 150; and Jno. S. Smiley to Sidney M. Finger, September 5, 1887, box 153, SPI Correspondence. These are only a small sampling of the hundreds of complaint letters that arrived in the superintendent's office.

35. "The Need for Education," *Wilson Advance*, August 19, 1882; J. P. Caldwell to Charles D. McIver, August 6, 1888, box 1, Charles McIver Papers; and "A Protest against the Graded School," *Wilson Advance*, May 4, 1883. In 1900, black teachers attending a summer institute in Elizabeth City adopted a resolution declaring that "the responsibility of preparing children for good citizenship rests more upon teachers than upon parents." See *Biennial Report, 1898–99/1899–1900*, p. 196.

36. King, "Era of Progressive Reform," p. 182; *Biennial Report, 1896–97/1897–98*, pp. 70–71, 260–61; and *Biennial Report, 1898–99/1899–1900*, p. 227.

37. Edmonds, *Negro and Fusion Politics*, p. 59; King, "Era of Progressive Reform," p. 171; Bode, *Protestantism and the New South*, pp. 61–94; Gobbel, *Church-State Relationships*, p. 145; and *Biblical Recorder*, November 11, 1896. One lone Silverite in the House of Representatives accounted for the twenty-first seat lost by Democrats.

38. J. M. Spainhour to Charles D. McIver, November 12, 1896, box 3, Charles McIver Papers.

39. Goodwyn, *Democratic Promise*, pp. 387–514; King, "Era of Progressive Reform," pp. 173–74; and Josephus Daniels, *Editor in Politics*, pp. 219–20.

40. J. M. Spainhour to Charles D. McIver, November 12, 1896, box 3, Charles McIver Papers; Harlan, *Separate and Unequal*, pp. 51–52; King, "Era of Progressive Reform," pp. 171–72; and Charles H. Mebane to John C. Kilgo, January 4, 1897, John Kilgo Papers. Mebane's defection to the Populists was never forgiven. He appears in none of the state biographical dictionaries produced in the early twentieth century, and the standard history of public education in North Carolina fails even to mention his name. See Knight, *Public School Education in North Carolina*. For a particularly unflattering view of Mebane, see Wagstaff, *Impressions of Men and Movements*, p. 61.

41. King, "Era of Progressive Reform," pp. 180–87; *Biennial Report, 1896–97/1897–98*, pp. 9–10, 17, 100–102; and *Biennial Report, 1898–99/1899–1900*, p. 231.

42. *Biennial Report, 1896–97/1897–98*, pp. 260–61, and *Biennial Report, 1898–99/1899–1900*, p. 234.

43. King, "Era of Progressive Reform," p. 182; *Biennial Report, 1896–97/1897–98*, pp. 70–71, 260–61; and *Biennial Report, 1898–99/1899–1900*, p. 227.

44. *Biennial Report, 1898–99/1899–1900*, pp. 227, 238, and *Biennial Report, 1896–97/1897–98*, pp. 70–71.

45. *Biennial Report, 1898–99/1899–1900*, p. 227, and *Biennial Report, 1896–97/1897–98*, p. 14.

46. King, "Era of Progressive Reform," pp. 180–81; *Biennial Report, 1892–93/1893–94*, p. 12; *Public School Law of North Carolina, 1897*, pp. 44–48; and *Biennial Report, 1896–97/1897–98*, pp. 198–99.

47. King, "Era of Progressive Reform," pp. 179–80; *Biennial Report, 1896–97/1897–98*, pp. 70–71; and Charles D. McIver to Edwin A. Alderman, October 23, 1894, box 2, and Charles D. McIver to Charles H. Mebane, [1896], box 9, Charles McIver Papers.

48. *Raleigh News and Observer*, July 14, 28, and 31, 1897; *Biennial Report, 1896–97/1897–98*, p. 75; T. A. Sharpe to Charles H. Mebane, July 2, 1897, box 190, SPI Correspondence; Charles H. Mebane to E. W. Flake, July 22, 1897, and Charles H. Mebane to D. Matt Thompson, July 31, 1897, SPI Letterbook 106; and King, "Era of Progressive Reform," p. 189.

49. Walter H. Page to Catherine R. Page, October 16, 1872, American Period file 813, Walter Hines Page Papers; *State Chronicle*, September 15, 1883; and Cooper, *Walter Hines Page*, pp. 3–251.

50. Page, "Forgotten Man," pp. 1–47.

51. Cooper, *Walter Hines Page*, p. 144; *Raleigh News and Observer*, May 20, 1897; *Biennial Report, 1896–97/1897–98*, p. 134; election report, box 71, State Board of Education Papers; and King, "Era of Progressive Reform," p. 191.

52. Charles L. Coon to Charles D. McIver, June 28, 1897, box 10, Charles McIver Papers; B. Williams to Charles H. Mebane, July 2, 1897, Zeb Walser to Charles H. Mebane, July 14, 1897, box 190; R. W. Simpson to Charles H. Mebane, June 21, 1897, T. S. Rollins to Charles H. Mebane, June 26, 1897, and D. L. Ellis to Charles H. Mebane, June 26, 1897, box 189; and R. W. Moore to Charles H. Mebane, September 1, 1897, box 192, SPI Correspondence.

53. Josephus Daniels to Charles D. McIver, July 29, 1897, box 3, Charles McIver Papers.

54. Lefler and Newsome, *North Carolina*, p. 557; Furnifold Simmons to F. C. Pritchard, open letter published in the *Raleigh News and Observer*, October 30, 1898; and S. M. Hill to Charles H. Mebane, May 17, 1897, box 189, SPI Correspondence.

55. Lefler and Newsome, *North Carolina*, pp. 557–58; King, "Era of Progressive Reform," pp. 199–20; Escott, *Many Excellent People*, pp. 255–59; Prather, *Re-*

surgent *Politics and Educational Progressivism*, pp. 133–72; Edmonds, *Negro and Fusion Politics*, pp. 136–57; Kousser, *Shaping of Southern Politics*, pp. 182–95; Hamilton, *North Carolina since 1860*, p. 287; and Prather, *We Have Taken a City*.

56. Kousser, *Shaping of Southern Politics*, p. 190; Edmonds, *Negro and Fusion Politics*, p. 187; Escott, *Many Excellent People*, pp. 258–59; *Public Laws and Resolutions of the State of North Carolina, 1899*, chap. 732; Zeb Walser to Charles H. Mebane, December 8, 1899, box 215, SPI Correspondence; *Biennial Report, 1898–99/1899–1900*, pp. 75, 84–86; and King, "Era of Progressive Reform," pp. 205–7, 209–11. The Fusion principle of local home rule held such popular appeal that the Democrats dared not undermine it completely. For that reason, the school law of 1899 required that appointed school directors stand for election two years after they first took office. The confusion in school administration continued until 1900 because the Democratic attorney general ruled that the law did not abolish the old county boards of education but only changed their names. The old boards therefore remained viable legal entities and had the right to perform their duties until the next election. For the hundreds of complaints about the dual boards that flooded Superintendent Mebane's office, see boxes 209–10, 212, and 215, SPI Correspondence.

57. *Raleigh News and Observer*, January 29 and February 3, 1899; *Charlotte Observer*, quoted in Escott, *Many Excellent People*, p. 259; and Josephus Daniels, *Editor in Politics*, pp. 312, 374–80.

58. Untitled, undated manuscript, box 9, Charles McIver Papers, and Charles D. McIver to Samuel A. Ashe, August 17, 1897, box 3, Samuel Ashe Papers. Charles Mebane had also favored suffrage restrictions since at least 1896. He wrote to a friend in 1900, "I expect to support [disfranchisement] for three special reasons. . . . First—As a great incentive to Education for the rising and the future generations. Second—Because it will remove a great mass of ignorant negro voters who form a dangerous power in the hands of designing politicians. Third—It will force the white people of this State to spend more money for public education, and finally force them to send their children to school." See Charles H. Mebane to J. Allen Holt, March 7, 1900, box 4, Charles McIver Papers. By this time, Mebane was especially eager to denounce black voters, since he was making a bid to be nominated for reelection as a Democrat. See King, "Era of Progressive Reform," pp. 211–15.

59. *Raleigh News and Observer*, March 5, 1899; Ashe et al., *Biographical History of North Carolina*, 2:475–80; Kousser, *Shaping of Southern Politics*, pp. 191–92; and Lefler and Newsome, *North Carolina*, pp. 559–60. For a first-hand account of the design of the disfranchisement amendment, see Rippy, *F. M. Simmons*, pp. 26–30.

60. *Public Laws and Resolutions of the State of North Carolina, 1899*, pp. 539–40; Furnifold Simmons, quoted in Cell, *Highest Stage of White Supremacy*, p. 121; and Escott, *Many Excellent People*, p. 260. See also Williamson, *Crucible of Race*, pp. 249–55.

61. Connor and Poe, *Life and Speeches of Charles Brantley Aycock*, pp. 3–60, 218–19, 225. See also Orr, *Charles Brantley Aycock*.

62. Connor and Poe, *Life and Speeches of Charles Brantley Aycock*, p. 229; Orr,

Charles Brantley Aycock, p. 155; Waddell, quoted in Josephus Daniels, *Editor in Politics*, p. 368; and Kousser, *Shaping of Southern Politics*, p. 193.

63. Dabney, "Public School Problem in the South," pp. 61–62; Connor and Poe, *Life and Speeches of Charles Brantley Aycock*, p. 258; Aycock to Henry Groves Connor, November 10, 1898, Henry Groves Connor Papers, Southern Historical Collection, University of North Carolina at Chapel Hill, quoted in Steelman, "Progressive Era in North Carolina," p. 187; Murphy, *Basis of Ascendancy*, pp. 29–30; and Josephus Daniels, *Editor in Politics*, p. 469. I am indebted here to John W. Cell's incisive discussion of the alternative courses southern race relations might have followed at the turn of the century. See Cell, *Highest Stage of White Supremacy*, especially chapter 7, "A note on Southern moderates and segregation."

64. "Address of W. H. Page," *Proceedings of the Seventh Conference for Education in the South*, pp. 105–6; Reverend John E. White, "Prohibition: The New Task and Opportunity of the South," *South Atlantic Quarterly* 7 (April 1908): 136, quoted in Link, *Paradox of Southern Progressivism*, p. 59; Page to Wallace Buttrick, February 10, 1907, American Period file 187, Walter Hines Page Papers; and Alderman, "The Child and the State," p. 59. For the attitudes of reformers toward rural whites, see Link, *Paradox of Southern Progressivism*, pp. 58–63.

65. Jabez Lamar Monroe Curry, "Address before the General Assembly of South Carolina," December 13, 1894, Curry Papers, Library of Congress, quoted in Theodore R. Mitchell, "From Black to White," p. 348; "Address of W. H. Page," *Proceedings of the Seventh Conference for Education in the South*, pp. 105–6; and Page to Wallace Buttrick, February 10, 1907, American Period file 187, Walter Hines Page Papers.

Chapter Five

1. Connor and Poe, *Life and Speeches of Charles Brantley Aycock*, pp. 233–38.

2. Poland, *Twentieth Century Statesmen*, p. 28; *Minutes of the Seventy-Second Annual Meeting of the Baptist State Convention*, p. 50; and *Biennial Report, 1896–97/1897–98*, pp. 9–10. Simmons had engaged in similar deal-making in 1898. In order to prevent Josiah Bailey and the Baptists from disrupting that year's campaign by again agitating the state-aid issue, he promised not to increase appropriations for the university and the Normal School. Charles McIver and his friends felt betrayed. "All of us," he wrote to his wife, "feel that Simmons has treated us very badly." For Edwin Alderman, the compromise encouraged a decision to give up the presidency of the university, a post he had just acquired in 1896, for the same office at Tulane. He complained to an old friend that the political battles of the 1890s had sorely tried his "local love and pride of state. North Carolina has always been a hard [master] to serve, exacting much for little, and subject to hurtful spasms of conservatism." See Rippy, *F. M. Simmons*, pp. 23–24, 29; Charles D. McIver to Lula McIver, February 22, 1899, box 7, Charles McIver Papers; Malone, *Edwin A. Alderman*, pp. 71, 97; and Alderman to Cornelia Phillips Spencer, January 17, 1895, box 2, Cornelia Phillips Spencer Papers (Raleigh).

3. *Raleigh News and Observer*, March 16, 1901, and Harlan, *Separate and Unequal*, pp. 111–13.

4. *Raleigh News and Observer*, quoted in Harlan, *Separate and Unequal*, pp. 113–14; and Harlan, *Separate and Unequal*, pp. 117–18.

5. Memorandum in the Rockefeller Family Papers, record group 2, quoted in E. Richard Brown, *Rockefeller Medicine Men*, p. 46. On the ideas of efficiency, bureaucratic management, and expert knowledge and their role in the turn-of-the-century restructuring of American business and economic life, see Chandler, *Visible Hand*, and Sklar, *Corporate Reconstruction of American Capitalism*.

6. For a comparison with women's educational work outside the South, see Reese, *Power and the Promise of School Reform*, pp. 30–62. The best overview of these two reform cultures and their implications for politics and state development on the national level is Baker, "Domestication of Politics."

7. GEB policy statement, n.d., series 1.2, box 304, folder 3176, GEB Papers, and Alderman, "Life and Work of Dr. Charles D. McIver," p. 6. For more on regional reconciliation, see H. B. Frissell to Walter Hines Page, March 18, 1899, American Period file 396, Walter Hines Page Papers, and Walter Hines Page to George Barnard, n.d., series 1.5, box 718, folder 7401, GEB Papers. On the origins of the Conference for Southern Education and Ogden's influence on its development, see Dabney, *Universal Education*, 2:3–31; Rose, "Educational Movement in the South," pp. 359–62, 365–69; and Philip Whitwell Wilson, *Unofficial Statesman*.

8. Dabney, *Universal Education*, 2:32–33; King, "Era of Progressive Reform," p. 224; and *Proceedings of the Fourth Conference for Education in the South*.

9. *Review of Reviews* 23 (June 1901): 646, and Dabney, *Universal Education*, 2:40–43.

10. Rose, "Educational Movement in the South," pp. 365–90; Dabney, *Universal Education*, 2:74–88; *Proceedings of the Fourth Conference for Education in the South*; and letter to Frederick T. Gates, June 17, 1903, series 1.5, box 720, folder 7414, GEB Papers. For biographical information on Claxton, Coon, and Eggleston, see Lewis, *Philander Priestley Claxton*; Powell, *Dictionary of North Carolina Biography*, 1:384–85, 427–29; and *National Cyclopaedia of American Biography*, 42:550–51.

11. *Proceedings of the Fourth Conference for Education in the South*, p. 6; *Proceedings of the Second Capon Springs Conference for Education in the South*, pp. 72, 74; James D. Anderson, *Education of Blacks*, pp. 33–78, 238–78; and Sherer, *Subordination or Liberation?*, pp. 114–48. The industrial philanthropists argued that the missionary colleges "should be 'Hamptonized' as far as possible, they should eliminate Latin, Greek, etc.[,] . . . they should teach agriculture and related industries with consistent and growing appreciation of the educational values of such courses, in a word, they should . . . [train] the negro for the life that now is [and should] make of him a producer—a servant—of his day and generation." See Wallace Buttrick to Frederick T. Gates, October 14, 1904, series 1.5, box 716, folder 7386, GEB Papers.

12. Dabney, *Universal Education*, 2:534. Edwin Alderman stated the SEB's position plainly in a news conference in New Orleans several months after the Winston meeting. "The highest welfare of the Negro," he advised reporters, "[lies] in the

education of the white man even more than in his own education." See the *New Orleans Times-Democrat*, November 17, 1901, quoted in Malone, *Edwin A. Alderman*, pp. 142–43.

13. Dabney, *Universal Education*, 2:33, and *New York World*, April 28, 1901, quoted in King, "Era of Progressive Reform," p. 227. See also Nicholas Murray Butler to Charles D. McIver, March 14, 1899, box 3, Charles McIver Papers. Butler, a professor of philosophy and education and later president of Columbia University, wrote, "I wish that the generous men and women who have poured out so much money in the South for the education of the negro, could now be induced to see that a mere fraction of that vast fund, if expended along the line that you are developing . . . would be an almost unequaled service to the cause of an advanced and more effective civilization."

14. Charles D. McIver to Edwin A. Alderman, January 13, 1902, Edwin Alderman Papers, quoted in Link, *Hard Country*, p. 101, and Robert Bingham to Charles D. McIver, February 22, 1902, box 5, Charles McIver Papers.

15. Woodward, *Origins of the New South*, pp. 402–3; Fosdick, *John D. Rockefeller, Jr.*, pp. 117–18; "Organization of the General Education Board," series 1.2, box 329, folder 3463, and "Historical Review 1902–1951," series 1.2, box 329, folder 3467, GEB Papers. For more on the founding of the GEB and its work outside the South, see Dabney, *Universal Education*, 2:123–52; Fosdick, *Adventure in Giving*; *General Education Board*; and Madison, "John D. Rockefeller's General Education Board." The goal of systematizing educational philanthropy is discussed in "Historical Statement," n.d., series 1.2, box 337, folder 3542, Robert C. Ogden to F. W. Boatwright, May 29, 1905, series 1.5, box 718, folder 7400, and Wallace Buttrick to E. B. Preston, July 27, 1906, series 1.5, box 720, folder 7414, GEB Papers. From 1902 to 1915, the GEB provided the SEB with grants totaling more than $97,000. See *General Education Board*, p. 17. Gates and Buttrick were both Baptist ministers who pursued long careers in educational and social reform. See *Dictionary of American Biography*, 2:377–78, 4:182–83.

16. Frederick T. Gates to John D. Rockefeller Jr., May 7, 1924, box 3, folder 59, and "Philanthropy and Civilization," box 4, folder 79, vol. 2, Frederick Gates Papers; Dabney, *Universal Education*, 2:138; GEB policy statement, n.d., and Wallace Buttrick, speech before the New England Society, December 22, 1925, series 1.2, box 304, folder 3176, GEB Papers. See also Chester Barnard, memorandum of October 11, 1950, series 1.2, box 194, folder 1844, GEB Papers, and E. Richard Brown, *Rockefeller Medicine Men*, pp. 13–59.

17. Harlan, *Separate and Unequal*, pp. 85–86; *General Education Board*, pp. xiii–xiv, 9–11; press release, Rockefeller Family Papers, record group 2, quoted in E. Richard Brown, *Rockefeller Medicine Men*, p. 46; and Charles W. Dabney to V. W. Brierley, April 6, 1933, series 1.5, box 721, folder 7420, GEB Papers. The Peabody Fund was established in 1867 by George Peabody, a Boston financier (not to be confused with George Foster Peabody). Both the Peabody and the Slater Funds focused on black education. On the Peabody Fund, see Dabney, *Universal Education*, vol. 1, chap. 7. For more on the Slater Fund, see below, chap. 6.

18. Minutes of the SEB, November 6 and 7, 1901, vol. 38, SEB Papers; invitation to the Raleigh Educational Conference, cited in King, "Era of Progressive Reform," p. 237; and *Biennial Report, 1900–01/1901–02*, pp. lii–liii.

19. *Biennial Report, 1900–01/1901–02*, pp. lxvii–lxx.

20. *Biblical Recorder*, February 10 and November 12, 1902, January 21, 1903, and July 29, 1908; Harlan, *Separate and Unequal*, pp. 119–20, 127–28; and Powell, *Dictionary of North Carolina Biography*, 1:84–85.

21. Elmer Johnson, "James Yadkin Joyner," pp. 363–67; Ashe et al., *Biographical History of North Carolina*, 6:337–38; Bowles, *Good Beginning*, pp. 32, 40; and King, "Era of Progressive Reform," pp. 240–41.

22. Gatewood, *Eugene Clyde Brooks*, pp. 37–40, and King, "Era of Progressive Reform," pp. 238, 241. In 1919, Brooks was appointed state superintendent of public instruction to replace James Joyner, who retired in 1918. Brooks won election to a full term in 1920 and held the office until 1923.

23. F. C. Abbott, "To the Delegates to the Educational Convention at Greensboro," box 11 (filed under "Greensboro"), Charles McIver Papers; *Greensboro Patriot*, April 9, 1902; and Charles D. McIver to Miss J. E. Davis, May 13, 1902, SEB Letterbook, box 17, Charles McIver Papers. For the list of Greensboro contributors, see box 11, Charles McIver Papers. McIver solicited the GEB pledge. See Rose, "Educational Movement in the South," p. 381.

24. *Charlotte Observer*, April 8, May 3, and May 16, 1902; Wallace Buttrick to Frederick T. Gates, April 18, 1902, series 1.5, box 716, folder 7386; Wallace Buttrick to Robert C. Ogden, May 5, 1902, series 1.5, box 718, folder 7399; and Leah D. Jones to Wallace Buttrick, August 9, 1905, series 1.5, box 105, folder 946, GEB Papers. The GEB abandoned its program of local matching grants in 1903, placing its money instead in statewide programs for better school supervision and curriculum enhancement. For the North Carolina reformers' disappointment in their inability to aid specific communities, see Wallace Buttrick to James Y. Joyner, January 26, 1903, and Charles D. McIver to James Y. Joyner, January 29, March 13, 1903, box 32, James Yadkin Joyner Series, SEB Papers.

25. Report to the Southern Education Board, [January 1903], box 16, Charles McIver Papers.

26. Clipping from the *Roanoke Chowan Times*, May 8, 1902, vol. 10, Woman's College Scrapbook, and undated and untitled speech, box 9, Charles McIver Papers. On the growth of white women's clubs in postbellum North Carolina, see Sims, "Feminism and Femininity."

27. Eugene Clyde Brooks, "Women Improving School Houses," p. 7937, and undated, untitled speech, box 9, Charles McIver Papers. For a more detailed account of the meeting, see Lathrop, "Alumnae for 'School Betterment,'" p. 11.

28. Connor, *Woman's Association*; Lathrop, "Alumnae for 'School Betterment,'" pp. 10–11; and Eugene Clyde Brooks, "Women Improving School Houses," p. 7937. A survey of the Records of the Woman's Association for the Betterment of Public School Houses in North Carolina indicates that the organization fared best in counties with large towns or cities—counties such as Alamance, Buncombe,

Cumberland, Durham, Edgecombe, Forsyth, Guilford, Mecklenburg, New Hanover, Wake, and Wayne.

29. Speech before the Wake County Betterment Association, August 8, 1902, p. 10, folder 5, and manuscript of a lecture at the Garner School, folder 6, Elvira Moffitt Papers; "For Better School Houses," *Raleigh News and Observer*, September 14, 1902; Lula M. McIver, untitled essay, n.d., box 1, Records of the Woman's Association; and Sue V. Hollowell to Charles D. McIver, December 21, 1903, box 11, Charles McIver Papers.

30. *Constitution and By-Laws*, p. 5, and "Report of Women's Work in North Carolina," *Proceedings of the Ninth Conference for Education in the South*, p. 59.

31. Lathrop, "Alumnae for 'School Betterment,'" pp. 10–11; Connor, *Woman's Association*, p. 15; "Woman's Association," *Raleigh Morning Post*, October 19, 1902; and Joyner, "Ways and Means of Carrying on the Work," pp. 326–31. On SEB funding, see Knight, *Public School Education in North Carolina*, p. 336, and Lula M. McIver, manuscript of an address before the North Carolina Teachers' Assembly, n.d., box 1, Records of the Woman's Association.

32. The Raleigh Township association, for example, had three subdivisions that managed the needs of the city's five schools. See Elvira Moffitt, note, October 30, 1903, vol. 19, Elvira Moffitt Papers; "Improve School Houses," *Raleigh Morning Post*, November 5, 1903; and "To Improve School Houses," *Raleigh News and Observer*, November 5, 1903. On the responsibilities of district organizations, see Lucy B. Patterson to Charles D. McIver, December 27, 1902, box 10, Charles McIver Papers.

33. Elvira Moffitt, "Address to Patrons and Pupils—Reddish School House," 1904, folder 7, and Wake County Association for the Betterment of Public School Houses, open letter, March 7, 1908, vol. 18, Elvira Moffitt Papers; Emma Servis Speight to Mary Taylor Moore, n.d., box 2, Records of the Woman's Association; and "Medals Awarded to Happy Pupils," *Raleigh News and Observer*, June 1, 1906. For more on fund-raising activities, see Jennie J. White to Lula M. McIver, December 4, 1908, box 1, Records of the Woman's Association, and untitled note, December 2, 1903, vol. 19, Elvira Moffitt Papers.

34. "Report of Women's Work in North Carolina," *Proceedings of the Ninth Conference for Education in the South*, p. 58; Elvira Moffitt, "Address to Patrons and Pupils—Reddish School House," 1904, folder 7, Elvira Moffitt Papers; and Turlington, *Child Study*, pp. 14–15.

35. Mrs. Gordon Wilfong to L. C. Brogden, December 6, 1913, box 3, Edwin Alderman Papers.

36. "Survey of the Elvira Evelyna Moffitt Papers," Elvira Moffitt Papers, and Ashe et al., *Biographical History of North Carolina*, 8:349–53.

37. Ashe et al., *Biographical History of North Carolina*, 2:350–56; Rogers, *Tar Heel Women*, pp. 169–74; and Patterson, "Old Patterson Mansion."

38. In addition to her work for the WABPS, Moffitt held leadership positions in the Daughters of the Revolution, the United Daughters of the Confederacy, the Colonial Dames, the King's Daughters, the Virginia Dare Association, the State

Confederate Monument Association, the North Carolina Literary and Historical Society, the YMCA Ladies' Auxiliary, and the North Carolina Peace Society. She also served on the editorial board of the *North Carolina Booklet*, a historical publication of the Daughters of the Revolution. See "Survey of the Elvira Evelyna Moffitt Papers," Elvira Moffitt Papers, and Ashe et al., *Biographical History of North Carolina*, 8:349–53. Lucy Patterson was active in the Daughters of the American Revolution, helped found the North Carolina Federation of Women's Clubs, organized the Winston Embroidery Club, and served as the state's representative on the Republican National Executive Committee just prior to her death in 1942. See Rogers, *Tar Heel Women*, pp. 169–74. Moffitt and Patterson both held a variety of state and county offices within the WABPS. They each served on the executive committees of their respective county associations; Moffitt worked as vice president of the state association; and Patterson held the presidency of the Interstate Association for the Betterment of Public School Houses. See Lucy B. Patterson to Charles D. McIver, December 27, 1902, box 10, and Elvira E. Moffitt to Charles D. McIver, April 22, 1903, box 11, Charles McIver Papers; Connor, *Woman's Association*, p. 9; and N. A. Edwards, *North Carolina Congress of Parents and Teachers*, p. 117.

39. Lucy Bramlette Patterson to Charles D. McIver, August 1, 1903, box 11, Charles McIver Papers. See also Edith Royster to Charles D. McIver, September 9, 1903, box 11, Charles McIver Papers.

40. Leah D. Jones, newspaper clipping, "Better School Houses," n.p., n.d., box 3, Records of the Woman's Association.

41. R. D. W. Connor to Charles D. McIver, August 1, 1906, box 32, James Yadkin Joyner Series, SEB Papers, and Knight, *Public School Education in North Carolina*, p. 336. On the SEB's work outside North Carolina, see Dabney, *Universal Education*, 2:74–88, 320–35, 348–407, and Link, *Hard Country*, pp. 108–12.

42. *Manufacturer's Record*, April 28, 1904, p. 320; and Edward Ingle, *The Ogden Movement, an Educational Monopoly in the Making*, and *Charleston News and Courier*, April 4, 1906, quoted in Patton, "Southern Reaction to the Ogden Movement," pp. 73, 75. On issue of black education, see also John William Larkins to Charles D. McIver, April, 16, 1903, box 5, Charles McIver Papers.

43. *Manufacturer's Record*, September 28, 1905, and Warren A. Chandler, *Dangerous Donations and Degrading Doles, or a Vast Scheme for Capturing and Controlling the Colleges of the Country*, quoted in Patton, "Southern Reaction to the Ogden Movement," p. 74. Warnings about the "deeply-laid plans on the part of the Rockefeller interests to control education in the United States and particularly in the southern United States" continued to crop up throughout the next decade. See, for example, Paul H. Hanus to Abraham Flexner, December 18, 1917, series 1.4, box 615, folder 6502, and *New York Evening Post*, editorial, August 25, 1920, clipping in series 1.2, box 270, folder 2796, GEB Papers.

44. Genevieve Jennings to Lula M. McIver, December 10, 1908, box 1, Records of the Woman's Association. Elvira Moffitt's manuscript lists of Raleigh Township and Wake County members provide some indication of the average length of mem-

bership. The lists lack the information necessary for a systematic analysis; many of them are either undated or do not specify which of the county's various district organizations they describe. They do suggest, however, that most women remained in the association for a period of five to ten years. See manuscript lists of Raleigh Township and Wake County members, vols. 18 and 19, Elvira Moffitt Papers.

45. "A Work for the Girls," series 1.4, box 694, folder 7152, GEB Papers; Robert C. Ogden to Charles D. McIver, March 18, 1904, box 14; Charles D. McIver to Robert C. Ogden, March 23, 1904, SEB Letterbook, box 19; and Robert C. Ogden to Charles D. McIver March 16, 22, and April 25, 1906, box 15, Charles McIver Papers; *Proceedings of the Tenth Conference for Education in the South*, pp. 109–11; Connor, *Woman's Association*, pp. 6, 13, 17; Lathrop, "Alumnae for 'School Betterment,'" p. 22; and Edgar Gardner Murphy to Wallace Buttrick, November 14, 1907, box 2, Edwin Alderman Papers. For an internal critique of the SEB's early operations, see [Charles Coon to William Baldwin], January 6, 1903, series 1.2, box 303, folder 3169, GEB Papers.

46. "Rural Organization Service," [1913], series 1.4, box 695, folder 7159, GEB Papers. See also undated notes for a speech, box 1, biographical materials, Walter Hines Page Papers; "Summary by the Chairman," [1927], series 1.5, box 721, folder 7424, GEB Papers; Wickliffe Rose to Walter Hines Page, October 19, 1910, and Walter Hines Page to Wickliffe Rose, November 1, 1910, series 1, box 3, folder 37, RSC Papers. Page viewed school reform as the key to "the reconstruction and reorganization of country life in general."

47. *Biennial Report, 1900–01/1901–02*, pp. xiv, 292, and Connor, *Woman's Association*, p. 12.

48. Elvira Moffitt, "Address to Patrons and Pupils—Reddish School House," 1904, folder 7, Elvira Moffitt Papers. For the WABPS's schoolhouse ideal, see Connor, *Woman's Association*, photographs following pp. 30, 38, 54, and Mebane, *Woman's Association*, photographs following pp. 8, 16, 24, 40. For a revealing account of other long-forgotten efforts "to bring homelike nurturing into public life," see Hayden, *Grand Domestic Revolution*.

49. *Biennial Report, 1900–01/1901–02*, pp. xv–xvi, and "How the Southern Education Board Has Helped and Can Help the South," 1908, series 1.5, box 720, folder 7417, GEB Papers.

50. The changes in reform thought during the Progressive Era are traced in Boyer, *Urban Masses and Moral Order*; Bremner, *From the Depths*; Lubove, *Professional Altruist*; and Thelen, *New Citizenship*.

51. Clipping, Mary Taylor Moore, "Woman's Association for the Betterment of Public Schoolhouses in North Carolina," *Southern School and Home*, n.d., box 3, Records of the Woman's Association, and Elvira Moffitt, "Which Name?" August 1902, vol. 18, Elvira Moffitt Papers.

52. "Tenants' Children to Be Looked After," June 1903, untitled clipping, n.p., August 27, 1902, clipping, "South's Summer School," n.p., 1902, vol. 18, and "To Teachers' Institute," August 1902, folder 5, Elvira Moffitt Papers; clipping, J. O.

Kern, "School Sanitation and Decoration," n.p., n.d., box 3, Records of the Woman's Association; and "How the Southern Education Board Has Helped and Can Help the South," 1908, series 1.5, box 720, folder 7417, GEB Papers.

53. Untitled history of the Wake County Association for the Betterment of Public School Houses, p. 11, folder 48, and Elvira Moffitt, manuscript of a lecture at the Garner School, April 1903, folder 6, Elvira Moffitt Papers; *Biennial Report, 1908–09/1909–10*, p. 14; and *Bulletin of the North Carolina Department of Agriculture*, December 1912, pp. 80–81. See also "School Gardens," *North Carolina Education* 1 (June 1907): 10, and Mrs. Charles Price, speech, "A Long School House," box 3, Records of the Women's Association. For more on the efforts of the state Department of Agriculture and the *Progressive Farmer* to foster commercial farming practices, see Lu Ann Jones, " 'Task That Is Ours,' " pp. 69–94, and Young, "History of Agricultural Education in North Carolina," pp. 227–41. Clarence Poe described his role in Poe, *My First Eighty Years*.

54. Woodward, *Origins of the New South*, pp. 409–12; Bailey, *Seaman A. Knapp*; Scott, *Reluctant Farmer*, pp. 206–42; and Knapp, "Farmers' Cooperative Demonstration Work," pp. 607–8.

55. *General Education Board*, pp. 18–70, and manuscript, "Address of Wallace Buttrick," Conference for Education in the South, 1913, series 1.2, box 304, folder 3176, GEB Papers.

56. *General Education Board*, pp. 18–70; V. W. Brierley to Russell Lord, August 16, 1939, series 1.4, box 694, folder 7152, GEB Papers; and *Biennial Report, 1912–13/1913–14*, pp. 12–16. The best account of the club work and its place among other efforts to reform country life is Lu Ann Jones, " 'Task That Is Ours.' " The tomato club work was directed by Jane Simpson McKimmon, the daughter of a Raleigh pharmacist. Born in 1867, she attended Peace Institute and planned to pursue a career as a commercial artist, but her father objected to her traveling alone to New York for advanced study. McKimmon married and raised four children, turning to school improvement only after they had left home. She was introduced to the tomato club idea by her neighbor, I. O. Schaub, a GEB agent and professor at the state Agricultural and Mechanical College who served as the first organizer of the boys' corn clubs. McKimmon found in the work a release for her long-repressed ambitions. She used it as a springboard for returning to college, earning both a bachelor's and a master's degree in her early sixties. "Thus did the young woman, thwarted in her personal desires," wrote one of McKimmon's biographers, "find new freedom in the lives of others." See Rogers, *Tar Heel Women*, pp. 278–84.

57. *Biennial Report, 1912–13/1913–14*, p. 13; *General Education Board*, pp. 59–60; and *Progressive Farmer*, July 1, 1911. See also Dabney, *Universal Education*, 2:191–204.

58. Dabney, *Universal Education*, 2:195, 203; Jane S. McKimmon to Dr. John A. Ferrell, with attached clipping, "Doing a Good Work for the Girls of North Carolina is Mrs. M'Kimmon of Raleigh," September 3, 1913, series 2, box 6, folder 119, RSC Papers; "A Work for the Girls," series 1.4, box 694, folder 7152, GEB

Papers; *General Education Board,* p. 66; *Biennial Report, 1910–11/1911–12,* pp. 12–13; and *Biennial Report, 1912–13/1913–14,* pp. 14–16.

59. Dabney, *Universal Education,* 2:195; *Biennial Report, 1912–13/1913–14,* p. 15; *General Education Board,* p. 65; Martin, *Demonstration Work,* p. 193; Lu Ann Jones, " 'Task That Is Ours,' " pp. 72–94; and Walter Hines Page to Wickliffe Rose, November 1, 1910, series 1, box 3, folder 37, RSC Papers. See also Wallace Buttrick to Edwin Alderman, May 20, 1913, series 1.2, box 295, folder 3077; "A Work for the Girls," and Grace E. Frysinger, "Home Demonstration Work," series 1.4, box 694, folder 7152, GEB Papers.

60. "Germ of Laziness Found," *New York Sun,* December 5, 1902; Bickett, "Higher Conception of Crime," pp. 346–47; Lay, "Sanitary Privy," p. 27; "Memoranda From the Old Man Buttrick," January 17, 1924, series 1.2, box 329, folder 3463, GEB Papers; *Fourth Annual Report of the International Health Board,* p. 126, and *Second Annual Report of the Rockefeller Sanitary Commission,* p. 15, series 4, RSC Papers. "Ignorance" and "filthy" habits, however, were not limited to rural folk. The university at Chapel Hill had "no sanitary conveniences" until 1892, "when the basement of the library building was fitted up for that purpose with a fair number of water closets, urinals, bath tubs and shower baths." Even then, conditions remained less than ideal. Waste from the facilities was "discharged into a small branch about one thousand feet from the buildings." See Washburn, *History of the North Carolina State Board of Health,* p. 28.

61. Rankin, "Importance of the Recognition of Physically Defective Children by the Teacher," pp. 243–44; Elvira Moffitt, "Address to Patrons and Pupils—Reddish School House," 1904, folder 7, Elvira Moffitt Papers; and Paul Anderson, "Mental Hygiene in the Young," p. 383.

62. Washburn, *History of the North Carolina State Board of Health,* pp. 4–37; Allen, "Public Health Work in the Southeast"; and *Second Annual Report of the Rockefeller Sanitary Commission,* p. 56, series 4, RSC Papers. The state health agency, chartered in 1877, began its work in 1879.

63. Washburn, *History of the North Carolina State Board of Health,* p. 5, and Elvira Moffitt, "Which Name?," August 1902, vol. 18, Elvira Moffitt Papers. See also Mary Hunter to Lula M. McIver, March 6, 1912, box 1, Records of the Woman's Association. For a description of lectures by physicians R. H. Lewis and Dixon Carroll, see Elvira Moffitt's notes on the meeting of the centennial division of the Raleigh Township association, March 8, 1904, vol. 19, Elvira Moffitt Papers. For more on the association's efforts to control childhood diseases, see Lula M. McIver, speech, n.d., box 1, and Mary Taylor Moore, speech, n.d., box 2, Records of the Woman's Association.

64. "Citizenship and Public Health," *Bulletin of the North Carolina Board of Health* 25 (June 1910): 102–3.

65. Ettling, *Germ of Laziness,* pp. 9–48, 97–121, and Watson S. Rankin to Wickliffe Rose, January 15, 1912, series 2, box 6, folder 118, RSC Papers. On the expected economic rewards of the work, see Frederick T. Gates to John D. Rocke-

feller, December 12, 1910, record group 2, box 30, folder 230, Rockefeller Family Papers. The improvement of rural life was a national as well as a southern concern. On the Country Life Commission, see Bowers, *Country Life Movement in America*.

66. Ettling, *Germ of Laziness*, pp. 142–43; Charles Stiles to Wickliffe Rose, August 15, 1912, series 1, box 3, folder 47, and report of John Ferrell, September 30, 1910, series 4, RSC Papers. The best account of the North Carolina campaign is Washburn, *As I Recall*. See also Wickliffe Rose, "Work of the Rockefeller Sanitary Commission," 1914, pp. 2–6, series 1, box 2, folder 6, and reports of John Ferrell, June 30, 1910, September 30, 1910, and September 30, 1911, series 4, RSC Papers. Dispensary work in North Carolina and Alabama served as a model for other southern states. See Wickliffe Rose to Frederick T. Gates, August 14, 1911, record group 2, box 30, folder 230, Rockefeller Family Papers.

67. Wickliffe Rose to Walter Hines Page, October 29, 1910, series 1, box 3, folder 37, John Ferrell to Wickliffe Rose, October 12, 1910, series 2, box 5, folder 115; minutes of the North Carolina fieldworkers meeting, January/February 1911, series 2, box 5, folder 116; "Organization, Acts, Results," series 4; John Ferrell to Wickliffe Rose, April 23, 1910, series 2, box 5, folder 114; *Second Annual Report of the Rockefeller Sanitary Commission*, p. 101, series 4; and report of John Ferrell, June 30, 1910, series 4, RSC Papers. For more on the WABPS's involvement, see James Y. Joyner to Frederick T. Gates, December 23, 1909, series 2, box 5, folder 114; Charles Stiles to Wickliffe Rose, November 7 and 9, 1910, series 1, box 3, folder 45; and John Ferrell to Wickliffe Rose, March 7, 1911, series 2, box 5, folder 116, RSC Papers. On the role of the WABPS, see also Link, " 'Harvest Is Ripe,' " pp. 8–9. For examples of the health catechism and privy plans, see Nash County Board of Health, *A Catechism of Public Health*, and Lay, "Sanitary Privy."

68. Washburn, *As I Recall*, pp. 12–14; Frederick T. Gates, "The Colleges and Rural Life," series 1.5, box 717, folder 7388, GEB Papers; and *Second Annual Report of the Rockefeller Sanitary Commission*, p. 21, series 4, RSC Papers.

69. Benjamin Washburn to C. L. Pridgen, July 6, 1913, series 2, box 6, folder 119, and *Second Annual Report of the Rockefeller Sanitary Commission*, p. 116, series 4, RSC Papers. See also H. O. Hyatt to John Ferrell, March 30, 1911, series 2, box 5, folder 116, and J. W. Williams to John Ferrell, September 24, 1911, series 2, box 6, folder 118, RSC Papers.

70. On the RSC's long-range objectives and the founding of county health departments, see "Recommendation of Plan for Closing the Work of the Rockefeller Sanitary Commission in the Southern States," 1914, series 1, box 2, folder 6; *Fifth Annual Report of the Rockefeller Sanitary Commission*, p. 24, series 4; Frederick T. Gates to Wickliffe Rose, August 21, 1914, series 1, box 1, folder 2; Wickliffe Rose to Frederick T. Gates, November 22, 1911, series 1, box 2, folder 1; Wickliffe Rose to Charles Stiles, August 24, 1912, series 1, box 2, folder 37, RSC Papers; and Washburn, *History of the North Carolina State Board of Health*, p. 60. For the founding of model communities, see letter to John Ferrell, received September 22, 1914, series 2, box 6, folder 121; C. L. Pridgen to John Ferrell, April 3, 1914, series 2, box 6, folder 120; and newspaper clipping, "Community Organization Tested Out at

Salemburg," series 2, box 6, folder 120, RSC Papers; *Biennial Report, 1912–13/ 1913–14*, pp. 17–19; and *Biennial Report, 1914–15/1915–16*, pp. 13–16. Maps of the projects in the Salemburg and Philadelphus communities can be found in the *Fifth Annual Report of the Rockefeller Sanitary Commission*, pp. 96–99, series 4, RSC Papers.

71. "The Country School of Tomorrow," series 1.2, box 270, folder 2796, GEB Papers, and C. L. Pridgen to John Ferrell, April 3, 1914, series 2, box 6, folder 120, RSC Papers.

Chapter Six

1. "The Negro and the Future," *Charlotte Observer*, October 25, 1903; "Lynch Law and Its Logical Outcome," *North Carolina Presbyterian*, March 10, 1908; and Bassett, "Stirring Up the Fires of Racial Antipathy," p. 304. See also Greenwood, *Bittersweet Legacy*, pp. 215–17, and Link, *Paradox of Southern Progressivism*, pp. 58–70. The epigraph was originally used for the same purpose by Bertha Maye Edwards, a black teacher, in her history of Wake County's Berry O'Kelly Teacher Training School. See *Little Place*, p. 21.

2. "Col. A. M. Waddell at Newberry College," *The State*, Columbia, South Carolina, June 15, 1905, clipping in box 1, folder 3, Waddell Papers.

3. Orr, *Charles Brantley Aycock*, pp. 208–11, and Westin, "State and Segregated Schools," pp. 192–99.

4. Walter B. Hill, "Negro Education in the South," p. 209; Josephus Daniels, "Progress of Southern Education," p. 144; "The Negro and the Future," *Charlotte Observer*, October 25, 1903; "The Old-Time Negro Preacher," *Charlotte Observer*, December 30, 1902; "Passing of a Black Mammy," *Charlotte Observer*, February 10, 1904; "The Negro as a Laborer," *Charlotte Observer*, January 27, 1901; and Simmons, "The Race Problem in the South," *Raleigh News and Observer*, May 31, 1903. See also Winston, "Industrial Training in Relation to the Negro Problem," and *Biennial Report, 1902–03/1903–04*, pp. 72–83.

5. *Biennial Report, 1900–01/1901–02*, pp. vii–ix.

6. Connor and Poe, *Life and Speeches of Charles Brantley Aycock*, pp. 225 and 258; Orr, *Charles Brantley Aycock*, pp. 208–9, 245–46; and "Governor's Message to the General Assembly of North Carolina of 1905," Governor's Letter Books, no. 109, p. 141.

7. Connor and Poe, *Life and Speeches of Charles Brantley Aycock*, pp. 247–51.

8. Shepard, "Message to the Negro Race," *Charlotte Observer*, November 8, 1903. On the lily-white movement in the Republican party, see Greenwood, *Bittersweet Legacy*, pp. 222–40, and Williamson, *Crucible of Race*, pp. 341–63.

9. Leo Favrot to Jackson Davis, January 22, 1917, series 1.1, box 24, folder 215, GEB Papers, and *Star of Zion*, October 2, 1902. For more on these matters of tactics and survival, see Greenwood, *Bittersweet Legacy*; McMillen, *Dark Journey*; and Cell, *Highest Stage of White Supremacy*, pp. 230–75.

10. Dabney, "Public School Problem in the South," p. 62; Winston, "Industrial

Training in Relation to the Negro Problem," p. 106; Walter B. Hill, "Negro Education in the South," pp. 208–9; Baldwin, "The Present Problem of Negro Education, Industrial Education," p. 68; and Josephus Daniels, "Progress of Southern Education," p. 143.

11. Walter B. Hill, "Negro Education in the South," pp. 208–9, 216–17, and Winston, "Industrial Training in Relation to the Negro Problem," p. 106. See also Hoke Smith, "Popular Education as the Primary Policy of the South," pp. 48–49.

12. *Southern Workman,* quoted in James D. Anderson, *Education of Blacks,* pp. 37 and 46, and Walter B. Hill, "Negro Education in the South," p. 208. For excellent accounts of the origins and purposes of industrial education, see Anderson, *Education of Blacks,* pp. 33–78, and Theodore R. Mitchell, "From Black to White."

13. Josephus Daniels, "Progress of Southern Education," p. 145; Winston, "Industrial Training in Relation to the Negro Problem," p. 105; Walter B. Hill, "Negro Education in the South," p. 209; and Alderman, "The Child and the State," pp. 60–61.

14. Winston, "Industrial Training in Relation to the Negro Problem," pp. 106–7; Alderman, "The Child and the State," p. 61; and "Address of Lyman Abbott, D.D.," *Proceedings of the Fourth Conference for Education in the South,* pp. 111–15.

15. Newbold to Wallace Buttrick, February 27, 1914, series 1.1, box 115, folder 1038, GEB Papers. See also Abraham Flexner to James Yadkin Joyner, July 1, 1914, Correspondence of the Director, box 1, DNE Papers. On the GEB's support of state agents across the South, see Dabney, *Universal Education,* 2:447–49.

16. On Newbold's family background, see Powell, *Dictionary of North Carolina Biography,* 4:362–63, and Proctor, "N. C. Newbold, '95, and Negro Education." The quotation is from untitled notes on an address to a conference of county superintendents, July 27, 1938, Articles and Speeches, box 2, DNE Papers.

17. Westin, "State and Segregated Schools," p. 197; Williamson, *Crucible of Race,* pp. 261–71; Powell, *Dictionary of North Carolina Biography,* 4:362–63; Edgar Gardner Murphy, *Problems of the Present South,* quoted in Fredrickson, *Black Image in the White Mind,* p. 287; and Allen Barwick to J. Elwood Cox, July 2, 1908, Correspondence of the Director, box 1, DNE Papers.

18. James Yadkin Joyner to Wallace Buttrick, April 25, May 6, and May 31, 1912, Correspondence of the Director, box 1, DNE Papers; untitled notes on an address to a conference of county superintendents, July 27, 1938, Articles and Speeches, box 2, DNE Papers; and Newbold to Wallace Buttrick, June 1 and 7, 1912, series 1.1, box 115, folder 1038, GEB Papers.

19. Untitled notes on an address to a conference of county superintendents, July 27, 1938, Articles and Speeches, box 2, DNE Papers, and Newbold to Wallace Buttrick, June 8, 1914, series 1.1, box 115, folder 1038, GEB Papers.

20. Lance G. E. Jones, *Jeanes Teacher,* pp. 11–21 (quotation from p. 19); Dabney, *Universal Education,* 2:445–47, 451–54; "Informational and Explanatory Letter about Industrial Work in Public Schools of the State," Correspondence of the Director, 1913 Reports, box 1, DNE Papers; "First Biennial Report of State Agent of Negro Rural Schools for North Carolina," *Biennial Report, 1912–13/1913–14,*

pp. 123–29; and "Negro Rural School Fund, Jeanes Foundation, Statement for Month of January, 1917," attached to Gertrude C. Mann to Newbold, March 29, 1917, Correspondence of the Director, box 3, DNE Papers.

21. *Raleigh Morning Post,* June 14, 1903, and *Raleigh News and Observer,* October 28, 1910, clippings in file 1903–1914, box 14, Charles N. Hunter Collection; *Biennial Report, 1898–99/1899–1900,* pp. 288–89; *Biennial Report, 1912–13/1913–14,* part 1, p. 73; "Jeanes Fund Workers, 1917–1918," Correspondence of the Director, Reports, box 3, DNE Papers; and Newbold to Washington Catlett, July 21, 1916, Correspondence of the Director, box 2, DNE Papers.

22. T. Fletcher Bulla to Newbold, June 16, 1916, and Newbold to Bulla, June 17, 1916, Correspondence of the Director, box 2; Newbold to Washington Catlett, July 21, 1916, Correspondence of the Director, box 2; and James H. Dillard to Newbold, August 14, 1914, Correspondence of the Director, box 1, DNE Papers.

23. T. G. Williamson to Newbold, September 5, 1916, Correspondence of the Director, box 3, DNE Papers.

24. Pankey, "Life Histories," pp. 23, 36–37, 41–42, 49, and 58. On Turner as a Jeanes teacher, see Williams et al., *Jeanes Story,* p. 153.

25. Pankey, "Life Histories," pp. 71–72, and Annie Holland to Newbold, October 15, 1914, Correspondence of the Director, box 1, DNE Papers.

26. J. R. Faison to Newbold, June 11, 1913, and J. N. Bennett to Newbold, June 16, 1913, Correspondence of the Director, Jeanes Reports, box 1, DNE Papers.

27. Hine, *Black Women in America,* 1:569–70; Powell, *Dictionary of North Carolina Biography,* 3:174; and Newbold, *Five North Carolina Negro Educators,* pp. 61–70 (quotation from p. 70).

28. Newbold, *Five North Carolina Negro Educators,* pp. 71–72, and 74–75; Powell, *Dictionary of North Carolina Biography,* 3:174; and Holland to Newbold, May 8, 1916, Correspondence of the Director, box 2, DNE Papers.

29. Powell, *Dictionary of North Carolina Biography,* 3:174, and "Items Gathered from the Year's Work in North Carolina, July 1, 1916–June 30, 1917," series 1.1, box 115, folder 1044, GEB Papers.

30. Newbold to E. C. Sage, January 11, 1916, series 1.1, box 115, folder 1038, and "Summary of Reports of Mr. N. C. Newbold, January 1, 1916 to December 31, 1916," series 1.1, box 115, folder 1044, GEB Papers. See also "Second Biennial Report of State Agent of Negro Rural Schools," *Biennial Report, 1914–15/1915–16,* pp. 119–23.

31. Circular letter from J. Y. Joyner, E. E. Sams, and N. C. Newbold, November 28, 1913, Correspondence of the Director, box 1, DNE Papers; "First Biennial Report of State Agent of Negro Rural Schools for North Carolina," *Biennial Report, 1912–13/1913–14,* pp. 123 and 125; Thomas J. Morgan to Wallace Buttrick, February 1, 1901, series 1.5, box 717, folder 7388, GEB Papers; and "Second Biennial Report of State Agent of Negro Rural Schools," *Biennial Report, 1914–15/1915–16,* p. 119. For more on the history of North Carolina's private black colleges, see "Brief History of Johnson C. Smith University"; "Centennial Founders Day Convocation"; *Record of Fifty Years;* Griffin, *Black Theology,* pp. 89–116;

Stowell, *Methodist Adventures*, pp. 155–61; and Tupper, *Narrative of Twenty-Five Years' Work*.

32. Minutes of State Board of Examiners, June 30, 1903, box 490, SPI Reports; Westin, "State and Segregated Schools," pp. 210–24 and 260–61; T. F. Toon to J. L. M. Curry, September 11, 1901, box 118, SPI Letterbooks; J. Y. Joyner to Wallace Buttrick, October 10, 1905, box 137, SPI Letterbooks; John Duckett to H. L. Cook, September 25, 1908, and E. E. Smith to John Duckett, October 26, 1908, Correspondence of the Director, box 1, DNE Papers; and *Report of the State Board of Examiners for the Two Years Ending January 1, 1905*, pp. 28–30.

33. D. P. Allen to John Duckett, September 3, 1907, Correspondence of the Director, box 1, DNE Papers.

34. Newbold to J. T. Woofter, July 4, 1914, Correspondence of the Director, box 1, DNE Papers.

35. Chance to Newbold, September 1, 1922, Correspondence of the Director, box 6, DNE Papers, and Powell, *Dictionary of North Carolina Biography*, 1:352–53.

36. *Biennial Report, 1914–15/1915–16*, pp. 62–68.

37. Fisher, *John F. Slater Fund*, pp. 1–14; Redcay, *County Training Schools*, pp. 4–5, 8, 24–28; and *Suggested Course of Study for County Training Schools*, p. 5.

38. "Report on Parmele Industrial School," Correspondence of the Director, 1913 Reports, box 1; Anson Phelps Stokes to William C. Chance, November 4, 1913, Correspondence of the Director, 1913 Reports, box 1; Newbold to A. J. Manning, September 7, 1922, Correspondence of the Director, box 6; T. J. Woofter, Jr., to Newbold, August 17, 1914, Correspondence of the Director, box 1; A. J. Manning to Newbold, August 20, 1914, Correspondence of the Director, box 1; "List of County Training Schools in N.C. 1915–16," Correspondence of the Director, box 3; and James H. Dillard to Newbold, July 28, 1919, Correspondence of the Director, box 4, DNE Papers.

39. "Report on Parmele Industrial School," Correspondence of the Director, 1913 Reports, box 1; Chance to Newbold, June 7, 1920, Newbold to Chance, June 11, 1920, Manning to Newbold, June 26, 1920, and Newbold to Manning, June 30, 1920, Correspondence of the Director, box 4; Newbold to A. J. Manning, September 7, 1922, Correspondence of the Director, box 6; and Newbold to Jno. H. Small, August 15, 1916, Correspondence of the Director, box 2, DNE Papers.

40. Newbold to Manning, September 7, 1922; Manning to Newbold, October 3, 1922; The Community, Parmele, N.C., to The Honorable Board of Education, Martin County, Williamston, N.C., October 5, 1922; To the Board of Education of Martin County, October 9, 1922; Chance to The Honorable Board of Education, November 7, 1922; to The Hon. Board of Education of Martin County, November 8, 1922; Chance to Newbold, November 10, 1922; Chance to Newbold, November 16, 1922; Chance to Newbold, November 17, 1922; and In Re: W. C. Chance, November 17, 1922, Correspondence of the Director, box 6, DNE Papers.

41. Newbold to Manning, September 26, 1922; Newbold to Chance, September 30, 1922; Newbold to Manning, October 11, 1922; Newbold to Chance, November 15, 1922; Chance to Newbold, January 2, 1923; Chance to Newbold, January 6,

1923; Newbold to Manning, January 12, 1922 (misdated and filed accordingly in box 5); Wiley C. Rodman to Newbold, January 23, 1923; and Chance to Newbold, February 21, 1923, Correspondence of the Director, box 6, DNE Papers. On Manning's promise to resign rather than admit defeat, see Chance to Newbold, November 17, 1922, Correspondence of the Director, box 6, DNE Papers.

42. Newbold to Manning, January 12, 1922 (misdated), Correspondence of the Director, box 5, and Newbold to Manning, March 2, 1923, Correspondence of the Director, box 6, DNE Papers.

43. Newbold to J. D. Murphy, June 14, 1916, Correspondence of the Director, box 2, and Newbold to W. M. Hinton, September 9, 1914, Correspondence of the Director, box 1, DNE Paper.

44. "Progress of the Orange County Training School," *The Orange Jewel*, October 29, 1925, and Noble to Newbold, March 27, 1918, series 1.1, box 115, folder 1044, GEB Papers. See also "Items Gathered from the Year's Work in North Carolina, July 1, 1916–June 30, 1917," series 1.1, box 115, folder 1044, GEB Papers.

45. Untitled report, April 18, 1918, attached to Newbold to Mrs. R. E. Malone, April 22, 1918, Correspondence of the Director, Reports, box 3, DNE Papers; "The English Club," and "Forward," *The Orange Jewel*, October 29, 1925. See also the only other extant issue of the *Jewel*, April 15, 1926.

46. M. C. S. Noble to Newbold, March 27, 1918, series 1.1, box 115, folder 1044, GEB Papers; untitled report, April 18, 1918, attached to Newbold to Mrs. R. E. Malone, April 22, 1918, Correspondence of the Director, Reports, box 3, DNE Papers; and T. B. Attmore to Newbold, January 21, 1916, Correspondence of the Director, box 2, DNE Papers.

47. Lines, "Orange County Commencement."

48. Brawley, *Doctor Dillard*, p. 60; Glenda Gilmore, "Gender and Jim Crow," p. 336; O. B. Martin to Newbold, December 3, 1913, Correspondence of the Director, box 1, DNE Papers; Newbold to Mrs. Maggie Hester, March 8, 1916, Correspondence of the Director, box 2, DNE Papers; "Summary of Reports of Mr. N. C. Newbold, State Agent for Negro Rural Schools of North Carolina, January 1, 1916, to December 31, 1916," series 1.1, box 115, folder 1044, GEB Papers; and Lucy E. Pritchard to Newbold, June 10, 1913, Correspondence of the Director, 1913 Jeanes Reports, box 1, DNE Papers. For a perspective on other parts of the South, see Neverdon-Morton, "Self-Help Programs as Educative Activities."

49. "Summarized Statement of Home Makers' Club Work for the Summer of 1918," series 1.1, box 116, folder 1048, GEB Papers; Mrs. M. L. Petty to Newbold, March 13, 1916, Correspondence of the Director, box 2, DNE Papers; S. L. Delany to Newbold, June 20, 1913, and Lucy E. Pritchard to Newbold, June 10, 1913, Correspondence of the Director, 1913 Jeanes Reports, box 1, DNE Papers; and "Hundreds of Girls Join Canning Clubs in North Carolina," *Globe and Commercial Advertiser*, clipping in series 1.1, box 116, folder 1048, GEB Papers.

50. "Summary of Reports of Mr. N. C. Newbold, State Agent for Negro Rural Schools of North Carolina, January 1, 1916, to December 31, 1916," series 1.1, box 115, folder 1044, GEB Papers; Newbold to E. C. Sage, January 11, 1916, series 1.1,

box 115, folder 1038, GEB Papers; "Report of N. C. Newbold, State Supervisor of Negro Rural Schools for North Carolina for the Month of August, 1917," and "Report of N. C. Newbold, State Supervisor of Negro Rural Schools for North Carolina for the Month of September, 1917," series 1.1, box 115, folder 1044, GEB Papers; Newbold to L. B. McBrayer, September 22, 1917, Correspondence of the Director, box 3; and circular letter from Newbold, October 1, 1917, Correspondence of the Director, Reports, box 3, DNE Papers.

51. Pankey, "Life Histories," pp. 69, 77–81.

52. Newbold to E. C. Sage, January 11, 1916, series 1.1, box 115, folder 1038, and "Summarized Statement of Home Makers' Club Work for the Summer of 1918," series 1.1, box 116, folder 1048, GEB Papers; "The Jeanes Supervising Industrial Teachers, Some Things They Helped to Do Last School Year," Correspondence of the Director, box 3, and Annie Holland to Newbold, August 10, 1914, Correspondence of the Director, box 1, DNE Papers; and J. H. Smith, "Brief Sketch of the Industrial Work of the Colored Schools of Bertie County for Session 1910–11," pamphlet in box 474, SPI Papers.

53. "Report of N. C. Newbold, State Agent Rural Schools for Negroes for North Carolina, for the Month of April, 1915," series 1.1, box 115, folder 1043, and "Items Gathered from the Year's Work in North Carolina, July 1, 1916–June 30, 1917," box 115, folder 1044, GEB Papers. See also Newbold, "Negro County-School Commencements." See also "Report of N. C. Newbold, State Agent Rural Schools for Negroes for North Carolina, For the Month of March, 1916," series 1.1, box 115, folder 1044, GEB Papers.

54. "Report of N. C. Newbold, State Agent Rural Schools for Negroes for North Carolina, for the Month of April, 1915," series 1.1, box 115, folder 1043, GEB Papers. The exhibits are well documented in photographs. See folder NC 236, Photographic File, GEB Papers.

55. "Industrial Education," *Star of Zion*, January 7, 1887; "Report of N. C. Newbold, State Agent Rural Schools for Negroes for North Carolina, for the Month of April, 1915," series 1.1, box 115, folder 1043, GEB Papers; and John Skorupski, *Symbol and Theory: A Philosophical Study of Theories of Religion in Social Anthropology*, quoted in Ryan, "American Parade," p. 132. For more on the black perspective on industrial education, see W. G. Pearson to Newbold, August 8, 1916, Correspondence of the Director, box 2, DNE Papers; and "Trials and Achievements of the Afro-American Race," January 5, 1899; "Has Been Misunderstood," February 24, 1898; and "Expressions and Addresses," August 2, 1899, *Star of Zion*. Industrial education drew regular attention from the *Star*'s editors and contributors at the turn of the century. For this reading of the commencement parades, I am also indebted to Susan G. Davis, *Parades and Power*, and White, " 'It Was a Proud Day.' "

56. "Report of N. C. Newbold, State Agent Rural Schools for Negroes for North Carolina, for the Month of March, 1916," and "Items Gathered from the Year's Work in North Carolina, July 1, 1916–June 30, 1917," box 115, folder 1044, GEB Papers.

57. L. S. Inscoe to Newbold, August 25, 1919, Correspondence of the Director, box 4; W. H. Hinton to Newbold, July 17, 1915, Correspondence of the Director, box 1; and Spencer to Newbold, May 28, 1923, Correspondence of the Director, box 6, DNE Papers.

58. "Report of N. C. Newbold, State Agent Rural Schools for Negroes for North Carolina, for the Month of April, 1919," series 1.1, box 115, folder 1044, and "Extract from Letter of Mr. Newbold, State Agent of North Carolina," series 1.2, box 221, folder 2122, GEB Papers; Battle to Newbold, July 6, 1916, Correspondence of the Director, Training Schools, box 2; J. E. Debnam to Newbold, February 21, 1917, Correspondence of the Director, box 3, DNE Papers; and Minutes, Greene County Board of Education, July 5, 1915.

59. Battle to Newbold, March 9, 1915, Correspondence of the Director, box 1, and Battle to Newbold, July 13–16, 1916, Correspondence of the Director, box 2, DNE Papers; and *Biennial Report, 1914–15/1915–16*, part 2, pp. 76, 79, 84, 87, 117, 120.

60. Minutes, Greene County Board of Education, June 5, 1916; Newbold to Thomas Jesse Jones, January 18, 1917, Correspondence of the Director, box 3; Battle to Newbold, July 13–16, 1916; and Debnam to Newbold, June 17, 1916, Correspondence of the Director, box 2, DNE Papers.

61. Newbold to Battle, July 18, 1916, and Battle to Newbold, July 14, 1916, Correspondence of the Director, box 2, DNE Papers.

62. Battle to Newbold, July 13–16, 1916, and Battle to Newbold, July 14, 1916, Correspondence of the Director, box 2, DNE Papers. In the original, the phrase "live down" is underlined twice for emphasis.

63. "Report of N. C. Newbold, State Agent Rural Schools for Negroes for North Carolina, for the Month of April, 1919," series 1.1, box 115, folder 1044, GEB Papers.

64. *Biennial Report, 1914–15/1915–16*, part 2, p. 92; J. E. Debnam to Newbold, May 17, 1916, Correspondence of the Director, box 2; and "Report of W. F. Credle, Supervisor of the Rosenwald Fund, May, 1924," Special Subject File, box 8, DNE Papers.

65. U.S. Department of Labor, Division of Negro Economics, *Negro Migration in 1916–17*, p. 100, and Grossman, *Land of Hope*, p. 4, passim.

66. U.S. Department of Labor, Division of Negro Economics, *Negro Migration in 1916–17*, pp. 73–74, 96, and "Race Restlessness," *Star of Zion*, March 20, 1919. See also *Star of Zion*, October 26, 1916. The paper suggested that "the South can stop the emigration if it wills. The remedy is to recognize the Negro as a human being, protect his family, improve his educational facilities, give him opportunities for recreation under healthful conditions, and remove the constant dread and suspicion that hamper him."

67. Grossman, *Land of Hope*, pp. 16, 38–65; U.S. Department of Labor, Division of Negro Economics, *Negro Migration in 1916–17*, pp. 34–35; and "Race Restlessness," *Star of Zion*, March 20, 1919.

68. Circular letter to county superintendents and boards of education, from

Newbold and E. C. Brooks, April 15, 1919, series 1.2, box 212, folder 2038, GEB Papers; "Race Restlessness," *Star of Zion*, March 20, 1919; U.S. Department of Labor, Division of Negro Economics, *Negro Migration in 1916–17*, pp. 9–10, 112–13; Scott, *Negro Migration during the War*, pp. 18–19; "Eminent Sociologists Try to Lift Lid on Negro Exodus," *Star of Zion*, October 4, 1917; and *Five Letters of the University Commission on Southern Race Questions*, pp. 10–11. On the origins of the Southern University Commission, see Brough, "Work of the Commission of Southern Universities on the Race Question."

69. Werner, *Julius Rosenwald*, pp. 3–6, 114–15, 136, and John Graham Brooks, *American Citizen*, pp. 203–40.

70. Grossman, *Land of Hope*, pp. 4, 200–207; Werner, *Julius Rosenwald*, pp. 119–23; and Rosenwald, "You Can't Keep a Man in the Ditch."

71. Werner, *Julius Rosenwald*, pp. 123–36; "Evolution of the Schoolhouse Construction Program by the Julius Rosenwald Fund," box 331, folder 1, Rosenwald Fund Papers; S. L. Smith, *Builders of Goodwill*, pp. 63–66; and Embree and Waxman, *Investment in People*, pp. 28–29. See also R. R. Moton, Emmett J. Scott, and James L. Sibley, "Plan for the Erection of Rural Houses," September 20, 1917, box 331, folder 1, Rosenwald Fund Papers.

72. Newbold, "Common Schools for Negroes," p. 221; and John A. McLeod to Newbold, October 4, 1915, Correspondence of the Director, box 2, DNE Papers.

73. "Report from Lemley District No. 2," attached to J. M. Matthews to Newbold, February 24, 1916, Correspondence of the Director, box 2; and George Davis to William Credle, February 20, 1926, Correspondence of the Rosenwald Supervisor, box 2, DNE Papers. See also L. N. Hickerson to Newbold, March 28, 1916, Correspondence of the Director, box 2, DNE Papers.

74. Murray, *History of the North Carolina Teachers Association*, pp. 32–33; "Summary of Reports of N.C. Newbold, State Agent Negro Rural Schools for North Carolina, July 1, 1915–June 30, 1916," Correspondence of the Director, box 2, DNE Papers; Arnett, *For Whom Our Public Schools Were Named*, pp. 109–10; and "Professor C. H. Moore, M.A., the People's Choice for President of the Colored Agricultural and Mechanical College," *Africo-American Presbyterian*, August 20, 1891. On Moore's hiring, see also "Report of N. C. Newbold, State Supervisor of Negro Rural Schools for North Carolina for the Month of July 1915," and "Report of N. C. Newbold, State Supervisor of Negro Rural Schools for North Carolina for the Month of September 1915," series 1.1, box 115, folder 1043, GEB Papers. Moore's patron was the son of Edward Kidder, who moved to Wilmington from New Hampshire in 1825 and established himself as a successful commission merchant and sawmill owner. Edward held fast to his Whig sensibilities throughout the Civil War, and during Reconstruction he became an active member of the Republican Party. See *Directory of the City of Wilmington, North Carolina, 1889*, p. 84, and McDuffie, "Politics in Wilmington," p. 131.

75. Arnett, *For Whom Our Public Schools Were Named*, pp. 110–16. The college was a by-product of the efforts that had established a similar institution for whites in 1887. The Agricultural and Mechanical College in Raleigh admitted its first stu-

dents in 1889, but under a special provision of the Second Morrill Act, adopted by Congress one year later, North Carolina could claim no additional land-grant funds for the school's operation until it also provided a comparable facility for blacks. Bowing to that necessity, the state legislature passed a bill in March 1891 authorizing an "A. and M. College for the Colored Race." But the act specified no location for the school, and that, of course, set off a bidding war. When lawmakers named Moore to the college's board of trustees, he immediately began to ply his influence among Greensboro's white business and political elite to ensure that the city outmaneuvered Durham, Winston, and other centers of black urban population. Adopting the pen name "Justice," he wrote a series of articles for the *Greensboro Daily Record* assuring white merchants and property owners that the new school's stimulus to trade warranted public investment. He also reminded readers that black voters had supported Greensboro's recent campaign to host the State Normal and Industrial College, even though they had no direct interest in the education of white women. "Will the white people, with their centuries of moral and intellectual training back of them, be less generous and more selfish than their 'brother in black,'" Moore asked rhetorically. "We think not." That appeal—together with considerable politicking behind the scenes—eventually paid off. In early 1892, the Greensboro city council and a committee of leading white citizens submitted a winning bid of fourteen acres of land and a start-up appropriation of $11,000 backed by municipal bonds. The school accepted its first students one year later. For more on the college's origins and early history, see Gibbs, *History of the North Carolina Agricultural and Technical College*, pp. 1–26.

76. Charles H. Moore, *Report of Professor Charles H. Moore*, pp. 2–3; Newbold to Abraham Flexner, June 18, 1919, Correspondence of the Director, box 4; Newbold to Clinton J. Calloway, n.d., September 1919 to August 1920 division, folder C, Correspondence of the Director, box 4; and "Notes on the Rosenwald Fund," undated stories about the fund filed in 1923–25 correspondence folder, Correspondence of the Director, box 7, DNE Papers.

77. "Attempting to Solve Problems of Negro Education by Deliberative Processes in North Carolina; Explanation of Some Procedures That Have Been Used in this Interesting Enterprise," August 12, 1943, Articles and Speeches, box 2; George E. Davis to William Credle, August 6, 1924, Correspondence of the Rosenwald Supervisor, box 1, DNE Papers; Rev. W. V. Collins to E. C. Brooks, July 5, 1923, General Correspondence, Office of the Superintendent, box 90; William Credle to George Davis, March 3, 1923, General Correspondence, Office of the Superintendent, box 87, Department of Public Instruction Papers; and George Davis to William Credle, September 28, 1927, Correspondence of the Rosenwald Supervisor, box 4, DNE Papers.

78. Charles H. Moore, *Report of Professor Charles H. Moore*, p. 6.

79. E. L. Best to Newbold, April 17, 1917; Newbold to Best, April 18, 1917; and E. L. Best to A. M. Moore, April 21, 1917, Correspondence of the Director, box 3; and Newbold to E. C. Brooks, August 4, 1920, Correspondence of the Director, box 4, DNE Papers.

80. E. C. Brooks to Julius Rosenwald, December 30, 1921, General Correspondence, Office of the Superintendent, box 82, Department of Public Instruction Papers; Robert R. Moton to Abraham Flexner and Julius Rosenwald, April through July 1919, box 331, folder 1, Rosenwald Fund Papers; and T. H. Harris to Abraham Flexner, March 30, 1920, series 1.2, box 212, folder 2039, GEB Papers.

81. "Brief of Features of Rural School Audit, Recommendations, and Correspondence on Method of Administering Rural School Construction"; James H. Dillard to Julius Rosenwald, March 4 and 11, 1919, box 331, folder 1, Rosenwald Fund Papers; T. H. Harris to Abraham Flexner, March 30, 1920; Abraham Flexner to Julius Rosenwald, April 24, 1920; Robert R. Moton to Wallace Buttrick, May 20, 1920; Margaret Washington to Wallace Buttrick, May 24, 1920, series 1.2, box 212, folder 2039, GEB Papers; Robert R. Moton to Abraham Flexner and Julius Rosenwald, April through July 1919, box 331, folder 1; clipping from the *Peabody Reflector and Alumni News*, January 1932, box 127, folder 15, Rosenwald Fund Papers; and Embree and Waxman, *Investment in People*, pp. 40–41. On the decision to reorganize the Rosenwald work, see also Wallace Buttrick to Fletcher B. Dresslar, June 16, 1919, series 1.2, box 212, and William C. Graves to Abraham Flexner, September 9, 1919, series 1.2, box 212, 2039, GEB Papers.

82. Hanchett, "Rosenwald Schools in North Carolina," p. 400, and *Community Schools Plans*, Bulletin No. 3, issued by the Julius Rosenwald Fund, Nashville, Tenn., 1924, copy in Special Subject File, Rosenwald folder, box 8; Newbold to Clinton J. Calloway, November 24, 1919, Correspondence of the Director, box 4; and S. L. Smith to William Credle, September 8, 1924, Correspondence of the Rosenwald Supervisor, box 1, DNE Papers.

83. Westin, "State and Segregated Schools," pp. 342–43. On the creation of the Division of Negro Education and the general reorganization of the superintendent's office and the state Department of Public Instruction, see Prince, "History of the State Department of Public Instruction," pp. 235–68, 289–90.

84. Newbold to Byrd I. Satterfield, August 16, 1927, Correspondence of the Director, box 8, DNE Papers, and Newbold to A. T. Allen, July 16, 1926, Office of the Superintendent, General Correspondence, Division of Negro Education folder, box 98, Department of Public Instruction Papers. On the Lincoln County affair, see T. F. Reinhart to William Credle, September 14, 1925; anonymous to Credle, September 14, 1925; Credle to Reinhart, September 19, 1925; Beam to Credle, July 9, 1925; George Davis to Credle, November 3, 1925; Credle to Davis, November 5, 1925; and Harvey Foster to Credle, November 25, 1925, Correspondence of the Rosenwald Supervisor, box 2; Newbold to Beam, November 24, 1925; and Beam to Newbold, November 27, 1925, Correspondence of the Director, box 8, DNE Papers.

85. Newbold to S. L. Smith, September 7, 1920, Correspondence of the Director, box 5; A. M. Moore to Newbold, August 11, 1920, Correspondence of the Director, box 4; and Arnett, *For Whom Our Public Schools Were Named*, pp. 116–17.

86. Hanchett, "Rosenwald Schools in North Carolina," pp. 409–11.

87. T. H. Harris to Abraham Flexner, March 30, 1920, series 1.2, box 212, folder 2039, GEB Papers; Davis to William Credle, November 3, 1925, Correspondence of the Rosenwald Supervisor, box 2; "Detail" of Davis's speech, attached to his monthly report for May–June 1931, Special Subject File, box 8, DNE Papers.

88. Newbold to F. Harrison Hough, January 10, 1924, Correspondence of the Director, box 7; "Report of Dr. G. E. Davis," March 1929, Special Subject File, box 8, DNE Papers; and Hanchett, "Rosenwald Schools in North Carolina," pp. 409–16.

89. "Report of Dr. G. E. Davis," March 1929, and "Conference of Trustees and Guests Julius Rosenwald Fund, April 29, 1928," Special Subject File, box 8, DNE Papers.

90. Circular letter, March 27, 1928, and dedication program, Special Subject File, box 8, DNE Papers; "First Biennial Report of State Agent of Negro Rural Schools for North Carolina," *Biennial Report, 1912–13/1913–14,* pp. 123 and 125; S. L. Smith, "Report on Negro Rural Schools," September 1, 1928, box 331, folder 1, Rosenwald Fund Papers; and "The Julius Rosenwald Fund in North Carolina, speech of W. F. Credle at Dedication of 4000th School," Special Subject File, box 8, DNE Papers.

91. "Effects of the Rosenwald Work in North Carolina," Special Subject File, box 8, and Newbold to Governor Angus W. McLean, October 30, 1925, Correspondence of the Director, box 8, DNE Papers; Newbold to Edwin R. Embree, September 2, 1031, box 341, folder 5, and Jackson Davis to S. L. Smith, March 24, 1927, box 331, folder 1, Rosenwald Fund Papers; Clinton J. Calloway to Abraham Flexner, September 6, 1919, series 1.2, box 212, folder 2038, GEB Papers; and "Minutes of Committee Meeting on Negro Education in North Carolina," April 1, 1927, Special Subject File, box 8, DNE Papers.

92. Newbold to Philip Boden, November 24, 1925, Correspondence of the Director, box 8, DNE Papers; Williams and Palmer, *Dictionary of National Biography, 1951–1960,* pp. 715–16; Basil Mathews, *Clash of Color,* pp. 21–24, 72–75, 152, 159–61; and "Minutes of Committee Meeting on Negro Education in North Carolina," April 1, 1927, Special Subject File, box 8, DNE Papers. In 1927, Newbold reported that he had also hosted visits by the president of the University of South Africa; a member of the British Commission on Native Affairs in South Africa; the principal of the teacher-training college in Nairobi; Belgian officials from the Congo; English and Scottish missionaries from Rhodesia, Uganda, Nigeria, Nyasaland, and Nigeria; and the Commissioner of Education from British Guiana. See "Minutes of Committee Meeting on Negro Education in North Carolina," April 1, 1927, Special Subject File, box 8, DNE Papers. For more on those exchanges and the efforts to transplant southern models to Africa, see Thomas Jesse Jones, *Education in Africa* and *Education in East Africa*; Thomas Jesse Jones to Trevor Arnett, October 28, 1931, box 188, folder 4; "Lecture-Seminar-Conference on the Education of the American Negroes and the African Natives," an outline of a conference sponsored at Chapel Hill in 1937 by Yale University, the University of North

Carolina, and Hampton Institute, box 311, folder 3, Rosenwald Fund Papers; and Dabney, *Universal Education*, 2:517–28.

93. "Negro Common School in North Carolina," and *Biennial Report, 1926–27/1927–28*, part 3, p. 269. The value of the average white schoolhouse was $23,461, as compared to $4,215 for blacks. On the concern the article caused in Newbold's office, see George Davis to William Credle, April 28, 1927, Correspondence of the Rosenwald Supervisor, box 3, DNE Papers.

94. "Negro Common School in North Carolina," p. 135; "The Julius Rosenwald Fund in North Carolina, speech of W. F. Credle at Dedication of 4000th School," and "Rosenwald Schools in North Carolina," Special Subject File, box 8, DNE Papers; and Hart, "Negro Builds for Himself," p. 565.

95. "First Biennial Report of State Agent of Negro Rural Schools for North Carolina," *Biennial Report, 1912–13/1913–14*, pp. 124–25; Washington to Buttrick, May 24, 1920, series 1.2, box 212, folder 2039, GEB Papers; and Hart, "Negro Builds for Himself." The black students who sang Rosenwald's praises in 1928 made a similar point in the full text of their song:

> In a bright school room
> Built for Negro boys and girls,
> We will be happy
> Through the days of toil.
> Rosenwald has blessed us,
> Edgecombe, too, has done her part
> We will ever love her
> With an honest heart.
>
> Edgecombe, dear old Edgecombe,
> On your soil we love to dwell,
> We'll ne'er forsake you
> But will serve you well.
> With your help we'll conquer
> And will battle for the right,
> Always we'll remember
> Edgecombe does the right.

See Pankey, "Life Histories," p. 83.

96. Charlotte Hawkins Brown, "Some Incidents in the Life and Career of Charlotte Hawkins Brown Growing Out of Racial Situations at the Request of Dr. Ralph Bunche," box 1, folder 24, Charlotte Hawkins Brown Papers, quoted in Smith and West, "Charlotte Hawkins Brown," p. 200.

97. Todd, "Historical Development of the North Carolina Teachers Association," pp. 31–33, and Powell, *Dictionary of North Carolina Biography*, 4:363. Newbold retired in 1950 at the age of seventy-nine; he died in December 1957.

98. Interview with Joseph McNeil, 1978, quoted in Chafe, *Civilities and Civil Rights*, p. 112.

Afterword

1. *Biennial Report, 1924–25/1925–26*, part 2, pp. 149, 163, and part 3, pp. 153, 172.

2. Dabney, *Universal Education*, 1:ix; Knight, *Public School Education in North Carolina*, p. vi; Knight, *Public Education in the South*, p. vii; and Knight, *Documentary History*. Dabney's research and writing was supported over a period of eight years by a series of grants from the General Education Board and other Rockefeller philanthropies. The story of the funding can be traced through letters in series 1.5, box 721, folders 7419 through 7421 of the GEB Papers.

3. Knight, *Public School Education in North Carolina*, p. 368. Archival copies of the master's theses are cataloged by county in the North Carolina Collection at the University of North Carolina at Chapel Hill.

4. "Study of the Public Schools in Orange County," pp. 13, 17, 23, and 32.

5. "Report of the Committee on the Course of Study, City Superintendents' Association of North Carolina, January 22–24, 1902," box 2, folder 25, Coon Papers; Williford, "Relationship between Classroom Teaching Performance and Attrition," pp. 49–52; North Carolina Department of Public Instruction, *North Carolina Public Schools: Statistical Profile, 1993*, p. 31; Reich, *Work of Nations*; and Reich, *Education for the Next Economy*.

6. "E. Mitchell for himself and for Messrs. Hubbard and Phillips," quoted in Cherry, "Bringing Science to the South," p. 80, and Swett, *Methods of Teaching*, pp. 1–22.

Bibliography

Manuscript Collections

Cambridge, Massachusetts
  Manuscript Collection, Houghton Library, Harvard University
    Walter Hines Page Papers
Chapel Hill, North Carolina
  North Carolina Collection, Louis Round Wilson Library, University of North Carolina
    Manuscript census, population schedule, Gaston County, North Carolina, 1880. Microfilm.
    Manuscript census, population and agricultural schedules, Lenoir County, North Carolina, 1860. Microfilm.
    Manuscript census, population and agricultural schedules, Lenoir County, North Carolina, 1870. Microfilm.
    Manuscript census, population schedule, New Hanover County, North Carolina, 1870. Microfilm.
    "Orange County Commencement." Handwritten broadside.
  Southern Historical Collection, Louis Round Wilson Library, University of North Carolina
    Battle Family Papers
    Charles Lee Coon Papers
    Lawrence Dusenberry Diary
    Ernest Haywood Collection
    Sally Long Jarman Papers
    Elvira Evelyna Moffitt Papers
    Edward Pearson Moses Papers
    Southern Education Board Papers
    Cornelia Phillips Spencer Papers
    David Lowry Swain Papers
    Francis P. Venable Papers
    Alfred Moore Waddell Papers
    Calvin Henderson Wiley Papers

University Archive, Louis Round Wilson Library, University of North Carolina
  Student Organizations and Activities, Dialectic and Philanthropic Society
    Records
  University Papers
Charlottesville, Virginia
  Manuscript Collection, Edwin Anderson Alderman Library, University of Virginia
    Edwin Anderson Alderman Papers
Durham, North Carolina
  Manuscript Collection, William R. Perkins Library, Duke University
    Charles N. Hunter Collection
  University Archive, William R. Perkins Library, Duke University
    John Carlisle Kilgo Papers
Greensboro, North Carolina
  Special Collections, Walter Clinton Jackson Library, University of North Carolina at Greensboro
    Charles Duncan McIver Papers
    Records of the Woman's Association for the Betterment of Public School
      Houses in North Carolina
    Woman's College Scrapbook
Nashville, Tennessee
  Special Collections, Fisk University Library
    Julius Rosenwald Fund Papers
Pocantico Hills, North Tarrytown, New York
  Rockefeller Archive Center
    Frederick T. Gates Papers
    General Education Board Papers
    Rockefeller Family Papers
    Papers of the Rockefeller Sanitary Commission for the Eradication of Hookworm
Raleigh, North Carolina
  North Carolina Division of Archives and History
    Samuel A'Court Ashe Papers
    John Heritage Bryan Collection
    Governor's Letter Books, Charles Brantley Aycock
    Greene County Board of Education, Minutes
    Department of Public Instruction, Division of Negro Education Papers
    Department of Public Instruction, Office of the Superintendent, General
      Correspondence
    Cornelia Phillips Spencer Papers
    State Board of Education Papers
    State Superintendent of Public Instruction, Correspondence
    Superintendent of Public Instruction Correspondence, Letterbooks, and Reports

Government and School Documents

Acts of Assembly, Establishing and Regulating Common Schools in North Carolina, 1853. Raleigh: William W. Holden, 1853.

Annual Report of the Board of School Commissioners of the City of Winston, for the School Year Ending May 23, 1895. Winston: Stewarts' Printing House, 1895.

Annual Report of the Superintendent of Public Instruction of North Carolina, 1868. N.p., n.d.

Annual Report . . . 1878. Raleigh: The Observer, 1879.

Annual Report . . . 1879. Raleigh: P. M. Hale and Edwards and Broughton, 1880.

Annual Report . . . 1880. Raleigh: P. M. Hale and Edwards and Broughton and Company, 1881.

Annual Reports of the Public Schools of Raleigh Township, Wake County, N.C., 1885– 86. Raleigh: E. M. Uzzell, 1886.

Biennial Report of the State Superintendent of Public Instruction of North Carolina, for the Scholastic Years 1881–82. Raleigh: Ashe and Gatling, 1883.

Biennial Report . . . 1883–84. Raleigh: Ashe and Gatling, n.d.

Biennial Report . . . 1885–86. Raleigh: P. M. Hale, 1887.

Biennial Report . . . 1887–88. Raleigh: Josephus Daniels, 1889.

Biennial Report . . . 1889–90. Raleigh: Josephus Daniels, 1890.

Biennial Report . . . 1891–92. Raleigh: Josephus Daniels, 1893.

Biennial Report . . . 1892–93 and 1893–94. Raleigh: Josephus Daniels, 1895.

Biennial Report . . . 1896–97 and 1897–98. Raleigh: Guy V. Barnes, 1898.

Biennial Report . . . 1898–99 and 1899–1900. Raleigh: Edwards and Broughton and E. M. Uzzell, 1900.

Biennial Report . . . 1900–01 and 1901–02. Raleigh: Edwards and Broughton, 1902.

Biennial Report . . . 1902–03 and 1903–04. Raleigh: E. M. Uzzell and Company, 1904.

Biennial Report . . . 1908–09 and 1909–10. Raleigh: E. M. Uzzell and Company, 1910.

Biennial Report . . . 1910–11 and 1911–12. Raleigh: Edwards and Broughton, n.d.

Biennial Report . . . 1912–13 and 1913–14. Raleigh: Edwards and Broughton, n.d.

Biennial Report . . . 1914–15 and 1915–16. Raleigh: Edwards and Broughton, 1917.

Biennial Report . . . 1918–19 and 1919–20. Raleigh: Edwards and Broughton, 1921.

Biennial Report . . . 1920–21 and 1921–22. Raleigh: State Superintendent of Public Instruction, n.d.

Biennial Report . . . 1926–27 and 1927–28. Raleigh: State Superintendent of Public Instruction, n.d.

Catalogue of the Trustees, Faculty, and Students of the University of North Carolina, 1848–49. Fayetteville: Edward J. Hale, 1849.

Catalogue of the Trustees, Faculty, and Students of the University of North Carolina, 1875–76. Raleigh: News Publishing Company, 1876.

Catalogue of the University of North Carolina, at Chapel Hill, Ninety-First Year,
  1885–86. Raleigh: Edwards and Broughton, 1886.
Connor, Robert Diggs Wimberly. *The Woman's Association for the Betterment of*
  Public School Houses in North Carolina. Raleigh: Office of the State Super-
  intendent of Public Instruction, 1905.
Coon, Charles L. *A Statistical Record of the Progress of Public Education in North*
  Carolina, 1870–1906. [Raleigh]: Office of the State Superintendent of Public
  Instruction, 1907.
Division of Negro Economics, U.S. Department of Labor. *Negro Migration in*
  1916–17. Washington: Government Printing Office, 1919.
Eighth Annual Catalogue of the North Carolina State Normal and Industrial College,
  Greensboro, N.C., 1899–1900. Greensboro: Jos. J. Stone, 1900.
Fifth Annual Catalogue of the State Normal and Industrial College, Greensboro, N.C.,
  1896–97. Winston: M. I. and J. C. Stewart, 1896.
Fifth Annual Report of the General Superintendent of Common Schools. N.p.: Holden
  and Wilson, n.d.
First Annual Catalogue of the State Normal and Industrial School. Greensboro, N.C.,
  1892–93. N.p.: C. F. Thomas, n.d.
First Annual Report of the General Superintendent of Common Schools. Raleigh:
  W. W. Holden, 1854.
Fourth Annual Catalogue of the State Normal and Industrial School, Greensboro,
  N.C., 1895–96. Winston: M. I. and J. C. Stewart, 1896.
Journal of the House of Representatives of the General Assembly of the State of North
  Carolina, 1887. Raleigh: Josephus Daniels, 1887.
Journal of the House of Representatives of the General Assembly of the State of North
  Carolina, 1889. Raleigh: Josephus Daniels, 1889.
Journal of the House of Representatives of the General Assembly of the State of North
  Carolina, 1891. Raleigh: Josephus Daniels, 1891.
Journal of the Senate of the General Assembly of the State of North Carolina, 1887.
  Raleigh: P. M. Hale, 1887.
Journal of the Senate of the General Assembly of the State of North Carolina, 1889.
  Raleigh: Josephus Daniels, 1889.
Journal of the Senate of the General Assembly of the State of North Carolina, 1891.
  Raleigh: Josephus Daniels, 1891.
Laws and Resolutions of the State of North Carolina, 1881. Raleigh: Ashe and Gat-
  ling, 1881.
Laws and Resolutions of the State of North Carolina, 1885. Raleigh: P. M. Hale,
  1885.
Laws and Resolutions of the State of North Carolina, 1887. Raleigh: Josephus
  Daniels, 1887.
Laws and Resolutions of the State of North Carolina, 1889. Raleigh: Josephus
  Daniels, 1889.
Laws and Resolutions of the State of North Carolina, 1891. Raleigh: Josephus
  Daniels, 1891.

Mayo, Amory Dwight. "The Final Establishment of the American Common School System in North Carolina, South Carolina, and Georgia, 1863–1900." In *Annual Reports of the Department of the Interior. Report of the Commissioner of Education, for the Fiscal Year Ended June 30, 1904*, vol. 1, pp. 999–1090. House Documents, vol. 25, no. 5, 58th Congress, 3d sess. Washington: Government Printing Office, 1905.

Mebane, Charles H. *The Woman's Association for the Betterment of Public School Houses in North Carolina*. [Raleigh: Office of the State Superintendent of Public Instruction, 1908].

Nash County Board of Health. *A Catechism of Public Health*. N.p., n.d.

Ninth Annual Catalogue of the North Carolina State Normal and Industrial College, Greensboro, N.C., 1900–1901. Greensboro: C. F. Thomas, n.d.

North Carolina Department of Public Instruction. *North Carolina Public Schools: Statistical Profile, 1993*. N.p., n.d.

North Carolina Reports. Vol. 94, February Term, 1886. N.p.: Nash Brothers, 1909.

Office of Education, U.S. Department of Health, Education, and Welfare. *Biennial Survey of Education in the United States, 1956–58*. Chapter 2, *Statistics of State School Systems: 1957–58. Organization, Staff, Pupils, and Finances*. Washington: Government Printing Office, 1961.

Public Documents of the State of North Carolina, 1893. Raleigh: Josephus Daniels, 1893.

Public Laws and Resolutions of the State of North Carolina, 1871–72. Raleigh: Theo. N. Ramsay, 1872.

Public Laws and Resolutions of the State of North Carolina, 1895. Winston: M. I. and J. C. Stewart, 1895.

Public Laws and Resolutions of the State of North Carolina, 1897. Winston: M. I. and J. C. Stewart, 1897.

Public Laws and Resolutions of the State of North Carolina, 1899. Raleigh: Edwards and Broughton and E. M. Uzzell, 1899.

Public School Law of North Carolina, 1881. N.p., n.d.

Public School Law of North Carolina, 1885. Raleigh: P. M. Hale, 1885.

Public School Law of North Carolina, 1889. Raleigh: Josephus Daniels, 1889.

Public School Law of North Carolina, 1897. Winston: M. I. and J. C. Stewart, 1897.

Report of the State Board of Examiners for the Two Years Ending January 1, 1905, together with the Report of the Superintendent of the Colored State Normal Schools for 1904–05. Raleigh: E. M. Uzzell and Company, 1905.

Report of the Superintendent of Common Schools of North Carolina, for the Year 1859. Raleigh: W. W. Holden, 1860.

Report of the Superintendent of Common Schools of North Carolina, for the Year 1860. N.p.: John Spelman, n.d.

Report of the Winston Graded Schools, for the Year Ending May 17th, 1888. Winston: Stewarts' Job Office, 1888.

Rose, Wickliffe. "The Educational Movement in the South." In *Annual Reports of the Department of the Interior. Report of the Commissioner of Education, for the Fis-*

cal Year Ended June 30, 1903, vol. 1, pp. 359–90. House Documents, vol. 25, no.
    5, 58th Congress, 2d sess. Washington: Government Printing Office, 1904.
Second Annual Catalogue of the State Normal and Industrial School, Greensboro,
    N.C., 1893–4. N.p.: C. F. Thomas, n.d.
Seventh Annual Catalogue of the North Carolina State Normal and Industrial College,
    Greensboro, N.C., 1898–9. Greensboro: Jos. J. Stone, 1899.
Sixth Annual Catalogue of the State Normal and Industrial College, Greensboro, N.C.,
    1897–8. Raleigh: Edwards and Broughton, 1898.
Special Report of the General Superintendent of Common Schools of North Carolina,
    1854. Raleigh: W. W. Holden, 1855.
Third Annual Catalogue of the State Normal and Industrial School, Greensboro, N.C.,
    1894–5. N.p.: C. F. Thomas, n.d.
Turlington, Mrs. Ira T. [Hortense Rose]. *Child Study as an Aid to Discipline.*
    Raleigh: Office of the State Superintendent of Public Instruction, 1910.
U.S. Commissioner of Education. "Francis Wayland Parker and His Work for Ed-
    ucation." In *Annual Reports of the Department of the Interior for the Fiscal Year*
    Ended June 30, 1902. Report of the Commissioner of Education. Vol. 1, pp. 231–84.
    House Document No. 5, 57th Congress, 2d sess. Washington: Government
    Printing Office, 1903.
U.S. Department of Commerce, Bureau of the Census. *Fourteenth Census of the*
    United States. Vol. 3, *Population*. Washington: Government Printing Office, 1922.
U.S. Department of Labor, Division of Negro Economics. *Negro Migration in*
    1916–17. Washington: Government Printing Office, 1919.
The University of North Carolina Catalogue, 1894–95. Chapel Hill: University of
    North Carolina, 1895.
The University of North Carolina Catalogue, 1896–97. Chapel Hill: University of
    North Carolina, 1895.
Washburn, Benjamin E. *A History of the North Carolina State Board of Health,*
    1877–1925. Raleigh: North Carolina State Board of Health, 1966.
Weeks, Stephen B. "The Beginnings of the Common School System in the South;
    or, Calvin Henderson Wiley and the Organization of the Common Schools of
    North Carolina." In *Annual Reports of the Department of the Interior. Report of the*
    Commissioner of Education, for the Fiscal Year Ended June 30, 1897, vol. 2, pp.
    1379–1474. House Documents, vol. 22, no. 5, 55th Congress, 2d sess. Wash-
    ington: Government Printing Office, 1898.
Williams, Robin M., and Olaf Wakefield. "Farm Tenancy in North Carolina,
    1880–1935." North Carolina Agricultural Experiment Station. Agricultural Ex-
    periment Research Station Information Series No. 1. September 1937.

Directories and Biographical Dictionaries

Alumni History of the University of North Carolina, 1795–1924. Chapel Hill: Gen-
    eral Alumni Association of the University of North Carolina, 1924.
Ashe, Samuel A'Court, et al., eds. *Biographical History of North Carolina*. 8 vols.
    Greensboro: Charles L. Van Noppen, 1905–17.

Branson, Levi, ed. *Branson's North Carolina Business Directory for 1884*. Raleigh: Levi Branson, 1884.

——. *The North Carolina Business Directory, 1877 and 1878*. Raleigh: L. Branson, 1878.

Dictionary of American Biography. 10 vols. New York: Charles Scribner's Sons, 1929–30.

Directory of the City of Wilmington, North Carolina, 1889. Wilmington: Julius A. Bonitz, 1889.

Hine, Darlene Clark, ed. *Black Women in America: An Historical Encyclopedia*. 2 vols. Brooklyn, N.Y.: Carlson Publishing Co., 1993.

National Cyclopaedia of American Biography. Vol. 42. New York: James T. White and Company, 1958.

Powell, William S., ed. *Dictionary of North Carolina Biography*. 7 vols. Chapel Hill: University of North Carolina Press, 1979–.

Williams, E. T., and Helen M. Palmer, eds. *Dictionary of National Biography, 1951–1960*. London: Oxford University Press, 1971.

Newspapers and Periodicals

Africo-American Presbyterian
Alamance Gleaner (Graham)
Alumni Bulletin of the University of Virginia
Biblical Recorder (Raleigh)
Bulletin of the North Carolina Board of Health
Bulletin of the North Carolina Department of Agriculture
Carolina Messenger (Durham)
Carolina Watchman (Salisbury)
Caucasian
Charlotte Observer
Christian Educator (Durham)
Greensboro Patriot
The Land We Love
Manufacturer's Record
Morning Post (Raleigh)
The Nation
News and Observer (Raleigh)
New York Sun
North Carolina Education
North Carolina Journal of Education
North-Carolina Planter
North Carolina Presbyterian
North Carolina Teacher
Orange Jewel
Progressive Farmer

Review of Reviews
Schoolteacher
Southern Literary Messenger
Star of Zion (Salisbury)
State Chronicle (Raleigh)
State Normal Magazine
Tarboro Southerner
University Magazine
University Monthly
University of North Carolina Record
Weekly Globe (Durham)
Wilson Advance

Conference Proceedings

Minutes of the Seventy-Second Annual Meeting of the Baptist State Convention of North Carolina, Held at Durham, N.C., December 9–14, 1902. Raleigh: Edwards and Broughton, 1902.
Proceedings of the Fourth Conference for Education in the South, 1901. Harrisburg, Pa.: Mount Pleasant Press, J. Horace McFarland Company, 1901.
Proceedings of the Ninth Conference for Education in the South, 1906. Richmond: Executive Committee of the Conference [Times Printing Company], 1906.
Proceedings of the North Carolina Teachers Assembly, 1884. Raleigh: Uzzell and Gatling, 1884.
Proceedings of the North Carolina Teachers Assembly, Fourth Annual Session, 1887. Raleigh: E. M. Uzzell, 1887.
Proceedings of the Second Capon Springs Conference for Education in the South, 1899. N.p., n.d.
Proceedings of the Seventh Conference for Education in the South, 1904. New York: Conference Committee on Publication, 1904.
Proceedings of the Tenth Conference for Education in the South, 1907. Richmond: Executive Committee of the Conference, n.d.

Books, Articles, Pamphlets, and Addresses

Agnew, Jean-Christophe. *Worlds Apart: The Market and the Theater in Anglo-American Thought, 1550–1750.* New York: Cambridge University Press, 1986.
Alderman, Edwin A. "The Child and the State." In *Proceedings of the Fifth Conference for Education in the South, 1902,* pp. 55–62. Knoxville, Tenn.: Gaut-Ogden Company, 1902.
———. "Higher Education in the South." In *National Educational Association, Journal of Proceedings and Addresses, Session of the Year 1895,* pp. 979–87. St. Paul, Minn.: National Educational Association, 1895.
———. *J. L. M. Curry: A Biography.* New York: Macmillan, 1911.

———. "The Life and Work of Dr. Charles D. McIver." *North Carolina Journal of Education* 1 (December 15, 1906): 4–6.

———. "Obligations and Opportunities of Scholarship." In *National Educational Association, Journal of Proceedings and Addresses of the Thirty-Ninth Annual Meeting*, pp. 266–76. Chicago: University of Chicago Press, 1900.

———. "The University: Its Work and Its Needs." *University Record*, n.s. 1, no. 2 (1901–2): 46–54.

———. "The University of To-day: Its Work and Needs." *University Magazine*, n.s. 17 (June 1900): 287–97.

———. *Woodrow Wilson. Memorial Address Delivered before a Joint Session of the Two Houses of Congress, December 15, 1924, in Honor of Woodrow Wilson, Late President of the United States*. Garden City, N.Y.: Doubleday, 1925.

Anderson, Gary L. "Critical Ethnography in Education: Origins, Current Status, and New Directions." *Review of Educational Research* 59 (Fall 1989): 249–70.

Anderson, James D. *The Education of Blacks in the South, 1865–1935*. Chapel Hill: University of North Carolina Press, 1988.

Anderson, Paul. "Mental Hygiene in the Young." *Bulletin of the North Carolina Board of Health* 25 (November 1910): 375–83.

Apple, Michael W. *Cultural and Economic Reproduction in Education: Essays on Class, Ideology, and the State*. Boston: Routledge and Kegan Paul, 1982.

———. *Education and Power*. Boston: Routledge and Kegan Paul, 1982.

———. *Ideology and Curriculum*. London: Routledge and Kegan Paul, 1979.

———. *Teachers and Texts: A Political Economy of Class and Gender Relations in Education*. New York: Routledge, 1988.

———. "Teaching and 'Women's Work': A Comparative Historical and Ideological Analysis." In *Expressions of Power in Education: Studies in Class, Gender and Race*, edited by Edgar B. Gumbert, pp. 29–49. Atlanta: Center for Cross-Cultural Education, 1984.

———. "Work, Class, and Teaching." In *Gender, Class, and Education*, edited by Stephen Walker and Len Barton, pp. 53–67. Sussex: The Falmer Press, 1983.

Arnett, Ethel Stephens. *For Whom Our Public Schools Were Named*. Greensboro, N.C.: Piedmont Press, 1973.

Aronowitz, Stanley, and Henry A. Giroux. *Education under Siege: The Conservative, Liberal and Radical Debate over Schooling*. South Hadley, Mass.: Bergin and Garvey, 1985.

Bailey, Joseph Cannon. *Seaman A. Knapp, Schoolmaster of American Agriculture*. New York: Columbia University Press, 1945.

Baker, Paula. "The Domestication of Politics: Women and American Political Society, 1780–1920." *American Historical Review* 89 (June 1984): 620–47.

Baldwin, William H. "The Present Problem of Negro Education, Industrial Education." In *Proceedings of the Second Capon Springs Conference, 1899*, pp. 67–77. N.p., n.d.

Barney, Hiram H. *Report on the American System of Graded Free Schools*. Cincinnati: Office of the Daily Times, 1851.

Bassett, John Spencer. "Stirring Up the Fires of Racial Antipathy." *South Atlantic Quarterly* 2 (October 1903): 297–305.

Bateman, Fred, and Thomas Weiss. *A Deplorable Scarcity: The Failure of Industrialization in the Slave Economy.* Chapel Hill: University of North Carolina Press, 1981.

Battle, Kemp Plummer. *History of the University of North Carolina.* 2 vols. Raleigh: Edwards and Broughton Printing Company, 1912.

——. "Lives of the University Presidents." In *Biennial Report of the Superintendent of Public Instruction, 1898/99–1899/1900,* pp. 400–427. Raleigh: Edwards and Broughton and E. M. Uzzell, 1900.

——. "Old or Extinct Schools of North Carolina, Supplemental." In *Biennial Report of the Superintendent of Public Instruction, 1898/99–1899/1900,* pp. 428–43. Raleigh: Edwards and Broughton and E. M. Uzzell, 1900.

——. "Recollections of the University of North Carolina of 1844." *University Magazine* 13 (March–April 1896): 289–318.

——. *Sketches of the History of the University of North Carolina, Together with a Catalogue of Officers and Students, 1789–1889.* Chapel Hill: University of North Carolina, 1889.

——. "Struggle and Story of the Re-Birth of the University." *University Magazine* 17 (June 1900): 305–21.

Bergen, Barry H. "Only a Schoolmaster: Gender, Class, and the Effort to Professionalize Elementary Teaching in England, 1870–1910." *History of Education Quarterly* 22 (Spring 1982): 1–21.

Berkeley, Kathleen C. " 'Ladies Want to Bring About Reform in the Public Schools': Public Education and Women's Rights in the Post–Civil War South." *History of Education Quarterly* 24 (Spring 1984): 45–58.

Bickett, Thomas W. "The Higher Conception of Crime." *Bulletin of the North Carolina Board of Health* 25 (November 1910): 346–47.

Billings, Dwight B., Jr. *Planters and the Making of a "New South": Class, Politics, and Development in North Carolina, 1865–1900.* Chapel Hill: University of North Carolina Press, 1979.

Bledstein, Burton J. *The Culture of Professionalism: The Middle Class and the Development of Higher Education in America.* New York: W. W. Norton, 1976.

Bode, Frederick A. *Protestantism and the New South: North Carolina Baptists and Methodists in Political Crisis, 1894–1903.* Charlottesville: University Press of Virginia, 1975.

Bond, Horace Mann. *Negro Education in Alabama, A Study in Cotton and Steel.* Washington, D.C.: Associated Publishers, 1939.

Booth, A. E. "Teaching as a Profession." *North Carolina Teacher* 4 (November 1886): 109–12.

Bordin, Ruth. *Woman and Temperance: The Quest for Power and Liberty, 1873–1900.* Philadelphia: Temple University Press, 1981.

Bowers, William L. *The Country Life Movement in America, 1900–1920.* Port Washington, N.Y.: Kennikat Press, 1974.

Bowles, Elisabeth Ann. *A Good Beginning: The First Four Decades of the University of North Carolina at Greensboro.* Chapel Hill: University of North Carolina Press, 1967.

Boydston, Jeanne, Mary Kelley, and Anne Margolis. *The Limits of Sisterhood: The Beecher Sisters on Women's Rights and Woman's Sphere.* Chapel Hill: University of North Carolina Press, 1988.

Boyer, Paul. *Urban Masses and Moral Order in America, 1820–1920.* Cambridge: Harvard University Press, 1978.

Boykin, J. Robert III, comp. *Wilson County, North Carolina, 1880 Census.* Wilson: Toisnot Historical Company, 1984.

Brabham, Robin. "Defining the American University: The University of North Carolina, 1865–1875." *North Carolina Historical Review* 57 (October 1980): 427–55.

Brawley, Benjamin. *Doctor Dillard of the Jeanes Fund.* New York: Fleming H. Revell, 1930.

Bremner, Robert Hamlett. *From the Depths: The Discovery of Poverty in America.* New York: New York University Press, 1956.

Brewer, Fisk P. *The Library of the University of North Carolina.* N.p., n.d.

"A Brief History of Johnson C. Smith University." *Johnson C. Smith University Bulletin* 1 (May 30, 1935).

Brooks, Eugene Clyde. "Some Forgotten Educational History." *North Carolina Education* 9 (May 1915): 3–4.

——. "Status of the Graded School." *North Carolina Journal of Education* 1 (February 1907): 5–7.

——. "Women Improving School Houses." *World's Work* 12 (September 1906): 7937.

Brooks, John Graham. *An American Citizen: The Life of William Henry Baldwin, Jr.* Boston: Houghton Mifflin, 1910.

Brooks, Lucy. "A Day in My School Room." *North Carolina Journal of Education* 2 (December 1907): 10–12.

Brough, Charles Hillman. "Work of the Commission of Southern Universities on the Race Question." *Annals of the American Academy of Political and Social Science* 49 (September 1913): 46–57.

Brown, Cecil Kenneth. *A State Movement in Railroad Development: The Story of North Carolina's First Effort to Establish an East and West Trunk Line Railroad.* Chapel Hill: University of North Carolina Press, 1928.

Brown, E. Richard. *Rockefeller Medicine Men: Medicine and Capitalism in America.* Berkeley: University of California Press, 1979.

Bruce, Robert V. *The Launching of Modern American Science, 1846–1876.* Ithaca: Cornell University Press, 1987.

Buchanan, J. R. *The New Education.* Boston: n.p., 1882.

Burrow, James G. *Organized Medicine in the Progressive Era: The Move toward Monopoly.* Baltimore: Johns Hopkins University Press, 1977.

Burton, Orville Vernon. "The Effects of the Civil War and Reconstruction on the

Coming of Age of Southern Males, Edgefield County, South Carolina." In *The Web of Southern Social Relations: Women, Family, and Education*, edited by Walter J. Fraser Jr., R. Frank Saunders Jr., and Jon L. Wakelyn, pp. 204–24. Athens: University of Georgia Press, 1985.

Calhoun, Daniel. *The Intelligence of a People*. Princeton: Princeton University Press, 1973.

Campbell, Jack K. *Colonel Francis W. Parker: The Children's Crusader*. New York: Teachers College Press, 1967.

Cell, John W. *The Highest Stage of White Supremacy: The Origins of Segregation in South Africa and the American South*. Cambridge: Cambridge University Press, 1982.

"Centennial Founders Day Convocation and Announcement of Barber-Scotia College." Special issue of *The Barber-Scotia Index* (January 1967).

Chafe, William H. *Civilities and Civil Rights: Greensboro, North Carolina, and the Black Struggle for Freedom*. New York: Oxford University Press, 1980.

Chamberlain, Hope Summerell. *Old Days in Chapel Hill*. Chapel Hill: University of North Carolina Press, 1926.

Chandler, Alfred D., Jr. *The Visible Hand: The Managerial Revolution in American Business*. Cambridge: Belknap Press of Harvard University Press, 1977.

Cherry, Thomas Kevin B. "Bringing Science to the South: The School for the Application of Science to the Arts at the University of North Carolina." *History of Higher Education Annual* 14 (1994): 73-99.

Coates, Albert, and Gladys Hall Coates. *The Story of Student Government in the University of North Carolina at Chapel Hill*. Chapel Hill: Professor Emeritus Fund, 1985.

Cohen, Patricia Cline. *A Calculating People: The Spread of Numeracy in Early America*. Chicago: University of Chicago Press, 1982.

Connor, Robert Diggs Wimberly, comp. *A Documentary History of the University of North Carolina, 1776–1799*. 2 vols. Chapel Hill: University of North Carolina Press, 1953.

Connor, Robert Diggs Wimberly, and Clarence Poe. *The Life and Speeches of Charles Brantley Aycock*. Garden City, N.Y.: Doubleday, Page and Company, 1912.

Constitution and By-Laws: Woman's Association for the Betterment of Public School Houses in North Carolina. Greensboro: J. M. Reece, [1902].

Coon, Charles Lee. "The Beginnings of the North Carolina City Schools, 1867–1887." *South Atlantic Quarterly* 12 (July 1913): 235-47.

——, ed. *Public Education in North Carolina: A Documentary History, 1790–1840*. 2 vols. Raleigh: Publications of the North Carolina Historical Commission, Edwards and Broughton Printing Company, 1908.

Cooper, John Milton. *Walter Hines Page: The Southerner as American, 1855–1918*. Chapel Hill: University of North Carolina Press, 1977.

Cox, Monty Woodall. "Freedom during the Fremont Campaign: The Fate of One

North Carolina Republican in 1856." *North Carolina Historical Review* 45 (October 1968): 357–83.

Cremin, Lawrence A. *The Transformation of the School: Progressivism in American Education, 1876–1957.* New York: Vintage Books, 1964.

Crow, Jeffrey J., and Robert F. Durden. *Maverick Republican in the Old North State: A Political Biography of Daniel L. Russell.* Baton Rouge: Louisiana State University Press, 1977.

Cubberly, Ellwood. *Public Education in the United States.* Boston: Houghton Mifflin, 1934.

Curry, Jabez Lamar Monroe. *A Brief Sketch of George Peabody, and a History of the Peabody Education Fund through Thirty Years.* Cambridge: Cambridge University Press, 1898.

Curtis, Bruce. *Building the Educational State: Canada West, 1836–1871.* Philadelphia: The Falmer Press, 1988.

Dabney, Charles William. "The Public School Problem in the South." *Proceedings of the Fourth Conference for Education in the South, 1901*, pp. 39–64. Harrisburg, Pa.: Mount Pleasant Press, J. Horace McFarland Company, 1901.

———. *Universal Education in the South.* 2 vols. Chapel Hill: University of North Carolina Press, 1936.

Dale, George W. "About Normal Colleges." *North Carolina Teacher* 5 (February 1888): 243–44.

Daniels, Frank A. "The New South." *University Monthly* 2 (April 1883): 99–110.

Daniels, Josephus. *Editor in Politics.* Chapel Hill: University of North Carolina Press, 1941.

———. "The Progress of Southern Education." In *Proceedings of the Sixth Conference for Education in the South, 1903*, pp. 142–55. N.p., n.d.

———. *Tar Heel Editor.* Chapel Hill: University of North Carolina Press, 1939.

Danylewycz, Marta, and Alison Prentice. "Teachers, Gender, and Bureaucratizing School Systems in Nineteenth-Century Montreal and Toronto." *History of Education Quarterly* 24 (Spring 1984): 75–100.

———. "Teachers' Work: Changing Patterns and Perceptions in the Emerging School Systems of Nineteenth- and Early Twentieth-Century Central Canada." *Labour/Le Travail* 17 (Spring 1986): 59–80.

Danylewycz, Marta, Beth Light, and Alison Prentice. "The Evolution of the Sexual Division of Labour in Teaching: A Nineteenth-Century Ontario and Quebec Case Study." *Histoire Social—Social History* 16 (May 1983): 81–109.

Davis, Natalie Zemon. *Society and Culture in Early Modern France.* Stanford: Stanford University Press, 1975.

Davis, Susan G. *Parades and Power: Street Theatre in Nineteenth-Century Philadelphia.* Philadelphia: Temple University Press, 1986.

Dean, Pamela. "Learning to be New Women: Campus Culture at the North Carolina Normal and Industrial College." *North Carolina Historical Review* 68 (July 1991): 286–306.

DeGarmo, Charles. *Herbart and the Herbartians*. New York: Scribner's Sons, 1896.

Desmond, William J. "The Evolution of the Educator." *North Carolina Teacher* 7 (January 1890): 247–48.

Dey, William Morton. "The Beginnings of the Philological Club, A Paper Read before the Philological Club at Its Semi-Annual Celebration, January 20, 1943." *University Record* 383 (October 1942): 7–13.

Dickinson, J. W. "Results of Methods Teaching." In *The Addresses and Journal of Proceedings of the National Educational Association, Session of the Year 1880*, pp. 95–102. Salem, Ohio: National Educational Association, 1880.

Diehl, Carl. *Americans and German Scholarship, 1770–1870*. New Haven: Yale University Press, 1978.

Downs, Robert Bingham. *Friedrich Froebel*. New York: Twayne, 1978.

———. *Johann Heinrich Pestalozzi: Father of Modern Pedagogy*. Boston: Twayne, 1975.

Drake, William E. *Higher Education in North Carolina before 1860*. New York: Carlton Press, 1964.

Du Bois, W. E. Burghardt. "The Economic Revolution in the South." In W. E. B. Du Bois and Booker T. Washington, *The Negro in the South: His Economic Progress in Relation to His Moral and Religious Development, Being the William Levi Bull Lectures for the Year 1907*, pp. 77–102. Philadelphia: George W. Jacobs and Company, 1907.

———. *The Education of Black People*, edited by Herbert Aptheker. Amherst: University of Massachusetts Press, 1973.

Dunkel, Harold Baker. *Herbart and Education*. New York: Random House, 1969.

Durden, Robert F. *The Climax of Populism: The Election of 1896*. Lexington: University of Kentucky Press, 1965.

Edmonds, Helen G. *The Negro and Fusion Politics in North Carolina, 1894–1901*. New York: Russell and Russell, 1973.

Edwards, Bertha Maye. *The Little Place, and the Little Girl*. New York: Carlton Press, 1974.

Edwards, N. A. *North Carolina Congress of Parents and Teachers: History*. [Greensboro: n.p., 1945].

Eggleston, Edward. *The Hoosier School-Master. A Novel*. New York: Orange Judd and Company, 1871.

Eklof, Ben. *Russian Peasant Schools: Officialdom, Village Culture, and Popular Pedagogy, 1861–1914*. Berkeley: University of California Press, 1986.

Eller, Adolphus Hill. "The New University, An Oration Delivered by Adolphus Hill Eller, at the One Hundredth Annual Commencement of the University of North Carolina, June 5th, 1895." N.p., n.d.

Embree, Edwin R., and Julia Waxman. *Investment in People: The Story of the Julius Rosenwald Fund*. New York: Harper and Brothers, 1949.

Engelhard, Joseph A. "Address of Hon. J. A. Engelhard, before the Philanthropic and Dialectic Societies of the University of North Carolina, June 1878." Raleigh: Edwards, Broughton, and Company, 1879.

Escott, Paul D. *Many Excellent People: Power and Privilege in North Carolina, 1850–1900.* Chapel Hill: University of North Carolina Press, 1985.

Ettling, John. *The Germ of Laziness: Rockefeller Philanthropy and Public Health in the New South.* Cambridge: Harvard University Press, 1981.

Fink, Leon. *Workingmen's Democracy: The Knights of Labor and American Politics.* Urbana: University of Illinois Press, 1983.

Fisher, John E. *The John F. Slater Fund: A Nineteenth Century Affirmative Action for Negro Education.* Lanham, Md.: University Press of America, 1986.

Five Letters of the University Commission on Southern Race Questions. Occasional Papers, no. 24. N.p.: Trustees of the John F. Slater Fund, 1927.

Forney, E. J., Fodie Buie, and Emily Semple Austin. *Leaves from the Stenographers' Notebooks.* Greensboro: Harrison Printing Company, n.d.

Fosdick, Raymond B. *Adventure in Giving: The Story of the General Education Board, A Foundation Established by John D. Rockefeller.* New York: Harper and Row, 1962.

———. *John D. Rockefeller, Jr., A Portrait.* New York: Harper, 1956.

Foucault, Michel. *Discipline and Punish: The Birth of the Prison.* New York: Vintage Books, 1979.

Foushee, Alexander Roundtree. *Reminiscences: A Sketch and Letters Descriptive of Life in Person County in Former Days.* Roxboro, N.C.: The Seeman Printery, [Durham], 1921.

Fredrickson, George M. *The Black Image in the White Mind: The Debate on Afro-American Character and Destiny, 1817–1914.* New York: Harper and Row, 1971.

Garibaldi, Mrs. Joseph. "Work of Parent-Teacher Associations in North Carolina." *North Carolina Education* 14 (June 1920): 7–8.

Gaston, Paul M. *The New South Creed: A Study in Southern Mythmaking.* New York: Vintage Books, 1973.

Gatewood, Willard B. *Eugene Clyde Brooks: Educator and Public Servant.* Durham: Duke University Press, 1960.

The General Education Board: An Account of Its Activities, 1902–1914. New York: General Education Board, 1915.

Genovese, Eugene D. *The Political Economy of Slavery: Studies in the Economy and Society of the Slave South.* New York: Vintage Books, 1967.

———. *The Slaveholders' Dilemma: Freedom and Progress in Southern Conservative Thought, 1820–1860.* Columbia: University of South Carolina Press, 1992.

Gibbs, Warmoth T. *History of the North Carolina Agricultural and Technical College.* Dubuque, Iowa: Wm. C. Brown Book Company, 1966.

Gilbert, Edith F., and Jule B. Warren. "Teachers Association Reorganized," "Wanted—A Normal School," and "Assembly Moves to the Beach." *North Carolina Teacher* (North Carolina Educational Association) 5 (September–November 1928): 7, 34, 49, 80, 95, 122.

Gilmore, William J. *Reading Becomes a Necessity of Life: Material and Cultural Life in Rural New England, 1780–1835.* Knoxville: University of Tennessee Press, 1989.

Gleason, Abbott. *Young Russia: The Genesis of Russian Radicalism in the 1860s.* Chicago: University of Chicago Press, 1980.

Gobbel, Luther L. *Church-State Relationships in Education in North Carolina since 1776.* Durham: Duke University Press, 1938.

Goodwyn, Lawrence. *Democratic Promise: The Populist Moment in America.* New York: Oxford University Press, 1976.

Graff, Harvey J. *The Legacies of Literacy: Continuities and Contradictions in Western Culture and Society.* Bloomington: Indiana University Press, 1987.

Greenwood, Janette Thomas. *Bittersweet Legacy: The Black and White "Better Classes" in Charlotte, 1850–1910.* Chapel Hill: University of North Carolina Press, 1994.

Griffen, Clyde. "Reconstructing Masculinity from the Evangelical Revival to the Waning of Progressivism: A Speculative Synthesis." In *Meanings of Manhood: Constructions of Masculinity in Victorian America,* edited by Mark C. Carnes and Clyde Griffen, pp. 183–204. Chicago: University of Chicago Press, 1990.

Griffin, Paul R. *Black Theology as the Foundation of Three Methodist Colleges: The Educational Views and Labors of Daniel Payne, Joseph Price, Isaac Lane.* Lanham, Md.: University Press of America, 1984.

Groom, Ruth. "North Carolina Journals of Education—A History." *North Carolina Education* 8 (May 1914): 8–10, 15.

Grossman, James R. *Land of Hope: Chicago, Black Southerners, and the Great Migration.* Chicago: University of Chicago Press, 1989.

Grumet, Madeleine R. *Bitter Milk: Women and Teaching.* Amherst: University of Massachusetts Press, 1988.

Gutek, Gerald Lee. *Pestalozzi and Education.* New York: Random House, 1968.

Hall, Jacquelyn Dowd. "Disorderly Women: Gender and Labor Militancy in the Appalachian South." *Journal of American History* 73 (September 1986): 354–82.

Hall, Jacquelyn Dowd, James Leloudis, Robert Korstad, Mary Murphy, Lu Ann Jones, and Christopher B. Daly. *Like a Family: The Making of a Southern Cotton Mill World.* Chapel Hill: University of North Carolina Press, 1987.

Hamilton, Joseph Gregoire de Roulhac. *North Carolina since 1860.* A History of North Carolina, vol. 3. Chicago: Lewis Publishing Company, 1919.

Hamlin, Charles Hunter. *Ninety Bits of North Carolina Biography.* New Bern, N.C.: Owen G. Dunn Company, 1946.

Hanchett, Thomas W. "The Rosenwald Schools and Black Education in North Carolina." *North Carolina Historical Review* 65 (October 1988): 387–427.

Harlan, Louis R. *Separate and Unequal: Southern School Campaigns and Racism in the Southern Seaboard States, 1901–1915.* New York: Atheneum, 1968.

Harrington, Karl Pomeroy. *Shall the Classics Have a Fair Chance?* N.p., n.d.

Hart, Joseph K. "The Negro Builds for Himself: The Rosenwald Schools—An Episode in the Epic of Education." *The Survey* 52 (September 1, 1924): 563–67, 596.

Hayden, Dolores. *The Grand Domestic Revolution: A History of Feminist Designs for American Homes, Neighborhoods, and Cities.* Cambridge, Mass.: MIT Press, 1981.

Henderson, Archibald. *Campus of the First State University.* Chapel Hill: University of North Carolina Press, 1949.

Highsmith, Edwin M. "State Normal School Idea in North Carolina." *Meredith College Quarterly Bulletin,* series 7 (November 1923): 4–38.

Hill, Daniel Harvey. "Education" [a three-part article]. *The Land We Love* 1 (May 1866): 1–11; (June 1866): 83–91; (August 1866): 235–39.

Hill, Walter B. "Negro Education in the South." *Proceedings of the Sixth Conference for Education in the South, 1903,* pp. 206–17. N.p., n.d.

Hoffman, Nancy. *Woman's "True" Profession: Voices from the History of Teaching.* Old Westbury, N.Y.: Feminist Press, 1981.

Hogan, David John. *Class and Reform: School and Society in Chicago, 1880–1930.* Philadelphia: University of Pennsylvania Press, 1985.

———. "The Market Revolution and Disciplinary Power: Joseph Lancaster and the Psychology of the Early Classroom System." *History of Education Quarterly* 29 (Fall 1989): 381–417.

Holbeck, Elmer S. *Analysis of the Activities and Potentialities for Achievement of the Parent-Teacher Association, with Recommendations.* [New York: n.p., 1934].

Holder, Rose Howell. *McIver of North Carolina.* Chapel Hill: University of North Carolina Press, 1957.

Horowitz, Helen Lefkowitz. *Campus Life: Undergraduate Cultures from the End of the Eighteenth Century to the Present.* New York: Knopf, 1987.

Hoskin, Keith W., and Richard H. Macve. "Accounting and the Examination: A Genealogy of Disciplinary Power." *Accounting, Organizations and Society* 11, no. 2 (April 1986): 105–36.

Hughes, James Laughlin. *Froebel's Educational Laws for All Teachers.* New York: D. Appleton and Company, 1897.

Inauguration of Edwin Anderson Alderman, President of the University of North Carolina, January 27, 1897. N.p., n.d.

James, J. T. "Historical and Commercial Sketch of Wilmington, N.C." In *Smaw's Wilmington Directory,* compiled by Frank D. Smaw Jr. Wilmington: Frank D. Smaw Jr., [1867].

Johnson, Elmer D. "James Yadkin Joyner, Educational Statesman." *North Carolina Historical Review* 33 (July 1956): 359–83.

Johnson, Guion Griffis. *Ante-Bellum North Carolina, A Social History.* Chapel Hill: University of North Carolina Press, 1937.

Johnson, Norris Brock. *West Haven: Classroom Culture and Society in a Rural Elementary School.* Chapel Hill: University of North Carolina Press, 1985.

Jones, Lance G. E. *The Jeanes Teacher in the United States, 1908–1933.* Chapel Hill: University of North Carolina Press, 1937.

Jones, Thomas Jesse. *Education in Africa: A Study of West, South and Equatorial Africa by the African Education Commission.* New York: Phelps-Stokes Fund, 1922.

———. *Education in East Africa: A Study of East, Central and South Africa by the Second African Education Commission.* New York: Phelps-Stokes Fund, 1925.

Joyner, James Yadkin. "Ways and Means of Carrying on the Work." In *Proceedings and Addresses of the Twenty-Fifth Annual Session of the North Carolina Teachers Assembly*, pp. 326–31. Raleigh: Edwards and Broughton, 1909.

Kaestle, Carl F. *Pillars of the Republic: Common Schools and American Society, 1780–1860*. New York: Hill and Wang, 1983.

Katz, Michael B. *The Irony of Early School Reform: Educational Innovation in Mid-Nineteenth Century Massachusetts*. Cambridge: Harvard University Press, 1968.

——. "The 'New Departure' in Quincy, 1873–1881: The Nature of Nineteenth-Century Educational Reform." *The New England Quarterly* 40 (March 1967): 3–30.

——. *Reconstructing American Education*. Cambridge: Harvard University Press, 1987.

Kellogg, Eva D. *Teaching Reading in Ten Cities*. Boston: Educational Publishing Company, 1900.

Kenzer, Robert C. *Kinship and Neighborhood in a Southern Community: Orange County, North Carolina, 1849–1881*. Knoxville: University of Tennessee Press, 1987.

Kimball, Bruce. *Orators and Philosophers: A History of the Idea of Liberal Education*. New York: Teachers College Press, 1986.

Knapp, Seaman A. "Farmers' Cooperative Demonstration Work in the South." In *The South in the Building of the Nation*, edited by Samuel C. Mitchell, vol. 10, *The History of the Social Life of the Southern States*, pp. 603–13. Richmond: Southern Historical Publication Society, 1909.

Knight, Edgar W., ed. *A Documentary History of Education in the South before 1860*. 5 vols. Chapel Hill: University of North Carolina Press, 1950.

——. *Public Education in the South*. Boston: Ginn and Company, 1922.

——. *Public School Education in North Carolina*. Boston: Houghton Mifflin, 1916.

Kolchin, Peter. *Unfree Labor: American Slavery and Russian Serfdom*. Cambridge: Belknap Press of Harvard University Press, 1987.

Kousser, J. Morgan. "Progressivism—For Middle-Class Whites Only: North Carolina Education, 1880–1910." *Journal of Southern History* 46 (May 1980): 169–94.

——. *The Shaping of Southern Politics: Suffrage Restriction and the Establishment of the One-Party South, 1880–1910*. New Haven: Yale University Press, 1974.

Kramnick, Isaac. *Republicanism and Bourgeois Radicalism: Political Ideology in Late Eighteenth-Century England and America*. Ithaca: Cornell University Press, 1990.

Labaree, David E. *The Making of an American High School: The Credentials Market and the Central High School of Philadelphia, 1838–1939*. New Haven: Yale University Press, 1988.

Lasch, Christopher. "Origins of the Asylum." In *The World of Nations: Reflections on American History, Politics, and Culture*, edited by Christopher Lasch, pp. 3–17. New York: Basic Books, 1973.

Lathrop, Virginia Terrell. "Alumnae for 'School Betterment,' 1902." *Alumni News: The University of North Carolina at Greensboro* 60 (Spring 1972): 10–13, 22.

——. *Educate a Woman: Fifty Years of Life at the Woman's College of the University of North Carolina*. Chapel Hill: University of North Carolina Press, 1942.

Lay, George W. "The Sanitary Privy." *Bulletin of the North Carolina Board of Health* 25 (April 1910): 20–29.

Lefler, Hugh Talmage. *History of North Carolina*. 4 vols. New York: Lewis Historical Publishing Company, 1956.

Lefler, Hugh Talmage, and Albert Ray Newsome. *North Carolina: The History of a Southern State*. Chapel Hill: University of North Carolina Press, 1973.

Leloudis, James L. "School Reform in the New South: The Woman's Association for the Betterment of Public School Houses in North Carolina, 1902–1919." *Journal of American History* 69 (March 1983): 886–909.

Lewis, Charles Lee. *Philander Priestley Claxton, Crusader for Public Education*. Knoxville: University of Tennessee Press, 1948.

Lincoln, W. Bruce. *In the Vanguard of Reform: Russia's Enlightened Bureaucrats, 1825–1861*. DeKalb: Northern Illinois University Press, 1982.

Link, William A. *A Hard Country and a Lonely Place: Schooling, Society, and Reform in Rural Virginia, 1870–1920*. Chapel Hill: University of North Carolina Press, 1986.

——. " 'The Harvest Is Ripe, but the Laborers Are Few': The Hookworm Crusade in North Carolina." *North Carolina Historical Review* 67 (January 1990): 2–27.

——. *The Paradox of Southern Progressivism, 1880–1930*. Chapel Hill: University of North Carolina Press, 1992.

——. "Privies, Progressivism, and Public Schools: Health Reform in the Rural South, 1909–1920." *Journal of Southern History* 54 (November 1988): 622–42.

Logan, Frenise. "The Legal Status of Public School Education for Negroes in North Carolina, 1877–1894." *North Carolina Historical Review* 32 (July 1955): 346–57.

Lortie, Dan Clement. *Schoolteacher: A Sociological Study*. Chicago: University of Chicago Press, 1975.

Lubove, Roy. *Professional Altruist: The Emergence of Social Work as a Career, 1880–1930*. Cambridge: Harvard University Press, 1965.

McCorkle, Samuel Eusibius. *The Work of God for the French Republic*. Salisbury: Francis Coupee, 1798.

McCosh, James. "American Universities—What They Should Be. Inaugural Address Delivered by President James McCosh at the College of New Jersey, Princeton, October 27, 1868." San Francisco: Turnbull and Smith, 1869.

McLachlan, James. "The *Choice of Hercules*: American Student Societies in the Early 19th Century." In *The University in Society*, edited by Lawrence Stone, 2:449–94. Princeton: Princeton University Press, 1974.

McMath, Robert C. *Populist Vanguard: A History of the Southern Farmers' Alliance*. Chapel Hill: University of North Carolina Press, 1976.

McMillen, Neil R. *Dark Journey: Black Mississippians in the Age of Jim Crow*. Urbana: University of Illinois Press, 1989.

McVaugh, Michael R. "Elisha Mitchell's Books and the University of North Carolina Library." *The Bookmark* 55 (1987): 27–54.

Madison, James H. "John D. Rockefeller's General Education Board and the Rural School Problem in the Midwest, 1900–1930." *History of Education Quarterly* 24 (Summer 1984): 181–200.

Malone, Dumas. *Edwin A. Alderman: A Biography*. New York: Doubleday, Doran and Company, 1940.

Martin, O. B. *The Demonstration Work*. Boston: The Stratford Company, 1921.

Mathews, Basil. *The Clash of Color: A Study in the Problem of Race*. New York: Missionary Education Movement of the United States and Canada, 1924.

Mathews, Mitford M. *Teaching to Read, Historically Considered*. Chicago: University of Chicago Press, 1966.

Mauskopf, Seymour H. "Elisha Mitchell and European Science: The Case of Chemistry." *Journal of the Elisha Mitchell Scientific Society* 100 (Summer 1984): 57–60.

Mayo, Amory Dwight. "The New Education and Col. Parker." *Journal of Education* 18 (August 9, 1883): 84–85.

A Memorial to the General Assembly of North Carolina, from the State Teachers Assembly, Praying the Establishment of a North Carolina Normal College for Training the Men and Women of the State Who Are Preparing to Teach, Together with the Proposed Act to Establish a Normal College. N.p., n.d.

Meyer, Harold D. *The Parent-Teacher Association: A Handbook for North Carolina*. [Chapel Hill: n.p., 1922].

Miller, Howard. *The Revolutionary College: American Presbyterian Higher Education, 1707–1837*. New York: New York University Press, 1976.

Miller, Pavla. *Long Division: State Schooling in South Australian Society*. Netley, South Australia: Wakefield Press, 1986.

Mitchell, Elisha. *The Other Leaf of the Book of Nature and the Word of God*. N.p., 1848.

——. *Statistics, Facts, and Dates, for the Sunday Recitations of the Junior Class in the University*. Raleigh: Raleigh Register, 1843.

Mitchell, Theodore R. "From Black to White: The Transformation of Educational Reform in the New South, 1890–1910." *Educational Theory* 39 (Fall 1989): 337–50.

——. *Political Education in the Southern Farmers' Alliance, 1887–1900*. Madison: University of Wisconsin Press, 1987.

Monroe, Will S. *History of the Pestalozzian Movement in the United States*. Syracuse: C. W. Bardeen, 1907.

Montgomery, David. *Beyond Equality: Labor and the Radical Republicans, 1862–1872*. New York: Knopf, 1967.

Moore, Charles H. *Report of Professor Charles H. Moore, State Inspector of Negro Schools*. Durham: Press of the Durham Reformer, n.d.

Moore, John Robert. *Senator Josiah William Bailey of North Carolina: A Political Biography*. Durham: Duke University Press, 1968.

Murphy, Edgar Gardner. *The Basis of Ascendancy: A Discussion of Certain Princi-*

ples of Public Policy Involved in the Development of the Southern States. New York: Longmans, Green, and Company, 1910.

Murray, Percy. *History of the North Carolina Teachers Association.* N.p., n.d.

Nathans, Sydney. *Quest for Progress: The Way We Lived in North Carolina, 1870–1920.* Chapel Hill: University of North Carolina Press for the North Carolina Department of Cultural Resources, 1983.

"Negro Common School in North Carolina." *The Crisis* 34 (June 1927): 117–18, 133–35.

Neverdon-Morton, Cynthia. "Self-Help Programs as Educative Activities for Black Women in the South, 1895–1925: Focus on Four Key Areas." *Journal of Negro Education* 51 (Summer 1982): 207–21.

Newbold, N. C. "Common Schools for Negroes in the South." *Annals of the American Academy of Political and Social Science* 140 (November 1928): 209–23.

———. "Negro County-School Commencements." *Southern Workman* 45 (December 1916): 662–67.

———, ed. *Five North Carolina Negro Educators.* Chapel Hill: University of North Carolina Press, 1939.

Noble, Marcus Cicero Stephens. *A History of the Public Schools of North Carolina.* Chapel Hill: University of North Carolina Press, 1930.

North Carolina State Board of Health. *The Sanitary Privy: Plans for Construction, Bill of Materials, Sanitary Privy Ordinances.* Raleigh: E. M. Uzzell and Company, 1912.

Novak, Steven J. *The Rights of Youth: American Colleges and Student Revolt, 1798–1815.* Cambridge: Harvard University Press, 1977.

Olmsted, Frederick Law. *A Journey in the Seaboard Slave States, with Remarks on Their Economy.* New York: Dix and Edwards, 1856.

Orr, Oliver H., Jr. *Charles Brantley Aycock.* Chapel Hill: University of North Carolina Press, 1961.

Page, Walter Hines. "The Forgotten Man." In *The Rebuilding of Old Commonwealths, Being Essays towards the Training of the Forgotten Man in the Southern States,* pp. 1–47. New York: Doubleday, Page and Company, 1902.

———. "The Rebuilding of Old Commonwealths." In *The Rebuilding of Old Commonwealths, Being Essays towards the Training of the Forgotten Man in the Southern States,* pp. 105–53. New York: Doubleday, Page and Company, 1902.

———. "School That Built a Town." In *The Rebuilding of Old Commonwealths, Being Essays towards the Training of the Forgotten Man in the Southern States,* pp. 49–103. New York: Doubleday, Page and Company, 1902.

———. "Study of an Old Southern Borough." *Atlantic Monthly* 47 (May 1881): 648–58.

Parker, Francis W. *Talks on Pedagogics: An Outline of the Theory of Concentration.* New York: E. L. Kellogg and Company, 1894.

Paschal, George Washington. *History of Wake Forest College.* 3 vols. Wake Forest, N.C.: Wake Forest College, 1935–43.

Patridge, Lelia E. *The "Quincy Methods" Illustrated: Pen Pictures from the Quincy Schools*. New York: E. L. Kellogg and Company, 1885.

Patterson, Mrs. Lindsay [Lucy Bramlette]. "The Old Patterson Mansion, The Master and His Guests." *Pennsylvania Magazine of History and Biography* 39, no. 1 (1915): 80–97.

Patton, James W. "Southern Reaction to the Ogden Movement." In *Education in the South: Institute of Southern Culture Lectures at Longwood College, 1959*, edited by R. C. Simonini Jr., pp. 63–82. Richmond: Cavalier Press, 1959.

Peele, W. J. "Pen-Pictures of the Times of '75." *University Record*, n.s. 1, no. 2 (1901–2): 32–45.

Perry, Percival. "The Naval Stores Industry in the Old South, 1790–1860." *Journal of Southern History* 34 (November 1968): 509–26.

Piaget, Jean. *Six Psychological Studies*. New York: Vintage Books, 1968.

Poe, Clarence H. *My First Eighty Years*. Chapel Hill: University of North Carolina Press, 1963.

Poland, C. Beauregard. *Twentieth Century Statesmen: North Carolina's Political Leaders, 1900–1901*. N.p., n.d.

Prather, H. Leon, Sr. *Resurgent Politics and Educational Progressivism in the New South: North Carolina, 1890–1913*. Rutherford, N.J.: Fairleigh Dickinson University Press, 1979.

———. *We Have Taken a City: Wilmington Racial Massacre and Coup of 1898*. Rutherford, N.J.: Fairleigh Dickinson University Press, 1984.

Prentice, Alison. "The Feminization of Teaching in British North America and Canada, 1845–1875." *Histoire Social—Social History* 8 (May 1975): 5–20.

Prentice, Alison, and Marjorie R. Theobold, eds. *Women Who Taught: Perspectives on the History of Women and Teaching*. Toronto: University of Toronto Press, 1991.

Proctor, A. M. "N. C. Newbold, '95, and Negro Education." *Trinity Alumni Register* 10 (April 1924): 158–60.

Purvis, J. "Women and Teaching in the Nineteenth Century." In *Education and the State: Politics, Patriarchy and Practice*, edited by R. Dale et al., pp. 359–75. Sussex: The Falmer Press, 1981.

Rankin, Watson S. "The Importance of the Recognition of Physically Defective Children by the Teacher." *Bulletin of the North Carolina Board of Health* 25 (September 1910): 243–54.

Raymond, Zillah. *Then and Now, or Hope's First School*. Wilmington, N.C.: Jackson and Bell, 1883.

A Record of Fifty Years, 1867–1917, St. Augustine's School. Raleigh: Edwards and Broughton, n.d.

Redcay, Edward E. *County Training Schools and Public Secondary Education for Negroes in the South*. Washington, D.C.: The John F. Slater Fund, 1935.

Reese, William J. *Power and the Promise of School Reform: Grass-Roots Movements during the Progressive Era*. Boston: Routledge and Kegan Paul, 1986.

Reich, Robert B. *Education for the Next Economy*. Washington, D.C.: National Education Association, 1988.

———. *The Work of Nations: Preparing Ourselves for 21st-Century Capitalism.* New York: Knopf, 1991.

Rippy, J. Fred. *F. M. Simmons, Statesman of the New South: Memoirs and Addresses.* Durham: Duke University Press, 1936.

Robinson, Blackwell P. *William R. Davie.* Chapel Hill: University of North Carolina Press, 1957.

Robinson, T. M. "What Can a Woman Do to Earn a Living?" *State Normal Magazine* 3 (February 1899): 391–94.

Rogers, Lou. *Tar Heel Women.* Raleigh: Warren Publishing Company, 1949.

Rosenwald, Julius. "You Can't Keep a Man in the Ditch without Staying In with Him." *Collier's National Weekly,* July 4, 1925.

Ryan, Mary. "The American Parade: Representations of the Nineteenth-Century Social Order." In *The New Cultural History,* edited by Lynn Hunt, pp. 131–53. Berkeley: University of California Press, 1989.

Saenger, Paul. "Silent Reading: Its Impact on Late Medieval Script and Society." *Viator* 13 (1982): 367–414.

Satterfield, Frances Gibson. *Charles Duncan McIver, 1860–1906.* Atlanta: Ruralist Press, 1942.

Scott, Emmett J. *Negro Migration during the War.* New York: Oxford University Press, 1920.

Scott, Roy V. *The Reluctant Farmer: The Rise of Agricultural Extension to 1914.* Urbana: University of Illinois Press, 1970.

Sherer, Robert G. *Subordination or Liberation?: The Development and Conflicting Theories of Black Education in Nineteenth Century Alabama.* University: University of Alabama Press, 1977.

Silber, Katie. *Pestalozzi: The Man and His Work.* New York: Schocken Books, 1973.

Sklar, Martin J. *The Corporate Reconstruction of American Capitalism, 1890–1916: The Market, the Law, and Politics.* Cambridge: Cambridge University Press, 1988.

Smith, Henry Lester, Merrill T. Eaton, and Kathleen Dugdale. "One Hundred Fifty Years of Arithmetic Textbooks." *Bulletin of the School of Education, Indiana University* 21, no. 1 (January 1945): 1–149.

Smith, Hoke. "Popular Education as the Primary Policy of the South." In *Proceedings of the Fifth Conference for Education in the South, 1902,* pp. 43–51. Knoxville, Tenn.: Gaut-Ogden Company, 1902.

Smith, Ronald A. *Sports and Freedom: The Rise of Big-Time College Athletics.* New York: Oxford University Press, 1988.

Smith, S. L. *Builders of Goodwill: The Story of the State Agents of Negro Education in the South, 1910 to 1950.* Nashville: Tennessee Book Company, 1950.

Smith, Sandra N., and Earle H. West. "Charlotte Hawkins Brown." *Journal of Negro History* 51 (1982). Reprinted in *Black Women in American History: The Twentieth Century,* edited by Darlene Clark Hine, 4:191–206. New York: Carlson Publishing, 1990.

Smith, William C., Viola Boddie, and Mary Settle Sharpe, eds. *Charles Duncan McIver*. Greensboro: J. J. Stone and Company, 1907.

Storm, A. V. "Discipline as the Result of Self-Government." In *National Educational Association, Journal of Proceedings and Addresses, Session of the Year 1894*, pp. 764–72. St. Paul, Minn.: National Educational Association, 1895.

Stowe, Harriet Beecher. *My Wife and I; or, Harry Henderson's History*. New York: J. B. Ford and Company, 1871.

Stowe, Steven M. *Intimacy and Power in the Old South: Ritual in the Lives of the Planters*. Baltimore: Johns Hopkins University Press, 1987.

Stowell, Jay S. *Methodist Adventures in Negro Education*. New York: The Methodist Book Concern, 1922.

Strayhorn, J. T. "Southern Development." *University Monthly* 2 (January 1883): 19–21.

Strober, Myra, and David B. Tyack. "Why Do Women Teach and Men Manage?" *Signs* 5 (Spring 1980): 494–503.

"A Study of the Public Schools in Orange County, North Carolina." *The University of North Carolina Record* 166 (June 1919).

A Suggested Course of Study for County Training Schools for Negroes in the South. Occasional Papers, no. 18. N.p.: Trustees of the John F. Slater Fund, 1917.

Sumner, James. "The North Carolina Inter-Collegiate Foot-Ball Association: The Beginnings of College Football in North Carolina." *North Carolina Historical Review* 65 (July 1988): 263–86.

Swett, John. *Methods of Teaching: A Hand-Book of Principles, Directions, and Working Models for Common-School Teachers*. New York: Harper and Brothers, 1887.

Swetz, Frank J. *Capitalism and Arithmetic: The New Math of the 15th Century*. LaSalle, Ill.: Open Court, 1987.

[Taylor, Charles E.] *How Far Should a State Undertake to Educate?: Or, A Plea for the Voluntary System in the Higher Education*. Raleigh: Edwards and Broughton, 1894.

Thelen, David P. *The New Citizenship: Origins of Progressivism in Wisconsin, 1885–1900*. Columbia: University of Missouri Press, 1972.

———. *Paths of Resistance: Tradition and Dignity in Industrializing Missouri*. New York: Oxford University Press, 1986.

Thompson, Holland. *The New South: A Chronicle of Social and Industrial Evolution*. New Haven: Yale University Press, 1919.

Towers, Frederick. "The Ancient Greek and Modern Elizabethan Drama Compared." *University Magazine*, n.s. 13 (October 1893): 1–15.

Tupper, H[enry] M[artyn]. *A Narrative of Twenty-Five Years' Work in the South, 1865–1890*. N.p., n.d.

Turner, R. Steven. "University Reformers and Professional Scholarship in Germany, 1760–1806." In *The University in Society*, edited by Lawrence Stone, 2:495–531. Princeton: Princeton University Press, 1974.

Tyack, David B. *The One Best System: A History of American Urban Education.* Cambridge: Harvard University Press, 1974.

——. "The Tribe and the Common School: Community Control in Rural Education." *American Quarterly* 24 (March 1972): 3–19.

Ulrich, Laurel Thatcher. *Good Wives: Image and Reality in the Lives of Women in Northern New England, 1650–1750.* New York: Oxford University Press, 1983.

Veysey, Laurence R. *The Emergence of the American University.* Chicago: University of Chicago Press, 1965.

Vicinus, Martha. *Independent Women: Work and Community for Single Women.* Chicago: University of Chicago Press, 1985.

Waddell, Alfred M. "Address of Hon. A. M. Waddell, before the Philanthropic and Dialectic Societies of the University of North Carolina, June 1876." N.p., n.d.

——. "The Ante-Bellum University. Oration Delivered at the Celebration of the Centennial of the University of North Carolina, June 5th, 1895." Wilmington: Jackson and Bell, 1895.

Wagstaff, Henry McGilbert. *Impressions of Men and Movements at the University of North Carolina.* Chapel Hill: University of North Carolina Press, 1950.

Wakelyn, Jon L. "Antebellum College Life and the Relations between Fathers and Sons." In *The Web of Southern Social Relations: Women, Family, and Education,* edited by Walter J. Fraser Jr., R. Frank Saunders Jr., and Jon L. Wakelyn, pp. 107–26. Athens: University of Georgia Press, 1985.

Waller, Altina L. *Feud: Hatfields, McCoys, and Social Change in Appalachia, 1860–1900.* Chapel Hill: University of North Carolina Press, 1988.

Washburn, Benjamin E. *As I Recall.* New York: Office of Publications, The Rockefeller Foundation, 1960.

Weaver, Richard. *The Ethics of Rhetoric.* South Bend, Ind.: Gateway Editions, 1953.

Werner, M. R. *Julius Rosenwald: The Life of a Practical Humanitarian.* New York: Harper and Brothers, 1939.

White, Shane. " 'It Was a Proud Day': African Americans, Parades, and Festivals in the North, 1741–1834." *Journal of American History* 81 (June 1994): 13–50.

Wiener, Jonathan M. *Social Origins of the New South: Alabama, 1860–1885.* Baton Rouge: Louisiana State University Press, 1978.

Williams, Charles B. *A History of the Baptists in North Carolina.* Raleigh: Edwards and Broughton, 1901.

Williams, Lester Alonzo. "A Study of the Public Schools in Orange County, North Carolina." *University of North Carolina Record,* no. 166 (June 1919): 3–32.

Williams, Mildred M., Kara Vaughn Jackson, Madie A. Kiney, Susie W. Wheeler, Rebecca Davis, Rebecca A. Crawford, Maggie Forte, and Ethel Bell. *The Jeanes Story: A Chapter in the History of American Education, 1908–1968.* Jackson, Miss.: Southern Education Foundation, 1979.

Williamson, Joel. *The Crucible of Race: Black-White Relations in the American South since Emancipation.* New York: Oxford University Press, 1984.

Wilson, Louis Round, ed. *Selected Papers of Cornelia Phillips Spencer.* Chapel Hill: University of North Carolina Press, 1953.

Wilson, Peter Mitchel. *Southern Exposure.* Chapel Hill: University of North Carolina Press, 1927.

Wilson, Philip Whitwell. *Unofficial Statesman—Robert C. Ogden.* Garden City, N.Y.: Doubleday, Page and Company, 1924.

Winston, George T. "The First Faculty: Its Work and Its Opportunity." *University Record* n.s. 1, no. 2 (1901–2): 18–31.

———. "Industrial Training in Relation to the Negro Problem." In *Proceedings of the Fourth Conference for Education in the South, 1901,* pp. 103–7. Harrisburg, Pa.: Mount Pleasant Press, J. Horace McFarland Company, 1901.

———. "The University of To-Day." *University Magazine* 13 (March–April 1894): 325–28.

Wood, Phillip J. *Southern Capitalism: The Political Economy of North Carolina, 1880–1980.* Durham: Duke University Press, 1986.

Woods, Peter. *Inside Schools: Ethnography in Educational Research.* New York: Routledge and Kegan Paul, 1986.

Woodward, C. Vann. *Origins of the New South, 1877–1913.* A History of the South, vol. 9. Baton Rouge: Louisiana State University Press, 1951.

Wright, Gavin. *Old South, New South: Revolutions in the Southern Economy since the Civil War.* New York: Basic Books, 1986.

Wyatt-Brown, Bertram. *Southern Honor: Ethics and Behavior in the Old South.* New York: Oxford University Press, 1982.

Dissertations, Theses, and Unpublished Papers

Allen, Francis Robbins. "Public Health Work in the Southeast, 1872–1941: The Study of a Social Movement." Ph.D. diss., University of North Carolina at Chapel Hill, 1947.

Ayers, Edward. "Toward a New Synthesis of the New South." Paper presented at the annual meeting of the Organization of American Historians, Reno, Nevada, March 1988.

Butchart, Ronald E. "Educating for Freedom: Northern Whites and the Origins of Black Education in the South, 1862–1875." Ph.D. diss., State University of New York at Binghamton, 1976.

Carlton, David L. "The Revolution from Above: The National Market and the Beginnings of Industrialization in North Carolina." Unpublished paper.

Copelman, Dina Mira. "Women in the Classroom Struggle: Elementary Schoolteachers in London, 1870–1914." Ph.D. diss., Princeton University, 1985.

Dean, Pamela. "Covert Curriculum: Class and Gender at a New South Woman's College, 1892–1910." Ph.D. diss., University of North Carolina at Chapel Hill, 1994.

Ford, Paul Henry Michael. "Calvin H. Wiley and the Common Schools of North Carolina, 1850–1869." Ph.D. diss., Harvard University, 1960.

Gilmore, Glenda Elizabeth. "Gender and Jim Crow: Women and the Politics of White Supremacy in North Carolina, 1896–1920." Ph.D. diss., University of North Carolina at Chapel Hill, 1992.

Harris, Robert Chalmers. "Development of the Rural Public Schools in Cabarrus County." M.A. thesis, University of North Carolina at Chapel Hill, 1932.

Hurt, Alfred Burman. "Educational Development of Ashe County." M.A. thesis, University of North Carolina at Chapel Hill, 1929.

Jones, Lu Ann. "'The Task That Is Ours': White North Carolina Farm Women and Agrarian Reform, 1886–1914." M.A. thesis, University of North Carolina at Chapel Hill, 1983.

Kemal, Mustafa. "Moral Education in America, 1830–1990: A Contribution to the Sociology of Moral Culture." Ph.D. diss., Harvard University, 1989.

King, William Eskridge. "The Era of Progressive Reform in Southern Education: The Growth of Public Schools in North Carolina, 1885–1910." Ph.D. diss., Duke University, 1970.

Kyriakoudes, Louis. "The Southern City: Merchants and Boosterism in Antebellum Wilmington, North Carolina." Honors thesis in history, University of North Carolina at Chapel Hill, 1985.

Lamport, Harold Boyne. "A History of the Teaching of Beginning Reading." Ph.D. diss., University of Chicago, 1935.

McDuffie, Jerome A. "Politics in Wilmington and New Hanover County, 1865–1900: The Genesis of a Race Riot." Ph.D. diss., Kent State University, 1979.

Pankey, George E. "Life Histories of Rural Negro Teachers in the South." M.A. thesis, University of North Carolina at Chapel Hill, 1927.

Pippin, Kathryn A. "The Common School Movement in the South, 1840–1860." Ph.D. diss., University of North Carolina at Chapel Hill, 1977.

Prince, David Hyde. "A History of the State Department of Public Instruction in North Carolina, 1852–1956." Ph.D. diss., University of North Carolina at Chapel Hill, 1959.

Shreve, Clark Gerow. "The Development of Education to 1900 in Wilson, North Carolina." M.A. thesis, University of North Carolina at Chapel Hill, 1941.

Sims, Anastatia. "Feminism and Femininity in the New South: White Women's Organizations in North Carolina, 1883–1930." Ph.D. diss., University of North Carolina at Chapel Hill, 1985.

Steelman, Joseph Flake. "The Progressive Era in North Carolina, 1884–1917." Ph.D. diss., University of North Carolina at Chapel Hill, 1955.

Thompson, Samuel Hunter. "The Legislative Development of Public School Support in North Carolina." Ph.D. diss., University of North Carolina at Chapel Hill, 1936.

Todd, Irma. "The Historical Development of the North Carolina Teachers Association." M.A. thesis, North Carolina Agricultural and Technical University, 1952.

Westin, Richard B. "The State and Segregated Schools: Negro Public Education in North Carolina, 1863–1923." Ph.D. diss., Duke University, 1966.

Williford, Lynn E. "The Relationship between Classroom Teaching Performance and Attrition from Teaching." Ph.D. diss., University of North Carolina at Chapel Hill, 1992.

Young, Wade Phillips. "A History of Agricultural Education in North Carolina." Ph.D. diss., University of North Carolina at Chapel Hill, 1934.

Index

lature, 109, 110, 135; and Democrats, 109, 110, 135–36; and opposition to New South educational reforms, 109–25 passim, 135–36; race relations among, 117–19, 133; political divisions among, 124–25, 133; decline of, 125, 135

Gaston County, 8–9, 122
Gates, Frederick Taylor, 150, 175, 271 (n. 15)
Gates County, 189, 191
Gender roles: expansion and redefinition of, 73–74, 76; classroom as a focal point for debate over, 229–30
General Assembly. *See* Legislature
General Education Board (GEB), 213, 291 (n. 2); creation and purpose of, 150; and SEB, 150, 271 (n. 15); and Rockefellers, 150–51; significance of work of, 151; and rural school construction, 153, 272 (n. 24); and WABPS, 162, 166, 171; promotes "scientific farming," 166–67, 175, 276 (n. 56); promotes public health work, 171, 175; and RSC, 172, 175; and creation of model communities, 175; and education of blacks, 181, 183, 184, 191, 202
George Peabody College for Teachers, 172, 220
George Peabody Fund, 150–51, 254 (n. 73), 271 (n. 17)
Goldsboro, 91, 153, 255 (n. 4); graded schools in, 22–23, 137; Alderman in, 71, 72, 112; Joyner in, 72, 152; racially divided tax funds for schools in, 121
Graded schools. *See* Schools—graded
Grady, Henry, 52, 88
Graham, 90
Graham, Alexander, 1–2, 80, 84, 238 (n. 2)

Granville County, 144
Great Migration, 211–12, 213, 285 (n. 66)
Greene County, 207–11
Greensboro, 19, 156, 228, 259 (n. 46); graded schools in, 22, 147–48; as site of Normal School, 90, 93–94, 103, 154, 193, 287 (n. 75); Central Campaign Committee activity in, 153, 154; as site of North Carolina Agricultural and Technical College for Negroes, 194, 217, 287 (n. 75); Charles Moore in, 217, 222
Greensboro Daily Record, 287 (n. 75)
Greenville, 193
Guilford County, 70, 175, 272–73 (n. 28)

Hackney's Industrial and Educational Institute, 199–200
Halifax, 96
Halifax County, 197
Hallsboro, 175
"Hampton Idea," 182–83, 270 (n. 11)
Hampton Institute, 148, 180, 182, 189
Harrell, Eugene G., 111–13, 264 (n. 13)
Harrington, Karl Pomeroy, 58, 251 (n. 45)
Hedrick, Benjamin Sherwood, 51
Henderson County, 153
Herbart, Johann Friedrich, 28
Hickory, 153
Higher education. *See* Education—higher
Hill, Daniel Harvey, 52–53, 70
History of the University of North Carolina (Battle), 246 (n. 5)
Holland, Annie Welthy, 189–91
Homemakers' Clubs, 202–4, 207
Hookworm, 169, 171–75
Howard Grammar School (Fayetteville), 74
Howard University, 194, 215, 222

Amendments Committee (House), 137; Jim Crow laws enacted by, 137; and campaign for universal white education, 144; and education of blacks, 179, 192–93, 221; and establishment of North Carolina Agricultural and Technical College for Negroes, 286–87 (n. 75)

Lenoir County, 65, 71

Lincoln County, 221

Literary Fund, 6

Livingstone College, 192

Localism: and opposition to New South educational reforms, xiii, 78–79, 115–16, 120–21, 268 (n. 56); and common schools, 6, 17

Locke, John, 28

Louisburg, 219

Lumberton, 193–94

McCorkle, Samuel Eusebius, 247 (n. 7)

McIntyre, Edith, 93

McIver, Charles Duncan, 107, 109, 119, 125, 133, 144, 161, 254 (n. 77); as student at UNC, 37, 60, 67, 70, 80, 87; and Alderman, 37–38, 60, 68, 71–72, 79–91 passim, 258 (n. 33); and Joyner, 37–38, 60, 71–72; family and formative years of, 62–63; at UNC Summer Normal School, 71; early teaching jobs of, 71, 75, 99; and North Carolina Teachers Assembly, 72, 76; and campaign to establish a state-supported teachers college, 75, 79, 89, 255 (n. 6); as itinerant teaching institute conductor, 79–91 passim, 258 (n. 33); and Finger, 80–81, 89, 110, 112; wife and children of, 82–83, 98–99, 257 (n. 16), 261 (n. 58); as president of Normal School, 90–112 passim, 117, 262 (n. 65), 269 (n. 2); death of, 102;

Baptist/Fusionist critics of, 111–13, 152; supports local school tax, 130, 133; and disfranchisement, 136–37; and Aycock, 137, 146, 151; and northern philanthropists, 146, 147, 149; and SEB, 151; and improvement of rural schools, 151, 154; and WABPS, 155

McIver, Lula Martin, 83, 98–99, 257 (n. 16), 261 (n. 58); correspondence with Charles McIver, 82–83, 87–89, 90, 119–20; and Normal School, 93, 103, 119–20

McKinley, William, 125

Manhood: educational reform and shaping of new notions of, xii, 229; notions of among UNC students, 46–50, 60, 67–68

Manning, Asa J., 197–99

Manufacturer's Record, 160

Martin County, 195, 196–99

Mathews, Basil, 225–26

Maxton, 90

Mayo, Amory Dwight, 2

Mebane, Charles H., 125–27, 128, 129, 266 (n. 40), 268 (n. 58); school reforms of, 127–30, 135

Mecklenburg County, 10, 87, 110, 123, 215, 272–73 (n. 28)

Men: ratio of vs. women as public school teachers, xiii, 11, 74, 76–78, 187, 256 (n. 10); as administrators vs. women as teachers in public education, xiii, 76–78, 106, 155–56; salaries of as teachers, 77–78, 187; on Normal School faculty, 91–92; and gender relations within the household, 97–98, 106; and female sexuality/independence, 105–6; in WABPS, 156; as Jeanes teachers, 187–88

Mendenhall, Gertrude, 92

Method, 224

Methodist Episcopal Church, 217

Methodist Episcopal Church, South, 161

Methodists, 23, 98, 124

Middle class: white women of as advocates of graded schools, xiii, 73–74, 78, 145; college diploma as professional credential for, 53; sons of at UNC, 60; and conflict with older rural ways, 62, 82, 132; and changing view of woman's sphere, 99; educational reform shaped by conventions of, 163, 169; and white abandonment of public schools, 234

Mitchell, Elisha, 248 (nn. 14, 16)

Moffitt, Elvira Evelyna, 155–56, 159, 165, 169, 171, 273–74 (n. 38)

Monroe, 153

Montgomery County, 87

"Moonlight schools," 202–3

Moore, Charles Henry, 215–17, 218–19, 221–22, 234, 287 (n. 75)

Moore County, 63, 89, 215

Moravians, 98, 159

Morehead City, 89

Morganton, 90, 170

Morrill Act (1862), 53

Moses, Edward Pearson, 34, 112–13, 264 (n. 13)

Moton, Robert R., 220

Murphy, Edgar Gardner, 162

My Wife and I (Stowe), 99, 261 (n. 58)

Nash County, 206–7

National Association for the Advancement of Colored People, 180

Native Americans: normal school for, 74

Neighborhood schools. *See* Schools—common

Neighbors/Neighborhood: and personal identity, 6; and common schools, 8; as supplement to formal schooling, 13; and social value of education, 16; diminished importance of in commercial economy, 20, 33; and graded schools, 24, 33, 78, 123, 127, 128, 152, 176; and Southern Farmers Alliance, 108; as check on individual, 116; WABPS involvement with, 157, 158, 161, 162, 163–65; Jeanes teachers' involvement with, 186, 188, 189, 202, 203; and black commencement festivals, 205. *See also* Community; Friends/Friendship

New Bern, 65, 74, 238 (n. 1), 255 (n. 4)

Newbold, Nathan Carter: and GEB, 183, 191, 290 (n. 97); background and temperament of, 183–85; and Jeanes program, 185–88, 191, 199, 203, 206–7; and Holland, 191; and training of black teachers, 191–92, 193; and Parmele Industrial Institute, 196–99; and commencement festivals, 204–6; and Battle, 207–11; and Rosenwald program, 214–28 passim; and Moore, 215, 217, 218–19, 221; and Division of Negro Education, 221, 228

New education. *See* Schools—graded

New Hanover County, 272–73 (n. 28)

New South: public education as agency for making of, xii, xiv, 71, 146, 165, 229; economic views of promoters of, 18; graded school as institution for realization of, 20–21, 23–24, 27, 29, 33, 89, 140, 145; ideology of promoted at UNC, 38, 52–53; ideology of as bond between educators and businessmen, 89, 140–41, 145–46; women and, 97–98, 99; opponents of ideology of, 107, 115–16; Page as promoter of, 130, 140–41; racism among promoters of, 135; disfranchisement as a tool for realization of, 136; and commercial agriculture, 166; blacks and, 181, 182–83, 184, 185, 203–4

Newton, 74, 158, 238 (n. 1)

Noble, Marcus, 71, 80, 200

Normal Department (University of North Carolina), 75

Normal schools. *See* Schools—normal

North Carolina Agricultural and Mechanical College, 111, 166, 276 (n. 56), 286–87 (n. 75)

North Carolina Agricultural and Technical College for Negroes, 194, 217, 287 (n. 75)

North Carolina Baptist State Convention, 117

North Carolina Board of Health, 169, 203

North Carolina College for Negroes, 180

North Carolina Department of Agriculture, 156, 166, 167

North Carolina Department of Health, 156

North Carolina Department of Public Instruction, 156, 191, 228

North Carolina Journal of Education, 34

North Carolina Normal and Industrial School for Women, 130, 146, 154, 175, 287 (n. 75); campaign leading to establishment of, 73, 75–76, 79, 84, 89–90, 255 (n. 6); choice of site for, 90; choice of president for, 90–91; faculty of, 91–93; and commitment to female education, 91–93, 100; buildings and grounds of, 93–94; selection and arrival of first students, 93–94; background and motivation of students, 94–98, 99–100; curriculum, 100–101; students' love for, 101–2; student conduct and discipline, 102–5, 262 (n. 65); as foundry for new images of womanhood and teach-

ing, 105–6, 107; Baptist/Fusionist attack on, 109, 110–19, 269 (n. 2); promotion of New South ideology, 113; criticism of graduates of, 115, 123–24; teaching certification of graduates of, 115, 129; legislative appropriations for, 193

North Carolina Supreme Court, 122, 265 (n. 31)

North Carolina Tax Commission, 218

North Carolina Teacher, 24, 30, 111–12

North Carolina Teachers Assembly, 29, 72, 76, 78, 89, 155, 169

North Carolina Teachers Association, 186, 191, 217, 218, 228

Ogden, Robert Curtis, 146, 148, 149, 160

Orange County, 7, 88, 93, 231

Orange County Training School, 199–200, 201

Orange Jewel, The, 200

Oxford, 153

Page, Walter Hines, 130–32, 140–41, 146, 150, 171, 275 (n. 46)

Pamlico County, 87

Pamlico Training School, 200

Parents: and control of common schools, 7, 17; desire for schools to reflect their own views, 9, 38; relations with teachers in common schools, 11–12, 13, 17; and children's attendance at common schools, 13–14; and social value of education, 16, 17; relations with teachers in graded schools, 25, 32, 115, 123–24; and resistance to reforms of graded school advocates, 73, 79, 123–24, 127–28; of Normal School students, 96, 103

—black: and private normal schools, 194; and commencement festivals, 205, 206; and Rosenwald schools,

214, 215, 217, 218, 227; teachers'
   view of role of, 266 (n. 35)
   See also Family
Parker, Francis Wayland, 28–29
Parmele Industrial Institute, 194,
   195–99
Pasquotank County, 183, 207
Patterson, Lucy Bramlette, 159, 274
   (n. 38)
Peabody, George, 254 (n. 73), 271
   (n. 17)
Peabody, George Foster, 146, 149
Peabody Fund. *See* George Peabody
   Fund
Peace Institute, 75, 83, 276 (n. 56)
Pembroke, 74
Pender County, 223–24
People's Party. *See* Populists
Person County, 17, 122
Pestalozzi, Johann Heinrich, 28
Philadelphus, 175
Philanthropists, northern: as allies of
   New South educational reformers,
   xiv, 145–47, 150–51, 181, 183; and
   Page, 130; racial attitudes among,
   148–49, 181, 270–71 (n. 12); and
   "scientific philanthropy," 150; and
   education of blacks, 181, 183, 196,
   270 (n. 11), 271 (nn. 13, 17). *See
   also* Anna T. Jeanes Fund; General
   Education Board; John F. Slater
   Fund; Julius Rosenwald Fund;
   Rockefeller Sanitary Commission;
   Southern Education Board
Philological Club (University of North
   Carolina), 58, 251 (n. 45)
Pitt County, 88, 197
Pleasant Grove, 158
Plymouth, 74, 238 (n. 1)
Poe, Clarence Hamilton, 166
Polk, James K., 40
Polk, Leonidas L., 108
Polk County, 85
Pool, Solomon, 54

Populists, 124, 126, 135, 266 (n. 40);
   and opposition to New South educational reforms, xiii, 109–10, 117;
   and Farmers Alliance, 108–9; and
   Republicans, 109 (*see also* Fusionists); and Democrats, 109, 125, 133,
   137; racial attitudes among, 118–19,
   133; decline of, 125, 133, 136, 138,
   140
Presbyterians, 63, 222, 247 (n. 7), 248
   (n. 16)
Pritchard, Jeter C., 125
Progressive Farmer, 166
Prussia: schools in as model for New
   South schools, 29
Public education. *See* Education—
   public
Public health, 169–75, 203

Quakers, 23, 185, 186
"Quincy System," 28

Race: and common schools, 6, 21; and
   selection of school district committeemen, 7; and Baptist/Fusionist
   attacks on the new education, 117–
   19; and division of tax funds for
   school financing, 121–22, 208–9;
   consciousness of among blacks,
   201; classroom as a focal point
   for debate over, 229–30. *See also*
   Blacks; Race relations; Whites
Race relations: schools and the disci-
   plining of, xii, xiv, 140, 179, 194,
   203–4, 213, 214, 224–25, 226, 228;
   within Fusion alliance, 117–19, 133;
   and northern philanthropists, 148–
   49; industrial education as a means
   of managing, 182–83, 192, 206,
   225–26; Newbold's view of, 183–
   84, 204, 206, 209, 221, 223, 224–25,
   226, 228; challenge to posed by
   World War I, 211–13; Rosenwald's
   view of, 213–14. *See also* Disfran-

chisement; Segregation; White supremacy

Railroads, 3, 18–19, 108–9, 144

Raleigh, 3, 19, 29, 72, 75, 102, 130, 151, 166, 179, 192, 213, 223, 224; graded schools in, 22, 34, 112; as site of North Carolina Agricultural and Mechanical College, 111, 286 (n. 75); WABPS activity in, 158, 165, 171, 273 (n. 32), 274–75 (n. 44)

Raleigh News and Observer, 109

Randolph County, 187

Rankin, Watson S., 169–70

Reconstruction, 74, 145, 211; and New South educational reformers, xiii; and education of blacks, 6, 192 (*see also* Freedmen); UNC and the politics of, 53–54; Democratic overthrow and reversal of, 120

Red Oak, 175

"Red Shirts," 135, 138

Republicans, 74, 117, 135, 138, 217, 286 (n. 74); and control of common schools, 9; and UNC during Reconstruction, 54; and Populists, 109 (*see also* Fusionists); and rift within Fusion alliance, 125, 133

—black: and public schooling for blacks, 6; and tension within Fusion alliance, 117–19; Democratic efforts to stifle, 120; purged from party, 180

Robeson County, 193

Rockefeller, John D., Sr., 149–50, 172

Rockefeller, John D., Jr., 146, 149–50

Rockefeller philanthropies, 150, 230, 291 (n. 2). *See also* General Education Board; Rockefeller Sanitary Commission; Southern Education Board

Rockefeller Sanitary Commission (RSC), 172–75

Rose, Wickliffe, 20, 172

Rosenwald, Julius, 213–14, 220, 224, 227, 290 (n. 95)

Rosenwald Fund. *See* Julius Rosenwald Fund

Rosenwald program/schools, 214–27 passim

Rountree, George, 136–37

Roxboro, 184

Rule of Three, 14–15

Salem, 159

Salem Academy, 159

Salemburg, 175

Salisbury, 74, 118, 148, 238 (n. 1)

Sanford, 89

Sanitation. *See* Hookworm; Public health; Students, health of

Scarborough, John C., 120, 124

School for the Application of Science to the Arts (University of North Carolina), 51

Schools: as instruments of social change/reproduction, xii; vis-à-vis family, church, and community, xv, 229; township system for administration of, 127–28; Rosenwald Fund and construction of for blacks, 211, 212–25, 226–27, 290 (n. 95); monetary value of buildings for whites vs. blacks, 211, 226, 290 (n. 93)

—common: predominance of before 1880s, xii; and freedmen, 6; local control of, 6, 17, 120–21, 127; as a reflection of rural society, 6, 17, 229; construction and funding of, 7–8, 239 (n. 8); physical appearance/conditions of, 8, 16; and local politics, 8–9, 78, 127; considerations affecting employment of teachers in, 9–12; background and qualifications of teachers in, 11; calendar, 12–13; student attendance, 12–13, 14; curriculum and methods of instruction in, 13–16, 23, 25, 27,

208–9, 218–19, 226–27; reformers' campaign to promote local collection of, 129–30, 132–33, 151–52, 160; as supplement to SEB funds, 153; as supplement to Rosenwald funds, 226–27

Teachers: ratio of men vs. women, xiii, 11, 74, 76–78, 105, 187, 256 (n. 10); women as, vs. men as administrators, xiii, 76–78, 106; certification of, 9–10, 84, 85, 115, 129; professionalism among, 23, 73–74, 75, 76, 77, 79, 84, 88, 106, 115, 127, 128–29, 254–55 (n. 1); difficulties inherent in lives of, 71–72; UNC graduates as, 71–72; resistance to graded school reforms among, 73; salaries of, 77–78, 187, 226; style of women vs. men, 78; commitment to public service, 105; and corn clubs and tomato clubs, 167, 168–69; problems and role of in today's schools, 232–33

—black: use classroom to forge sense of racial dignity and consciousness, xiv, 180–81, 199–204, 228; trained as race leaders at Hampton Institute, 182; shortage of, 191–92, 195; and commencement festivals, 204; and Rosenwald schools, 215, 227; and obligation to create good citizens, 266 (n. 35)

—in common schools: control over hiring of, 7; conditions facing, 8; considerations affecting employment of, 9–12; emphasis on moral character of, 10; relations with parents, 11–12, 13, 17; goals and methods of, 13–16, 23, 25, 27, 31, 241 (n. 28); and social value of education, 16, 17; and discipline, 16–17

—in graded schools: evaluation of students by, 23–25; relations with parents, 25, 32, 115, 123–24; goals and methods of, 27–28, 29–35; and discipline, 34; limitations placed on, 232

See also Jeanes program/teachers; Teacher training

Teacher training: professionalization of, xii, 84, 254–55 (n. 1); lack of among common school teachers, 11, 16, 85; emphasized by graded school advocates, 23, 73, 84; early efforts to define a science of, 29; via itinerant teaching institutes, 79, 80, 84, 85–86, 89; GEB and, 151

—for blacks, 23, 226; at public normal schools, 74, 192–93; at private black colleges, 191, 192; at private normal schools, 193–95; at county training schools, 195–97, 208

See also Schools—normal

Tenants, 3–6, 108, 191

Then and Now (Raymond), 94–95, 106

Thirteenth Amendment, 18

Thomasville, 19, 90

Tobacco, 3, 18, 107–8; manufacturing/factories, 19, 20, 146, 149; falling prices for, 96; in WABPS school gardens, 166

Tomato clubs, 167, 168–69, 276 (n. 56)

Tomlinson, Julius, 23, 24

Toon, Thomas Fentress, 144, 151, 152

Transylvania County, 85

Trinity College (later Duke University), 122, 130, 184

Troy, 82

Tuberculosis, 169, 203

Tulane University, 185, 269 (n. 2)

Turner, Mamie, 188–89

Tuskegee Institute, 148, 182, 214, 219, 220, 227

U.S. Bureau of Animal Husbandry, 171

U.S. Department of Agriculture (USDA), 167, 202

Universal Education in the South (Dabney), 230

University Monthly (University of North Carolina), 66

University of Berlin, 28

University of North Carolina (UNC), 76, 126, 215, 222, 230, 231, 255 (n. 6); graduates of as graded school advocates, xiii, 37, 38, 238 (n. 2); promotion of New South ideology, 38, 113; curriculum, 38–40, 43–44, 46, 51–52, 53, 55–57, 107; antebellum conservatism of, 38–44, 51–52; student conduct and discipline, 39, 40, 45, 48–49, 59, 66–69; teaching methods, 44, 45, 57–58, 59–60; college library of, 44–45, 59, 248 (n. 14); student societies, 46–48, 66–67; significance of a degree from, 50, 60; modernization of organization and curriculum of, 52–53, 54–57; and Reconstruction politics, 53–55; Summer Normal School at, 70, 74, 238 (n. 1), 254 (n. 73); Baptist/Fusionist attack on, 109, 110–11, 113–19, 269 (n. 2); political power of alumni, 117; sanitation at, 277 (n. 60)

—board of trustees: antebellum conservatism of, 39–40; and moral character of instructors, 45; and curriculum changes, 50–51, 52, 54–55, 57; and Reconstruction politics, 54–55

—faculty: relations with students, 39, 45, 46, 48, 49–50, 59, 60, 66, 69–70, 248 (n. 16); and Enlightenment pedagogy, 39–40; antebellum conservatism of, 40–44, 52; goals and teaching methods of, 44, 45, 57–58, 59–60; background and

qualifications of, 45, 57; and curriculum changes, 50–51, 52–53, 55–58

—students: Alderman, Joyner, and McIver as, 37–38, 60, 65–71, 80, 87; background of, 38, 60; boisterous behavior of, 39, 43, 48–49, 68–69; relations with faculty, 39, 45, 46, 48, 49–50, 59, 60, 66, 69–70, 248 (n. 16); antebellum conservatism of, 40–43, 51; methods of instruction/learning for, 44, 45, 57–58, 59–60; and college library, 44, 59; attitudes toward scholarship and education among, 45–48, 49–50, 51–52, 58, 65–67, 71; notions of manhood among, 46–50, 60, 67–68; and curriculum change, 55–58; and honor code, 59; the new collegians, 65–70; and athletics, 67–68; and fraternities, 68–69, 253 (n. 67); and Summer Normal School, 70–71; education as career choice of, 71–72; growth in number of in 1890s, 111

Vance, Zebulon B., 121, 125

Venable, Francis Preston, 57

Vocational education. *See* Education—industrial vocational

Waddell, Alfred Moore, 49, 135, 138, 177, 178

Wake County, 155, 171, 187, 224, 272–73 (n. 28)

Wake Forest College, 110–11, 113

Washburn, Benjamin, 173, 174

Washington, Booker T., 148, 180, 182, 188, 213, 214

Washington, Margaret, 220, 227

Washington, N.C., 74, 153, 184, 185

Wayne County, 11, 158, 272–73 (n. 28)

Webster's Spelling Book, 11, 13, 31, 85

White-Government Unions, 135

Whites: rate of common school attendance among, 13; race consciousness among, 21; beginnings and growth of graded schools for, 23; teacher training for, 23 (*see also* Schools—normal: for whites); and Southern Farmers Alliance and Fusion movement, 108, 109, 137; and racially divided tax funds, 121–22; urged to return from Populists to Democrats, 130–31, 132, 136; universal education for, 143–44; priority of in educational efforts of northern philanthropists, 148, 270–71 (n. 12); and tolerance of southern racial attitudes in North, 149; education of blacks seen as responsibility of and in best interest of, 178–79, 181–83, 185, 214, 223–26, 228; salaries of as teachers, 187, 226; and black commencement festivals, 205, 206–7; monetary value of school buildings for, 211, 226, 290 (n. 93); Rosenwald funds diverted to schools for, 218; and establishment of North Carolina Agricultural and Technical College for Negroes, 286–87 (n. 75)

—poor: disfranchisement of, xiv, 120, 136, 137; and northern philanthropists, 145–46

—rural: as obstacles to reform and objects of uplift for graded school advocates, 140; WABPS efforts to improve schools for, 162–63 *See also* Race; Race relations; Teachers—white; Women—white

White supremacy: Democrats' appeal to as political weapon, 133–35, 137, 138–39; implications of for public education, 139–40, 177, 179, 187, 223; black responses to, 180, 223, 227–28

Whiteville, 207

Whitin Normal and Industrial Institute, 193

Wiley, Calvin Henderson, 6, 10, 21, 22, 241 (n. 27), 255 (n. 1), 261 (n. 62)

Wiley, Mary, 102, 103–4, 261 (n. 62)

Williamston, 197

Wilmington, 138, 222, 286 (n. 74); population and commerce of, 19, 60–62; graded schools in, 22; riot in, 135, 136–37; Charles Moore in, 215, 217

Wilson, 123; normal school in, 1, 74, 238 (n. 1); graded schools in, 2, 22–23, 24, 25–26, 32, 243 (n. 53)

Winston, Francis D., 136–37

Winston, George Tayloe, 57–58, 90, 91, 107, 117–19, 136, 181–82, 183

Winston, 244 (n. 55), 287 (n. 75); population and commerce of, 19, 20; McIver in, 71, 75, 99, 257 (n. 16); normal schools in, 74, 193; as site of Conference for Education in the South, 146–47, 148–50

Womanhood: educational reform and shaping of new notions of, xii, 229; Normal School and shaping of new image of, 105; WABPS understanding of, 155–56

Woman's Association for the Betterment of Public School Houses (WABPS), 155–73 passim, 272 (n. 28), 273–74 (n. 38)

Woman's Christian Temperance Union (WCTU), 89–90, 98

Women: ratio of vs. men as public school teachers, xiii, 11, 74, 76–78, 105–6, 187, 256 (n. 10); attractions/benefits of educational work for, xiii, 73–74, 78, 95, 98–100, 104–5, 145, 158–59, 189; as teachers vs.

men as administrators in public education, xiii, 76–78, 105–6, 155–56; as particularly qualified for educational work, 77–78, 154–56, 163, 187; salaries of as teachers, 77–78, 187; on Normal School faculty, 91–93; precarious economic position of, 95; New South ideology and role of, 97–98, 99; and gender relations within the household, 97–98, 106; and WABPS, 155–60, 161, 162–65, 168–70; and corn clubs and tomato clubs, 167, 168–69; and public health work related to schools, 169–70, 171, 172–73, 203

—black: as teachers who used classroom to forge sense of racial dignity, xiv, 180–81, 228; as Jeanes teachers, 186–89; and participation in public life, 189; and Homemakers' Clubs, 202–3

—white: as graded school advocates, xiii, 73–74, 78, 145; normal college for, xiii, 76 (*see also* North Carolina Normal and Industrial School for Women); and participation in public life, 74, 78, 98, 105, 145, 156, 159–60, 163; in voluntary associations designed to improve education, 154–73 passim

World War I, 211, 225

Worth, Jonathan, 159

Yadkin College, 63

Yale College, 38, 44

Yancey County, 86

Yeomen, 3–6, 19, 123–24

YMCAs/YWCAs, 213–14